CANADIAN COMBAT
AND SUPPORT AIRCRAFT
A MILITARY COMPENDIUM

CANADIAN COMBAT AND SUPPORT AIRCRAFT
A MILITARY COMPENDIUM

T.F.J. Leversedge

Vanwell Publishing Limited
St. Catharines, Ontario

Vanwell Publishing acknowledges the financial support of the Government of Canada through the Book Publishing Industry Development Program for our publishing activities.

Design: Carol Matsuyama
Cover design and layout: Carol Matsuyama
Front cover photo, CF-5 Freedom Fighter (CF); Back cover photo, F-86 Sabre (CF PL-55764)

Vanwell Publishing Limited
1 Northrup Crescent
P.O. Box 2131
St. Catharines, Ontario L2R 7S2
sales@vanwell.com
tel: 905-937-3100
fax: 905-937-1760

Printed in Canada

Library and Archives Canada Cataloguing in Publication
Leversedge, T.F.J., 1956–
Canadian combat and support aircraft: a military compendium/T.F.J. Leversedge.
Includes bibliographical references.
ISBN 978-1-55125-116-5
1. Airplanes, Military—Canada—Registers. I. Title.
UG1245.C3L38   2007   358.4'183'0971   C2007-900192-0

Table Of Contents
Alphabetical by Manufacturer

Canadian Forces aircraft announced or contracted for but not yet in use or delivered

Non-Canadian Forces aircraft (ie Civilian Leased, etc) flown by CF personnel during training, test or other military missions

Non-Canadian aircraft flown by Canadians in operations or combat missions while on exchange to other air forces ie RAF, NATO, USAF, USN, etc., or miscellaneous types

Airships

Missiles and Remotely Piloted Vehicles

Glossary

Photographic Credits

Bibliography

Table Of Contents
Alphabetical by Aircraft

Canadian Forces aircraft announced or contracted for but not yet in use or delivered

Non-Canadian Forces aircraft (ie Civilian Leased, etc) flown by CF personnel during training, test or other military missions

Non-Canadian aircraft flown by Canadians in operations or combat missions while on exchange to other air forces, ie RAF, NATO, USAF, USN, etc, or miscellaneous types

Airships

Missiles & Remotely Piloted Vehicles

Foreword

In 1968, Air Marshal C. Roy Slemon noted in his foreword to John Gordon's book *Of Men and Planes* that "Military aviation has contributed importantly to Canada's development as a great nation and to its national security." While there is no doubt that much in our world has changed since Slemon's day, when it comes to the importance of military aviation to Canadians, I believe his words remain as true now as when he wrote them 36 years ago.

LGen Campbell is a fighter pilot by training and a former Commander of Canada's Air Force. (CF)

While there have been a number of very useful Canadian military aviation histories produced over the years, the majority of these have tended to focus on personalities and events. But, to have a complete picture, it is also important to preserve information on the aircraft our military forces have flown over the years—and this is where Brigadier-General Leversedge's new book, *Canadian Combat and Support Aircraft*, comes in.

I first saw a pre-production version of the book in 2002 and was instantly impressed and surprised. Impressed, because the book is such a thorough, detailed and attractive compilation of information regarding the aircraft that have seen Canadian service during the past nine decades or so. Surprised, because—despite a 37 year association with the RCAF and CF and a professional and abiding personal interest in the subject—I personally found a number of aircraft in the book I had no idea our armed forces had ever operated!

In my view, Brigadier-General Leversedge, through his perseverance and attention to detail, has produced a very comprehensive and useful document that will prove to be of great value to military personnel, history buffs and aviation enthusiasts alike. It fills an important gap in our history and will do much to enhance overall knowledge of Canada's rich and proud tradition of military aviation.

Per Ardua Ad Astra

Lieutenant-General (Retired) Lloyd C. Campbell, CMM, CD
Ottawa, Ontario
June 2004

Preface

Canada's rich military aviation history reflects a proud tradition of excellence and valour displayed by its personnel throughout years of adversity, challenge and conflict. Canadian military aircraft include an exotic blend of types from many different manufacturers. Many of these aircraft types have been uniquely modified for Canadian service. This database is a brief summary of the majority of aircraft used by the various arms of the Canadian Forces, in an easy reference format. The data base draws heavily from several previously published works. The original inspiration for this work was a three-volume edition prepared in 1967 by John Gordon entitled *Of Men And Planes*. The definitive references for Canadian military aircraft are certainly the scholarly works of J.A. Griffin, published by the Canadian War Museum in 1969 and entitled *Canadian Military Aircraft (Serials & Photographs 1920-1968)*, and *Canadian Military Aircraft: Aircraft of the Canadian Armed Forces, Serials and Photographs, 1968–1998*, published by Vanwell Publishing (2005). The information contained in these works is updated here with later aircraft types, and some necessary corrections and additions. Special thanks, in particular, to the Comox Air Force Museum, the Royal Air Force, the United States Air Force and the Canadian Forces overall for supplying the bulk of the images.

Per Ardua Ad Astra

Explanation of Categories & Details.

What follows is a comprehensive list of all the aircraft types on strength by the Canadian Air Corps, Canadian Air Force, Royal Canadian Air Force, Royal Canadian Navy, Canadian Army and the Canadian Forces since 1914. It lists the aircraft name, year taken on strength, year struck off strength and the quantity acquired as well as providing a brief operational description and aircraft specifications. The years shown may in some cases not represent the actual service life of an aircraft as some aircraft were retained for ground instruction after their flying career had ended. Please note that many of the famous aircraft types flown by the RCAF personnel, including the Spitfire, Defiant, Beaufighter, Typhoon and others from the Second World War, though equipping RCAF squadrons, were not officially "on strength." As well, Canadian personnel were spread out through many Royal Flying Corps, Royal Naval Air Service, Royal Air Force and Fleet Air Arm squadrons both during the First and Second World War, flying British aircraft types. In the years following the Second World War, Canadians have also participated in many operational exchanges with other allied Air Forces. In the latter cases, it was virtually impossible to definitively detail all of the aircraft types in question. Consequently, a representative selection, of those types flown by Canadian aircrew in actual combat missions, have been included. Finally, contracting out services and leasing of aircraft for military use is another modern trend. Overall, this has resulted in four broad categorizations:

- Aircraft on strength with Canadian Forces *or* its predecessors
- Canadian Forces aircraft announced or contracted for but not yet in use or delivered
- Non-Canadian Forces (ie, civilian leased, etc) aircraft flown by Canadian personnel during training, test or other military missions
- Non-Canadian aircraft flown by Canadians in operations or combat missions while on exchange to other Air Forces ie RAF, NATO, USAF, USN, etc- or misc types

Brigadier-General T.F.J. Leversedge
December 2006

HISTORY OF THE MILITARY AIR SERVICES OF CANADA

The Beginning: 1909

Canada has had a proud aviation history. From those austere beginnings on 23 February 1909 on Bras-d'Or Lake, with J.A.D. McCurdy piloting Alexander Graham Bell's Silver Dart, through to the present day, Canada has rightfully been proud of her aviation history. But the country's military interest in aviation had slow beginnings. The first demonstration put on for the Department of the Militia and Defence (now the Department of National Defence) was at Camp Petawawa in August 1909, when J.A.D. McCurdy demonstrated the Silver Dart and the Baddeck No. 1 (another aircraft from A.G. Bell). However, after one aircraft was wrecked and the other crashed during the demonstration, the Department of the Militia and Defence did not show any interest in this new "fad." Over the ensuing years, several attempts were made to interest the Canadian government in aviation. But every time an attempt was made, it was frustrated on the grounds of "no funds available."

Canadian Aviation Corps, 1914–1915

On 16 September 1914 (while the original Canadian Expeditionary Force was forming up in Valcartier), Col Sam Hughes, Minister for the Militia and Defence, authorised the creation of the Canadian Aviation Corps (CAC). This corps was to consist of one mechanic and two officers. E.L. Janney of Galt, Ontario, was appointed as the Provisional Commander of the CAC with the rank of Captain. The expenditure of an amount not to exceed five thousand dollars for the purchase of a suitable airplane was approved. The aircraft selected was a float-equipped Burgess-Dunne bi-plane from the Burgess Aviation Company of Massachusetts. Captain Janney flew the aircraft back to Canada. Upon his arrival in Sorel, Quebec, Captain Janney was arrested by Customs officials and the aircraft was impounded. After Canada Customs received notification from the Department of the Militia and Defence, Captain Janney and the aircraft were released. As it turned out, this was to be the only flight of Canada's first military aircraft.

In the meantime the other two members of the CAC were recruited: Lieutenant W.F.N. Sharpe of Prescott, Ontario, and Staff Sergeant H.A. Farr of West Vancouver, British Columbia. Immediately after Captain Janney and the Burgess-Dunne were released from Customs, the aircraft was crated for shipping, and the CAC sailed on the S.S. *Athena* with the first Canadian contingent of the Canadian Expeditionary Force.

After landing at Plymouth, England, the aircraft was off-loaded and shipped to

Salisbury Plain were it was considered unsuitable for military service. It was placed in storage, where it eventually rotted and was written off. Captain Janney, now without an aircraft, resigned his commission and returned to Canada. Lieutenant Sharpe continued in England with the Royal Flying Corps. He was killed during a solo flight in a Maurice Farman bi-plane on 4 February 1915. This ended the first attempt at a national air force.

Royal Canadian Flying Corps, 1916

During 1916, there was a renewed interest in aviation within the Department of the Militia and Defence. The War Council and the Canadian Headquarters overseas thought that Canada should have its own air services supporting the war. Much effort was placed on realising this dream; however, Ottawa would not support this concept and the second attempt to create a national air force died.

Canadians in the Royal Flying Corps/Royal Naval Air Service, 1914–1918

Because Canada did not have a national air service during the First World War, many Canadians served with distinction in the Royal Flying Corps, the Royal Naval Air Service and later the Royal Air Force. Some of the more famous Canadians were Raymond Collishaw, William "Billy" Bishop, "Wop" May, Roy Brown, William Barker and Alan McLeod to name a few. This early link with British military aviation is where a great many of the current Air Force's customs, traditions and dress codes originated.

Royal Flying Corps in Canada, 1917–1918

The British War Office and the British Admiralty viewed Canada only as a potential source of recruits for their respective air services. Initially recruits had to have a valid pilot's licence before the RFC or the RNAS would consider recruiting them. This placed a strain on the small civilian training services available in Canada at that time. These civilian schools were inadequate to handle the increased demand for pilot training. At a cost of $400 for 500 minutes, these intrepid aviators paid for their own training at this time. As the demand for trained aviators increased, the RFC found that there were insufficient training facilities in Britain and they turned to Canada for assistance.

In 1917 the RFC decided to establish a training organisation in Canada. The original plan called for four training stations with one or more aerodromes at each station and up to five training squadrons per station. After consultation with Canada, the revised plan called for three stations: RFC Station Camp Borden, RFC Station Deseronto, and RFC Station North Toronto. RFC Station Camp Borden was the main training site and was accepted on 2 May 1917. In no time, all five squadrons and a school for aerial gunnery were operating at full capacity. RFC Station Deseronto consisted of aerodromes at Mohawk and Rathburn, and it was operating with five training squadrons by the end of May 1917. RFC Station North Toronto consisted of aerodromes at Long Beach, Leaside, and Armour Heights, and by the end of June 1917 there were three training squadrons operating.

With the United States's entry into the war in April 1917, a reciprocal agreement was established between the RFC and the U.S. Army's Signal Corps. This agreement brought Americans to Canada for training, and in turn it allowed the RFC to train in a snow-free environment. Fort Worth Texas was selected as the training centre, and the school of aerial gunnery and the wings from Camp Borden and Deseronto ceased training in Canada in November 1917 and moved to the Fort Worth area. RFC Station North Toronto remained open in Canada to test the feasibility of training personnel in a Canadian winter. This test was so successful it was decided that the training for the winter of 1918–19 was to be in Canada. Meanwhile, the other RFC training units proceeded on their 1600-mile rail-trip to Texas for the winter of 1917–18.

In April 1918, the RFC, now the Royal Air Force (by Royal decree, 1 April 1918), returned to Canada and re-established their stations. In addition, it was decided to establish several advanced flying training units in Canada. By the time the armistice was signed on 11 November 1918, the RAF establishment in Canada had a total strength of 11,928 all ranks. It was staffed by 993 officers and 6,158 other ranks, with 4,333 cadet pilots and 444 other officers under training. In its twenty and a half months in Canada the RFC/RAF training establishment had recruited 16,663 personnel and had graduated 3,135 pilots, of whom 2,539 went overseas and 356 remained in Canada as instructors, and 137 observers, of whom 85 were sent overseas. At the time of the armistice, it had an additional 240 pilots and 52 observers who were ready for overseas service. There had been 130 fatal crashes involving RFC/RAF aircraft in Canada during this same period.

Royal Canadian Naval Air Service, 1918

Because of the importance of Halifax to the war effort, and the threat posed by German submarines, the British Admiralty suggested the establishment of two air stations on the east coast; one at the Eastern Passage (Dartmouth) and one at Sydney, both in Nova Scotia. However, the Admiralty expressed regret that they could not provide any assistance in this endeavour and suggested that Canada create her own air service. Initially the Americans rendered assistance by providing two flying boats to patrol the area around Halifax and the Bedford Basin. On 5 September 1918, the Canadian government approved the Royal Canadian Naval Air Service. Personnel were to be trained on lighter-than-air airships (dirigibles) and heavier-than-air airships (aircraft). By the signing of the armistice, the RCNAS had 81 cadets of whom 60 were undergoing training in the United States, with 13 in the United Kingdom and 8 in Canada awaiting training. Additionally, 6 coxswains had enlisted for airship duties and were serving in the United Kingdom. However, on 5 December 1918 the RCNAS was disbanded and all the cadets and coxswains were demobilized.

The Original Canadian Air Force, 1918–1920

As early as 1915, the British Army Council had suggested that forces of the Dominions should raise their own air units. Even though the overseas headquarters and the War Council had made an attempt in 1916 to create the Royal Canadian Flying Corps, it was not until the spring of 1918 that any action was officially taken by Canada.

In a memorandum dated 30 April 1918, the Canadian High Commissioner in London suggested that the government consider forming a Canadian Air Force (CAF) in England. His proposal was based on the fact that so many Canadians were already serving in the Royal Air Force, and they had expressed a desire to serve in Canadian squadrons. In considering the proposal, the Canadian government made a study in July and discovered that some 13,000 Canadians were serving in the RAF, of whom 850 were on secondment from the Overseas Military Forces of Canada. This study finally prompted the Canadian Privy Council to discuss the possibility of forming Canadian squadrons within the RAF, with the eventual aim being the formation of the Canadian Air Force.

The original proposal was to form a Canadian Wing of up to eight squadrons to serve with the Canadian Corps in France and Belgium. The cost of equipping and maintaining this formation would be borne by the Canadian government. To raise these squadrons, it was proposed that a survey be conducted of current RAF squadrons to determine which squadrons were at 60 to 80 percent Canadian aircrew. From these squadrons eight would be selected for Canadian service. Unfortunately, the RAF and the British Air Ministry felt that this would unnecessarily disrupt the fighting ability of these units and the entire field force. In addition, it was pointed out that these units might have a large percentage of Canadian aircrew, but there were very few Canadian ground crews. Thus it was decided to train the required ground crew first before any Canadian squadrons could be formed.

On 5 August 1918 the Air Ministry authorized the formation of a Canadian fighter squadron and bomber squadron. On 22 August 1918, a CAF detachment was formed at the school of Technical Training at Halton, England, to train the required ground crew for these two Canadian squadrons. On 19 September 1918, the Canadian Privy Council approved the formation of the CAF in England, comprised of two squadrons and a CAF Directorate of Air Services. This directorate was a branch of the General Staff of the Overseas Military Forces of Canada, and Lieutenant-Colonel William Avery Bishop became the first commander of the CAF in England.

On 20 November 1918, nine days after the signing of the armistice, No. 1 Squadron (Fighter) was formed at Upper Heyford, Oxfordshire, England; it was followed on 25 November 1918 by No. 2 (Day Bombing) Squadron also at Upper Heyford. To administer these two squadrons, No. 1 Wing CAF was formed on 25 March 1919. However, No. 1 Wing did not assume its duties until 1 April, after the two squadrons had moved south to Shoreham-by-Sea.

The Canadian government then decided not to retain a permanent peacetime air force and orders were sent to cease flying and to package up all aircraft and equipment for shipment to Canada. No. 1 Squadron was disbanded on 28 January 1920 and No. 2 Squadron and the Wing disbanded on 5 February 1920. The directorate of Air Services was finally disbanded on 5 August 1920. Thus ended Canada's second attempt at creating a national air force.

Canadian Air Force, 1920–1923

On 18 February 1920 the second Canadian Air Force was authorized by the Privy Council. This home-based CAF was formed as a part of the Air Board (this Air Board consisted of three branches: Civil Aviation Branch, Civil Operations Branch and the Canadian Air Force), and was authorized to appoint six officers and men with temporary rank. This new CAF was a non-permanent organization to provide biennial 28-day refresher training to former officers and airmen of the wartime Royal Air Force. On 31 August 1920, a CAF association was established, with branches in all provinces to maintain a roster and select personnel for training. The program began at Camp Borden, using the installations erected by the RAF in Canada for their wartime training, and the aircraft and other equipment that had been donated by the British and Americans. By the end of 1922, when refresher training was suspended, 550 officers and 1,271 airmen had completed the course.

While the CAF was a non-permanent force, it did not embody any units and its primary mission was to provide service training. Many of its members were seconded to the Air Board for its Civil Operations Branch. One Air Board operation that deserves mention was the trans-Canada flight of 1920. The Civil Operations Branch of the Air Board flew relays of their branch personnel as well as CAF aircraft and crews from Halifax to Vancouver in ten days; total flying time was only 49 hours and seven minutes.

The Air Board took an early interest in Northern Canada and during the summer of 1922 sent Squadron Leader R.A. Logan, CAF, on a flying expedition of the Canadian Arctic with the Department of the Interior. By 1922 it was apparent that a non-permanent establishment was not what was required in a country the size of Canada, and a reorganization of the Air Board was undertaken. The final step to this reorganization was to combine the Civil Operations Branch and the Canadian Air Force to create a new air force.

The Royal Canadian Air Force, 1924–1968

The reorganization of the Canadian Air Board and the Canadian Air Force was completed on 1 April 1924, and the "Royal" prefix was granted by the Crown and added to the CAF. Thus, Canada's fifth attempt at creating an air force finally met with real success. The Royal Canadian Air Force was originally made up of three branches: a Permanent Active Air Force, a Non-permanent Active Air Force and a Reserve Air Force. The original establishment for the RCAF was set at 62 officers and 262 airmen. This early RCAF was unique amongst world air forces, as the majority of its work was non-military in nature. It performed the duties that today are often performed by civil agencies: photo-survey, casualty evacuation, airmail delivery, fisheries and border patrol, utility transport for government officials, etc. The RCAF assumed control of the original six stations of the Civil Operations Branch of the Air Board at Camp Borden (Ontario), Winnipeg (Manitoba), Vancouver (British Columbia), High River (Alberta), Ottawa (Ontario) and Dartmouth (Nova Scotia), and the headquarters was established in Ottawa. By 1927 there was strong opposition to the military performing these civil operations. Therefore, the Directorate of Civil Government Air Operations (DCGAO) was created to administer and control all air operations carried out by state aircraft, except for exclusively military operations. DCGAO was supposed to be a civilian organization, but in reality it was commanded, administered and staffed by RCAF personnel who were seconded to or attached to this new directorate. By 1927–28 the RCAF had been reduced to two air stations (Camp Borden and Vancouver) and a headquarters, the other stations being transferred to DCGAO. As money was scarce and DCGAO had assumed most of the flying operations in Canada, this RCAF organization was essentially a paper force. The RCAF was in effect training personnel for DCGAO.

In 1932, after seeing gradual growth, the RCAF was slashed by one-fifth, releasing 78 officers and 100 airmen because of the worldwide depression at the time. This left the total strength at 103 officers and 591 airmen. For three years the RCAF was barely able to survive, but in 1935 the situation began to gradually improve. This time period also heralded a major change to the concept of operations. For years the RCAF had been engrossed in civil aviation; now it was about to become a military air force.

On 1 November 1936 the Department of Transport was created, and this relieved the burden of civil aviation from the RCAF. The RCAF returned to many of the air stations that had been civil in nature for so many years and formed military type squadrons (bomber, fighter and torpedo). In addition, RCAF Station Trenton, Ontario, was constructed at this time. As the RCAF saw real expansion, it was realized that the infrastructure to control this vast organization was stretched to its limit and it was time to decentralize. Four new regional commands were set up to report to RCAF HQ in Ottawa. These new commands were:

> Eastern Air Command in Halifax, Nova Scotia, with operational command of all units in Nova Scotia, Prince Edward Island, and New Brunswick (Newfoundland was still a British colony at the time);

Central Air Command in Winnipeg, Manitoba, with operational command of all units in Manitoba, Saskatchewan, and northern Ontario;

Western Air Command in Vancouver, British Columbia, with operational command of units in British Columbia, and Alberta; and

Air Training Command in Toronto, Ontario, with control of all basic aircrew and ground crew training, and responsibility for Camp Borden and Trenton.

RCAF HQ in Ottawa exercised command over all units in Ontario (except the northwest) and Quebec. With the growing concern over a conflict in Europe, funding now became available for expansion and as a result of its reorganization, the RCAF was fairly well prepared for the coming war. As of 19 December 1938, the RCAF no longer reported to the army Chief of the General Staff. They now had their own chief, the Chief of the Air Staff, who reported directly to the Minister of National Defence.

Although the Non-permanent Active Air Force (Auxiliary Air Force) was authorized in 1924, it was not until 1932 that it became a reality. Three squadrons were formed that year: No. 10 Squadron Toronto, No. 11 Squadron Vancouver and No. 12 Squadron Winnipeg. In 1934 two more squadrons were formed: No. 15 and 18 Squadron Montreal. In 1935 two more squadrons were formed: No. 19 Squadron Hamilton and No. 20 Squadron Regina. On 15 November 1937 to facilitate expansion in the Permanent Force, the Non-permanent Force squadrons were all re-numbered to the 100 block of designators, i.e. No. 10 Squadron became No. 110 Squadron. In 1938 the last three Non-permanent Force squadrons were formed: No. 114 Squadron London, No. 116 Squadron Halifax, and No. 117 Squadron St John, N.B. In September 1939, when the RCAF mobilized, the Non-permanent Force represented about one-third of the total air force strength.

The Second World War

From the modest force at the outbreak of the Second World War, the RCAF grew to be the fourth largest air force in the world. On the eve of the outbreak of war, the RCAF had twenty squadrons on strength (eight Permanent Force and twelve Non-permanent Force) with authority to form three more Permanent Force squadrons. These squadrons had a total of 270 aircraft of twenty different types; of these only 124 could be termed operational service types and then only 29 could be deemed first-line equipment (19 Hurricane fighters and 10 Battle bombers). From this start the RCAF expanded into three major elements: the British Commonwealth Air Training Plan, the Home War Establishment, and the Overseas War Establishment with elements in Western Europe, the Mediterranean and the Far East.

The British Commonwealth Air Training Plan (BCATP)

On 10 October 1939 it was announced that Canada, Australia, New Zealand and the United Kingdom had agreed in principle to a combined and co-ordinated training plan based in Canada, similar to the First World War plan. Aircrew training would be conducted far from the battle zone. On 17 December 1939 the British Commonwealth Air Training Plan agreement was signed; Canada would be turned into a giant training mill.

Under the BCATP agreement the RCAF would administer 40,000 trained personnel and instruct (and provide ground crew for) 20,000 aircrew annually in 74 training schools. At the time the RCAF had only 4,061 officers and airmen (including the

Non-permanent Force) and had only trained 45 pilots in 1939. The BCATP was to become a major undertaking, as the first schools were to be open by 29 April 1940, a mere four months away.

To meet the demand, the RCAF called upon the seventeen civilian flying schools in Canada to provide the elementary flying training for the plan, and a group of commercial and bush pilots were assembled to train observers. The Department of Transport assumed the responsibility for selecting suitable sites and arranging contracts for the construction of these stations.

The first schools were opened as planned on 29 April 1940 and training began. By the end of September 1941, seven months ahead of schedule, all but three schools were opened. The first students from the plan were not expected to graduate until early 1941, but because accelerated training was possible in Canada, on 27 October 1941 the first 39 graduate pilots passed out of Camp Borden, followed by the first observers from Trenton and the first air gunners from Jarvis.

The plan was expanded in June 1942 to include 67 training schools (including 21 double schools, stations that had 2 schools) and 10 specialist schools. The RCAF was still responsible for the administration of an additional 27 RAF schools in Canada. By the close of 1943, the BCATP had reached its peak with four training commands, operating 97 schools and 184 ancillary units on 231 sites. It was now graduating an average of 3,000 students a month.

The program was so successful that, because of a backlog of trained aircrew, on 16 February 1944, the signatories agreed to begin a gradual reduction in the plan. The RCAF in June 1944 ceased recruiting aircrews and by October the closure of schools was stepped up. As an example of the excessive number of aircrews, during 1944 and 1945, it was common practice for aircrew to receive an Army commando course prior to proceeding overseas and as a result of a shortage of flight engineers, a second pilot course (pilots, however, were in short supply as late as 1943) with flight engineer training was initiated. On 31 March 1945 the British Commonwealth Air Training Plan came to an end, having produced 49,707 pilots, 29,963 various navigators, 15,673 air bombers, 18,696 wireless operator/air gunners, 15,700 air gunners and 1913 flight engineers. The total trained aircrew from the BCATP was 131,552. The BCATP was credited as a major contributing factor to winning air superiority in Europe.

Home War Establishment

When the war began in 1939, the RCAF had two operational commands (Eastern and Western Command) and seven under-strength squadrons equipped with a variety of obsolete aircraft. Because of the importance placed on the sea link between Canada and the United Kingdom, Eastern Air Command was given top priority for re-equipping and up-grading. When Japan entered the war in December 1941, the priority was reversed and the Western Air Command became top priority.

Because of the nature of Canadian geography, poor communications, lack of infrastructure and the isolation of many RCAF stations, command and control became very difficult. This necessitated the creation of smaller sub-headquarters. These became groups; odd numbered groups were designated for Eastern Air Command and even numbered groups were designated for Western Air Command.

In November 1943, the Home War Establishment reached its peak with 37 operational squadrons: 19 in Eastern Air Command and 18 in Western Air Command. Eastern Air Command's primary concern was the eastern sea approaches and the U-boat threat. As the war effort would depend largely on the ability of the Allies to ship the required supplies from North America to the U.K. or to other theatres, the North Atlantic was an essential roadway/seaway to victory. Eastern Air Command based their planning on this premise and accordingly equipped the bomber-reconnaissance squadrons with Hudson, Bolingbroke and Catalina aircraft, and later with Liberators. During the early stages of the Battle of the Atlantic, Eastern Air Command squadrons had to be satisfied with patrols and escort duties out to several hundred miles over the Atlantic; it was not until 1944 that they were able to fly patrols and escort convoys across the Atlantic. Their primary targets were the German U-boats that were attacking Allied shipping, some of which were actually venturing into the Gulf of St. Lawrence to sink vessels. The most critical period was from early 1942 to mid-1943 when enemy submarine activity reached its peak. Although aircraft from Eastern Air Command had only six confirmed U-boat kills, this cannot be the sole measure of the contribution of the command. Because of the patrols flown, the U-boats were always on their guard. Therefore, many opportunities were lost that otherwise would have been taken and many more Allied ships would have gone down; this in itself might have jeopardized the war effort and delayed victory.

In contrast, the Western Air Command generally was a quieter area. The first eighteen months of the war were spent flying patrols and identifying ships. When Japan attacked Pearl Harbour on 7 December 1941, things changed rapidly. Because of the seriousness of the situation and the lack of reinforcements in Alaska, Canada agreed to assist in the defence of Alaska. In May 1942, two squadrons were sent to Prince Rupert to defend this important seaport. In June 1942 a second formation was sent to Anchorage, Alaska. After the Japanese forces landed on Kiska Island in the Aleutian chain, this formation started flying offensive operations against the Japanese. On one of these missions Squadron Leader K.A. Boomer became the only member of a home unit to score a confirmed victory against an enemy aircraft. With the total withdrawal of the Japanese forces in the summer of 1943, the Canadian squadrons moved back south to British Columbia.

The RCAF Overseas

When the war began, the Royal Canadian Air Force was represented in England by a small liaison staff in London and various personnel attending training courses. As early as 1939, senior RCAF officers were pressing for the formation of overseas units, and in November the Chief of the Air Staff wrote a memorandum to the Minister of National Defence stating it was essential that the RCAF take more affirmative action in the war effort in addition to the British Commonwealth Air Training Plan. His proposal was to establish an overseas command to operate under RAF headquarters; the command would operate two major air groups in England, a bomber group and a fighter group, each containing three wings of two squadrons.

This proposal, when presented to the British Air Ministry, was received with mixed emotion. The bomber group was well received, but because of the organizational make-up of the U.K. (it was divided into RAF Fighter Command defence sectors with an associated air group assigned), the fighter group was not supported. However, Canadian fighter squadrons were welcome to become an integral part of the RAF fighter team. Under an amendment to the BCATP agreement signed on 17 December 1939 and a supplemental agreement (7 January 1940), it was agreed that the RCAF would form 25 overseas squadrons in the U.K.

The first RCAF squadrons overseas were No. 1, 110 and 112 Squadron. Of these, No. 1 was a fighter squadron and No. 110 and 112 were army co-operation units. The two army co-operation squadrons were to support the 1st Canadian Division in France, but by the time they arrived in England the Canadian Army had returned to

England after a failed excursion to France to support the British Expeditionary Force (BEF), then evacuating from Dunkirk.

Because of the large number of Dominion squadrons that were expected to form-up in the U.K., there was a great potential for mass confusion; imagine having command of five squadrons, all numbered No. 1 from each of the RAF, RCAF, RAAF(Australia), SAAF(South Africa) and RNZAF(New Zealand). To alleviate this confusion, the British Air Ministry assigned blocks of squadron numbers to the Dominions: 400–445 to Canada, 450–467 to Australia and 485–490 to New Zealand. The original three RCAF squadrons were then renumbered: No. 1 became No. 401 Sqn, No. 110 Sqn became No. 400 Sqn and No. 112 Sqn became No. 402 Sqn. Eventually, the RCAF had 44 of the "400 block" squadrons, along with three Army Observation Post squadrons (No. 664,665 and 666 Sqn) and one Home Defence Establishment squadron (No. 162 Sqn on detachment from Eastern Air Command), for a total of 48 squadrons serving overseas. They served on all fronts and in all theatres, and consisted of 15 bomber squadrons, 11 day fighter squadrons, three fighter-bomber squadrons, three fighter reconnaissance squadrons, three night fighter squadrons, one intruder squadron, six coastal patrol squadrons, three transport squadrons and three army co-operation (AOP) squadrons.

When the first RCAF squadrons arrived overseas, it was a bleak period on the continent. The Battle of France was almost over and the Battle of Britain was about to begin. No. 1 (401) Sqn RCAF pilots, equipped with Hurricanes, commenced an intensive training period and by August 1940 were participating in the Battle of Britain. In addition, because of the number of Canadians serving with or seconded to the RAF, the RAF converted one of its squadrons to a Canadian unit: No. 242 (Canadian) Sqn, commanded by Squadron Leader J.E. Johnson, RAF. These two squadrons gave a good account of themselves during the battle; No. 242 Sqn scored 68.5 confirmed victories and No. 401 Sqn scored 28.5 confirmed victories. However, Canadian participation in fighter operations did not terminate at the end of the Battle of Britain; it continued throughout the war. The RCAF formed night fighter (No. 406, 409 and 410) squadrons and an intruder (No. 418) squadron. These squadrons were operational in the summer of 1941 and were patrolling/prowling the night skies with great effect; night fighters patrolled the skies around the U.K. using ground controllers and airborne radar to intercept incoming bombers, while intruders prowled around German airfields at night waiting for returning German bombers or night fighters. After the Allied invasion in June 1944, these night squadrons continued their nocturnal work on the continent; and when the German "Buzz Bombs" started arriving in England, two of the night fighter squadrons turned their efforts against this new threat. By war's end, No. 409 Sqn was credited with 10 V-1 "Buzz-Bombs" and No. 418 Sqn had 77 kills over the English Channel credited to them and another five over England.

As in the First World War, Canadian fighter pilots wrote a page for themselves in history with their brilliant exploits. The first Canadian fighter squadron to arrive overseas was commanded by Squadron Leader E.A. McNab who was later awarded the first Distinguished Flying Cross bestowed on a member of the RCAF. In air battles over the continent, many Canadian pilots won distinction, including R.W. McNair, D.R. Morrision and K.L.B. Hodson. In Malta, G.F (Buzz) Beurling, became Canada's top fighter ace with 31 victories. Both R.W. McNair and H.W. McLeod won the Distinguished Service Order and Distinguished Flying Cross. In the night skies, Squadron Leader Russ Bannock and Flying Officer R.R. Bruce formed an outstanding night fighter team. They were also credited with destroying 18.5 V-1 flying bombs.

Prior to the war, the doctrine of the RAF did not include the concept of close support to land operations, but was strictly strategic (the RAF would bomb the bridges and factories while the army took care of the front line). After the lessons learned from the German war machine in their Battle of France, this doctrine was re-thought and army co-operation squadrons were formed. Initially these squadrons were equipped for light liaison duties (artillery spotting similar to WW1 and light transport). With the experience of the German Stuka still fresh in their memories, these squadrons were soon taking a more active role in army co-operation, including missions for photo-reconnaissance, sweep "rhubarbs", escort and close air support. When the RCAF started participating in this new form of warfare, the units were posted to Army Co-operation Command. After 6 June 1944, Army Co-operation Command was disbanded and the Second Tactical Air Force was landed on the continent.

Canada and RCAF Headquarters Overseas had envisioned providing all of the required air support for the First Canadian Army on the continent, but this undertaking would have totally drained the RCAF's resources overseas, and with their commitments to Coastal Command and Bomber Command to think about, a compromise was reached. The RCAF would provide units for the Second Tactical Air Force (2 TAF) in the hopes they eventually would form an all Canadian (Composite) Group. This did not materialize, but the Canadian squadrons in 2 TAF were assigned to No. 83 (Composite) Group and this group was assigned to the First Canadian Army.

As previously stated, Canada had volunteered to form bomber squadrons in the U.K. as part of Bomber Command. These squadrons were originally paid (at Canadian rates of pay) and equipped by the British Air Ministry. The first Canadian bomber squadrons were formed in late 1941 and were a part of No. 4 Group RAF in Yorkshire. By late 1942, with five bomber squadrons operational and six more on the way, plans went ahead to create No. 6 (RCAF) Group. On 1 January 1943 No. 6 Group assumed operational command of the RCAF bomber squadrons overseas. This group eventually operated 14 squadrons on eight different stations. On 1 April 1943, the Canadian government assumed the responsibility for pay and equipment for its overseas bomber force. Throughout the entire bombing offensive, the bomber organization was highly centralized and controlled by Bomber Command Headquarters. At the time, the groups were responsible for ensuring the crews were briefed according to Bomber Command's instructions (routes to and from the targets, altitudes, numbers of aircraft and bomb load), while the stations provided the domestic support and the squadrons provided administration and aircraft maintenance only.

However, this changed in March 1943, when Bomber Command reorganized into the Bomber Operational Base System; this system brought several small bases under one station commander and it centralized the administration and maintenance on this new large station. This reorganization reduced squadrons to the aircrew and basic servicing capabilities only (gas, oil, starts and parks). From the start, the Canadians in Bomber Command and later in No. 6 (RCAF) Group suffered under the operational workload placed upon them from Bomber Command and the lack of operational experience within their ranks; many losses were heartfelt during this time and morale suffered. However, as experience grew and equipment improved, the losses dropped and there was a corresponding increase in morale. By war's end No. 6 (RCAF) Group had a most enviable record of successes.

The RCAF Overseas contributed many units and personnel directly to the war effort in Europe. These were not the only contributions made by Canada or Canadians overseas. In addition to the combat squadrons supplied to the various RAF Commands, the RCAF also established transport squadrons outside Canada. In the late summer of 1944, No. 437 Squadron was established as a part of Transport

Command and almost immediately participated in the airborne assault on Arnhem with their Dakota aircraft. They provided glider-tow and airborne re-supply services for the airborne landings at Arnhem. After this operation they continued to provide transport services to the armies on the continent, bringing supplies in and casualties out. The RCAF also provided two other transport squadrons (No. 435 and 436) in the South East Asian Theatre of operations. These squadrons were formed in India and provided vital services to the British 14th Army in India and Burma. After the cessation of hostilities, the three transport squadrons were consolidated in England and flew supplies, mail and personnel to the Canadian occupation forces in Germany.

While the Home Defence Establishment was providing coastal patrols on the Canadian side of the Atlantic, there were Canadian squadrons flying the same missions from the United Kingdom. Eventually this establishment (Canada's contribution to Coastal Command's effort) would reach six squadrons with another on detachment from the Home War Establishment. Their mission was to protect the vital North Atlantic sea lanes by patrolling for U-boats and surface raiders. In addition, Canada also supplied one coastal patrol squadron for the South East Asian theatre. Shortly after their arrival in Ceylon (now Sri Lanka), a member of No. 413 Sqn (S/L L.J. Birchall) discovered the Japanese invasion fleet, which was headed for Ceylon. Because of this warning, the island's defences were alerted and the fleet was driven off, thus starting the great Japanese reversal in the Pacific.

Although the RCAF contributed 48 overseas squadrons to the war effort, the actual contribution by Canada was far greater. Of the RCAF personnel who served overseas, only about 40 percent actually served on Canadian squadrons, the remaining 60 percent served in RAF units. In addition to this, many Canadians joined the RAF before the RCAF was recruiting people (George Beurling originally joined the RAF before he transferred to the RCAF). During the defence of Malta, it was estimated that one in every four pilots who flew a mission was a Canadian. The RCAF officially has only two Victoria Cross winners (P/O A.C. Mynarski and F/L D.E. Hornell) and four George Cross winners, but there were a total of four Victoria Crosses (S/L I.W. Bazalgette, RAF, and Lt(N) R.H. Gray, RCNVR) and five George Crosses were won by Canadian airmen.

For a country the size of Canada with a population of only 16 million, it was quite an impressive contribution: 249,662 personnel served with the RCAF during the war, of which a total of 93,844 served overseas. 17,100 people lost their lives, of which 14,544 occurred overseas.

"Tiger Force" Pacific

From the earliest days of the Second World War, the primary goals were victory in Europe, phase one, and defeat of Japan, phase two. By late 1944 an Allied victory in Europe was assured and planning for phase two was implemented.

On 20 October 1944 a very large bomber force code named "Tiger Force," was proposed. It was to consist of three bomber groups: one RAF, one RCAF and one a composite of RAF, RAAF, RNZAF and SAAF squadrons. Each group would consist of twenty-two bomber, fighter and transport squadrons. The Canadian group was to be based upon 6 Group. Later the bomber strength of these groups was reduced from twelve squadrons to ten and finally to eight.

On 8 May 1945, when Germany surrendered, the plans for the creation of Tiger Force were stepped up. The RCAF squadrons selected for the Tiger Force were converted to the Canadian built Lancaster X which the crews ferried back to Canada. The training stations were RCAF Station Debert, RCAF Station Greenwood, RCAF Station Dartmouth, and RCAF Station Yarmouth, all in Nova Scotia. However, before these squadrons could commence training, the atomic bombs were dropped on Hiroshima (6 August 1945) and Nagasaki (9 August 1945) and Japan surrendered (14 August 1945). The RCAF Tiger Force was ordered to cease flying on 6 September 1945 and was then disbanded.

Post-War Era

At the cessation of hostilities the RCAF had 164,846 all ranks (the peak was in 1944 with 215,200) serving; this was to be reduced to an authorized strength of 16,000 all ranks. This demobilization was to take place over a two-year period. On 6 February 1946 the Cabinet approved a peacetime RCAF of four components: a Regular Force, an Auxiliary, a Reserve and the Royal Canadian Air Cadets (the RCAC was established during the war to provide basic military training to Canadian youth, so that training costs could be reduced when they joined the regular force). On 30 September 1947, when this organization came into effect, the RCAF was stood down from active service.

The post-war Regular Force RCAF was not all that different from the pre-war RCAF. Eight squadrons were authorized, but only five stood-up. These were to form the professional nucleus of the air force. Their primary tasks were again aerial photography, air transport and communications (utility). A new task that the RCAF assumed was search and rescue. In addition, Air Force Headquarters decided that the squadrons that did stand-up would be from the "400 Overseas" block of squadrons.

By 1947 the post-war world was not the utopia everyone had hoped for. The relationship between the democratic dominated western nations and the communist eastern bloc were cooling rapidly. So, after the post-war rush to demobilize, there came a new resurgence of the RCAF. The Department of National Defence (DND) announced in mid-January 1947 that the services would be built up. In late September 1948, the first post-war pilot course commenced (the first course since 1944).

From a post-war low of 11,569 officers and airmen in December 1947, the RCAF commenced a steady growth until January 1955 when a ceiling of 51,000 officers and airmen was authorized (this was a first, as the RCAF was now larger than the army's 47,000 strength). The post-war RCAF peaked in the mid-50s with twenty-nine regular force squadrons and twelve auxiliary squadrons. This continued until 1962 when the CF-100 squadrons were withdrawn without replacement.

The post-war infrastructure changed dramatically. Initially Canada was divided into two geographic commands: Central Air Command, located in Trenton, with No. 10 Group in Halifax and North Western Air Command, located in Edmonton, with No. 11 Group in Winnipeg and No. 12 Group in Vancouver. At this time while the regular force was trying to settle into their post-war organization, the auxiliary air force (now primary reserves) was being re-established. In April 1946 the auxiliary air force was authorized an establishment of 4500 officers and airmen and 15 squadrons. The auxiliary air force's role was air defence; this role they kept until 1958.

With the expansion of the RCAF came a corresponding increase in the infrastructure. Beginning in 1948, the RCAF began to restructure along operational commands rather than regional commands: No. 9 Transport Group became Air Transport Command and No.1 Air Defence Group was formed. In 1949 Maintenance Command became Air Material Command and Central Command became Training Command. Additionally in 1949, No. 10 and 11 Groups became Maritime and Tactical Group respectively. In the early 1950s, with world tension increasing, expansion continued, No.1 Air Division in Europe, No. 5 Air Division (formerly No. 12 Group) and No. 14 (Training) Group were formed, while other groups were elevated to command status: Air Defence Command, Maritime Air Command and Tactical Air Command.

Air Transport Command

Since the earliest days of aviation in Canada, air transport has played an important role. The Canadian Air Force and then the RCAF have always been involved in this aspect of opening up Canada's vast interior.

During the Second World War, air transport played a vital role in the support of the Allied efforts in Europe. Large quantities of supplies were flown over to the United Kingdom. In addition to freight, the ferrying of aircraft to Europe came under the umbrella of Air Transport and a western terminus for the ferry service was constructed at Goose Bay.

In the immediate post-war years air transport, including aerial photography of the north, was a major role for the RCAF. No. 9 (Transport) Group was formed to meet all of its transport requirements. As the RCAF expanded in the late 1940s, so did No. 9 (Transport) Group, until 1 April 1948 when Air Transport Command was established, headquartered in Rockcliffe. The headquarters moved to Lachine, Quebec, in August 1951 and later to Trenton, Ontario, in September 1959. This command continued through unification until 2 September 1975, when Air Command was formed and Air Transport Command became Air Transport Group. Throughout its long service Air Transport Command/Group has provided Canada with its primary Search and Rescue and strategic airlift capabilities. Some of the major operations that Air Transport Command has participated in have been Korea, support to No. 1 Air Division in Europe, UN operations (including Suez crisis 1956, Gaza 1956–67, Belgian Congo 1960, New Guinea and Yemen 1962, Cyprus and India-Pakistan 1964, Kashmir 1971, Egypt 1974, Golan Heights 1973, Persian Gulf 1991), Mercy operations (including 1960 earthquakes in Morocco and Chile, 1961 forest fires in Brazil, 1970 earthquake in Peru, 1973 drought in sub-Sahara Africa, 1979 uprising in Iran and Vietnamese boat-people) and northern re-supply. Air Transport Group continued to live up to their motto of "Versatile and Ready."

Air Defence Command

The original post-war concept called for air defence to be the responsibility of the auxiliary squadrons. These squadrons, augmented by auxiliary mobile radar squadrons, were equipped with Vampire jet interceptors or Mustang fighters and later with Sabre Mk 5s; no regular force units were involved in air defence. However, with the deteriorating international situation of the late 1940s, Canada decided to equip regular force squadrons for air defence. In December 1948, No. 1 Air Defence Group was created in Ottawa. In November 1949 the headquarters moved to St Hubert, Quebec. The Group became Air Defence Command in June 1951 and was integrated into North American Air Defence Command (NORAD) in September 1957. The Command finally moved to North Bay, Ontario, in August 1966. In September 1975 Air Defence Group was formed as an operational group of Air Command, and in 1984 Fighter Group was created and assumed the responsibility for all fighter operations within the Canadian Forces.

By 1955 Air Defence Command had reached its peak strength with nine Regular Force squadrons (flying CF-100s) and ten Auxiliary squadrons (flying Vampires and Mustangs). During this period, as radar warning lines were being erected across Canada, Canadian and American officials considered how best to optimize their defences. The concept of an international radar system gradually evolved into a single command structure and the North American Air Defence (NORAD) agreement was the final development. Canada had three radar warning lines, the Distant Early Warning (DEW) in the North West Territories, and the CADIN/ PINE-TREE and the Mid-Canada lines stretching across Canada at different latitudes. Under the NORAD agreement, there would be an American Commander in Chief with a Canadian as his deputy, and the backup NORAD command centre would be in Canada.

As equipment capabilities increased and the requirement for numbers decreased, the nine CF-100 squadrons were replaced by five CF-101 squadrons (later three squadrons) and the combat control system was modernized with the Semi-Automatic Ground Environmental (SAGE) system, thus eliminating many of the manual control centres. During this time, the auxiliary lost its air defence role and was re-equipped for light transport and liaison duties. Its mobile radars were disbanded. This trend has continued into the 1980s and 1990s with the Regional Operational Control Centre (ROCC) replacing SAGE, the North Warning System (NWS) replacing the DEW line, and the coastal radars replacing the remaining CADIN/PINETREE and Mid-Canada radars.

Fighter Group then became responsible for all fighter operations in the Canadian Forces and was prepared to deploy a wing of CF-18s to any region in the world. It continued to live up to the motto of Air Defence Group, *Detegere et Destruere* (To Detect and To Destroy) with its own motto, *Proponere et Posse* (Purpose and Power). In 1997, with the further re-organization of the Air Force, 1 Canadian Air Division assumed responsibility for all fighter forces and for the Canadian NORAD Region air defence operations.

Maritime Air Command

The original post-war RCAF plans did not include a plan for the defence of Canada's coasts; this was to be left to the Royal Canadian Navy. Therefore, only a small head-quarters was set up in Halifax in April 1947 (No. 10 Group, Central Air Command). However, as the growing Soviet submarine fleet increased the threat to the northern sea-lanes, the RCAF was required to augment the RCN. This increase in responsibility led to the formation of Maritime Group in April 1949 and finally Maritime Air Command in January 1951. Maritime Air Command was absorbed into the Canadian Forces Maritime Command in January 1966 and then was separated again as Maritime Air Group when Air Command was formed in September 1975.

On 1 April 1952 Maritime Group became an integral part of the newly formed Allied Command Atlantic of the North Atlantic Treaty Organization. In July 1952 its area of operations was increased to include the Pacific Coast. Over the years MG/MAC/MAG have patrolled both coasts and provided yeoman service with the detection of submarines to the RCN/Maritime Command and Allied Commanders in the Atlantic and the Pacific. Their motto was fittingly "Over the Seas."

No. 1 Air Division Europe

With the increasing tension between the east and the west in Europe after the Second World War, the western European communities started discussing a plan for a united defence.

From these discussions came the North Atlantic Treaty Organization. No. 1 Air Division was formed as Canada's air contribution to NATO. It was to consist of four wings of day fighters. These wings were to be located on the continent and, because of the damage to the established airfields, new airfields were to be constructed.

Canada would deploy two wings to France (Marville and Grostenquin) and two wings to Germany (Zweibrucken and Furstenfeldbruck). Until these airfields were ready, the first wing would initially go to England (North Luffenham) and the headquarters for No. 1 Air Division would be located in Metz, France.

The first two squadrons of No. 1 Wing crossed the Atlantic onboard the aircraft carrier HMCS *Magnificent* in November 1951. Upon their arrival in England they deployed to RAF North Luffenham, where they stayed until Marville was ready for occupation in March 1955. The third squadron of No. 1 Wing flew across the Atlantic in Operation Leapfrog I, flying to Labrador, Greenland, Iceland, Scotland and to England. As the remaining wings were formed in Canada, their new homes on the continent were being completed.

Operation Leapfrog II in October 1952, saw all three squadrons of No. 2 Wing fly across the Atlantic to arrive at their new home at Grostenquin, France. Considered ready for occupation by the French, it was far from ready by Canadian standards and life on the continent for these intrepid aviators was far from easy. Leapfrog III (April 1952) saw the three squadrons of No. 3 Wing fly across the Atlantic to their new home at Zweibrucken, Germany. In early 1952 it was realized that when No. 4 Wing was ready to leave Canada, their new home in Furstenfeldbruck would not be complete. The French Air Force offered Canada one of her deployment bases in Germany and alternate plans were devised. Therefore, in September 1952 (Leapfrog IV), No. 4 Wing arrived at their new base at Baden-Soellingen, Germany.

By 1955 NATO realized that there was a shortage of all-weather interceptor capability and Canada responded by volunteering four CF-100 squadrons for service to NATO. Between October 1956 and August 1957, one Sabre squadron per wing was stood-down and replaced by a CF-100 squadron from Canada. In the fall of 1959, the Canadian government announced that starting in the fall of 1962 the Sabre squadrons of the Air Division would be re-equipped with CF-104 Starfighters and the CF-100 squadrons would be disbanded.

This new equipment brought a new role to the Air Division. Instead of the day/all-weather interceptor role, the Canadian squadrons would now be involved with nuclear strike and reconnaissance. However, during 1964 the cold winds of change were blowing and the French government announced that all nuclear weapons located on French soil would fall under French control. Therefore, in late 1964 after being recently re-equipped with the CF-104, No. 2 Wing sent their two squadrons to the two wings in Germany and closed their doors at Grostenquin. The other wing in France (No. 1 Wing Marville) converted to strictly reconnaissance, and the communications flight (103 KU) for the Air Divisions moved to Marville from Grostenquin. In March 1966, the French government announced the withdrawal of their military forces from NATO and the NATO forces stationed in France must leave (or fall under French command). New quarters were found for No. 1 Wing and 1 Air Division HQ at Base Arienne 139 Lahr, West Germany. The move of the operational equipment was accomplished by March 1967. Because the French were loath to move out of Lahr, the dependants and schools were moved later.

As an austerity measure, in 1968 No. 3 Wing Zweibrucken was closed and its two squadrons were moved to No. 1 and 4 Wing. In 1969 came the announcement of the amalgamation of the Canadian Forces in Europe to one command and two bases, and that the Canadian army in northern Germany (Zoest area) would be moving south to No. 1 and 4 Wing. This meant that No. 1 Wing Lahr would close its doors and the air force in Europe would be reduced in strength (from 6 to 3 squadrons) and concentrated at Baden-Soellingen, and to be named 1 Canadian Air Group (CAG). The Group remained until 1988 when Canada increased her commitment to NATO

(3 squadrons in theatre and two squadrons in Canada) and No. 1 Canadian Air Division stood-up again. However, shortly after this, relations with eastern Europe eased and Canada made another announcement; Canadian forces stationed in Europe would be withdrawn and their two bases closed by 1994. The Air Division, reduced to three squadrons then to two and finally one, ceased flying operations on 1 January 1993. This ended a major era of Canada's Air Force. *Ad Custodiendam Europam* (For the Defence of Europe).

Training Command

Training Command was formed at Trenton in October 1949; it controlled No. 14 (Training) Group in Winnipeg. In September 1958 Training Command moved to Winnipeg and absorbed No. 14 (Training) Group.

Training Command was responsible for the training of all personnel in the RCAF. In addition, under a mutual aid program, it assumed the responsibility for training aircrew for Belgium, Denmark, France, Italy, the Netherlands, Norway, Portugal, and the United Kingdom. Later, this arrangement included Turkey, Greece and West Germany. Between May 1951 and July 1957, the RCAF trained 4600 pilots and navigators for our NATO allies. This arrangement was extended for another three years for Denmark, the Netherlands and Norway, and in 1958, Canada was contracted by West Germany to train an additional 360 aircrew. Some of the RCAF Stations used during this period were Penhold and Claresholm in Alberta; MacDonald, Gimli, Portage la Prairie, and Winnipeg in Manitoba; Moose Jaw in Saskatchewan; and Trenton and Centralia in Ontario.

Training Command survived unification in 1968 and was responsible for all individual training, including flying and trades training. In 1975, when Air Command formed in Winnipeg, Training Command was reduced in size, became Training Systems, and moved back to Trenton. Their motto was *Exercendum Usque ad Optimum* (One must train up to the highest standard).

The RCAF in Korea

Because the RCAF was rebuilding its fighter forces at the time of the Korean conflict (four wings of three squadrons each for NATO), it did not contribute any fighter squadrons. However, the RCAF did make significant contributions to the war effort. Soon after the outbreak of hostilities in Korea, Canada committed her primary transport squadron (No. 426 Squadron) to United Nations service. In July 1950 the RCAF ordered No. 426 Squadron stationed at RCAF Station Lachine (Dorval) up to wartime strength (12 North Star transport aircraft) and in late July its personnel were detached to McChord AFB Washington. From 25 July 1950 until 9 June 1954, No. 426 (T) Squadron provided outstanding service to the UN in Korea, completing 599 missions for a total of over 34,000 flying hours. This was a feat which amazed the U.S. Military Air Transport Service, "how so few could do so much with so little."

Although Canada did not send any fighter squadrons to Korea, Canadian pilots were sent there on "exchange" with the United States Air Force. A total of 22 pilots served on Sabre squadrons and one RCN pilot served with a US Navy Panther Fighter Squadron in Korea. These pilots accounted for a total of 9 Mig-15s confirmed, 2 probables and 10 damaged. RCAF pilots were awarded seven US Distinguished Flying Crosses, one Commonwealth Distinguished Flying Cross, four U.S. Air Medals, and flew a total of 1,036 sorties in Korea. Of these pilots, only one was shot down and became a POW (S/L Andy MacKenzie was accidentally shot down by a USAF pilot). In addition, because the US could not produce the numbers of Sabres needed to sustain the war effort, Canada supplied the USAF with 60 F-86 Sabre Mk 2s (USAF F-86E-6).

Aviation in the Royal Canadian Navy, 1943–1968

Although Canadians had been involved with naval aviation since the First World War, the RCN did not officially form an aviation division until after the Second World War. During the first war, both the Royal Navy and the Royal Naval Air Service viewed Canada strictly as a potential source of recruits. Indeed the RNAS's top scoring ace came from Canada: Raymond Collishaw was from North Vancouver. Naval aviation then remained very low-key until the Second World War when it returned to the forefront.

Although Canada then had no naval aviation division, the RCN did man two RN escort carriers, HMS *Nabob* (commissioned September 1943) and HMS *Puncher* (commissioned February 1944). HMS *Nabob* was torpedoed in August 1944, and although she made Scapa Flow she was paid off, while HMS *Puncher* served through to VE Day. With the experience gained in wartime the RCN decided to start a naval aviation division immediately post-war. Initially two fleet carriers were considered by the RCN and after accepting the use of HMS/HMCS *Warrior* it was decided, because of cost, that the RCN would operate only one carrier. HMS *Warrior* was returned to the RN and, after HMCS *Bonaventure* (ex-HMS *Powerful*) was purchased and while "Bonny" was being finished to Canadian specifications, the RCN borrowed HMS/HMCS *Magnificent*.

Canada's aircraft carriers were in order of service:

> HMCS *Warrior* on loan to Canada from the United Kingdom (in Canadian service from January 1945–February 1947),

> HMCS *Magnificent* again on loan to Canada (from April 1948–April 1957) for operations had a straight flight deck and no mirror landing system; and

> HMCS *Bonaventure* the hull of which was laid down at the same time as that of *Magnificent* but was not completed; Canada then bought her and she was completed as a modern carrier in the Harland & Wolfe Shipyards, Belfast. She had an angled flight deck and stabilized mirror landing system. She was commissioned on 17 January 1957 and remained in service until 1969.

In the spring of 1944, a Naval Air Division was set up at Naval Headquarters in Ottawa to advise the naval staff on developments in the field of naval aviation and to formulate plans for the day when Canada would expand her fleet with the addition of an aircraft carrier. Early in 1945, four Royal Naval Air Flying Squadrons were formed in the United Kingdom for service on the Canadian carrier then under construction. These Squadrons were No. 803, 825, 826 and 883.

On 15 May 1947, the 18th Carrier Air Group (CAG), consisting of 826 and 883 Squadron, was formed at Royal Canadian Naval Air Station (RCNAS) Dartmouth, NS, and on 1 May 1951, VF 803 and VS 825 Squadron were re-designated VF-870 and VS-880 respectively and formed the 31st C.A.G. while 826 and 883 became VS-881 and VF-871 and formed the 30th C.A.G.

It was decided that the interests of the service would best be served by renumbering the air squadrons to give them a Canadian identity within the Commonwealth system, and to provide a logical means of identifying additional squadrons and air groups in the event of expansion. Thus squadron numbers 880 to 889 were allocated for antisubmarine squadrons and 870 to 879 for fighter squadrons, and existing squadrons were re-designated in June 1951. These squadrons remained in being until 7 July 1959 when VS-880 and VS-881 were amalgamated to form VS-880, the largest air unit in the RCN. Further manpower cutbacks resulted in the amalgamation of VF-870 and VF-871 into VF-870 shortly thereafter.

The Naval Air Stations and Squadrons were as follows:

HMCS *Shearwater*—the shore station home of Canadian Naval Air Operations since 1948, was the largest naval establishment in Canada;

VS-880 and VS-881 antisubmarine squadrons, which flew Barracuda, Swordfish, Firefly, Avenger and Tracker aircraft; and

VF-870 and VF-871 Fighter squadrons, which flew Wildcat, Hellcat, Seafire, Sea Fury and Banshee aircraft.

There were 5 auxiliary Naval Air Squadrons formed in order to maintain the operational efficiency of the reservist who would be of vital importance to the RCN in time of war:

VC—920 HMCS *York*	Toronto, ON	30 September 1953
VC—911	Kingston, ON	
VC—922 HMCS *Malahat*	Victoria, BC	1 December 1953
VC—923 HMCS *Montcalm*	Quebec, PQ	1 June 1954
VC—924 HMCS *Tecumseh*	Calgary, AB	1 June 1954

Naval Air Squadron HU-21 was formed at HMCS *Shearwater* in November 1952. The squadron had the following aircraft on its inventory: Bell HTL-4 & 6, Sikorsky HO4S-2 & 3, Piasecki HUP-3 and CHSS-2 Sea King Helicopters;

VT-40 All Weather Training Squadron was amalgamated with VU-32 Utility Squadron on 4 May, 1959. They flew Beechcraft 18 (Expeditors), Harvard, Avenger, Sea Fury and T-33 Silver Star aircraft;

VU-33, a Utility Squadron operated from Patricia Bay, Vancouver Island with Avenger, Piasecki HUP-3 helicopter, T-33 Silver Star and Tracker aircraft;

VX-10, a Naval Experimental Squadron, based at *Shearwater* but responsible to NDHQ Ottawa, had a least one of each type of naval aircraft in use at any time and tested for acceptance all aircraft and products utilized in naval air; and

HS-50, an Anti-Submarine Helicopter Squadron formed at *Shearwater* on 4 July, 1955 to operate Sikorsky HO4S-2 and 3, later converted to CHSS-2 Sea Kings and operated from HMCS *Bonaventure* and later the first DDEs.

The first flying unit of the RCN was in fact Fleet Requirements Unit (FRU) 743, a fleet refresher unit tasked with refresher training for some of the wartime aviators who were returning to the RCN or recruited from the ranks of demobilized RCAF pilots. In the post-war period, however, the primary role of the aviation division of the RCN was antisubmarine warfare.

In 1951 as their primary ASW platform, the RCN selected an updated version of the USN Avenger aircraft and the Sea Fury continued as the fighter. These aircraft served with 880 Sqn (RCN) and 870 Sqn (RCN) on board HMCS *Magnificent* (825 and 803 Sqn reverted to the RN). In 1952, the RCN adopted the USN designators for its squadrons, so "V" was heavier than air, "S" was antisubmarine and "F" was fighter. In 1955, the RCN expanded its aviation division and created VS 881 as its Airborne Early Warning unit, VF 871 (another fighter squadron) and HS 50, the RCN's first helicopter squadron. In 1974 HS 50 was split and HS 423 and 443 were created. As the follow-on ASW aircraft, the RCN selected a Canadian-built version of the Grumman S-2F Tracker; VS 880 and VS 881 were equipped with this aircraft type. The arrival of these aircraft coincided with the acceptance of HMCS *Bonaventure* (commissioned January 1957). The "Bonny" had been modified from her original plans and included many new innovations; steam catapults, an angled deck and mirror landing system to name a few. These advances meant higher performance aircraft could be carried as part of the ship's complement. To replace the piston-engined Sea Furies flown from the *Magnificent*, ex-USN Banshee jet fighter aircraft were selected; VF 870 and VF 871 Squadron were equipped with this aircraft type.

However, by the early 1960s budgetary restrictions meant that the RCN would be strictly an antisubmarine force; the two fighter squadrons were reduced to nil strength and the Banshees were mothballed. As another austerity measure, the two ASW squadrons were amalgamated into VS 880 Squadron. In 1970, after a major refit, it was decided that HMCS *Bonaventure* would be paid off. This was not the end of naval aviation in Canada, because in the early 1960s Canada had been working on a helicopter destroyer (DDH), capable of landing, securing and supporting helicopter operations. These were to be the future of naval aviation in Canada. From the mid-1960s through to the present, naval aviation has been primarily helicopter-based ASW.

On 1 February 1968, the RCN's naval aviation division was absorbed into Maritime Air Group, a part of Maritime Command, and in September 1975, MAG became a part of Air Command.

Army Aviation, 1944–1968

The roots of Canadian Army aviation go back to British practices. The First World War RFC trained its own pilots in all the military arts including artillery spotting, target marking, battlefield reconnaissance and identification. With the formation of the RAF, army aviation was carried out by RAF aircrew for the years between the world wars. Development of concepts and doctrines was the responsibility of The Joint School of Army Cooperation, located at Old Sarum on the Salisbury Plain, in which both the British army and RAF shared responsibility.

In Canada, military aviation did not receive much attention in the early days. The Air Board and early RCAF concentrated their efforts on providing civil air service to the entire government. There are a few examples of army cooperation in coastal defence artillery spotting, and air support of militia concentrations, but both these activities were rare. After the big cut of 1933, the RCAF shifted from Civil Government Air Operations (CGAO) to more military tasks. At the time, the tiny air force was in effect an organic part of the Canadian Army with the Director of the Air Force reporting to the Chief of the General Staff. It should come as no surprise that aviation in support of the army received a high priority within the Canadian defence establishment. The army cooperation course at Old Sarum was one of the most popular professional development courses for up-and-coming RCAF officers between the wars. An RCAF school of army cooperation was established at RCAF Camp Borden in the early 1930s and a flight of Atlas army cooperation aircraft was located at RCAF Station Trenton in 1930. In addition, Canada's emerging aircraft procurement strategy involved manufacture of Lysander aircraft, the front line RAF army cooperation aircraft of the time. Canada's first air contribution to the war in Britain was two Lysander squadrons, which arrived at Oldpost in Salisbury Plain in l940.

Unfortunately the Old Sarum doctrine for army cooperation during the opening days of the war was a failure. The Lysander had been developed from first war concepts for a Corps support aircraft and could do all those functions desired by the RFC to support operations under Western front conditions in a superior manner, but the rules of the game had changed. The new German concept of war, the blitzkrieg, made trench warfare obsolete, and the Lysander was withdrawn from direct army aviation support roles shortly after the fall of France. Canada converted its two RCAF Lysander squadrons, which arrived in England in 1940, to fighter aircraft, which continued in a new army cooperation role that emphasized photo reconnaissance and interdiction. Many of the traditional army cooperation roles simply disappeared. Among these was artillery spotting functions, one of the major roles of the old Corps support aircraft.

Air Observation Post Units

The Air Observation Post (AOP) Squadron was an idea of Captain HC Bazeley, RA. Bazeley was the secretary of the Royal Artillery Flying Club and had put forward the idea, before the war, of providing batteries and brigades of the Royal Artillery with the same sort of light aircraft that officers of the flying club flew for pleasure. The aircraft would be flown by qualified Royal Artillery officers who would use their ordinary procedures for ranging a battlefield and spotting the fall of shot. Originally the RAF was not convinced on the idea of an army aviation component. However, an experimental flight was formed in February 1940 using an American designed light aircraft, the Taylorcraft Auster, which was built under license in England. The aircraft took no part in the campaign in France during 1940, but a squadron of the aircraft went out to Algeria in July 1941 and proved to be most successful. It was the first of some 15 squadrons of AOP aircraft using the Auster that had become part of the military aviation scene during the Second World War. The Auster was also used as a light transport aircraft and a few were assigned to the RCAF fighter wings for transport and training.

During the Italian campaign it became obvious to the Canadian Army field commanders that AOP was definitely needed. Canadian Overseas Headquarters approached army headquarters in Ottawa during 1944 to form army AOP squadrons. After considerable discussion it was agreed that their squadrons would form, but on the RAF pattern.

The approach taken by the British to organize the AOP squadrons was somewhat peculiar. It reflected the political decision taken just before the war that the Air Ministry would remain responsible for all air materiel and support. The squadrons were on the order of battle of the RAF with RAF administration and ground crew but with pilots and squadron commanders drawn from the Royal Artillery. The Canadian war cabinet decided to follow the same approach and three squadrons No. 664, 665 and 666, were authorized as RCAF units in September 1944.

The first squadron, 664, formed on 1 December 1944 at RAF Station Andover. The Squadron Adjutant, an RCAF Administrative Officer, was Flight Lieutenant LE Crowe. On 8 December 1944, the advance party of Royal Canadian Artillery arrived with a full complement of motor transport equipment, and on 9 December 1944, the main party of RCAF ground crew, some 54 personnel—mainly airframe and aero-engine technicians with a scattering of cooks, instrument mechanics and nursing orderlies. The squadron was roughly half army and half air force and was billeted together. By 31 December the squadron's strength included nine officers (one of which was RCAF), eight senior NCOs (two of which were RCAF), and 72 other ranks, (65 of which were RCAF). On the 6 January 1945, the squadron received its first Auster aircraft from 29 Maintenance Unit and the rest followed shortly thereafter.

On 2 February 1945, the squadron moved from Andover to RAF Parkhurst in Kent, a satellite field of Kenley. It formed a separate servicing flight and carried out squadron level operational training. Also during this time, the CO indicated that he wanted the RCAF troops in khaki battle dress rather than blue. He took this subject up with RCAF overseas headquarters, which granted permission on 2 February. Finally on 17 March the entire squadron was on its way overseas to Tilbury and Breda in Holland. The squadron started operations at the end of March 1945, which interestingly enough included missions to take recce photographs. By the middle of April 1945 the squadron had accumulated 434 operational hours and 266 hours of non-operational flying. The ground crew was faced with hard work in open field conditions. Often they had to work all night to put down metalized strips for a landing strip, since mud was a major enemy. The war came to an end before the squadron had gained much experience. After a short period of time at Wiliamshafen, Oldenburg and Apeldoorn it was time for the squadron to stand down. All aircraft were returned to the maintenance unit on 20 May and all personnel were struck off strength by 31 May 1946.

No. 665 Squadron was formed on 5 February 1945 and followed a similar evolution to 664 Squadron. The aircraft arrived at Leis in Holland on 15 April 1945 and commenced operations. The squadron encountered some difficulty getting appropriate fuel. The aircraft was designed to use 73-octane gasoline but the only fuel available was 80-octane motor transport fuel. The 80-octane fuel created some serious valve and servicing problems in the field. When the war ended the squadron changed from an AOP role to a military services and communications role. Ten volunteers for the Far East remained and the squadron continued to do good work until early October 1945 when it disbanded. No. 666 Squadron started up on 3 March 1945 and had a very short life, being disbanded on 31 October 1945.

Post-War Development

An AOP squadron was part of the approved plan for the post-war structure of the RCAF. The AOP squadron was organized on the same basis as the wartime overseas AOP squadrons, the army providing the pilots and the RCAF providing the ground support. The AOP squadron relied upon the central maintenance facilities at the Canadian Joint Air Training Center (CJATC) in Rivers, Manitoba, since a dedicated RCAF squadron maintenance organization was not provided. It was a system that worked reasonably well and provided routine inspection services, however there was a continuous problem in looking after snagged aircraft. For exercises, ad hoc arrangements were made. For example, AOP aircraft flew out of the NRC flight test center at Arnprior in support of Petawawa with airmen from the AFHQ Piston Practice Flight for maintenance support. The squadron was equipped with Auster Mk 4 aircraft and AMCHQ supported the procurement of spares, the issue of maintenance schedules and such other activities as were needed to support the aircraft in the field.

CJATC Rivers

Manitoba and army aviation were synonymous terms in the beginning days. The

Canadian Army's first direct involvement with aviation took place at Shilo, Manitoba in September 1942 with the start of Canadian Paratroop Parachute training. After the war, a joint air school was established at Shilo on 3 May 1947 which moved to Rivers on 1 April 1949 where it formed the initial cadre of CJATC. There were several components to the school at Rivers, including: a transport support school, which taught the theory and practice of moving armed forces by air, and consisted of a transport support section, an air portability section and an air supply section; an offensive support school; a joint air photo interpretation school; and an air training wing. Initially the air training wing was known as No. 20 Tactical Wing and consisted of a flying control section, a met section, 417 (Fighter) Squadron, 416 (Bomber) Squadron, 122 (Transport) Flight, and 444(AOP) Squadron. On 1 April 1949, the tactical wing was renamed the Air-Training Wing. No. 417 Squadron became the Fighter Tactical Flight, 112 (T) became the Air Transport School, 444(AOP) the Light Aircraft and Helicopter Conversion School. The Transport School had eight Dakotas and eight Horsa gliders, the Tactical Flight was equipped with Mustangs and Harvards and was involved in Operation Sweetbrier. The AOP consisted of one squadron at Rivers on a reduced scale, and one flight attached to the artillery school at Shilo. The AOP was equipped with Chipmunk and Auster fixed wing aircraft, and a few Bell and Sikorsky helicopters. There was an Air Support Signal Unit and the entire operation was mobile in trucks.

CJATC was commanded by an RCAF Group Captain with an army Lieutenant Colonel as second in command. The school was not just an army air force operation —the navy arrived every year to carry out air land maneuvers and in this regard was often moved from Dartmouth to Rivers by CJATC Dakotas. In August 1948 eight Seafire and eight Fireflies plus a Harvard and Norseman were used for navy training. Maintenance support at Rivers was on a central maintenance basis with a servicing squadron and a repair squadron. A separate armament squadron was later incorporated.

Canadian army pilots had been flying Bell 47 helicopters from late 1948. As part of CJATC, a helicopter school was established at Rivers and became the initial training ground for both army and air force helicopter pilots and maintainers.

By 1950, there were 230 people in the central maintenance organization with an average strength of 42 aircraft. During Operation Sweetbrier the station provided six Dakotas, eight Mustangs, and three Austers at Whitehorse along with 171 air technicians. In addition to their powered aircraft, the center had six Horsa gliders, which were used for a variety of roles until the early 1950s. In late 1951, C-119 Flying Box Car aircraft were deployed to Rivers along with Piasecki helicopters. There was no shortage of new and modern equipment at the center—perhaps more in quality than in quantity.

The carrier air groups spent approximately two months of each summer at the center. This was a very intensive operation involving extensive armament activities. For example during the RCN visit of 1953, VF-871 Squadron spent the period from 9-20 November at Rivers. During the course of its stay, it dropped 120 bombs (500 and 1,000 lb live ordinance) and expended 500 rockets.

The AMC newsletter in 1953 complimented Rivers on a well-organized smooth functioning maintenance team. It noted that helicopter maintenance was much more complicated and demanding than normal aircraft and engines. And it pointed out that this station was involved in an accelerated training scheme on the S-51 helicopter, which was new in service. CJATC at the time was the principal helicopter operator within the Canadian Forces.

The aircraft strength at CJATC Rivers in 1955 included one Dakota, four C-119s, five Auster Mk6s, four L-19s, two Bell 47s, four Sikorski S-51s, six Mustangs, and No. 2 AOP flight with three Auster 6s and two L-19As. This was a complicated maintenance organization by any standard. It was decided to introduce individual fitter/rigger flights for specific aircraft types with a C-119 flight, an L-19 and Auster flight, a Mustang flight, a helicopter flight and a transient servicing flight. These reported to an OC flights, and there was an OC services who looked after instrument, electrical and support services. During this period there was no army involvement with aircraft maintenance activities. In fact, the wartime agreement where the air force provided support and the army provided the pilots remained in effect.

No 1 THP RCASC (1 THUMP)

During the late 1950s the Canadian Army recognized the need for a heavy lift helicopter unit. The Department of National Defence estimates for 1957 included three requirements for heavy helicopters; ASW machines for the RCN; SAR helicopters for the RCAF; and transport helicopters for the Army. Government officials tried very hard to get the three services to agree to a common type and were partly successful when the army and air force agreed to a common variant of the Vertol Model 107 Voyageur helicopter. In due course, 12 aircraft were bought to support the army requirement. This was the largest aircraft ever procured by the Canadian Army, having a 5,000 pound lifting capacity.

The Army activated No. 1 Transport Helicopter Platoon, Royal Canadian Army Service Corps as an elite unit of the field force and in typical military shorthand, the unit became known as 1 THUMP. It was the largest and most complex aviation unit organized by the Canadian Army. Although it was an RCASC unit, it included representatives from several different force and arms—in particular a maintenance section of RCEME personnel who carried out all first and second line maintenance. The first aircraft was delivered early in1964 and was assigned to RCEME for technician training (a small cadre of RCEME craftsmen were also sent to Boeing Vertol at Morton, Pennsylvania and General Electric at Lynn, for factory training courses). The Platoon officially formed on 10 December 1964 and became operational at CJATC Rivers on 16 November 1964. The initial mission of the unit was to reach a stage of organization and training sufficient to allow it to be joined to a field formation as an operational unit by November 1965. No. 1 THUMP was successful in achieving its first assignment in a most commendable manner and was extended a full complement of 12 helicopters during the summer of 1966.

Transitions

It must be recognized that the formal organization of Canadian army aviation tended to overlap the unification and integration process. Mr. Paul Hellyer's March 1964 White Paper is chiefly remembered for the introduction of unification and integration but it also changed the roles and functions of the Canadian military. A functional system of control was adopted in which mobile command—principally the army— was assigned a global, mobile peacekeeping and peace-restoring role. Mobile Command then initiated a project to design its own Army Aviation Corps. The design goal seemed to be the US Air Calvary division model then being used in Southeast Asia. Several new equipment programs were started and an emphasis placed on air mobile operations including the purchase of close-support fighters (F-5/CF-116 Freedom Fighters), utility helicopters (CH-135 Twin Huey), light observation helicopters (CH-136 Kiowa), heavy lift helicopters (CH-147 Chinook) and transport aircraft (CC-115 Buffalo). There were even later plans for attack helicopters and Mohawk-type reconnaissance aircraft. The helicopter squadrons were located in Edmonton, Petawawa, Valcartier and Gagetown. The fighter squadrons were located at Cold Lake and Bagotville. The squadron of Buffaloes was originally intended for St. Hubert, however the assignment of transport aircraft to Mobile Command proved very transitory. While the RCAF and the RCN had long traditions of aircraft operations, the Canadian Army had become involved much later on. Indeed the early involvement with aircraft maintenance was not really achieved as a completely separate service function, but became caught up in the unification and integration process. With integration all of these tactical aviation units and squadrons were absorbed into Air Command.

Unification, 1968 to the Present Day

It was argued in 1964 that the command, logistics, administration and training functions of the three services of Canada could be streamlined and unified. In April 1964 the government introduced Bill C-90 "Integration of the Headquarters Staff" into the House. On 1 August this bill created a single commander of the armed services of Canada, the Chief of the Defence Staff; all element commanders reported to him instead of directly to the Minister of National Defence. This brought the functional command of the entire armed forces under one headquarters: Canadian Forces Headquarters (CFHQ). The Canadian Armed Forces were now broken down into six functional commands:

> Mobile Command was formed to maintain a combat-ready land and air force capable of rapid deployment.

> Maritime Command embodied all sea and air maritime forces on the Atlantic and Pacific.

> Air Transport Command would provide strategic airlift capability.

> Air Defence Command would contribute squadrons for the defence of North America.

> Training Command was responsible for all individual training.

> Material Command was to provide the necessary supply and maintenance support to the other functional commands.

There were two additional elements: Communications Systems (in 1970 elevated to command status), and Canadian Forces Europe, which was an independent organization reporting directly to CFHQ.

On 6 November 1966, Bill C-243, "The Canadian Forces Reorganization Act" was introduced to the House. This bill would amend the National Defence Act to reflect the unification process. Under the previous National Defence Act, Canada supported three separate forces (the Canadian Army, the Royal Canadian Navy and the Royal Canadian Air Force); under the amendment there would be only one force. The Canadian Forces Reorganization Act came into effect 1 February 1968. Unification brought many external and internal changes. The most visible change was the move to all green uniforms by most personnel and the standardization of ranks, with the air element adopting army style nomenclature for ranks. The post-unification period, however, also brought continuous changes in structure and evolution/devolution of responsibilities.

Some of the significant changes over the following years included:

Material Command became Associate Deputy Minister (Material) ADM (Mat)

Air Command was formed in September 1975. This change brought Air Transport and Air Defence Commands (both had became groups), Tactical Air Group and Maritime Air Group under overall command of Air Command.

The formation of Air Command also brought changes to Training Command with a name change to Training Systems and an associated move to Trenton.

1988 saw the re-introduction of distinctive environmental uniforms (DEU) and the Air Force returned to light blue uniforms.

In 1994 Canadian Forces Europe closed its doors, marking in part the end of the Cold War era.

Re-Formation of Wings

The basic organizational structures and nomenclature of Canada's military aviation were first established during the First World War. With the formation No. 1 Canadian Wing RAF in 1918, the wing unit became standard in air operations, along with commands, groups, squadrons and flights. In using this structure, Canada followed the well-established Royal Air Force model.

With Unification in February 1968, the RCAF structure, including wings, disappeared. The Canadian Armed Forces adopted a new organization structured on the Base concept. Nos. 1, 2, 3 and 4 Air Reserve Wings were re-established in the 1970s and No. 3 (Fighter) Wing, Lahr, and No. 4 (Fighter) Wing, Baden were also re-established in the late 1980s to meet NATO air force command and control requirements.

Finally, beginning in 1993 the Air Force re-established the wing structure and nomenclature across the entire organization. Each of the existing bases then received a numerical designation ranging from 1 to 22 (i.e. 19 Wing Comox) in some cases based on the previous historical affiliations of the base.

Re-Formation of 1 Canadian Air Division and Chief of Air Staff

The latest change in structure for the Air Force was brought about in 1997. Previous studies had established the need to eliminate at least one layer of headquarters in the overall establishment, which had gradually shrunk with periodic budget cutbacks and personnel reductions. The Air Force decided to eliminate the existing Air Command Headquarters in Winnipeg along with each of the Group Headquarters. In the their place, the Chief of the Air Staff (CAS) amalgamates the strategic level functions of each of the five previous HQs. 1 Canadian Air Division (1 CAD) in Winnipeg amalgamates the operational level functions of AIRCOM, 10 TAG, MAG, ATG and FG. In addition, 1 CAD assumed the responsibilities for Canadian NORAD Region (CANR) Headquarter functions and is officially known as 1 CAD/CANRHQ. The nomenclature for both CAS and 1 CAD re-introduces historical terminology in that both these entities previously existed in the RCAF/CF.

Persian Gulf

On 2 August 1990, Iraq invaded Kuwait. This act of aggression precipitated the Persian Gulf War. The world in unison chastised this act of violence and a coalition of forces was formed to liberate Kuwait. Diplomacy failed and the United Nations Security Council issued an ultimatum to Saddam Hussein: leave Kuwait by 15 January or suffer the consequences. Shortly after midnight, 17 January 1991, the coalition forces opened their strategic bombing campaign. This campaign lasted until the cease-fire on 28 February 1991. The ground assault started on 24 February 1991 after the most successful air assault in history. This ground assault swept through the Iraqi defensive lines and turned the battle into a rout.

Canada joined the coalition in condemning Iraq and committed her forces. Initially Canada's contribution was two helicopter destroyers (DDH) and a supply ship (AOR) to assist in the blockade in the Persian Gulf (Operation Friction); included in this task group were the ship's complement of Sea King helicopters. These aircraft flew many missions to investigate unknown sea traffic. To protect her men-of-war, Canada committed a squadron of 18 CF-18s (Operation Scimitar). After a long recce of the in-theatre airfields, Doha in Qatar was selected as the deployment base. The deployment to Doha started on 4 October 1990 from the available forces in Canadian Forces Europe, and the first operational missions were flown on 9 October 1990. The commitment later increased to 24 and then 28 CF-18s. The original task for Canadian Air Task Group Middle East (CATGME) was Combat Air Patrol (CAP) for the fleet in the Persian Gulf; this changed later to a coalition CAP of the Persian Gulf. This task continued until 24 January 1991 when sweep and escort missions were authorized and flown by the Canadian Forces, and then finally on 24 February 1991 air-to-ground missions were authorized and flown.

Included in our air commitment to the coalition was an air-to-air tanker. This arrived in-theatre on 8 January 1991 and joined the other tanker resources of the coalition. Their first mission was flown on 9 January 1991 and continued until the cease-fire.

In January 1991 it was decided to bring all of the Canadian Forces units deployed to the Persian Gulf under one Canadian Commander. The headquarters were set up in Bahrain and they were provided with a light transport/utility Challenger aircraft. Operational command of all Canadian resources was assigned to the Canadian commander, while operational control was delegated to the coalition.

After the cease-fire, Canada quickly repatriated her forces back to their original bases and the deployment bases in Bahrain and Doha were closed out in March 1991.

To the Present

In the face of ever decreasing budgets and resources, the Canadian Air Force has remained extremely busy ever since the first Gulf War, with operational deployments of every kind around the globe.

Airlift missions involving CC130 Hercules, CC137 Boeing, CC150 Airbus and CC144 Challenger aircraft into the former Yugoslavia, into Central America, African, Russia, the Persian Gulf and many other parts of the world have been a frequent occurrence in support of both operational deployments and humanitarian assistance.

CF-18 Hornets have been deployed operationally to NATO bases in support of missions in Bosnia and the former areas of Yugoslavia. On 24 March, 1999, just before midnight Adriatic time, four CF-18 Hornets of Task Force Aviano launched from Aviano Air Base in Italy en route to a pre-planned target located in Kosovo. These

Canadian tactical fighters were four of sixteen dedicated bombing aircraft situated in the centre of a much larger strike package of NATO aircraft. This mission, conducted on Day One of the Balkan air campaign, represented the first Canadian air combat mission in Europe since the end of the Second World War, and the beginning of the most extensive Canadian Air Force combat operation since the Persian Gulf War of 1991. Over the ensuing 78 days and nights, the six, then twelve, and eventually eighteen Canadian CF-18s from Aviano flew a total of 678 combat sorties over nearly 2600 flying hours. They delivered 532 bombs—nearly half a million pounds of high explosive munitions—including 361 laser-guided 500 and 2000 pound bombs on a variety of targets throughout Kosovo and the Federal Republic of Yugoslavia, without loss to participating Canadian aircrew and aircraft.

CH146 Griffon helicopters have been deployed on tactical aviation missions flown in Haiti in support of the UN and in Bosnia in support of SFOR.

CP-140 Aurora maritime patrol aircraft deployed to Italy in support of the UN maritime embargo on the former Yugoslavia and to the Gulf region as part of Canada's contribution to the war on terrorism.

As part of their naval contingents, CH124 Sea King helicopters have also deployed into "harm's way" in diverse locations such as Somalia, East Timor and the Gulf Region.

Closer to home, within Canada, Air Force missions in support of relief for various disasters such as the Manitoba and Saguenay region floods, the Quebec/Ontario ice storms, the Swiss Air crash, and the response to the 9/11 terror attacks to name a few have also added to the operational tempo.

Air Force personnel, particularly from the support echelon, have themselves been increasingly committed to CF operational deployments around the world. Regular deployments to Afghanistan by both Canadian Air Force aircrews and support personnel are now the norm. CC150 Polaris, CC130 Hercules and CU-161 Sperwer UAVs are regularly seen in these Middle East skies.

In all cases, the finest traditions of the Air Force have been and continue to be upheld.

X-35 Joint Strike Fighter (Lockheed Martin).

AIRCRAFT ON STRENGTH WITH THE CANADIAN FORCES

Airbus Industries
POLARIS (Airbus)

The Polaris is a twin-engine, high-speed jet which was originally a commercial airliner design. Three aircraft were acquired from Canadian Air Lines (ex–Wardair aircraft) and two additional aircraft were acquired from foreign sources. In CF service, they are easily converted to passenger, freight or medical transport. Stationed at 8 Wing Trenton, Ontario, 437 Squadron (The Huskies) is the only transport squadron equipped with the Polaris, which replaced the aging Boeing 707 starting in 1992. The five-plane fleet's primary role is long-range transport of personnel and equipment, up to 194 passengers or 32,000 kg of cargo. Four aircraft can be configured in the combi role, carrying both passengers and freight, and they are equipped with a large cargo door plus a strengthened floor and fuselage. One aircraft (CC150001) is permanently configured for VIP transportation duties. They have participated in operations supporting Canadian Forces, NATO and numerous United Nations and Red Cross initiatives. The squadron has earned an excellent reputation transporting high ranking government officials and foreign dignitaries, including members of the Royal Family, the Prime Minister, and the Governor General, around the world. The Huskies are proud of their motto, *Omnia Passim* (Anytime, Anywhere).

Two views of CC-150 Polaris aircraft from 437 (Transport) Squadron. Originally delivered in a 194-seat passenger configuration, four of the aircraft have now been modified into a combi-configuration that includes the addition of a large cargo door. A removable bulkhead also provides a compartment for 60 passengers in the back of the aircraft and for freight, which is loaded in the front. (CF Photos)

DETAILS

Designation: CC-150   **Model No:** A310   **Role:** Transport

TOS: 1992/93   **SOS:** In Service   **No:** 5   **Service:** Canadian Forces

SPECIFICATIONS

Manufacturer: Airbus Industries Ltd

Crew/Passengers: Maximum 194 passengers in standard configuration and 60 passengers in combi configuration

Powerplant: Two GE CF6-80C2A2 turbofans each with 24,265 kg thrust

Performance: Max Speed: Cruising Speed: Mach 0.80
Service Ceiling: 44,839 ft (13,667 m)   Range: 7,250 mi (11,668 km)

Weights: Gross: 152,616 lb (69,226 kg)   Cargo Load: 70,547 lb (32,000 kg)

Dimensions: Wing Span: 144 ft 0 in (43.9 m)   Length: 153 ft 0 in (46.66 m)
Height: 51 ft 10 in (15.8 m)   Wing Area: 2,360 sq ft (219 sq m)

Armament: None

Cost: Each 3 (cx-Cdn) aircraft at $51.2M, one a/c at $54.1 M and one a/c at $57.1 M

Airspeed
HORSA

The Horsa was a Second World War troop and vehicle carrying glider used by the British and their Allies during many of the airborne assault actions in the war. Designed and test flown in less than ten months, the glider was put into quantity production starting in 1940. Built virtually entirely of wood, the aircraft featured fairly complete cockpit instrumentation for flying at night or in cloud. The fuselage was built in three pieces and the main fuselage and tail sections featured quick-disconnect bolts to allow the aft section to be removed for rapid unloading of the payload. The main gear of the tricycle undercarriage could also be jettisoned and a nosewheel in combination with a central shock absorbing skid could be used for rough ground landings. The RCAF acquired a small number of Horsas for use in post-war evaluations.

Two views of an Airspeed Horsa under tow. In the lower photo, the Albermarle tow plane and the Horsa's central skid between the two main landing gears can just barely be discerned. (LAC Photos # PA-211504, PA-133492)

DETAILS

Designation: N/A	**Model No:** N/A	**Mark:** Mk II	**Role:** Glider
TOS: 1948	**SOS:** 1959	**No:** 3	**Service:** RCAF

SPECIFICATIONS

Manufacturer:	Airspeed
Crew/Passengers:	two pilots plus up to 25 troops or light vehicles (jeeps or motorcycles)
Powerplant:	None
Performance:	Max Towing Speed: 150 mph (241 km/h) Normal Towing Speed: 100 mph (161 km/h)
	Service Ceiling: Tow Plane Dependent Range: Tow Plane Dependent
Weights:	Empty: 8,370 lb (3,800 kg) Gross: 15,500 lb (7,030 kg)
	Payload: 6,900 lb (3,130 kg)
Dimensions:	Span: 88 ft (26.8 m) Length: 67 ft (20.4 m)
	Height: 19 ft 6 in (5.90 m) Wing Area: 1,104 sq ft (102.5 sq m)
Armament:	None
Cost:	Unknown

Airspeed
OXFORD

The Airspeed Oxford was a three-seat advanced trainer used for all aspects of aircrew training during the Second World War. The first versions were received in Canada from Great Britain in 1939 and were used in numerous roles for the British Commonwealth Air Training Plan. Among others, these roles included navigation training, communication training, radar calibration, air ambulance duties, and training of anti-aircraft crews.

An action view of an early Mk I Oxford aircraft at Comox. The Airspeed Oxford Mk I was fitted with Armstrong Siddeley Cheetah X powerplants. The RCAF had 27 aircraft of this mark on strength between May 1939 and April 1944. (Comox Air Force Museum Photo)

DETAILS
Designation: N/A   **Model No:** AS 10, AS46   **Marks:** Mk I, II & Mk V   **Role:** Trainer
TOS: 1939   **SOS:** 1947   **No:** 1425   **Service:** RCAF

SPECIFICATIONS (for Mark II aircraft)
Manufacturer: Airspeed
Crew/Passengers: three crew with space for four passengers
Powerplant: Two 370 hp Armstrong Siddeley Cheetah Mk X engines
Performance: Max Speed: 188 mph (303 km/h)
Service Ceiling: 19,500 ft (5,944 m)
Weights: Empty: 5,350 lbs (2,427 kg)   Gross: 7,600 lbs (3,447 kg)
Dimensions: Span: 53 ft 4 in (16.25 m)   Length: 34 ft 6 in (10.51 m)
Height: 11 ft 1 in (5.38 m)   Wing Area: 348 sq ft (32.33 sq m)
Armament: None
Cost: Unknown

Armstrong Whitworth
ATLAS

Designed for an all encompassing "Army Co-operation" role, the Armstrong Whitworth Atlas was a two-seat biplane. First acquired in 1927, the aircraft's excellent low-speed handling made it highly suitable in the ground liaison role. Message dropping and snatching techniques were routinely practiced. Additional reconditioned examples were purchased in 1934 after financial restrictions imposed for the Depression had eased. Badly outclassed by the eve of the Second World War, there were still sixteen Atlases on strength in the RCAF. The type was therefore pressed into reconnaissance coastal patrols in the Bay of Fundy at the outbreak of the war until they were passed on to No. 118 (Coast Artillery Co-operation) Squadron for brief use prior to their retirement.

The lineup of RCAF Armstrong Whitworth Atlas army cooperation aircraft seen here is probably at the Halifax Aero Club in the fall of 1939. (Author's Collection)

DETAILS

Designation: N/A   **Model No:** N/A   **Marks:** Mk I, Mk IIAC   **Role:** Army Co-op

TOS: 1927   **SOS:** 1942   **No:** 16   **Service:** RCAF

SPECIFICATIONS

Manufacturer:	Armstrong Whitworth
Crew/Passengers:	2 (pilot & observer or 2 pilots in dual control advanced trainer)
Powerplant:	one 450 hp Armstrong Siddeley Jaguar IVB radial engine

Performance:	Max Speed: 149 mph (240 kph)	Service Ceiling: 17,700 ft (5,395 m)
Weights:	Empty: 2,550 lbs (1,157 kg)	Gross: 4,020 lbs (1,823 kg)
Dimensions:	Span: 39 ft 6½ in (12.00m)	Length: 28 ft 6½ in (8.68 m)
	Height: 10 ft 6 in (3.20 m)	Wing Area: 391 sq ft (36.30 sq m)
Armament:	one fixed Vickers machine gun and two Lewis machine guns on a Scharffe ring in the observer's cockpit plus provisions for four 112 lb bombs on under wing racks	
Cost:	Unknown	

Armstrong Whitworth
SISKIN

The Armstrong Whitworth Siskin was perhaps the most important RCAF aircraft of the interwar years. Indeed, along with its cousin, the Armstrong Whitworth Atlas, it represented the only pure military aircraft design in service with the RCAF between 1929 and 1936. A fighter design, the Siskin originally served with the RAF in this role and when acquired by the RCAF in 1926, it represented a state of the art design. The aircraft received a great deal of exposure in the 1930s when the RCAF formed an aerobatic display team using the type. The three-plane Siskin aerobatic team put on popular displays from coast to coast. The Siskin also formed the basis of No. 1 Fighter Squadron. The aircraft remained with this unit until the outbreak of the Second World War, eventually to be replaced by modern Hawker Hurricanes in 1939. The airframes were then turned over to various technical establishments for use as instructional airframes.

The Siskin was the RCAF's front line fighter from 1926 until approximately 1938. The aircraft was also used for one of Canada's first military air demonstration teams. In the summer of 1929, the Siskin air demonstration team was formed at Camp Borden, Ontario, and toured the country. With its three Siskins, the team flew formation and solo displays until 1932. (CF Photo)

DETAILS

Designation: N/A	**Model No:**	**Marks:** Mk III, Mk IIIA	**Role:** Fighter
TOS: 1926	**SOS:** 1942	**No:** 12	**Service:** RCAF

SPECIFICATIONS

Manufacturer: Armstrong Whitworth
Crew/Passengers: 1 pilot or 2 pilots in dual-control advanced trainer
Powerplant: one 420/450 hp Armstrong Siddeley Jaguar IV radial engine
Performance: Max Speed: 156 mph (251 kph) at sea level and 143 mph (230 kph) at 15,000 ft
Service Ceiling: 27,000 ft (8,230 m)
Weights: Empty: 2,061 lbs (935 kg)   Gross: 3,012 lbs (1,366 kg)
Dimensions: Span: 33 ft 2 in (10.11 m)   Length: 25 ft 4 in (7.72 m)
Height: 10 ft 2 in (3.10 m)   Wing Area: 293 sq ft (27.20 sq m)
Armament: two fixed Vickers machine guns plus provisions for four 20 lb bombs on under wing racks
Cost: Unknown

Auster
TAYLORCRAFT

A light observation aircraft, the Auster Taylorcraft Mk IV was introduced by the Canadian Army during the fighting in Northwest Europe in 1945. The primary role of the aircraft was artillery spotting and the aircraft carried a pilot and observer in this role. Two Canadian squadrons, designated No. 664 and 665 Squadron, were equipped with these aircraft. 664 Squadron served in the Canadian Army Occupation Force in post-war activities until its disbandment in May 1946.

In the upper view is a Canadian Army Auster Taylorcraft AOP Mk V aircraft complete with D-Day invasion stripes. In the lower view is another AOP Mk I variant; note the difference in engine installations. (LAC Photo # PA-162286, RAF Photo)

DETAILS

Designation: N/A	**Model No:**	**Marks:** Mk IV, Mk V	**Role:** Army Co-op
TOS: 1944	**SOS:** 1946	**No:** 12	**Service:** Canadian Army

SPECIFICATIONS (for Mark V)

Manufacturer:	Auster	
Crew/Passengers:	1 pilot plus 1 observer or 2 passengers	
Powerplant:	One 130 hp 0-290-3 Lycoming flat-four piston engine	
Performance:	Max Speed: 130 mph (209 km/h)	Cruising Speed: 112 mph (180 km/h)
	Service Ceiling:	Range: 250 mi (402 km)
Weights:	Empty: 1,100 lb (499 kg)	Maximum Take-off: 1,850 lb (839 kg)
Dimensions:	Span: 36 ft 0 in (10.97 m)	Length: 22 ft 5 in (6.83 m)
	Height: 8 ft 0 in (2.44 m)	Wing Area: 167 sq ft (15.51 sq m)
Armament:	None	
Cost:	Unknown	

Auster
AOP

On 1 March 1947, the Canadian Army Air Component was formed and to equip it 36 Auster AOP Mark MI aircraft were ordered. The British Taylorcraft firm had changed its name to Auster Aircraft Ltd in the post-war period. Following the success of the Auster Taylorcraft in the Second World War, an improved and upgraded version of the aircraft, simply known as the Auster Mk VI, was introduced just prior to the Korean War. The Auster AOP Mk VI differed from its predecessors in its more powerful engine, protruding rear flaps, longer undercarriage legs and increased fuel capacity. Like the Taylorcraft, the primary roles of this aircraft were also artillery spotting, along with liaison and light observation duties. During the Korean War, Canadian Army crews were attached to the Commonwealth Division Air OP Flight.

An Auster AOP Mk VI aircraft is illustrated here on skis, at RCAF Station MacDonald, Manitoba in the 1950s. (Author's Collection)

DETAILS

Designation: N/A   **Model Nos:**   **Marks:** Mk VI, Mk VII   **Role:** Army Co-op
TOS: 1948   **SOS:** 1958   **No:** 42   **Service:** Canadian Army

SPECIFICATIONS

Manufacturer: Auster/Taylorcraft
Crew/Passengers: 1 pilot plus 1 observer or 2 passengers
Powerplant: One 145 hp De Havilland Gipsy Major VII engine
Performance: Max Speed: 124 mph (200 km/h)   Cruising Speed: 108 mph (174 km/h)
Service Ceiling: 14,000 ft (4,267 m)
Weights: Empty: 1,413 lbs (641 kg)   Gross: 2,160 lbs (980 kg)
Dimensions: Span: 36 ft 0 in (10.97 m)   Length: 23 ft 9 in (7.24 m)
Height: 8 ft 4½ in (2.55 m)   Wing Area: 184 sq ft (17.09 sq m)
Armament: None
Cost: Unknown

Avro
504

Originally designed in 1913 as an operational type, the Avro 504 provided the backbone for flying training throughout the First World War for Britain and her allies. In 1918, Canada ordered a substantial number of 504 aircraft to be built by the Canadian Aeroplanes Company. When the war ended the order was terminated and instead, in 1919, Canada received sixty-two Avro 504Ks as part of an Imperial gift of 114 aircraft from Britain. The type then served in a variety of roles for more than a decade. Additional examples were also acquired and the aircraft was progressively modified and improved.

A wartime design, the Avro 504K was the CAF and RCAF's basic post-First World War trainer. It served with both the early Canadian Air Force (CAF) and its successor, the RCAF, from 1920 until 1934. This fine colour view illustrates a restored example of the Avro 504K from the Canadian Aviation Museum. (CF Photo)

DETAILS

Designation: N/A   **Model No:** 504K, 504L, 504N   **Role:** Trainer
TOS: 1920   **SOS:** 1934   **No:** 97   **Service:** CAF/RCAF

SPECIFICATIONS 504K

Manufacturer:	Avro, and licence-built by Canadian Aeroplanes Company	
Crew/Passengers:	one or two pilots	
Powerplant:	Clerget 9B 130 hp radial engine	
Performance:	Max Speed: 100 mph (161 km/h)	Cruising Speed: 75 mph (121 km/h)
	Service Ceiling: 13,500 ft (4,115 m)	Range: 255 mi (410 km)
Weights:	Empty:	Gross: 1,829 lb (830 kg)
Dimensions:	Span: 36 ft 0 in (10.97 m)	Length: 28 ft 0 in (8.54 m)
	Height: 10 ft 5 in (3.17 m)	Wing Area: 330 sq ft (30.66 sq m)
Armament:	None	
Cost:	Unknown	

Avro (504 Mod)
VIPER & LYNX

After the First World War, the availability of thousands of cheap powerplants from the S.E. 5A fighter design in the form of 180 hp Wolseley Viper water-cooled engines complete with frontal radiators led to the modification and upgrade of the Avro 504 aircraft type. Considerable modifications were needed to the airframe to accommodate the new more powerful engine installation. In 1923, following the assembly of six long-range, single-seat Avro 552As at Camp Borden, the RCAF ordered another five single-seat and nine two-seat versions for forest fire patrol work.

An interesting view of an RCAF Avro Viper on floats being prepared for a patrol. This aircraft, G-CYGC was one of nine Avro Viper T.S. Seaplanes (T.S. meaning two-seat) acquired by the RCAF. This aircraft suffered a Category "A" accident at Bowden Lake, Alberta and was therefore struck off strength on 18 October 1927. (CF Photo)

DETAILS

Designation: N/A   **Model No:** 552A   **Role:** Trainer, Forest Fire Patrol
TOS: 1924   **SOS:** 1928   **No:** 14   **Service:** RCAF

SPECIFICATIONS

Manufacturer:	Avro and licence-built by Canadian Vickers Limited	
Crew/Passengers	one or two pilots	
Powerplant:	one 180 hp Wolseley Viper water-cooled engine	
Performance:	Max Speed:	Cruising Speed:
	Service Ceiling:	Range:
Weights:	Empty:	Gross: 2,260 lb (1,025 kg)
Dimensions:	Span: 36 ft 0 in (10.97 m)	Length: 28 ft 0 in (8.53 m)
	Height: 10 ft 5 in (3.20 m)	Wing Area: 330 sq ft (30.66 sq m)
Armament:	None	
Cost:	Unknown	

Avro
AVIAN

In 1929, the Ottawa Car Manufacturing Company assembled twenty-one Avro Avian light two-seat trainers for the Department of National Defence which, in turn, distributed them to the RCAF (ten) and to various flying clubs (eleven). Other aircraft were then acquired in 1930 for both the RCAF and additional flying clubs.

The RCAF began using the type for initial flying training but, surprisingly, no extensive use was made of the aircraft. Most had very few hours flown before being relegated as instructional airframes or being transferred to flying clubs.

This is one of 21 RCAF Avro Avian IVM aircraft which did not last long in regular RCAF service. (CF Photo)

DETAILS

Designation: N/A   **Model No:** 616   **Mark:** Mk IVM   **Role:** Trainer
TOS: 1929   **SOS:** 1945   **No:** 29   **Service:** RCAF

SPECIFICATIONS (for Avian IVM)

Manufacturer:	Ottawa Car Manufacturing Company under licence from Avro
Crew/Passengers:	2 pilots
Powerplant:	Seven cylinder 135 hp Genet Major 1 or Minor radial engine

Performance:	Max Speed: 100 mph (161 km/h)	Cruising Speed: 90 mph (145 km/h)
	Service Ceiling: 12,500 ft (3,810 m)	Range: 360 mi (579 km)
Weights:	Empty: 1,000 lb (454 kg)	Gross: 1,600 lb (726 kg)
Dimensions:	Span: 28 ft 0 in (8.53 m)	Length: 24 ft 3 in (7.39 m)
	Height: 8 ft 6 in (2.59 m)	Wing Area: 245 sq ft (22.76 sq m)
Armament:	None	
Cost:	Unknown	

Avro
TUTOR

The Avro Model 621 was initially known as the Trainer. It was a light initial pilot trainer, which originated as a private venture of the Avro Company in England. The type was eventually adopted as the standard trainer of the RAF under the service name of Avro Tutor. Standard model 621s were supplied to the Ottawa Car Co. Ltd for sale to the RCAF. Why the aircraft were ordered remains somewhat of a mystery. The RCAF already had three other trainers in service including the Hawker Tomtit, Gipsy Moth and Fleet Fawn. The Tutor aircraft were not as suitable as these other types in the basic training role and were converted instead to army co-operation training. The aircraft were modified with wireless sets and vertical cameras to facilitate this latter role. The type survived into the Second World War as ground instructional airframes.

Two RCAF Avro Tutors, following conversion to the army cooperation training role, as evidenced by the long hook (used to snag messages or packages) under the fuselages. (CF Photo)

DETAILS

Designation: N/A   **Model No:** 621   **Role:** Trainer
TOS: 1931   **SOS:** 1945   **No:** 13   **Service:** RCAF

SPECIFICATIONS

Manufacturer: Ottawa Car Company Limited under Avro Licence
Crew/Passengers: 2 pilots
Powerplant: one 240 hp Armstrong Siddeley Lynx IVC radial engine
Performance: Max Speed: 120 mph (193 km/h)   Cruising Speed: 97 mph (156 km/h)
Service Ceiling: 16,000 ft (4,877m)   Range: 250 mi (402 km)
Weights: Empty: 1,844 lb (836 kg)   Gross: 2,493 lb (1,131 kg)
Dimensions: Span: 34 ft 0 in (10.36 m)   Length: 26 ft 4½ in (8.04 m)
Height: 9 ft 7 in (2.92 m)   Wing Area: 301 sq ft (27.96 m)
Armament: None
Cost: Unknown

Avro
626

To satisfy the needs of air forces with limited financial resources, the Avro Company re-designed the Model 621 Tutor to make it suitable not only for initial flying training but also for bombing, photography, gunnery, wireless, night flying, navigation or instrument training as well. Although the machine remained a two-seater, a third cockpit or gunner's cockpit could be provided aft of the second cockpit. The RCAF placed a follow-on order for the 626 after experience with the 621 model. These aircraft could be equipped with twin metal skis, enclosed cockpits and "Arctic" cowlings with controllable shutters.

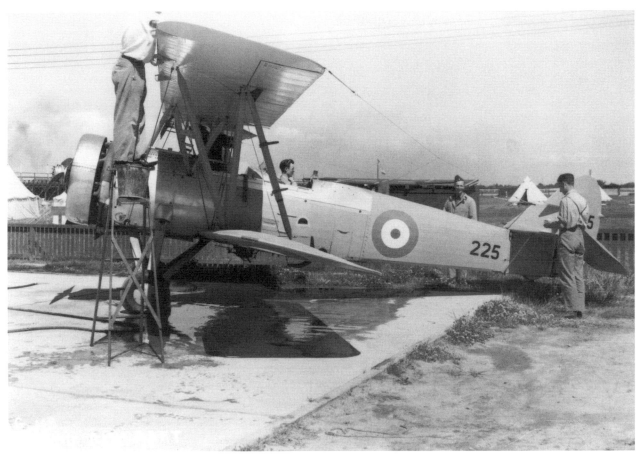

The Avro 626 trainer, shown here undergoing maintenance, served with No. 111 (Coastal Artillery Cooperation) Squadron at Vancouver, BC in 1939. (CF Photo)

DETAILS
Designation: N/A   **Model No:** 626   **Role:** Trainer
TOS: 1937   **SOS:** 1945   **No:** 12   **Service:** RCAF

SPECIFICATIONS
Manufacturer: Avro Aircraft Limited
Crew/Passengers: 2 pilots
Powerplant: one 240 hp Armstrong Siddeley Lynx IVC radial engine
Performance: Max Speed: 112 mph (180 km/h)   Cruising Speed: 95 mph (153 km/h)
                     Service Ceiling: 14,800 ft (4,511 m)   Range: 240 mi (386 km)
Weights: Empty: 1,765 lb (801 kg)   Gross: 2,750 lb (1,247 kg)
Dimensions: Span: 34 ft 0 in (10.36 m)   Length: 26 ft 6 in (8.08 m)
                     Height: 9 ft 7 in (2.92 m)   Wing Area: 300 sq ft (27.87 m)
Armament: None
Cost: Unknown

Avro Canada
ANSON

The Avro Anson was known by a number of nicknames including "Faithful Annie" or "Flying Greenhouse." It was the first aircraft to be flown by the RAF to have a retractable undercarriage, which was a comparative novelty in 1936. In 1940, a Canadian government-owned company, Federal Aircraft Limited, was created in Montreal to manufacture the Anson for Canadian use. Nearly, 3,000 Anson aircraft were produced and in the early days of the British Commonwealth Air Training Plan (BCATP), the Anson was the standard trainer for many pilots, observers, wireless operators and bomb aimers. More than 20,000 aircrew received training on the Anson. In Canadian service, the aircraft was substantially re-designed with the substitution of North American engines and many other airframe and equipment changes.

This photo illustrates an early model RCAF Anson as used in the BCATP. The yellow overall finish, which readily identified trainers, was typical of most BCATP aircraft. (CF Photo)

DETAILS

Designation: N/A   **Model No:** 652A   **Marks:** Mk I, II, III, IV, V, VA, VP, VT, VI   **Role:** Trainer
TOS: 1940   **SOS:** 1954   **No:** 4413   **Service:** RCAF/RCN

SPECIFICATIONS

Manufacturer: Avro Canada plus various other Canadian companies
Crew/Passengers: two pilots plus crew
Powerplant: two 450 hp Pratt & Whitney R-985AN-12B or 14B Wasp Jr radial engines
Performance: Max Speed: 190 mph (304 km/h)   Cruising Speed: 174 mph (280 km/h)
Service Ceiling: 20,550 ft (6,263 m)   Range: 1,130 miles (1,818.55 km)
Weights: Empty: 6,693 lb (3,039 kg)   Gross: 9,275 lb (4,210 kg)
Dimensions: Span: 56 ft 6 in (17.2 m)   Length: 42 ft 3 in (12.9 m)
Height: 13 ft 1 in (4 m)   Wing Area: 410 sq ft (38.1 sq m)
Armament: None, but provision for bomb and gunnery training in turret equipped with machine gun and using practice bombs in under wing bomb bays
Original Cost: Unknown

Avro Canada
CANUCK ("Clunk")

The RCAF named the CF-100 "Canuck" after the much earlier Curtis JN-4 Canuck trainer of the First World War. However, the name Canuck was never really accepted for the jet aircraft and the crews more often referred to the type as the "Clunk." The twin engine jet all-weather interceptor was all Canadian designed and built. The CF-100's good climb, excellent fire control and radar systems, twin engine reliability and all weather capability made the aircraft highly suitable for Canadian and NATO air defence roles of the Korean and Cold War eras. Belgium also selected the design for its NATO forces. After a successful career in the RCAF/CF as a fighter, the aircraft type was later modified as an electronic countermeasures (ECM) trainer and was fitted with electronic ECM and chaff dispensing equipment. A black paint scheme was chosen by

Avro for the prototype aircraft and to commemorate the type's retirement, a Mark V aircraft was repainted in this original colour scheme.

In the lower view, 18423 was a Canuck Mk. 4B, one of 144 on strength with the RCAF from 12 November 1954 until it was struck off strength on 3 October 1962. The aircraft belonged to 423 All-Weather Fighter Squadron, which operated out of RCAF Station St. Hubert, Quebec. In the upper image, CF-100, #18105, is seen performing a Jet Assisted Take Off while on detachment with the Experimental Proving Establishment at RCAF Station Uplands, 13 October 1952. (CF Photos)

DETAILS

Designation: CF-100   **Model No:**   **Marks:** Mk 1, 2, 3A/B, 4A/B, 5D/M, 6   **Role:** Fighter/EW Trainer
TOS: 1951   **SOS:** 1981   **No:** 692   **Service:** RCAF/CF

SPECIFICATIONS Mk IV

Manufacturer:	Avro Canada: designed and built
Crew/Passengers:	2 crew (pilot/navigator) in ejection seats
Powerplant:	Orenda Series 11 or 17 Turbojet

Performance:
Max Speed: 525 kts (972.3 km/h)	Cruising Speed: 400 kts (741 km/h)
Service Ceiling: 41,000 ft (12,496 m)	Range: 2000 nm (3,706 km)

Weights: Empty: 23,100 lbs (10,487 kg)   Gross: 33,000 lbs (14,969 kg)

Dimensions:
Span: 57 ft 6 in (16.31 m)	Length: 54 ft 2 in (16.5 m)
Height: 14 ft 6 in (4.43 m)	Wing Area: 526.6 sq ft (48.92 sq m)

Armament: Provisions for bombs, rockets (unguided), missiles
Original Cost: $660,000

Avro Canada
LANCASTER

The Avro Lancaster was derived from the unsuccessful twin-engine Avro Manchester bomber that first flew in 1939. The decision was made in late 1940 to replace the two Rolls Royce Vulture engines of the Manchester with four of the more reliable Rolls Royce Merlin (in Canada, Packard Merlin) engines, which had a proven record in the Hurricane and Spitfire fighter designs. The revised design was an immediate success and the Lancaster went on to carry the heaviest individual bomb loads of the Second World War. The Lancaster was manufactured in Canada by Victory Aircraft Ltd. in Malton, Ontario and 430 Mk 10 versions were built. In post-war use, the Canadian built Lancasters went on to serve in highly useful roles. Quickly converted into photographic reconnaissance variants for charting and mapping and into maritime patrol versions, the Lancaster soldiered on well into the Cold War era.

An Avro Lancaster MkX variant as employed in the post-war period by 407 Squadron for ASW/long range patrol duties in Comox, BC. (CF Photo)

DETAILS
Designation: N/A   **Model No:** 683   **Marks:** B.I, B.II, B.III, B.X, XPP; Mk 10 AP, AR, BR, DC; Mk 10 MP, MR, N; Mk 10 P, PR, S, SR

Role: Bomber/Photographic Reconnaissance/Maritime Patrol
TOS: 1944   **SOS:** 1965   **No:** 229   **Service:** RCAF

SPECIFICATIONS Mk X

Manufacturer:	Victory Aircraft Ltd which became Avro Canada	
Crew/Passengers:	one pilot and up to 6 crew	
Powerplant:	four 1,620 hp Packard Merlin 224 piston engines	
Performance:	Max Speed: 272 mph (438 km/h)	Cruising Speed: 200 mph (322 km/h)
	Service Ceiling: 24,700 ft (7,528 m)	Range: 2,530 mi (4,072 km)
Weights:	Empty: 35,240 lb (15,999 kg)	Gross: 60,000 lb (27,400 kg)
Dimensions:	Span: 102 ft 0 in (31.09 m)	Length: 69 ft 6 in (21.18 m)
	Height: 20 ft 0 in (6.10 m)	Wing Area: 1,297 sq ft (120.49 sq m)
Armament:	Provision for three gun turrets each with two or four .303 calibre machine guns; up to 14,000 lb (6,350 kg) bomb load	
Original Cost:	Unknown	

Avro Canada
LINCOLN

In 1943, an improved version of the Lancaster was proposed for the war in the Pacific. The aircraft featured larger dimensions, more powerful engines, better performance, heavier armament and longer range. Originally to be designated the Lancaster Mk IV, the eventual design was sufficiently different to warrant a new designation and name, and became known as the Avro 694 Lincoln.

Canada ordered home production of the Lincoln in order to re-equip Canadian bomber squadrons, and also the "Tiger Force," destined for the Pacific theatre. At the cessation of hostilities, the production order was terminated after only six aircraft had been started. Three Lincolns, including two borrowed from the RAF, were then briefly evaluated by the RCAF in post-war tests.

A view of the Lincoln illustrating its overall lineage from the Lancaster, some of which are parked in the background. (CF Photo)

DETAILS

Designation: N/A   **Model No:** 694   **Marks:** B. Mk I, B. Mk II, B. Mk XV   **Role:** Bomber
TOS: 1946   **SOS:** 1948   **No:** 3   **Service:** RCAF

SPECIFICATIONS B. Mk I

Manufacturer:	Licence-built from Avro by Victory Aircraft Ltd (later Avro Canada) in Malton
Crew/Passengers:	typical crew of seven
Powerplant:	Four 1,750 hp Rolls-Royce Merlin 85 piston engines
Performance:	Max Speed: 295 mph (475 km/h) Cruising Speed: 238 mph (383 km/h)
	Service Ceiling: 22,000 ft (6,706 m) Range: 3,750 miles (6,035 km)
Weights:	Empty: 43,778 lb (19,858 kg) Gross: 82,000 lb (37,195 kg)
Dimensions:	Span: 120 ft 0 in (36.58 m) Length: 78 ft 3½ in (23.86 m)
	Height: 17 ft 3½ in (5.27 m) Wing Area: 1,421 sq ft (132.02 sq m)
Armament:	Provisions for a 14,000 lb (6,350 kg) bomb load and self defence armament consisting of twin 20 mm or .50 in cal guns in nose, dorsal and tail powered turrets
Cost:	Unknown

Avro (Canadian Vickers)
WRIGHT

The Avro Wright was in fact simply another derivative of the Avro 504 series of aircraft. The rapid development of improved powerplants in wartime had meant that, in the post-war period, the Avro 504 aircraft could be significantly improved. Various engine installations were tried and other improvements were made to the aircraft type. Simply known as the Wright in the RCAF, this particular aircraft was a conversion of the 504 airframe with a Wright Whirlwind engine and Hamilton Standard variable pitch propeller installed. The single float design was completed by Canadian Vickers Ltd.

A view of the Avro Wright with a ski installation for RCAF service. (CF Photo)

DETAILS

Designation: N/A	**Model No:** 552A	**Role:** Amphibian	
TOS: 1925	**SOS:** 1930	**No:** 1	**Service:** RCAF

SPECIFICATIONS

Manufacturer:	Canadian Vickers Ltd
Crew/Passengers:	one pilot
Powerplant:	one 200 hp Wright J4/J5 Whirlwind radial engine

Performance:	Max Speed: 85 mph (137 kmh)	Cruising Speed:
	Service Ceiling:12,000 ft (3,657 m)	Range:
Weights:	Empty: 1,848 lb (839 kg)	Gross: 2,676 lb (1,221 kg)
Dimensions:	Span: 36 ft 0 in (10.97 m)	Length: 32 ft 8¾ in (9.97 m)
	Height: 11 ft 3½ in (3.44 m)	Wing Area: 330 sq ft (30.66 sq m)
Armament:	None	
Cost:	Unknown	

Barkley Grow

The Barkley Grow Model T8P-1 was a twin-engine, all-metal, low-winged transport monoplane with seating normally arranged for 6 passengers with a crew of two. Often mistaken for either a Beech 18 or Lockheed Electra, the Barkley Grow was designed around a patented "multi-spar" all-metal wing that provided exceptional bending and torsional strength. Unfortunately, the design proved to be less popular than its competitors and only a handful were built. The fixed landing gear was considered archaic by some but the design proved more popular in Canada where seasonal changes between wheels, skis and floats were facilitated by this arrangement. The RCAF acquired one Barkley Grow for use in the early part of the Second World War.

A ground view of the RCAF's Barkley Grow illustrating its fixed landing gear. (Comox AFM Photo)

DETAILS

Designation: N/A **Model No:** T8P-1 **Role:** Transport

TOS: 1939 **SOS:** 1941 **No:** 1 **Service:** RCAF

SPECIFICATIONS

Manufacturer: Barkley Grow

Crew/Passengers: 6 passengers with a crew of two

Powerplant: two Wasp Jr SB engines rated at 400 hp (450 hp for take-off)

Performance: Max Speed: 224 mph (361 km/h) Cruising Speed: 204 mph (328 km/h)

Service Ceiling: 20,000 ft (6,096 m) Range: 750 mi (1,207 km)

Weights: Empty: 5,448 lb (2,471 kg) Gross: 8,250 lb (3,742 kg)

Dimensions: Span: 50 ft 9 in (15.47 m) Length: 36 ft 2 in (11.02 m)

Height: 9 ft 8 in (2.95 m) Wing Area: 354 sq ft (32.89 sq m)

Armament: None

Cost: $37,500 US

Beechcraft
EXPEDITOR

The Beechcraft Expeditor was an American-built twin-engine aircraft that provided yeoman service to the RCAF over three decades. Originally serving as a light transport in the First World War, the Expeditor was the RCAF's basic multi-engine trainer after the war. The aircraft also served as a light communication, refresher training, liaison, VIP transport, and search and rescue aircraft. It was affectionately known by a variety of names such as the "Bug Smasher," "Twin Harvard," "Wichita Wobbler," or "Exploder." As a trainer, its many roles included multi-engine training for pilots, navigators and radio operators. Unification of the Canadian Armed Forces took place in 1968 with only 53 Expeditors remaining of the total of 398 once listed as on strength, and these were all retired along with the Dakota fleet.

An in-flight colour view of an RCAF Expeditor. 2340 was a Mk. III NM (later NMT) model Expeditor on strength with the RCAF and the CAF from 3 November, 1952 to 3 June, 1970. (CF Photo)

DETAILS

Designation: CT-128   **Model No:** C-45F, C45M   **Marks:** Mk I, II, III H, III NM, III T, III TM   **Role:** Transport
TOS: 1941   **SOS:** 1972   **No:** 398   **Service:** RCAF/RCN/CF

SPECIFICATIONS

Manufacturer:	Beech Aircraft
Crew/Passengers:	two crew and 5–7 passengers
Powerplant:	two 450 hp Pratt & Whitney Jr R-985-AN-14B radials

Performance:	Max Speed: 230 mph (370 km/h)	Cruising Speed: 205 mph (330 km/h)
	Service Ceiling: 20,500 ft (6,248 m)	Range: 1,200 miles (1,931 km)
Weights:	Empty: 4,600 lb (2087 kg)	Gross: 7,500 lb (3,402 kg)
Dimensions:	Span: 47 ft 8 in (14.52 m)	Length: 34 ft 3 in (10.43 m)
	Height: 9 ft 5 in (2.87 m)	
Armament:	None	
Original Cost:	$75,000	

Beechcraft
MENTOR

In early 1950, the RCAF initiated an evaluation program to select a new primary trainer as it struggled to define the pilot training program best suited to the needs of a "jet" air force. The Beechcraft T-34A Mentor training aircraft had been a development of the successful Beechcraft Bonanza light aircraft and in fact had many components in common with its civilian cousin. The T-34A Mentor was adopted by both the USAF and USN for primary training and in 1953, the USAF awarded a contract to Canadian Car and Foundry to build thirty-four T-34As. Shortly there-

after, perhaps somewhat reluctantly, the RCAF ordered twenty-five of the low-powered Mentors for its own use. An experimental course of student pilots was processed on the Mentor through normal training at No. 4 FTS in Penhold, Alberta. For a variety of reasons the Mentors were not considered suitable for RCAF training purposes. One aircraft was written off in a crash and the remaining aircraft were quickly disposed of to Greece and Turkey as part of a NATO Mutual Aid program.

A rare view of the short-lived RCAF Beechcraft Mentor. (CF Photo)

DETAILS

Designation: T-34A	**Model No:** 45	**Marks:**	**Role:** Trainer
TOS: 1954	**SOS:** 1956	**No:** 25	**Service:** RCAF

SPECIFICATIONS

Manufacturer:	Licence-built from Beechcraft by Canadian Car & Foundry
Crew/Passengers:	Two pilots: student and instructor in tandem
Powerplant:	one 225 hp Continental 0-470-13 piston engine

Performance:	Max Speed: 189 mph (304 km/h)	Cruising Speed: 173 mph (278 km/h)
	Service Ceiling: 21,200 ft (6,461 m)	Range: 975 mi (1,569 km)
Weights:	Empty: 2,170 lb (985 kg)	Gross: 2,900 lb (1,317 kg)
Dimensions:	Span: 32 ft 10 in (10.01 m)	Length: 25 ft 10 in (7.87 m)
	Height: 9 ft 7 in (2.92 m)	Wing Area: 177 sq ft (16.51 sq m)
Armament:	None	
Cost:	Unknown	

Beechcraft
MUSKETEER/SUNDOWNER (Musketeer II)

The Beech Model 23 was manufactured from 1961 until approximately 1980, under various names such as Sierra, Sundowner, Sport and Musketeer, to serve the market for a small, inexpensive private recreational aircraft. Beechcraft Musketeer aircraft were first purchased by the Canadian Forces in 1970 to replace the capable but increasingly difficult to maintain Chipmunk ab-initio trainers. Although not an ideal aircraft for the role, the Musketeer served capably in the guise of a pilot selection vehicle and primary flying trainer. Derived from the stock civilian Beechcraft, the Canadian military models featured a second access door. In 1981, primarily due to structural problems, the original Musketeers were replaced by a newer, improved version of the aircraft. Based on the commercial Sundowner version these later aircraft were designated CT-134A or Musketeer II in CF service.

The Musketeer fleet was originally bought in 1971 to replace the Chipmunk as a primary flight trainer. Based at CFB Portage la Prairie, Manitoba, they were used to initiate thousands of pilots until the second batch of aircraft were retired in 1992. (CF Photos)

DETAILS

Designation: CT-134/CT-134A   **Model No:** 23   **Role:** Trainer
TOS: 1970 CT-134/1981 CT-134A   **SOS:** 1992   **No:** 25 CT-134/25 CT-134A   **Service:** CF

SPECIFICATIONS

Manufacturer:	Beechcraft
Crew/Passengers:	2 pilots and up to 2 passengers
Powerplant:	Lycoming 0-360-A4K 360 cu in reciprocal engine with 180 hp
Performance:	Max Speed: 132 kts (245 km/h)
	Ceiling: 12,600 ft (3,840 m) Range: 690 m (1,110 km)
Weights:	Gross: 2,350 lbs (1,113 kg)
Dimensions:	Span: 32 ft 9 in (9.99 m) Length: 25 ft 9 in (7.85 m)
Armament:	None
Original Cost:	CT-134 $25,195 CT-134A $150,610

Bell
47

The Bell 47 helicopter was first flown in 1945 and was the first helicopter to be commercially licensed, reaching commercial production in 1947. It became one of the most successful and most numerous of the early helicopters. With its distinctive bubble canopy, the Bell 47 started off as a two-seat helicopter but it was successfully modified into three and four place versions. It served in a wide variety of roles and helped pioneer various uses for the helicopter. The RCN ordered is first three Bell 47D-1 (HTL-4) helicopters in 1951. These helicopters were later upgraded to HTL-6 status. Three more Bell 47G (HTL-6) helicopters joined the fleet in 1955. All of these RCN

helicopters served with HU-21 Squadron in HMCS Shearwater. These aircraft were used for rescue, light re-supply, photography, ice survey, training and for evaluation of dunking sonar. The Canadian Army also acquired Bell 47D helos for the Basic Helicopter Training Unit at the Canadian Joint Air Training Centre in Rivers, Manitoba. These aircraft were used for the transitioning of Canadian Army pilots from fixed wing to rotary wing operations. In addition, the aircraft were also used for wire laying, rescue and evacuation, topographic survey and light re-supply missions.

A Canadian Army Bell 47 helicopter on the ramp in Rivers, Manitoba. (Author's collection)

DETAILS

Designation: H-13, HTL-4, HTL-6   **Model No:** 47 D & G   **Role:** Light Utility Helicopter
TOS: 1948   **SOS:** 1965   **No:** 9   **Service:** RCN, Canadian Army

SPECIFICATIONS

Manufacturer:	Bell Helicopter Corporation
Crew/Passengers:	two pilots or one pilot and one passenger/observer
Powerplant:	one 200 hp Franklin 0-335-5 or 6U4-C32 or 210 hp 6B-33A piston engine

Performance:	Max Speed: 90 mph (145 km/h)	Cruising Speed: 77 mph (124 km/h)
	Service Ceiling: 10,000 ft (3,050 m)	Range: 190 mi (306 km)
Weights:	Empty: 1,380 lbs (626 kg)	Gross: 2,350 lb (1,066 kg)
Dimensions:	Rotor Diameter: 35 ft 1½ in (10.71 m)	Length: 41 ft 2½ in (12.56 m)
	Height: 9 ft 6 in (2.90 m)	
Armament:	None	
Cost:	Unknown	

Bell
IROQUOIS (HUEY)

The CH118 Iroquois was purchased after the success of the US UH-1 Huey in Vietnam. Unlike the US military, however, the CF purchased the "single" Huey exclusively for base rescue flight duties. (The use of the term "single" Huey was derived to differentiate this single-engine type from the later Twin Huey, the twin-engine version.) These duties involved primarily Search and Rescue (SAR), aero-medical support, casualty evacuation and general utility duties. The aircraft were consequently fitted with a rescue hoist and medivac equipment, and were flown in high visibility all-white or all-yellow rescue colour schemes. Only ten aircraft were purchased and following the loss of one helicopter in a crash, the remaining nine aircraft served faithfully in these roles until their retirement in 1995. The Iroquois served primarily in base rescue flights at Chatham, Moose Jaw, Bagotville and Cold Lake.

A CH-118 Iroquois Base Rescue Flight helicopter starting up. (CF Photo)

DETAILS

Designation: CH-118 **Model No:** 205 **Role:** SAR/Utility Helicopter
TOS: 1968 **SOS:** 1995 **No:** 10 **Service:** CF

SPECIFICATIONS

Manufacturer: Bell Helicopter Company
Crew/Passengers: 2 pilots and 1 flight engineer plus up to 11 passengers or 6 litters
Powerplant: one 1,400 shp AVCO Lycoming T-53-L-13B turbo-shaft engine
Performance: Max Speed: 147 mph (237 km/h) Cruising Speed: 113 mph (182 km/h)
  Hover Ceiling: 6,000 ft (1,829 m) Range: 318 mi (511 km)
Weights: Empty: 4,973 lb (2,256 kg) Gross: 9,500 lb (4,309 kg)
Dimensions: Rotor Diameter: 48 ft 0 in (14.63 m) Length: 41 ft 10¾ in (12.77 m)
  Height: 14 ft 6 in (4 .42 m) Rotor Disc Area: 1,809 sq ft (168.06 sq m)
Armament: None
Cost: Unknown

Bell
KIOWA

The Bell Kiowa was a significant improvement over the Hiller helicopter in both the light observation army co-operation and training roles. There was room for four in relative comfort. A high inertia rotor system and a light-weight turbine engine provided much needed modern-ization and performance. The helicopter provided excel-lent handling characteristics and reliability in the training role although high temperature, and high density altitude operation was less than satisfactory. The helicopter also provided valuable operational service in Europe and in Canada with both regular force and reserve units. The Kiowa was retired in 1996.

In 1970, 74 Bell CH-136 Kiowas were ordered to replace the Canadian Forces' 44 remaining Nomads and L-19s. Although the CH 136 is very similar in appearance to its Bell stable mate, the Jet Ranger, the two aircraft types are considerably different. The Kiowa was a purpose-built military variant; it could carry armament and was equipped, in later years, with a self-defence suite. (CF Photos)

DETAILS

Designation: CH-136   **Model No:** OH-58 or 206 BII   **Role:** Light Observation and Training Helicopter
TOS: 1971   **SOS:** 1996   **No:** 74   **Service:** CF

SPECIFICATIONS

Manufacturer:	Bell Helicopter Company	
Crew/Passengers:	two crew (pilots or pilot/observer) plus two passengers	
Powerplant:	Allison 250 C-18 317 shp turbine engine	
Performance:	Max Speed: 138 mph (222 km/h)	Cruising Speed: 117 mph (188 km/h)
	Service Ceiling:19,000 ft (5,791 m)	Range: 356 mi (573 km)
	Hover Ceiling: 6,000 ft (1,829 m)	
Weights:	Empty: 1,583 lb (718 kg)	Gross: 3,000 lbs (1,360 kg)
Dimensions:	Rotor Diameter: 35 ft 4 in (10.77 m)	Length: 40 ft 11¾ in (12.49 m)
	Height: 9 ft 6½ in (2.90 m)	Rotor Disc Area: 978.8 sq ft (90.93 sq m)
Armament:	Provisions for light 7.62mm machine guns and target marking rockets (unguided)	
Original Cost:	$150,000	

Bell
JET RANGER

Following successful experience with the Bell Kiowa, the CF selected the Bell 206 BIII Jet Ranger, an improved commercial derivative, for basic helicopter training duties. The Jet Rangers were essentially purchased "off the shelf" for delivery to the military. Primarily employed in this role at CFB Portage La Prairie in Manitoba, the Jet Rangers possessed more powerful engines and consequently better "hot and high" performance than their operational cousins. The performance of the helicopters spawned a helicopter display team flown by instructors who were known as the Dragonflies. As result of a UN mission to central America which required better performance, some of the Jet Rangers were rapidly modified for operational UN use and actively deployed. The entire Jet Ranger fleet was officially retired from the CF in 1992, only to re-emerge as contractor flown and maintained training aircraft in a now civilian, primary flying training facility in support of the CF program.

The photo illustrates a CF CH-139 Jet Ranger training helicopter in a United Nations colour scheme after preparation for an upcoming UN mission. Note the infrared countermeasures unit also installed on the lower rear fuselage. (CF Photo)

DETAILS

Designation: CH-139   **Model No:** 206 BIII   **Role:** Training Helicopter

TOS: 1981   **SOS:** 1992   **No:** 14   **Service:** CF

SPECIFICATIONS

Manufacturer: Bell Textron Helicopters

Crew/Passengers: two pilots plus up to three passengers

Powerplant: one 420 shp Allison 205-C20B turboshaft engine

Performance: Max Speed: 140 mph (225 km/h)   Cruising Speed: 133 mph (214 km/h)

Hover Ceiling: 13,200 ft (4,025 m)   Range: 430 mi (692 km)

Weights: Empty: 1,702 lb (722 kg)   Gross: 3,200 lbs (1,452 kg)

Dimensions: Rotor Diameter: 33 ft 4 in (10.16 m)   Length: 38 ft 9½ in (11.82 m)

Height: 9 ft 6 in (2.89 m)   Rotor Disc Area: 872.7 sq ft (81.07 sq m)

Armament: None

Original Cost: Unknown

Bell
TWIN HUEY

After the successful introduction of the CH118 Iroquois helicopter into CF service, a major improvement of the basic Bell model 204/205 was undertaken starting in 1968 on behalf of the US military. The uprated helicopter was based around the installation of the Canadian developed Pratt & Whitney PT-6T Twin-Pac powerplant. This involved two of the Canadian company's PT-6A turboshaft engines coupled to a common gear box which resulted in a significant increase in installed thrust with the benefit of enhanced twin-engine reliability. The Twin Huey development warranted a new model designation, and

the 212 versions or UH-1N, as it was known in the US military, proved to be highly successful. The CF recognized the potential of this new helicopter and ordered 50 Twin Hueys for general utility duties in support of Canadian land forces. The Twin Hueys were primarily flown in tactical aviation roles and were painted and equipped accordingly. The exceptions were three Twin Hueys which were devoted to Base Rescue Flight duties in Goose Bay, Labrador. Twin Hueys served with distinction in a wide variety of CF roles and missions.

In its day, the CH-135 Twin Huey was considered one of the finest utility tactical transport helicopters in the world. The fleet made up the backbone of the Air Force's 10 Tactical Air Group and was used primarily to support Army operations. Other variants were also used in the utility and search and rescue roles. This image illustrates an aircraft belonging to the Aerospace Engineering Test Establishment as evidenced by the red "X" on the tail. (CF Photo)

DETAILS

Designation: CH-135 **Model No:** 212 **Role:** Utility Helicopter
TOS: 1971 **SOS:** 1997 **No:** 50 **Service:** CF

SPECIFICATIONS

Manufacturer: Bell Textron Helicopters
Crew/Passengers: two pilots and one flight engineer plus up to thirteen passengers
Powerplant: one 1250 shp Pratt & Whitney T400-CP-400Twin-Pac turboshaft engine
Performance: Max Speed: 127 mph (204 km/h) Hover Ceiling: 9,300 ft (2,835 m)
Service Ceiling: 17,300 ft (5,273m) Range: 286 miles (460 km)
Weights: Empty: 6,000 lb (2,722 kg) Gross: 10,000 lb (4,536 kg)
Dimensions: Rotor Diameter: 48 ft 2½ in (14.69 m) Length: 57 ft 0 in (17.37 m)
Height: 14 ft 4¾ in (4.39 m)
Armament: Provisions for door-mounted 7.62 mm machine guns and two 19-tube CRV-7 rocket launchers
Cost: Unknown

Bell
GRIFFON

The CH146 Griffon was purchased to replace the Single and Twin Huey and the Kiowa helicopters. In addition to its military roles it has proved invaluable to civilian law enforcement, drug enforcement, support to firefighting and other special operations. The Griffon was selected by the army for its flexibility and its ability to perform more operations than the helicopters it replaced. Currently Canada's only land aviation helicopter, it is used for everything from airlift of equipment and troops, reconnaissance and surveillance missions through direction and control of fire. to aeromedical support, casualty evacuation and Search and Rescue (SAR). The four-bladed Griffon heli-

copter is powered by two Pratt Whitney Canada PT6T-3D Twin-Pac turboshaft engines. The Griffon has an all-up weight of 5,398 kgs (11,900 pounds) with standard seating for nine and maximum seating for ten plus the three crew members. The Griffon crew of two pilots and one flight engineer must be skilled in a wide range of battlefield and non-battlefield tasks. Their primary mission remains transporting troops and their equipment. Lightly armed with a C9 machine gun mounted in open doorways, the CH-146 Griffon can carry up to twelve lightly equipped troops or eight fully equipped troops.

The CH-146 Griffon tactical helicopter is essentially a commercial "off-the-shelf" acquisition by the CF. Its lineage from the Bell (single) Huey and Twin Huey design is readily apparent. It can easily be distinguished from the former by the four-bladed rotor. (CF Photo)

DETAILS

Designation: CH-146   **Model No:** 412 EP   **Role:** Utility Helicopter

TOS: 1995   **SOS:** In-Service   **No:** 100   **Service:** CF

SPECIFICATIONS

Manufacturer:	Bell Textron Mirabel
Crew/Passengers:	two pilots and one flight engineer plus up to thirteen passengers
Powerplant:	two Pratt Whitney Canada PT6T-3D Twin-Pac turboshaft engines

Performance:	Max Speed: 162 mph (269 km/h)	Cruising Speed: 136 mph (219 km/h)
	Hover Ceiling: 10,200 ft (3,109 m)	Range: 408 mi (656 km)
Weights:	Empty: 7,511 lb (3,407 kg)	Gross: 11,900 lb (5,398 kg)
Dimensions:	Rotor Diameter: 46 ft 0 in (14.02 m)	Length: 56 ft 2 in (17.12 m)
	Height: 15 ft 3 in (4.65 m)	
Armament:	Door mounted C9 (7.62 mm) machine guns	
Cost:	Unknown	

Bellanca
PACEMAKER

The Bellanca Pacemaker came from a long line of famous Bellanca monoplanes, which had been used on numerous record-breaking, long distance flights. This successful reputation for outstanding performance ensured Canadian interest in the design and the RCAF was able to acquire a total of 13 CH-300 Pacemakers. The CH-300 Pacemaker was a typical Bellanca design featuring a high wing monoplane with lifting struts. It combined wooden wings with a welded steel-tube fuselage and with tail surfaces featuring both wood and steel. The RCAF machines featured a wider than normal float track and a rear spreader bar that angled upward to a centre point which was strut-braced to the fuselage. This revised arrangement provided an improved view for a vertically-mounted camera. The RCAF aircraft served primarily in this photographic role where they proved to be reliable and stable platforms.

The Bellanca Pacemaker was a direct development of the Bellanca "Columbia", which was the first aircraft to make a double-crossing of the Atlantic. Shown here are two Bellanca Pacemakers (G-CYVB, foreground and G-CYVA) in RCAF colours while at Rockcliffe, Ont, on 29 May 1938. (LAC Photo #PA-062723)

DETAILS

Designation:	**Model No:** CH-300	**Role:** Utility	
TOS: 1929	**SOS:** 1944	**No:** 13	**Service:** RCAF

SPECIFICATIONS

Manufacturer: Bellanca Aircraft of Canada Ltd.
Crew/Passengers: one pilot and up to four passengers
Powerplant: one 300 hp Wright Whirlwind J-6E or one 300 hp P & W Wasp Jr piston engine

Performance:	Max Speed: 143 mph (230 km/h)	Cruising Speed: 110 mph (177 km/h)
	Service Ceiling: 17,000 ft (5,181 m)	Range: 500 mi (805 km)
Weights:	Empty: 2,647 lb (1,201 kg)	Gross: 4,300 lb (1,952 kg)
Dimensions:	Span: 46 ft 4 in (14.12 m)	Length: 27 ft 9 in (8.46 m)
	Height: 8 ft 4 in (2.54 m)	Wing Area: 272 sq ft (25.36 sq m)
Armament:	None	
Cost:	Unknown	

Blackburn
SHARK

The RCAF became interested in acquiring a torpedo bomber in 1935. It turned to the RAF for assistance and on the RAF's advice, acquired seven Blackburn Shark Mk II aircraft powered by 760 hp Armstrong Siddeley Tiger VI engines in 1937. These aircraft were tested and consequently uprated 840 hp Bristol Pegasus Mk IX engines were installed. Additional orders for these improved Mk III Shark aircraft were added in 1939. The Shark featured unequal-span folding biplane wings. Another unusual feature was full-span ailerons on both wings, which could be lowered together for landings or take-offs. The aircraft could be operated on wheels, skis and floats and it was also suitable for carrier operations. Pressed into operational service at the outbreak of war, the RCAF's Sharks primarily patrolled the West Coast. Only one Shark is known to have seen action, dropping depth charges on a suspected submarine during the course of its patrol duties. No aircraft were lost to enemy action, but more than a few were lost during training and landing accidents. After their useful operational service, the last RCAF Sharks ended their days serving as deck-handling practice aircraft for Royal Navy training purposes.

In all, 26 Sharks (7 Mk.IIs and 19 Mk.IIIs) served in the RCAF and established a reputation as a tough, well-liked aircraft. Though they could be mounted on wheels, as shown here, they were much more normally seen on floats. The only recorded RCAF Shark combat action during the Second World War occurred on 27 October 1942, when one attacked a submarine off the West Coast with no known results. (Comox AFM Photo)

DETAILS

Designation:	**Model No:**	**Marks:** Mk II, Mk III	**Role:** Torpedo Bomber
TOS: 1936	**SOS:** 1944	**No:** 26	**Service:** RCAF

SPECIFICATIONS

Manufacturer: Blackburn Aircraft & Boeing Aircraft of Canada

Crew/Passengers: one pilot and one observer/gunner

Powerplant: one 840 hp Bristol Pegasus Mk IX radial piston engine

Performance: Max Speed: 152 mph (245 km/h) Cruising Speed: 135 mph (217 km/h)
Service Ceiling: 16,100 ft (4,876 m)

Weights: Empty: 4,948 lb (2,246 kg) Gross: 8,300 lb (3,768 kg)

Dimensions: Upper Span: 46 ft 0 in (14.02 m) Lower Span: 36 ft 0 in (10.97 m)
Length: 35 ft 2¼ in (10.72 m) Height: 12 ft 1 in (3.68 m)
Wing Area: 489 sq ft (45.43 sq m)

Armament: One fixed forward .303 cal machine gun and one flexibly mounted .303 cal machine gun plus provisions for one 1,650 lb (749 kg) 18 in (46 cm) torpedo or equivalent bomb load

Cost: Unknown

Boeing
247D

The all-metal Boeing Model 247-D was a low-winged, twin-engined transport monoplane. It was the first of the "modern-day" airliners and made transports of its day virtually obsolete. The model 247-D featured newly developed supercharged engines mounted in streamlined nacelles with controllable-pitch propellers. The 247-D also had a new windshield that sloped backward instead of forward as on earlier 247 models. No. 121 (RCAF) Squadron flew seven Model 247-D aircraft as medium transports during the early part of the war.

An RCAF Boeing 247D, #7625, is illustrated here in an air-to-air formation with a Harvard trainer. It was flown by 121 Composite Squadron in Dartmouth, NS. This 247D was used by 121 Squadron for light transportation and target-towing duties during its two year career in the RCAF. (Comox AFM Photo)

DETAILS

Designation:	**Model No:** 247-D	**Role:** Transport
TOS: 1940	**SOS:** 1942	**No:** 8
Service: RCAF		

SPECIFICATIONS

Manufacturer:	Boeing Aircraft Company
Crew/Passengers:	crew of three and up to ten passengers
Powerplant:	two Pratt & Whitney Wasp S1H1-G engines rated at 550 hp
Performance:	Max Speed: 202 mph (325 km/h) Cruising Speed: 184 mph (296 km/h)
	Service Ceiling: 25,400 ft (7,742 m) Range: 745 miles (1,194 km)
Weights:	Empty: 8,940 lbs (4,055 kg) Gross: 13,650 lbs (6,192 kg)
Dimensions:	Span: 74 ft 0 in (22.56 m) Length: 51 ft 7 in (15.72 m)
	Height: 12 ft 2 in (3.71 m) Wing Area: 836 sq ft (77.67 sq m)
Armament:	None
Cost:	$69,000 US

Boeing
707

The Boeing 707 was the most successful and versatile of the early jet airliners. The Canadian Forces acquired a fleet of five used Boeing 707-320C jet transports to provide long range strategic transport. The aircraft were acquired to replace the Canadair Yukons in this same role. The aircraft were modified to a quick-change combi-configuration allowing the rapid change from passenger to cargo or combi configurations. This was facilitated by the installation of reinforced flooring and large dimension loading hatches. VIP interior configurations were also introduced. Two aircraft (137703 & 137704) were adapted as long range strategic refuellers by the installation of wing-tip mounted Fletcher-Sergeant "probe and drogue" refuelling pods. The CF 707's were retired in 1996 in favour of used A-300 Airbus aircraft and many of the ex-CF aircraft were bought to provide either the basis or spares for the J-Stars aircraft program.

First acquired in 1970, the Boeing CC-137 served the Canadian Forces both as a strategic airlifter and, as shown here, as an air-to-air refueller (two aircraft only) for fighter aircraft. The CC-137 fleet was retired in the summer of 1997. (CF Photo)

DETAILS

Designation: CC-137   **Model No:** 707-320C   **Role:** Strategic Transport and Refuelling
TOS: 1970   **SOS:** 1996   **No:** 5   **Service:** CF

SPECIFICATIONS

Manufacturer:	Boeing Aircraft Corporation
Crew/Passengers:	two pilots and crew plus up to 170 passengers and 88,900 lb (40,325 kg) cargo
Powerplant:	four Pratt & Whitney 19,700 lb thrust JT3D-7 turbofan engines

Performance:	Max Speed:	Cruising Speed: 618 mph (994 km/h)
	Service Ceiling: 39,000 ft (11,887 m)	Range: 7,638 mi (12,293 km)
Weights:	Empty:	Gross: 333,600 lb (151,321 kg)
Dimensions:	Span:	Length:
	Height:	Wing Area:
Armament:	None	
Cost:	Unknown	

Boeing
FLYING FORTRESS

The Boeing B-17 Flying Fortress was probably the most famous of all the American heavy bombers of the Second World War. Introduced into the US Army Air Corps prior to the war, the Flying Fortress was subsequently flown on US operations in all theatres of the war. In some theatres, war-weary B-17 bombers were converted to unarmed transport aircraft. It was in this latter less glamorous role that RCAF Flying Fortresses were employed. The RCAF acquired six used B-17 E and F aircraft from the US in 1943. Stripped of all armament and armour, the aircraft were employed by No. 168 (RCAF) Squadron on a trans-Atlantic mail service vital to the morale of overseas forces. The aircraft were progressively modified and improved for service in this transport role and some aircraft were subsequently stripped of paint and appeared in a polished bare metal finish. No. 168 Squadron delivered over two million pounds of mail between December 1943 and March 1946.

The Boeing B-17 Flying Fortress aircraft were bombers by design, but the RCAF versions, three B-17E models and three B-17F models, flew without armament since they were purely used as transport aircraft in Canadian service. (RCAF Photo)

DETAILS

Designation: B-17E, F **Model No:** 299-O, 299-P **Marks:** Mk II, Mk IIA **Role:** Transport
TOS: 1943 **SOS:** 1946 **No:** 6 **Service:** RCAF

SPECIFICATIONS

Manufacturer:	Boeing Aircraft Company	
Crew/Passengers:	two pilots and navigator and up to five additional crew	
Powerplant:	four 1,200 hp Wright Cyclone R-1820-65 radial engines	
Performance:	Max Speed: 317 mph (510 km/h)	Cruising Speed: 210 mph (338 km/h)
	Service Ceiling: 36,600 ft (11,156 m)	Range: 800 mi (1,287 km)
Weights:	Empty: 32,250 lb (14,629 kg)	Gross: 53,000 lb (24,041 kg)
Dimensions:	Span: 103 ft 9 in (31.62 m)	Length: 73 ft 10 in (22.50 m)
	Height: 19 ft 2 in (5.85 m)	Wing Area: 1,420 sq ft (131.92 sq m)
Armament:	None in Canadian service, but provision for 0.50 calibre machine guns in powered turrets and flexible positions plus carriage of bombs in an internal bomb bay	
Cost:	$276,000 US	

Boeing Vertol
LABRADOR/VOYAGEUR

Prior to the integration of the Canadian Forces, both the RCAF and the Canadian Army acquired versions of this large twin-rotor helicopter. The Army acquired the Voyageur CH-113A version for transport of troops and supplies. The RCAF acquired the Labrador CH-113 version of the aircraft primarily for search and rescue work. With integration, the two versions were merged and each type was progressively upgraded to a single standard for SAR work. The aircraft was to be replaced by the EH-101 Cormorant helicopter in 2001.

Two views of the CH113 Labrador as flown by 442 Squadron. (CF Photo & Author's collection)

DETAILS

Designation: CH-113 & CH113A   **Model No:** 107-11 & 107-11-9   **Role:** Transport/SAR Helicopter
TOS: 1963   **SOS:** In-service   **No:** 18   **Service:** RCA, RCAF, CF

SPECIFICATIONS

Manufacturer: Boeing Vertol
Crew/Passengers: two pilots and flight engineer plus SAR techs (up to 26 passengers)
Powerplant: two 1,350 eshp General Electric T-58-GE-85 turbine engines
Performance:

Max Speed: 148 kts (274 km/h)	Cruising Speed: 126 kts (233 km/h)
Service Ceiling: 10,600 ft (3,180 m)	Range: 599 nm (1,110 km)
Hover Ceiling: 6,525 ft (1,989 m)	

Weights: Empty: Gross: 18,700 lbs (8,482 kg)
Dimensions: Rotor Diameter: 52 ft 0 in (15.54 m)   Length: 84 ft 4 in (25.70 m)
Height:
Armament: None
Original Cost: CH113 Labrador $948,000   CH113A Voyageur $1,020,000

Boeing Vertol
CHINOOK

The Boeing Vertol CH-47C Chinook was a special uprated variant of the heavy-lift tandem-rotor helicopter acquired by the CF in 1974 and used primarily for Mobile Command operations. The first aircraft unfortunately crashed on its initial delivery flight. The remaining seven survivors were used extensively by the CF in transport duties associated with 10 Tactical Air Group (10 TAG). These included medium airlift requirements such as the transport of troops, rations, military supplies, transport, and weapons for mobility operations. Arctic re-supply and

special heavy-lift operations were also routinely undertaken. The Chinooks were based primarily with 447 and 450 Transport Helicopter Squadrons while employed by the CF. Although highly versatile, the CH-147 Chinooks eventually proved to be maintenance intensive and consequently expensive to operate so the CF retired the fleet as an economy measure in 1991. The ex-Canadian aircraft were eventually refurbished by Boeing Vertol and sold to the Dutch Armed Forces.

The heavy-lift Boeing Vertol CH-147 Chinook was the largest helicopter that has ever served with the CF to date. (Author's Collection)

DETAILS

Designation: CH-147   **Model No:** CH-47C   **Role:** Transport Helicopter

TOS: 1974   **SOS:** 1991   **No:** 8   **Service:** CF

SPECIFICATIONS CH-147 (CH-47C)

Manufacturer: Boeing Vertol

Crew/Passengers: four: two pilots and flight engineer and loadmaster plus up to 44 passengers, 33 troops or up 28,000 lb (12,700 kg) external loads

Powerplant: two AVCO Lycoming 3,300 shp T55-L-11C turboshaft engines

Performance: Max Speed: 180 mph (290 km/h) — Cruising Speed: 160 mph (257 km/h)

Hover Ceiling: 9,200 ft (2,804 m) — Range: 115 mi (185 km)

Weights: Empty: 20,616 lb (9,351 kg) — Takeoff: 39,000 lbs (17,781 kg)

Dimensions: Rotor Diameter: 60 ft 0 in (18.29 m) — Length: 99 ft 0 in (30.18 m)

Height: 22 ft 6 in (6.86 m)

Armament: None

Original Cost: Unknown

Boeing Vertol (Piaseki)
H-21

The Boeing Vertol (formerly Piasecki) H-21A was a single-engine, tandem rotor helicopter acquired by the RCAF in 1954 and used primarily for search and rescue work. The type was also used extensively by both the RCAF and commercial companies in transport duties associated with the construction of the various radar chains (i.e. Mid-Canada, DEW) across Canada. The H-21 B version was virtually identical to the H-21 A except for an increase in the available horsepower of the engine for take-off. The H-44 version was equipped with metal rotor blades and an advanced transmission and could be distinguished from the earlier versions by the covered struts of its landing gear. The H-21 was employed in the SAR role until replaced by another tandem rotor Boeing Vertol product, the CH-113 Labrador/Voyageur.

A 442 Squadron H-21 from Comox shown in operation and after restoration for the museum. (CF Photo and Author's collection)

DETAILS
Designation: CH-125, CH-127   **Model No:** H-21 A&B, H-44   **Role:** Transport/SAR Helicopter
TOS: 1954   **SOS:** 1968   **No:** 20   **Service:** RCAF

SPECIFICATIONS
Manufacturer: Originally designed and built by Piasecki Corporation, eventually part of Boeing Vertol
Crew/Passengers: Three: two pilots and flight engineer plus up to 20 passengers
Powerplant: one 1,425 hp Wright R-1820-103 engine
Performance: Max Speed: 131 mph (211 km/h)   Cruising Speed: 90 mph (145 km/h)
Service Ceiling: 8,450 ft (2,576 m)   Range: 350 m (563 km)
Weights: Empty: 8,000 lb (3,629 kg)   Gross: 13,500 lbs (6,123 kg)
Dimensions: Rotor Diameter: 44 ft 6 in (13.56 m)   Length: 86 ft 4 in (26.31 m)
Height: 15 ft 5 in (4.70 m)
Armament: None
Cost: $406,000 US

Boeing Vertol (Piaseki)
HUP-3

In 1949, after experimenting with two prototypes, the US Navy ordered 32 Piaseckis HUP helicopters for plane guard and utility duties. The RCN followed suit in 1954 with a more modest order of three helicopters. The PV-18 had been designed to suit a USN requirement for a carrier-based utility helicopter. In USN service, the helicopter was known as the Retriever. It had tandem rotors that could be folded for storage and that were interconnected by shafts to a rear fuselage mounted engine. A large floor-mounted hatch allowed for loads up to 400 lb (180 kg) to be hoisted using a winch. The RCN's HUP-3 helicopters all served with HU-21 Squadron in the general utility role and were based at HMCS *Shearwater* and on various RCN ships including the Arctic Patrol Vessel HMCS *Labrador*.

The RCN's diminutive HUP-3 helicopter in action. (CF Photo)

DETAILS

Designation: HUP-3   **Model No:** PV-18   **Role:** Helicopter

TOS: 1954   **SOS:** 1964   **No:** 3   **Service:** RCN

SPECIFICATIONS

Manufacturer:	Piasecki Helicopter Corporation (later Boeing Vertol)
Crew/Passengers:	one pilot and up to 5 passengers
Powerplant:	one 550 hp Continental R-975-46A piston engine

Performance:
Max Speed: 100 mph (161 km/h)   Cruising Speed: 80 mph (129 km/h)
Service Ceiling: 10,000 ft (3,050 m)   Range: 210 mi (338 km)

Weights: Empty: 4,132 lbs (1,874 kg)   Gross: 5,750 lb (2,608 kg)

Dimensions: Rotor Diameter: 35 ft 0 in (10.67 m)   Length: 32 ft 0 in (9.75 m)
Height: 12 ft 6 in (3.81 m)

Armament: None

Cost: Unknown

Brewster
BERMUDA

The Brewster Bermuda, or Buccaneer as it was known in the US, has the dubious distinction of being one of the least successful US combat aircraft put into production during the Second World War. The US Navy ordered a prototype of the new Brewster Model-340 design in 04 April 1939. The mid-wing, inward retracting undercarriage and internal weapon bay features were all very similar to the previous Brewster product for the Navy. The aircraft made its first flight on 17 June 1941. Desperate for modern aircraft designs, the British Purchasing Commission then ordered 750 aircraft of the type, to be known as Bermudas. But mediocre performance quickly relegated the aircraft type to only training duties. In 1943, the RCAF acquired three Bermudas for training and utility purposes in Canada. The aircraft saw no operational use and all were retired in the post-war period.

One of the lesser-known types in RCAF service, the Brewster Bermuda was a large single engine aircraft. (Comox AFM Photo)

DETAILS

Designation: SB2A-2   **Model No:** 340   **Marks:** Mk I   **Role:** Utility
TOS: 1943   **SOS:** 1946   **No:** 3   **Service:** RCAF

SPECIFICATIONS

Manufacturer:	Brewster Aeronautical Corporation	
Crew/Passengers:	Pilot and observer/gunner in tandem	
Powerplant:	one 1,700 hp Wright R-2600-8 radial engine	
Performance:	Max Speed: 274 mph (441 km/h)	Cruising Speed: 161 mph (259 km/h)
	Service Ceiling: 24,900 ft (7,589 m)	Range: 1,650 mi (2,656 km)
Weights:	Empty: 9,924 lb (4,502 kg)	Gross: 14,289 lb (6,481 kg)
Dimensions:	Span: 47 ft 0 in (14.33 m)	Length: 39 ft 2 in (11.94 m)
	Height: 15 ft 5 in (4.70 m)	Wing Area: 379 sq ft (35.21 sq m)
Armament:	Provisions for two fixed forward-firing 0.50 calibre machine guns in the fuselage and two 0.30 calibre guns in the wings along with two 0.30 calibre guns in a flexible dorsal mount; 1,000 lb (454 kg) internal bomb load	
Cost:	Unknown	

Bristol
BLENHEIM

In 1936, the RCAF was interested in obtaining a general reconnaissance aircraft and after evaluation selected the Bristol Bolingbroke in 1937. The Bolingbroke was in fact an improved version of the fast twin-engine Blenheim bomber being developed for the RAF. The Blenheim was rushed into front line service at the outbreak of the war. It was in a Blenheim that an RCAF officer, attached to the RAF, made the first flight by a member of the Canadian Forces over enemy territory. No. 404, 406, 407, 415 and 419 (RCAF) Squadrons all flew Blenheim bombers in action. Initial experience with the Blenheim models led to the subsequent adoption of the Bolingbroke style modifications, and later variants of the two aircraft were exter-

nally identical. On the home front, the RCAF maintained a small number of Blenheim aircraft, in addition to the far more numerous Bolingbroke type.

The Bristol Bolingbroke, shown in the lower image, was externally indistinguishable from the Bristol Blenheim Mk IV aircraft illustrated in the upper view. (RCAF and RAF photos)

DETAILS

Designation:	**Model No:** 142M	**Marks:** I, IV	**Role:** Bomber
TOS: 1941	**SOS:** 1945	**No:** 5	**Service:** RCAF

SPECIFICATIONS

Manufacturer:	Bristol Aircraft Ltd	
Crew/Passengers:	crew of three: pilot, bomb aimer and gunner	
Powerplant:	two 920 hp Bristol Mercury XV 2 radial engines	
Performance:	Max Speed: 262 mph (422 km/h)	Cruising Speed: 225 mph (362 km/h)
	Service Ceiling: 28,400 ft (8,660 m)	Range: 1,400 mi (2,253 km)
Weights:	Empty: 8,963 lb (4,065 kg)	Gross: 14,500 lb (6,576 kg)
Dimensions:	Span: 56 ft 4 in (17.17 m)	Length: 42 ft 7 in (13.03 m)
	Height: 9 ft 10 in (2.77 m)	Wing Area: 469 sq ft (43.57 sq m)
Armament:	Provisions for one fixed forward and twin flexible .303 cal machine guns in dorsal turret and in blister beneath the nose and up to 1,000 lb (454 kg) of bombs internally plus 320 lb (kg) externally	
Cost:	Unknown	

Bristol
BOLINGBROKE

In 1936, the RCAF was interested in obtaining a general reconnaissance aircraft and after evaluation selected the Bristol Bolingbroke in 1937. The Bolingbroke was an improved version of the Blenheim bomber being developed for the RAF. Although dropped by the RAF after the prototype version, the RCAF expressed interest in continuing the Bolingbroke's development. An order was subsequently placed with Fairchild Aircraft Ltd of Longueuil, Quebec. First introduced to active service in 1939, the type became the standard patrol bomber on Canada's east and west coasts during the war. The major operational use for the aircraft was in Western Air Command where the type equipped four bomber-reconnaissance squadrons, some of which were deployed to Alaska. Essentially obsolete before too long, the type was developed into bombing and gunnery training aircraft as well as target towing aircraft. It served useful British Commonwealth Air Training Plan functions in these training roles. A successful prototype float-plane version was also developed and this prototype was one of the largest float-planes of the period but no operational development followed. After the end of hostilities, the type was quickly scrapped.

An overhead fly-past by a Bristol Bolingbroke, likely on the west coast. (Author's collection)

DETAILS
Designation: **Model No:** 142M   **Marks:** I, II, III, IV, IVC, IVM, IVT, IVTT, IVW
Role: Bomber/Trainer/Float-plane
TOS: 1939   **SOS:** 1947   **No:** 626   **Service:** RCAF

SPECIFICATIONS
Manufacturer: Fairchild Aircraft Ltd
Crew/Passengers: crew of four
Powerplant: two 920 hp Bristol Mercury XV or two 750 hp P&W Twin Wasp Jr radial engines
Performance: Max Speed: 262 mph (422 km/h)   Cruising Speed: 225 mph (362 km/h)
Service Ceiling: 28,400 ft (8,660 m)   Range: 1,400 mi (2,253 km)
Weights: Empty: 8,963 lb (4,065 kg)   Gross: 14,500 lb (6,576 kg)
Dimensions: Span: 56 ft 4 in (17.17 m)   Length: 42 ft 9 in (13.03 m)
Height: 9 ft 1 in (2.77 m)   Wing Area: 469 sq ft (43.57 sq m)
Armament: Provisions for one fixed forward and one flexible .303 cal machine guns and up to 1,000 lb (454 kg) of bombs
Cost: Unknown

Bristol
BEAUFORT

The Beaufort was first flown in October 1938 and first used in action by the RAF's Coastal Command in 1939. Its main function was torpedo bombing, but it was also used in reconnaissance and mine-laying missions. Beauforts were used to attack enemy shipping in the North Sea, the English Channel and in the Mediterranean. Operating from Malta, Gibraltar and North African bases, the aircraft type did much to deprive the enemy forces in North Africa of valuable supplies, most notably gasoline. No. 415 (RCAF) Squadron flew Beauforts for a brief period and in Canada, No. 149 Squadron flew them in a training role from Patricia Bay, BC. Many more Beauforts were flown by Canadians in RAF service.

The Beaufort was designed in 1937 to combine the requirements of the British Air Ministry for a general reconnaissance bomber and a land-based torpedo bomber. The type served in the RCAF as torpedo bombers for No.149 (TB) Squadron at Patricia Bay, BC and with 415 Squadron in Coastal Command overseas. This particular Beaufort is a war-weary example from the Operational Training Unit in Patricia Bay. (Comox AFM Photo)

DETAILS

Designation:	**Model No:** 152	**Marks:** Mk I	**Role:** Torpedo Bomber
TOS: 1941	**SOS:** 1944	**No:** 15	**Service:** RCAF

SPECIFICATIONS Mark 1

Manufacturer:	Bristol Aircraft Company
Crew/Passengers:	crew of four
Powerplant:	two 1,130 hp (843 kW) Bristol Taurus VI, XII or XVI radial engines
Performance:	Max Speed: 260 mph (418 km/h) Cruising Speed: 200 mph (322 km/h)
	Service Ceiling: 16,500 ft (5,030 m) Range: 1,035 mi (1,666 km)
Weights:	Empty: 13,107 lb (5,945 kg) Maximum Take-off: 21,230 lb (9,630 kg)
Dimensions:	Span: 57 ft 10 in (17.63m) Length: 44 ft 7 in (13.59 m)
	Height: 12 ft 5 in Wing Area: 503 sq ft (46.73 sq m)
Armament:	four .303 in (7.7 mm) calibre machine guns: two each in nose and dorsal turrets plus three additional .303 guns in nose and beam stations. Provisions for up to 1,500 lb (680 kg) bombs or a 1,605 lb (728 kg) torpedo
Cost:	Unknown

Bristol
FIGHTER

The Bristol Fighter was an interesting departure from the standard single seat fighter design. A two-seat machine armed with both fixed and flexible machine guns, the Bristol Fighter or Brisfit as it was more affectionately known was fast, maneuverable and well suited to offensive operations. Modern for its day, the design proved to be very popular with crews. A number of Canadian aircrew achieved success with the Brisfit. A leading exponent of the Bristol Fighter was the Canadian ace, Major A.E. McKeever who accounted for most of his 30 victories with the type. Over 3,500 were built and with the end of the war, the wartime success of the type ensured its continuing use well into the next decade. In post war Canada, a number of F.2B's were acquired by the Canadian Air Board for aerial photographic work.

The Bristol Fighter in Canadian Air Board post war operational colours. (CF Photo)

DETAILS

Designation:	**Model No:** F.2B	**Marks:**	**Role:** two seat biplane fighter
TOS: 1920	**SOS:** 1922	**No:** 2	**Service:** RCAF

SPECIFICATIONS

Manufacturer:	Bristol Aeroplane Company Ltd	
Crew/Passengers:	crew of two: pilot and observer/gunner	
Powerplant:	one 275 hp Rolls Royce Falcon III twelve cylinder engine	
Performance:	Max Speed: 125 mph (201 km/h)	Cruising Speed:
Service Ceiling:	22,000 ft (6,710 m)	Range:
Weights:	Empty: 1,750 lb (793.7 kg)	Gross: 2,800 lb (1,270 kg)
Dimensions:	Span: 39 ft 3 in (11.96 m)	Length: 25 ft 9 in (7.85 m)
	Height: 10 ft 1 in (3.07 m)	Wing Area: 405 sq ft (37.63 sq m)
Armament:	one fixed forward Vickers machine gun and twin flexible Lewis machine guns on a Scarff ring and up to 240 lb (109 kg) of bombs	
Cost:	Unknown	

Bristol
FREIGHTER

The Bristol Freighter was a rugged and reliable transport designed for front-end loading through clam-shell doors which permitted the rapid handling of cargoes weighing as much as 12,000 lbs (5,443 kg). The high-wing construction allowed for efficient handling by reducing the distance that loads had to be moved vertically during loading and unloading. The box-like structure of the fuse-lage allowed for maximum utilization of cargo space. The RCAF acquired the type in July of 1952 and formed No. 137 (T) Flight at Lachine, Quebec to operate it. This flight was subsequently transferred to England where it served as the link between the Air Material Base at Langar, the four wings of Canada's NATO Air Division based in Europe and the air-firing range in Decimomannu, Sardinia.

A fine air-to-air portrait of the unusual looking Bristol Freighter clearly illustrating its massive bulbous fuselage and fixed landing gear. (CF Photo)

DETAILS

Designation:	**Model No:** 170	**Marks:** Mk 31C, Mk 31M	**Role:** Transport
TOS: 1952	**SOS:** 1967	**No:** 6	**Service:** RCAF

SPECIFICATIONS

Manufacturer:	Bristol Aircraft Company	
Crew/Passengers:	Crew of three	
Powerplant:	Two 1,980 hp Bristol Hercules 734 14 cylinder radial engines	
Performance:	Max Speed: 230 mph (370 km/h)	Cruising Speed: 166 mph (267 km/h)
	Service Ceiling:	Range:
Weights:	Empty: 24,000 lb (11,780 kg)	Gross: 36,500 lb (16,556 kg)
Dimensions:	Span: 98 ft 0 in (29.87 m)	Length: 68 ft 4 in (20.82 m)
	Height: 21 ft 8 in (6.60 m)	Wing Area: 1,405 sq ft (130.53 sq m)
Armament:	None	
Cost:	Unknown	

Burgess-Dunne

Canada's first air force consisted of just one aircraft, two pilots and one mechanic. The Canadian Aviation Corps came into being on 16 September 1914 under the auspices of the Minister of Militia and Defence, Colonel Sam Hughes. The entire corps was made up of two officers, Captain E.L. Janney and Lieutenant W.F. Sharpe, and one non-commissioned member, Staff Sergeant H.A. Farr who served as the ground crew. Their aircraft was a re-conditioned Burgess-Dunne hastily purchased from the US Navy. The Burgess-Dunne was a unique hydro-plane design with swept-back wings providing inherent stability. The aircraft had originally been designed by Lieutenant J.W. Dunne, an early British experimenter, and was

manufactured under licence in the United States by the Burgess Company, a boat-building firm which supplied several models to the US Navy. The aircraft was purchased and flown to Quebec City where Canada's First Contingent was forming. The design of the aircraft limited its military usefulness but it was, in fact, disassembled and shipped overseas to England with the First Canadian Contingent. Once there, the aircraft was never flown and it rotted into "a heap of worthless junk" on Salisbury Plain where the Canadian Contingent was in training. The Canadian Aviation Corps faded away in 1915 with the aircraft.

Canada's first military aircraft: the ungainly looking Burgess-Dunne floatplane. (CF Photo)

DETAILS

Designation:	**Model No:** AH-7	**Role:** Utility	
TOS: 1914	**SOS:** 1915	**No:** 1	**Service:** Canadian Aviation Corps

SPECIFICATIONS

Manufacturer: Burgess Company of Marblehead, Mass., USA
Crew/Passengers: two pilots
Powerplant: one 100 hp Curtiss OX piston engine
Performance: Max Speed: 55 mph (89 km/h) — Cruising Speed:
Service Ceiling: — Range:
Weights: Empty: — Gross:
Dimensions: Span: 46 ft 6 in (14.17 m) — Length:
Height: — Wing Area:
Sweepback Angle: 30 degrees
Armament: None
Cost: $5,000

Canadair
ARGUS

The Canadian-built, Canadair Argus was a unique hybrid that employed the wings, tail surfaces and undercarriage of the British designed Britannia transport, married to a completely new unpressurized fuselage of Canadian design and equipped with different American-designed engines. One of the most effective anti-submarine warfare aircraft of its day, the Argus was a mainstay for the RCAF in the maritime role. The principal difference between the Mark I and Mark II was in the different navigation, communication and tactical electronic equipment fitted internally. Externally, the Mk II exhibited a redesigned smaller nose radome and additional ECM antennae above the fuselage. The Argus replaced the Lancaster and Neptune aircraft types previously flown in the maritime roles and eventually, the Argus was itself replaced by the current CP-140 Aurora aircraft.

Adapted from the Bristol Britannia, the Argus entered service in 1957, giving the RCAF the most advanced anti-submarine aircraft in the world. It provided excellent service throughout a distinguished career. Although only 33 were built, there were still 31 in the Air Force inventory when it was retired in 1982 and replaced by the CP-140 Aurora. (RCAF Photo)

DETAILS

Designation: CP-107   **Model No:** CL-20   **Marks:** Mk I, II   **Role:** ASW
TOS: 1957   **SOS:** 1982   **No:** 33   **Service:** RCAF/CF

SPECIFICATIONS

Manufacturer: Canadair licence-built version of Bristol Britannia
Crew/Passengers: 15: two pilots, flight engineer, navigator, radio operator plus relief crew of four plus 6 operators for ASW equipment
Powerplant: four 3,700 hp Wright R3370 TC981 engines
Performance:
Max Speed: 288 mph (463 km/h)   Cruising Speed: 207 mph (333 km/h)
Service Ceiling: 24,200 ft (7,376 m)   Range: 4,420 nm (8,190 km)
Endurance: 26½ hrs
Weights: Empty: 81,000 lbs (36,744 kg)   Gross: 148,000 lbs (67,192 kg)
Dimensions:
Span: 142 ft 3½ in (43.38 m)   Length: 128 ft 3 in (39.09 m)
Height: 36 ft 8½ in (11.2m)   Wing Area: 2,075 sq ft (192.77 sq m)
Armament: 8,000 lbs of torpedos, bombs, depth charges, mines, etc
Original Cost: $5,513,00

Canadair (Bombardier)
CHALLENGER

The Challenger is a twin-engine executive jet used in the Canadian Forces both as a medium to long range transport and also originally as an electronic warfare (EW) training aircraft. Now, based in Ottawa but belonging to 8 Wing Trenton, Ont., the Challenger-equipped 412 Squadron provides high-ranking government officials and foreign dignitaries with air transportation worldwide. Two previous combat support grey Challengers are now assigned to the Squadron, bringing the total to six Challengers in the Canadian Forces. The grey Challengers are used for military transport and can be configured for medical evacuation for CF personnel on duty anywhere in the world. The type was previously used by 434 Combat Support Squadron at 14 Wing Greenwood, N.S. as an EW

training and combat support aircraft. In the combat support role, the Challenger was very similar to the CT-133 Silver Star, and EW training involved the same techniques, including chafe radar jamming, the dispersal of false targets to confuse enemy radar, and the creation and transmission of false radar signals. 434 Squadron's Challengers were also previously employed in the maritime patrol role.

Two views of the Challenger: on the bottom, CC144615, is one of the original four CC-144Bs (Model 601) flown by the Air Force, all of which belonged to 412 Squadron flying out of Uplands in Ottawa. These four Challenger 601s have General Electric instead of Avco Lycoming engines, the Electronic Flight Information System (EFIS) cockpit, and 700-800 extra miles in range. The upper view illustrates one of the Electronic Warfare combat support variants as indicated by the grey paint scheme. (CF Photos)

DETAILS

Designation: CC-144A, CE-144B, CX-144   **Model No:** CL-600, CL-601, CL-604   **Role:** Transport/EW
TOS: 1983   **SOS:** In-service   **No:** 18   **Service:** CF

SPECIFICATIONS 600 model

Crew/Passengers:	Up to four crew and twelve passengers
Powerplant:	Two Avco Lycoming ALP 502L-2C turbofans developing 7,500 lbs (3,405 kg) thrust
Performance:	Max Speed: Mach .83 576 mph (927 km/h) Cruising Speed: 544 mph (875 km/h)
	Service Ceiling: 49,000 ft (14,4935 m) Range: 3,176 mi (5,112 km)
Weights:	Empty: 15,085 lb (6,842 kg) Gross: 32,500 lb (14,061 kg)
Dimensions:	Span: 61 ft 10 in (18.83 m) Length: 68 ft 5 in (20.82 in)
	Height: 20 ft 9 in (6.33 m) Wing Area: 450 sq ft (41.7 sq m)
Armament:	None
Cost:	CL600 $11,371,000 CL601 $18,381,250 CL604 $24 M (US)

Canadair
COSMOPOLITAN

Canadair's parent company in the late 1950s was General Dynamics which also owned Convair Aircraft in the United States. When Convair phased out the Convair CV-440 twin-engine transport design, Canadair purchased the production jigs along with some uncompleted airframes. Canadair further refined the original design with 3,500 shp Napier Eland turboprop engines. These new variants were initially known as the Convair 540 since they were initially based on the uncompleted CV-440 airframes. New build aircraft were subsequently given the CL-66 Canadair designation. The RCAF became the launch customer for this new version by ordering ten CL-66B variants, which incorporated a reinforced floor, wide load doors and the ability for both cargo and passengers. The aircraft were introduced in Air Transport Command and were primarily used for most of the type's career for VIP transport duties. The aircraft were also deployed to Europe for Canadian NATO contingent support as well as to the US in support of Canadian NORAD operations. In 1966, eight of the RCAF Cosmopolitans were re-engined with Allison T-56 turboprops. After an avionics upgrade to "glass cockpit" status, the aircraft were retired in 1995.

The CC-109 Cosmopolitan was a turboprop version of the Convair-designed "Convairliner" passenger aircraft. The "Cosmo" was bought to be the standard VIP aircraft for the RCAF, replacing the Douglas DC-3 Dakota and the North American B-25 Mitchell, and it served exclusively in this VIP role. (RCAF Photo)

DETAILS

Designation: CC-109	**Model No:** CV-540, CL-66	**Role:** VIP Transport CV 540	
TOS: 1959	**SOS:** 1966	**No:** 3 CL-66B	
TOS: 1960	**SOS:** 1995	**No:** 10	**Service:** RCAF/CF

SPECIFICATIONS

Manufacturer: Canadair Aircraft Ltd

Crew/Passengers: crew of four with provisions for 40 passengers or up to 14,300 lb (6,486 kg) in cargo

Powerplant: two 3,500 eshp Napier Eland 504 turboprop engines

Performance:
Max Speed: 340 mph (547 km/h)   Cruising Speed: 322 mph (518 km/h)
Service Ceiling: 26,200 ft (6,220 m)   Range: 1,244 mi (1,996 km)

Weights: Empty: 32,333 lb (14,666 kg)   Gross: 47,000 lb (21,319 kg)

Dimensions:
Span: 105 ft 4 in (32.12 m)   Length: 81 ft 6 in (24.84 m)
Height: 28 ft 2 in (8.49 m)   Wing Area:

Armament: None

Cost: CV540 (used) - $880,000   CL-66B (new)—$2,000,000

Canadair
FREEDOM FIGHTER

In July 1965, the Canadian government selected the F-5 lightweight fighter as the new tactical aircraft in the midst of a great degree of disdain. The F-5 had been designed as a cheap, throwaway fighter for developing countries with limited technical expertise. For a country like Canada with a sophisticated aerospace industry, the aircraft selection was seen as a step backward. A substantial number of unique Canadian modifications were added to make the aircraft suitable and it was subsequently also adopted by the Dutch Air Force with further modifications. The aircraft went on to provide yeoman service for the Canadian Air Force both in the tactical fighter and advanced jet training role. Its small size also made it a valuable adversary training aircraft in exercises. After it was removed from front-line service, the aircraft became a lead-in fighter trainer for the CF-18, only to be retired after further extensive overhaul and avionics modification programs.

CF-116 Freedom Fighters in action: The Canadian aircraft were Canadair license-built versions of the original Northrop design significantly modified for RCAF use. (CF Photos)

DETAILS

Designation: CF-116   **Model No:** F-5, CL-219   **Marks:** 116A, 116D   **Role:** Tactical Fighter/Trainer

TOS: 1968   **SOS:** 1995   **No:** 89 CF-116A, 46 CF-116D   **Service:** RCAF, CF

SPECIFICATIONS   CF-116A

Manufacturer: License built by Canadair from Northrop

Crew/Passengers: one or two pilots in ejection seats

Powerplant: Two Orenda J-85-Can-15 Turbojets 2,925 lbs thrust (mil) 4,300 lbs thrust (A/B)

Performance: Max Speed: 650 kts (1,204 km/h)   Cruising Speed: 450 kts (834 km/h)

Service Ceiling: 41,000 ft (12,496 m)   Range: 195 m (314 km)

Weights: Empty: 8,681 lbs (3,938 kg)   Maximum Take-off: 20,390 lbs (9,249 kg)

Dimensions: Span: 25 ft 10 in (7.87 m)   Length: 47 ft 2 in (14.38 m)

Height: 13 ft 2 in (4.01 m)

Armament: Two 20 mm cannon and provisions for tanks, bombs, rockets (unguided), or missiles

Original Cost: Single $1,100,000 Dual $1,200,000

Canadair
NORTH STAR

The Canadair North Star was a unique Canadian development of the Douglas C-54 / DC-4 aircraft. Instead of radial piston engines found on the Douglas design, Canadair selected Rolls-Royce Merlin engines in order to achieve a 35 mph faster cruising speed. The prototype flew on 15 July 1946 and the type was selected by various airlines as well as by the RCAF. The RCAF North Stars were not pressurized and were used on a wide variety of general transport duties. They were also unfortunately infamous for the high level of interior cabin noise caused by the Merlin engines. The North Stars were assigned to 426 Transport Squadron initially deployed to Dorval, Quebec and then to Trenton, Ontario. During the Korean War, from 1950 to 1952 RCAF North Star aircraft were employed ferrying supplies to Korea across the Pacific. They flew 599 round trips over the Pacific and delivered seven million pounds of cargo and 13,000 personnel both ways. North Stars were also employed by 412 Squadron from Ottawa on various VIP transport duties. Overall the aircraft provided valuable and reliable long range transport services to the RCAF.

The Canadair C-54GM North Star served the RCAF for many years almost exclusively in the transport role. An exception was the aircraft shown here which was known as "The Rockcliffe Ice Wagon" and was used for icing trials. It replaced a similarly named Consolidated Privateer originally used for the same purpose. (RCAF Photo)

DETAILS

Designation:	**Model No:** C-54GM	**Marks:** Mk I	**Role:** Transport
TOS: 1947	**SOS:** 1965	**No:** 24	**Service:** RCAF

SPECIFICATIONS

Manufacturer:	Canadair Aircraft Ltd	
Crew/Passengers:	crew of seven with provisions for 44 passengers or 11,500 lbs (5,216 kg) of cargo	
Powerplant:	four 1,760 hp Rolls-Royce Merlin 622 piston engines	
Performance:	Max Speed: 353 mph (568 km/h)	Cruising Speed: 325 mph (523 km/h)
	Service Ceiling: 36,000 ft (10,970 m)	Range: 420 mi (677 km)
Weights:	Empty: 43,500 lb (19,731 kg)	Gross: 73,000 lb (33,112 kg)
Dimensions:	Span: 117 ft 6 in (35.81 m)	Length: 94 ft 9½ in (28.89 m)
	Height: 27 ft 6 in (8.38 m)	Wing Area: 1,462 sq ft (135.82 sq m)
Armament:	None	
Cost:	Unknown	

Canadair
C-5

Noise problems associated with the engine installation on the Canadair North Star led to the development of another variant of the Douglas C-54 / DC-4 aircraft. The C-5 was the final derivative of the North Star and reverted to the radial piston engines as found on the Douglas original design, Canadair having selected Pratt and Whitney Double Wasp R-2800 engines. The first and only C-5 was delivered to the RCAF in 1950 and it entered service with 412 Transport Squadron in Uplands, Ottawa. In RCAF service, the aircraft was specially outfitted for the transportation of VIP passengers. It was then used to transport the Canadian Prime Minister, the Queen and numerous other dignitaries on various high profile missions. It served faithfully for seventeen years before being retired and sold in the United States.

The Canadair C-5 was a one-of-a-kind hybrid drawing from both the Douglas DC-4 and DC-6 designs. It entered service in 1950 and was the RCAF's premier VIP transport aircraft. (CF Photo)

DETAILS

Designation:	**Model No:** C-5	**Marks:**	**Role:** Transport
TOS: 1950	**SOS:** 1967	**No:** 1	**Service:** RCAF

SPECIFICATIONS

Manufacturer: Canadair Aircraft Ltd
Crew/Passengers: crew of seven with provisions for 27 passengers
Powerplant: four 2,100 hp Pratt & Whitney Double Wasp R-2800-CA15 radial piston engines
Performance: Max Speed: 320 mph (568 km/h)   Cruising Speed: 303 mph (486 km/h)
Service Ceiling: 26,200 ft (6,220 m)   Range:
Weights: Empty: 49,475 lb (22,441 kg)   Gross: 86,000 lb (9,009 kg)
Dimensions: Span: 117 ft 6 in (35.81 m)   Length: 93 ft 5 in (28.47 m)
Height: 27 ft 6 in (8.38 m)   Wing Area: 1,462 sq ft (135.82 sq m)
Armament: None
Cost: Unknown

Canadair
SABRE

The North American F-86 Sabre was first flown on 1 October 1947 and the aircraft quickly proved to be a highly successful design. In 1949 with the formation of NATO the Canadian government made the decision to re-equip the RCAF's front-line fighter squadrons with modern aircraft and the F-86 Sabre was the type selected. Consequently, an agreement was reached between North American and Canadair Limited of Montreal to manufacture 100 F-86As in Canada. After the first prototype, designated CL-13 Sabre Mk I, Canadair immediately began production in earnest with an improved Mk II model. The Mark II was essentially an F-86E with an "all flying" tailplane to provide better flying characteristics, as well as a flat windscreen. The next major production model was the Mark IV which originally was to have been powered by an Orenda designed engine, but to retain commonality with the F-86E, it also carried the J47-GE-13. Various design improvements were incorporated throughout the aircraft. A total of 438 Mk IV Sabres rolled off the assembly lines. The Mark V Sabre was the first production model with a Canadian engine utilizing the Orenda 10 version

rated at 6,355 lbs thrust. The bigger Orenda engine necessitated a larger diameter opening in fuselage frames and stronger engine mounts. An important structural modification was the introduction of a fixed leading edge to replace the automatic slats on earlier versions. This change was designed to enhance the high altitude performance of the aircraft. Small wing fences were also introduced at the 70% span position. These modifications were successful but also resulted in a corresponding decrease in low speed handling characteristics. After the construction of 370 Mk V aircraft, Canadair moved on to the final (and best) version, the Mark VI. This version carried the two-stage Orenda 14 engine with a 7,275 lb thrust rating. The wing leading slats were re-introduced while retaining portions of the Mk V wing configuration. The Mk VI therefore acquired superb combat maneuvering. With this combination of engine and aerodynamics, the Mark VI was widely regarded as the best "dog-fighter" of its era. The RCAF's Golden Hawks team flew Mk V aircraft initially but were soon equipped with the excellent Mk VI aircraft.

Sabre 23757 was one of 390 Canadair CL-13B Sabre Mk. VI (the last version, with Avro Orenda 14 engines) that served with the RCAF. This Sabre is carrying the camouflage developed for all RCAF European-based operational aircraft. The photo was taken while the aircraft belonged to 1 Overseas Ferry Unit (OFU) (based at St. Hubert, Que.) formed in 1953 to ferry Sabres and T-33s across the North Atlantic.

These Sabres are en route to Europe via Greenland. (CF Photos)

DETAILS

Manufacturer: North American designed and built by Canadair   **Designation:** F-86

Model No: CL-13   **Marks:** Mk 1, 2, 3, 4, 5, 6   **Role:** Fighter

TOS: 1950   **SOS:** 1970   **No:** 1184   **Service:** RCAF, CF

SPECIFICATIONS Mk II

Crew/Passengers: one pilot in ejection seat

Powerplant: General Electric J-47-GE-13 turbojet at 5,200 lbs (2,360 kg) thrust

Performance: Max Speed: 590 mph (949 km/h)   Cruising Speed:

Service Ceiling: 47,200 ft (14,386 m)   Range:

Weights: Empty: 10,434 lbs (4,737 kg)   Gross: 14,577 lbs (6,618 kg)

Dimensions: Span: 37 ft 11½ in (11.57 m)   Length: 37 ft 6 in (11.43 m)

Height: 14 ft 9 in (4.50 m)   Wing Area: 287.9 sq ft (26.74 sq m)

Armament: Six .50 calibre machine guns plus provisions for tanks, bombs, and rockets (unguided)

Original Cost: Unknown

SPECIFICATIONS Mk V

Crew/Passengers: one pilot in ejection seat

Powerplant: Orenda Series 10 turbojet at 6,600 lbs (2,996 kg) thrust

Performance: Max Speed: 605 mph (973 km/h)   Cruising Speed:

Service Ceiling: 50,700 ft (15,453 m)   Range:

Weights: Empty: 10,662 lbs (4,840 kg)   Gross: 14,634 lbs (6,644 m)

Dimensions: Span: 37 ft 11½ in (11.57 m)   Length: 37 ft 6 in (11.43 m)

Height: 14 ft 9 in (4.50 m)   Wing Area: 302.3 sq ft (28.08 sq m)

Armament: Six .50 calibre machine guns plus provisions for tanks, bombs, and rockets (unguided)

Original Cost: Unknown

SPECIFICATIONS Mk VI

Crew/Passengers: one pilot in ejection seat

Powerplant: Orenda Series 14 Turbojet at 7,275 lbs (3,302 kg) thrust

Performance: Max Speed: 606 mph (975 km/h)   Cruising Speed: 489 mph (787 km/h)

Service Ceiling: 54,000 ft (16,458 m)   Range: 1,486 m (2,391 km)

Weights: Empty: 10,618 lbs (4,818 kg)   Gross: 14,613 lbs (6,634 m)

Dimensions: Span: 37 ft 11½ in (11.57 m)   Length: 37 ft 6 in (11.43 m)

Height : 14 ft 9 in (4.50 m)   Wing Area: 287.9 sq ft (26.74 sq m)

Armament: Six .50 calibre machine guns plus provisions for tanks, bombs, and rockets (unguided)

Original Cost: $360,000

Canadair
SILVER STAR

The Silver Star is more often referred to as the T-33 or T-Bird. The CT-133 Silver Star has a long and distinguished history with the Canadian Forces. The world's first purpose-built jet trainer, the T-33 evolved from America's first successful jet fighter, the Lockheed P-80 Shooting Star that briefly flew operationally during the Second World War. Initially known as the P-80C, the trainer variant was powered by an Allison J33-35 single-shaft, turbojet engine with a thrust rating of 5,200 lbs. and flew better than its single-seat cousins. The improvements to the trainer meant it climbed faster, cruised better and overall was slightly faster than the fighter version. In May 1949, the aircraft's designation was officially switched to T-33. The RCAF's first introduction to the aircraft followed two years later, when the first of twenty Lockheed built T-33As were delivered on loan. The aircraft was known to the RCAF as the Silver Star Mk 1. This first group was fol-

lowed by a second loan of ten more aircraft. On 13 September 1951, Canadair signed a licence agreement with Lockheed to build T-33 aircraft for the RCAF. The Canadair built version, known internally as the CL-30 (and as the T-33ANX by Lockheed and the USAF), was to be powered by an uprated Nene 10 engine licensed by Rolls Royce and supplied by Orenda Ltd. Once in production, the aircraft were designated T-33 Silver Star Mk 3 by the RCAF. Variations included versions for armament training (AT), photo-reconnaissance (PR) and pilot training (PT). Initially, the RCAF ordered 576 aircraft. Eventually, a total of 656 aircraft were delivered to the RCAF between 1952 and 1959. The "T-Bird" has been used by a wide variety of Air Force and Navy units and a few aircraft continued valuable service at the Aerospace Engineering Test Establishment in various test support roles after the majority of the fleet was retired.

The T-33 or CT-133 Silver Star in Canadian service was one of the longest serving aircraft types. This view of a "T-bird" in very early RCAF service illustrates an aircraft with a Delmar tow target installation, which explains the high visibility markings. (CF Photo)

DETAILS

Designation: CT-133 **Model No:** T-33 **Marks:** Mk I, II, III **Role:** Trainer, EW, Target Towing
TOS: 1953 **SOS:** 2005 **No:** 656 **Service:** RCAF & CF

SPECIFICATIONS Mk III

Manufacturer: Built by Canadair under licence from Lockheed Aircraft
Crew/Passengers: two crew in ejection seats
Powerplant: one 5,100 lb Rolls Royce Nene 10 turbojet
Performance: Max Speed: 570 mph (917 km/h) Cruising Speed: 190 mph (306 km/h)
Service Ceiling: 47,000 ft (14,325 m) Range: 1400 m (2,253 km) with tip tanks
Weights: Empty: 8,440 lbs (3,832 kg) Gross: 16,800 lbs (7,627 kg)
Dimensions: Span: 42 ft 5 in (12.93 m) Length: 37 ft 8½ in (11.49 m)
Height 11 ft 8 in (3.6 m) Wing Area: 238 sq ft (22.11 sq m)
Armament: none, but provisions for two .50 cal Browning machine guns and underwing pylons
Original Cost: $165,000

Canadair (Lockheed)
STARFIGHTER

Late in 1959, Canadair was selected to produce 200 strike, reconnaissance versions of the Lockheed designed F-104 Starfighter, designated as the CF-104, to replace the F-86 Sabres being flown by the RCAF in NATO. The aircraft was known by a wide variety of nicknames some flattering and some not so flattering (i.e. "missile with a man in it" referred to the design while "flying lawn dart" and "widow-maker" referred to the high number of crashes the type suffered in the early years). The CF-104s had a number of specialized changes and equipment for the Canadian role. The aircraft was capable of a nuclear strike role and reconnaissance packs could be carried in a special pod under the fuselage. Originally, the standard M-61 gun pod was replaced by a 120 US gallon (455 litre) fuel tank. Later in its CF career, the aircraft was returned to a conventional strike role and the 20mm cannon was re-installed. The CF-104 was replaced in service by the CF-18 Hornet.

A dramatic view of a CF-104 Starfighter from the Aerospace Engineering Test Establishment carrying a full load of BL-755 cluster bombs. (CF Photo)

DETAILS
Designation: CF-104 A/D   **Model No:** F-104G/CL-90   **Marks:** Mk I (A), Mk II (Dual)
Role: Fighter/Strike/Photo-Reconnaissance
TOS: 1961   **SOS:** 1984   **No:** 200   **Service:** RCAF, CF

SPECIFICATIONS
Manufacturer: Canadair licence-built version of Lockheed design
Crew/Passengers: one or two pilots in ejection seats
Powerplant: one General Electric (Orenda) J-79-OEL-7 turbojet with afterburning (10,000 lbst to 15,800 lbst in afterburner)
Performance: Max Speed: Mach 2.2, 1,450 mph (2,334 km/h)   Cruising Speed: Mach 1.2, 915 mph (1,473 km/h)
Service Ceiling: 58,000 ft (17,660 m)   Range: 2,180 miles (3,510 km)
Weights: Empty: 14,082 lb (6,387 kg)   Gross: 28,779 lbs (13,510 kg)
Dimensions: Span: 21 ft 11 in (6.68 m) w/o tip tanks   Length: 54 ft 9 in (16.69 m)
Height: 13 ft 6 in (4.11 m)   Wing area:196 sq ft (18.21 sq m)
Armament: Provision for one 20 mm M61A-1 cannon, plus bombs, rockets, or tanks on underwing or fuselage pylons
Original Cost: $1,200,000 single, $1,400,000 dual

Canadair
TUTOR

The CT-114 Tutor aircraft was designed and manufactured by Canadair Limited (now Canadair, Bombardier Inc.) to a Royal Canadian Air Force (RCAF) specification. In anticipation of a requirement by the RCAF for a basic jet trainer, Canadair began preliminary in-house studies in 1955. By 1957, Canadair had constructed a full-scale mock-up of the aircraft incorporating side-by-side seating and a single engine. After an evaluation by the RCAF, the CL-41 was selected as the RCAF's basic jet trainer and was ordered into production in September 1961 as the CT-114 Tutor in RCAF terminology. The CT-114 Tutor is a conventional all metal, low wing, single-engine turbojet aircraft designed for training student pilots. It features side-by-side ejection seats for a crew of two in a pressurized and air conditioned cockpit. The majority of the services are electrically operated, but the landing gear, wing flaps, speed brakes, nose wheel steering and wheel brakes are hydraulically operated. The aircraft is certified for Instrument Flight Rule (IFR) conditions and is equipped with all necessary instrumentation for navigation, instrument and night flying training. Canadair supplied 190 CT-114 aircraft to the Royal Canadian Air Force in the 1963-67 timeframe. Various changes were immediately made to the CL-41A prototype configuration. The most significant modification was the government directed use of the General Electric J-85 CAN 40 jet engine produced under licence by Orenda Ltd (now the Orenda Aerospace Corporation, a Magellan Aerospace Company) in Toronto. This engine is an axial flow turbojet developing approximately 2,700 pounds maximum continuous static thrust at sea level under standard atmospheric conditions.

This colour view illustrates the Canadair-designed and built CT-114 Tutor aircraft as it was originally delivered to the RCAF. (CF Photo)

DETAILS

Designation: CT-114 **Model No:** CL-41 **Role:** Trainer
TOS: 1963 **SOS:** In-service **No:** 190 **Service:** RCAF/CF

SPECIFICATIONS

Manufacturer: Canadair designed and built
Crew/Passengers: two crew (pilots) in ejection seats
Powerplant: Orenda J-85 CAN-40 Turbojet with 2,950 lbs thrust
Performance: Max Speed: 486 mph (782 km/h) Service Ceiling: 42,200 ft (12,863 m)
Range: 940 m (1,563 km)
Weights: Empty: 4,895 lbs (2,220 kg) Gross: 7,397 lbs (3,335 kg)
Dimensions: Span: 36 ft 6 in (11.13 m) Length: 32 ft 0 in (9.75 m)
Height 9 ft 4 in (2.84 m)
Armament: None, but provisions for under-fuselage tanks
Original Cost: $425,000

Canadair
YUKON

The Canadair-built Yukon was acquired to replace the North Star in order to provide the RCAF with modern long-range transport. Like the Canadair ASW aircraft the CC-107 Argus, the CC-106 Yukon also stemmed from the design of the Bristol Britannia transport. The fuselage was lengthened as compared to the Britannia and Rolls Royce Tyne engines were fitted to provide additional power. The Yukons had two large cargo doors fitted on the port side, both front and rear. The Yukons played a pivotal role in Canada's UN missions through the 1960s, delivering troops and supplies to countries such Ghana, Tanzania, Pakistan, India, Vietnam, and Cyprus as well as supporting Canada's NATO contingent in Europe. The aircraft were retired in the spring of 1971 in favour of a smaller fleet of Boeing 707 jet transports.

A unique, Canadian hybrid design, the Canadair CC-106 Yukon was the backbone of air transport for the RCAF for many years. Twelve aircraft faithfully served from 1959 until 1971, when they were retired from service. (RCAF Photo)

DETAILS

Designation: CC-106   **Model No:** CL-44   **Role:** Transport

TOS: 1959   **SOS:** 1971   **No:** 12   **Service:** RCAF/CF

SPECIFICATIONS

Manufacturer:	Canadair Aircraft Ltd
Crew/Passengers:	crew of ten with provisions for 134 passengers or up to 14,300 lb (6,486 kg) in cargo
Powerplant:	four 5,500 eshp Rolls Royce Tyne II turboprop engines

Performance:	Max Speed: 320 mph (515 km/h)	Cruising Speed: 288 mph (463 km/h)
	Service Ceiling: 30,000 ft (9,144 m)	Range: 3,550 mi (1,996 km)
Weights:	Empty: 91,000 lb (41,314 kg)	Gross: 205,000 lb (3,075 kg)
Dimensions:	Span: 142 ft 3⅝ in (43.35 m)	Length: 136 ft 8 in (41.65 m)
	Height: 38 ft 7⅝ in (11.77 m)	Wing Area: 2,075 sq ft (192.76 sq m)
Armament:	None	
Cost:	$6,491,115	

Canadian Vickers
VANCOUVER

The Canadian Vickers Vancouver was another twin-engine flying boat designed to an RCAF specification for an aircraft to replace the Varuna and capable of transporting men and equipment to forest fire locations. The resulting equal-span biplane had a metal hull manufactured from a new Alclad material. The remainder of the aircraft was of the conventional wood and fabric construction of the period. In 1929, the initial trials on the aircraft proved the suitability of the design and with some modest improvements additional aircraft were ordered as Vancouver II. These aircraft then provided long and faithful service. In the mid-1930s, the Vancouvers were modified to a military coastal patrol capability with the installation of flexible machine guns and provision for the carriage of light bombs. This resulted in the aircraft designation being amended to Mk IIS (S for Service). The aircraft also went through a progressive series of engine changes and improvements. The installation of Wright and Serval powerplants resulted in further designation amendments to Mk IIS/W and Mk IIS/S respectively. At the outbreak of the Second World War, Vancouver aircraft continued to serve on coastal patrol with No. 4 Squadron at Jericho Beach Air Station on the west coast. By 1940, however, the aircraft were clearly obsolete and were relegated briefly to training duties before being struck off strength.

In the 1920s, many aircraft that served the Civil Government Air Operations (CGAO) were transferred to the newly created RCAF. As funds were scarce during this period, proper RCAF markings were frequently neglected in favour of fuel and parts. Vancouver CV107, seen here at Rockliffe, is devoid of markings. (RCAF Photo)

DETAILS

Designation:	**Model No:**	**Marks:** Mk I, II	**Role:** Flying Boat
TOS: 1929	**SOS:** 1940	**No:** 6 Mk I (ea 1) Mk II (ea 5)	**Service:** RCAF

SPECIFICATIONS Vancouver IIS/S

Manufacturer:	Canadian Vickers
Crew/Passengers:	crew of nine: two pilots, plus seven passengers or crew
Powerplant:	two 340 hp Armstrong Siddeley Serval IV radial engines
Performance:	Max Speed: 94 mph (151 km/h)　　　Cruising Speed: 86 mph (138 km/h)
	Service Ceiling: 4,800 ft (1,463 m)　　　Range:
Weights:	Empty: 5,960 lb (2,706 kg)　　　Gross: 10,000 lb (4,540 kg)
Dimensions:	Span: 55 ft 0 in (16.76 m)　　　Length: 38 ft 3 in (11.66 m)
	Height: 15 ft 7 in (4.75 m)　　　Wing Area: 409.5 sq ft (38.04 sq m)
Armament:	provisions for three Lewis machine guns on flexible mounts (one in the nose and two in separate cockpits at the rear) plus up to four 250 lb (113.5 kg) bombs
Cost:	Unknown

Canadian Vickers
VANESSA

The Canadian Vickers Vanessa was a single-engine float plane designed as a private venture for the commercial market. The enclosed cabin fuselage was constructed of steel tubing as were various support structures along with the tail surfaces. The remainder of the aircraft was constructed of wood and the entire aircraft was fabric covered. The biplane wings were braced by interplane struts in the form of an "X", eliminating the need for traditional wire bracing. After completion of a prototype, the RCAF expressed an interest in the aircraft for general communication and transport duties. In service, the RCAF pi-

lots considered the aircraft's performance disappointing. his resulted in the installation of a more powerful Wright Whirlwind engine. In September 1927, the aircraft was used for a series of trial airmail runs and during the tests a float failed structurally, and the aircraft sank as a result. Despite a subsequent salvage, the aircraft was considered uneconomical to repair. Notwithstanding a very brief career, the Vanessa has the distinction of being one of the first enclosed cabin aircraft to be designed and built in Canada.

The inspiration behind the design for the Vickers Vanessa was a Stinson enclosed cabin biplane, which had been produced in the United States. One feature the Canadian Vickers Chief Engineer did not like about the Stinson was the usual wire bracing for biplanes, which interfered with easy cabin access. Consequently, he introduced a system of interplane struts, as seen here. (CF Photo)

DETAILS

Designation:	**Model No:**	**Role:** Float Plane	
TOS: 1927	**SOS:** 1927	**No:** 1	**Service:** RCAF

SPECIFICATIONS (Lynx powered version)

Manufacturer:	Canadian Vickers		
Crew/Passengers	one pilot		
Powerplant:	one 180 hp Armstrong Siddeley Lynx or 220 hp Wright J-5C Whirlwind radial engines		
Performance:	Max Speed: 103 mph (166 km/h)	Cruising Speed:	
	Service Ceiling: 12,000 ft (3,657 m)	Range	
Weights:	Empty: 2,120 lb (963 kg)	Gross: 3,400 lb (1,543 kg)	
Dimensions:	Span: 35 ft 3 in (10.74 m)	Length: 30 ft 0 in (9.14 m)	
	Height: 12 ft 4 in (3.76 m)	Wing Area: 410 sq ft (38.1 sq m)	
Armament:	None		
Cost:	Unknown		

Canadian Vickers
VARUNA

The Canadian Vickers Varuna was a twin-engine flying boat designed to an RCAF specification for an aircraft capable of transporting men and equipment to forest fire locations. The front cockpit was also to be capable of supporting photographic missions. The resulting unequal-span biplane was essentially an enlarged Vedette flying boat. The wing structure was constructed of steel tubing, as were various support structures and the tail surfaces. The remainder of the aircraft was of wood construction.

Initial tests on the prototype Varuna I proved the suitability of the design and with some modest improvements additional aircraft were ordered as Varuna II. The selection of lower powered engines for the Varuna II unfortunately resulted in decreased performance. In RCAF service, most of the Varuna II aircraft spent their working lives in the province of Manitoba filling their intended purpose. All of the Varuna II were struck off strength by 1930 but the sole Varuna I languished until 1932.

Varuna G-CYZT, shown here, was one of seven Mk. II versions in the RCAF and it served from 11 May 1927 to 9 October 1930, when it suffered an accident. The vast majority of Varuna IIs spent their working lives in the province of Manitoba. The aircraft's poor performance restricted it to flying only from large bodies of water and continued to plague its crews throughout its service life. (CF Photo)

DETAILS

Designation:	**Model No:**	**Marks:** Mk I, II	**Role:** Flying Boat
TOS: 1926	**SOS:** 1932	**No:** 8	**Service:** RCAF

SPECIFICATIONS Varuna II

Manufacturer:	Canadian Vickers	
Crew/Passengers:	crew of seven: two pilots, one photographer and four passengers or crew	
Powerplant:	two 180 hp Armstrong Siddeley Lynx IV radial engines	
Performance:	Max Speed: 81 mph (130 km/h)	Cruising Speed:
	Service Ceiling: 7,800 ft (2,377 m)	Range:
Weights:	Empty: 4,325 lb (1,963 kg)	Gross: 6,315 lb (2,867 kg)
Dimensions:	Upper Span: 55 ft 3 in (16.84 m)	Lower Span: 47 ft 4½ in (14.44 m)
	Length: 38 ft 3 in (11.66 m)	Height: 13 ft 9½ in (4.20 m)
	Wing Area: 715 sq ft (66.42 sq m)	
Armament:	None	
Cost:	Unknown	

Canadian Vickers
VEDETTE

The Canadian Vickers Vedette was the first aircraft in Canada designed and built to meet a Canadian specification for Canadian conditions. It was a single-engine flying boat purchased to meet an RCAF specification for an aircraft suitable for forestry survey and fire protection control work. The type went on to have a long and distinguished career in civil operations with the RCAF. Five versions of the Vedette were produced, including two amphibious versions and one with an enclosed cabin on an all-metal

hull. With the exception of these major changes however most of the remaining differences between versions were relatively minor and not externally visible. Each version was produced with a range of optional engine types. In RCAF service, the aircraft proved popular and versatile. It was able to perform photographic and forestry patrols satisfactorily and provided a backbone for RCAF flying operations through the difficult Depression years. The type lasted even until the outbreak of war.

Canada's sole Vedette Mk.VI flew out of Lac du Bonnet, first as G-CYWI and later as RCAF # 817. The only visible difference between this and other earlier Vedettes is the almost totally enclosed cockpit. However, this variant also had an all-metal hull rather than a wooden one. (CF Photo)

DETAILS

Designation:	**Model No:**	**Marks:** Mk I, II, V, VA, VI	**Role:** Flying Boat
TOS: 1925	**SOS:** 1941	**No:** 44 Mk I(1), II(20),V (11), VA (11), VI(1)	**Service:** RCAF

SPECIFICATIONS Vedette I

Manufacturer:	Canadian Vickers
Crew/Passengers:	crew of three: one pilot and two passengers
Powerplant:	one 200 hp Wolseley Viper, Rolls Royce Falcon or Wright J4 or 185 hp Armstrong Siddeley Lynx IVB radial engine

Performance:	Max Speed: 95 mph (153 km/h)	Cruising Speed: 87 mph (140 km/h)
	Service Ceiling: 13,000 ft (3,962 m)	Range:
Weights:	Empty: 2,140 lb (972 kg)	Gross: 3,155 lb (1,432 kg)
Dimensions:	Upper Span: 42 ft 0 in (12.8 m)	Length: 32 ft 10 in (10.0 m)
	Height: 11 ft 9 in (3.58 m)	Wing Area: 496 sq ft (46.04 sq m)
Armament:	None	
Cost:	Unknown	

Canadian Vickers
VELOS

The Canadian Vickers Velos was a twin-engine float plane designed to an RCAF specification for a photographic survey aircraft. The enclosed cabin fuselage was constructed of steel tubing as were various support structures along with the tail surfaces. The remainder of the aircraft was constructed of wood and the entire aircraft was fabric covered. Readied for initial water tests in 1927, the aircraft was noted to be overweight and sitting low in the water. Perhaps indicative of the aircraft's overall fate, it almost sank at its mooring. Flight tests were consequently postponed pending a redesign and weight re-

duction exercise. First flight occurred in 1928 but again the problems were numerous and the aircraft could not meet specifications. The RCAF test pilot considered the aircraft "unsuitable for any operation carried out in the Royal Canadian Air Force." In November 1928, the aircraft sank at its mooring after a heavy snowstorm. The RCAF and Canadian Vickers staff considered the aircraft a "dead loss" and consequently it was only salvaged for parts. The Velos therefore has the distinction of being one of the RCAF's worst aircraft types.

Canadian Vickers' Velos G-CYZX was the Air Force's one and only acquisition of this type. In 1926 the Department of National Defence awarded a contract to Canadian Vickers to design and construct an aircraft for photographic survey use. However, the resulting prototype was considered unsuitable for any operation carried out in the RCAF. (CF Photo)

DETAILS

Designation:	**Model No:**	**Role:** Float Plane	
TOS: 1927	**SOS:** 1928	**No:** 1	**Service:** RCAF

SPECIFICATIONS

Manufacturer: Canadian Vickers
Crew/Passengers: crew of three: one pilot, one photographer and one surveyor/navigator
Powerplant: two 304 hp Pratt & Whitney Wasp R-1340 radial engines
Performance: Max Speed: 85 mph (137 km/h)   Cruising Speed:
Service Ceiling: 8,000 ft (2,438 m)   Range:
Weights: Empty: 5,752 lb (2,611 kg)   Gross: 7,918 lb (3,595 kg)
Dimensions: Upper Span: 68 ft 0 in (20.72 m)   Lower Span: 27 ft 6 in (8.38 m)
Length: 41 ft 0 in (12.5 m)   Height: 16 ft 9 in (5.10 m)
Wing Area: 810 sq ft (72.25 sq m)
Armament: None
Cost: Unknown

Canadian Vickers
VIGIL

The Canadian Vickers Vigil was a single-seat patrol aircraft based on an RCAF specification for a forest fire patrol aircraft. The CAF/RCAF had been undertaking forest patrols since the early 1920s. In 1926, the RCAF issued a specification to replace aging D.H. 4 aircraft being used in this role. The Vigil was a strut-braced sesquiplane. The upper wing was instead made of steel spars and ribs with a corrugated aluminum skin. The aircraft was designed for operation on floats, wheels and skis. Unfortunately, the Vigil was considerably overweight when built and this deficiency significantly reduced the aircraft's performance and operational ceiling, making it unsuitable for its intended role. The aircraft was instead stationed at the Rockcliffe Air Station in Ottawa and used by pilots then stationed in Ottawa for proficiency flying. In January and February of 1929, the aircraft was used for experimental air mail delivery flights to the Maritimes. A little over a year later, the requirement for an overhaul and repairs led to the assessment that further effort was uneconomical and the aircraft was scrapped.

There was only one Vigil, G-CYZW, on strength with the RCAF but it was found unsuitable for the original intended role of forestry patrol. However, the RCAF decided to accept the machine because of its otherwise fine flying qualities. The Vigil was based at Rockcliffe Air Station and was used primarily by pilots assigned to administrative duties in Ottawa. The aircraft's unusual sesquiplane configuration is clearly visible in this photo. (CF Photo)

DETAILS

Designation:	**Model No:**	**Role:** Patrol aircraft	
TOS: 1928	**SOS:** 1930	**No:** 1	**Service:** RCAF

SPECIFICATIONS

Manufacturer: Canadian Vickers
Crew/Passengers: one pilot
Powerplant: one 180 hp Armstrong Siddeley Lynx IV radial engine
Performance: Max Speed: 116 mph (186 km/h)   Cruising Speed: 95 mph (153 km/h)
Service Ceiling: 13,000 ft (3,962 m)   Range:
Weights: Empty: 2,005 lb (910 kg)   Gross: 2,750 lb (1,248 kg)
Dimensions: Upper Span: 35 ft 5¼ in (10.8 m)   Lower Span: 16 ft 8 in (5.08 m)
Length: 27 ft 0 in (8.23 m)   Height: 11 ft 4 in (3.45 m)
Wing Area: 280 sq ft (26.01 sq m)
Armament: None
Cost: Unknown

Canadian Vickers
VISTA

The Canadian Vickers Vista was a single-seat flying boat and interestingly, the first Canadian monoplane design. The hull was made of duralumin sheet and the tail surfaces were made of sheet metal tubing. The wings were wood and both the wing and tail surfaces were fabric covered. Following prototype completion for the RCAF, a production order was subsequently cancelled. The design proved to have some less than desirable characteristics and the availability of DH 60 Cirrus Moth floatplanes probably sealed the Vista's fate. The prototype registered as "G-CYZZ", was shipped to the RCAF Station at Jericho Beach in Vancouver in 1930. It then became a training aid to provide aircrew with experience in water-taxiing and docking techniques. In this role, the Vista had its wings clipped in order to prevent the aircraft from getting inadvertently airborne. When not in use, the aircraft was continuously moored outside, in order to test the effects of corrosion on the duralumin hull. By 1931, the results of this testing dictated the scrapping of the aircraft.

G-CYZZ was the only Vista ever to appear on RCAF rolls although initially two had been ordered. The Vista was never put into production, likely because of the ready availability of the cheaper D.H. 60 Moth seaplane, which may have provided a more practical solution to the RCAF's needs. (CF Photo)

DETAILS

Designation:	Model No:	Role: Flying Boat	
TOS: 1927	SOS: 1931	No: 1	Service: RCAF

SPECIFICATIONS

Manufacturer:	Canadian Vickers		
Crew/Passengers:	one pilot		
Powerplant:	one 60 hp Armstrong Siddeley Genet radial engine		
Performance:	Max Speed: 88 mph (142 km/h)	Cruising Speed: 66 mph (297 km/h)	
	Service Ceiling: 12,000 ft (3,657 m)	Range:	
Weights:	Empty: 655 lb (297 kg)	Gross: 1,005 lb (456 kg)	
Dimensions:	Span: 29 ft 6 in (8.99 m)	Length: 23 ft 9 in (7.24 m)	
	Height: 7 ft 6 in (2.28 m)	Wing Area: 147 sq ft (13.65 sq m)	
Armament:	None		
Cost:	Unknown		

Cessna
L-182

The Cessna L-182 was essentially a commercial off-the-shelf purchase for the Canadian Army. In 1963, the Army purchased ten L-182 light commercial aircraft from Cessna. They were intended for use in the courier and liaison role and as such were distributed to the different Army commands of the period. Perhaps unusually for army aircraft, the L-182s were maintained in a highly polished, bare metal finish. Little data is available on overall Army use and experience with these aircraft.

The Canadian Army flew the commercial model Cessna L-182 models E, F and G, in the 1960s and early 1970s in utility and liaison roles. (CF Photo)

DETAILS

Designation:	**Model No:** L-182	**Role:** Utility Transport	
TOS: 1963	**SOS:** 1971	**No:** 10	**Service:** RCA

SPECIFICATIONS

Manufacturer: Cessna Aircraft Corporation
Crew/Passengers: one pilot with provisions for three passengers
Powerplant: one 230 hp Continental 0-470-L piston engine
Performance: Max Speed: 165 mph (266 km/h)   Cruising Speed: 135 mph (217 km/h)
Service Ceiling: 19,800 ft (6,035 m)   Range:
Weights: Empty: 1,560 lb (708 kg)   Gross: 2,650 lb (1,202 kg)
Dimensions: Span: 36 ft 0 in (10.97 m)   Length: 26 ft 0 in (7.92 m)
Height: 8 ft 6 in (2.59 m)   Wing Area:
Armament: None
Cost: Unknown

Cessna
BIRD DOG

The Cessna L-19 Bird Dog first entered service with the Canadian Army in late 1954. It replaced the British-made Auster aircraft in the Army co-operation role providing observation, communication, reconnaissance and artillery spotting duties. The Cessna was a much more modern piece of equipment than its predecessor. Being considerably more powerful, it provided better performance on take-off and climb and was more comfortable for the pilot and observer. After de-commissioning from Army service, the Cessna found a new lease on life as a glider tow plane for the Royal Canadian Air Cadet program.

Two Canadian Army Cessna L-19 aircraft are shown here in two slightly different paint schemes. The upper view illustrates the original scheme while the lower view illustrates a later version (CF Photos)

DETAILS

Designation: L-19A   **Model No:** O-1E   **Role:** Army Co-operation/Glider Towing
TOS: 1954   **SOS:** 1973 (by RCA)   **No:** 25   **Service:** RCA, Cadets

SPECIFICATIONS

Manufacturer:	Cessna Aircraft	
Crew/Passengers:	Pilot and observer	
Powerplant:	one 213 hp Continental O-470-11 engine	
Performance:	Max Speed: 130 mph (209 km/h)	Cruising Speed: 104 mph (167 km/h)
	Service Ceiling: 24,800 ft (7559 m)	Range:
Weights:	Empty: 1,498 lb (679 kg)	Gross: 2,430 lb (1,102 kg)
Dimensions:	Span: 36 ft 0 in (10.97 m)	Length: 24 ft 11½ in (7.61 m)
	Height: 6 ft 7 in (2.01 m)	Wing Area:
Armament:	None	
Original Cost:	Unknown	

Cessna
CRANE

The Cessna T-50 Crane, or Bobcat as it was known in US service, was a light twin-engine trainer procured in large numbers by both the RCAF and the US military during the Second World War. The aircraft was conventional for the period, featuring a low cantilever wing. It was of mixed material construction with the wings and tail made of wood and the fuselage made of welded steel tube. The skin featured a combination of lightweight wood and fabric. The retractable tail wheel and trailing edge flaps were electrically equipped. The type supplemented the Avro Anson in the BCATP service. The Crane provided valuable multi-engine training throughout the war. The vast majority of the Cranes were retired at the end of war, although a few lingered on in light communication duties.

The diminutive Cessna Crane in RCAF BCATP colours (predominately all-yellow). (CF Photos)

DETAILS

Designation:	**Model No:** T-50	**Marks:** Mk I, IA	**Role:** Trainer
TOS: 1941	**SOS:** 1949	**No:** 826	**Service:** RCAF

SPECIFICATIONS

Manufacturer:	Cessna Aircraft Corporation	
Crew/Passengers:	two pilots with provisions for three passengers	
Powerplant:	two 245 hp Jacobs R-755-9 radial engines	
Performance:	Max Speed: 195 mph (314 km/h)	Cruising Speed: 175 mph (282 km/h)
	Service Ceiling: 22,000 ft (6,705 m)	Range: 750 mi (1,207 km)
Weights:	Empty: 3,500 lb (1,588 kg)	Gross: 5,700 lb (2,585 kg)
Dimensions:	Span: 41 ft 11 in (12.78 m)	Length: 32 ft 9 in (9.98 m)
	Height: 9 ft 11 in (3.02 m)	Wing Area: 295 sq ft (27.41 sq m)
Armament:	None	
Cost:	Unknown	

Consolidated
LIBERATOR

During the Second World War, the Consolidated B-24 Liberator was manufactured in larger numbers than any other heavy bomber. In RCAF service, however, the type primarily served the long-range maritime reconnaissance and heavy transport roles although some RCAF personnel did fly this type of aircraft on heavy bomber operations in the South East Asia theatre of war. From Canada's east coast, the type was used primarily in the ASW role, providing convoys with air cover as far as the mid-Atlantic. An Operational Training Unit (OTU) using Liberators was also established on Canada's west coast.

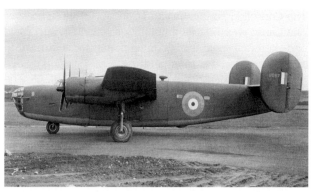

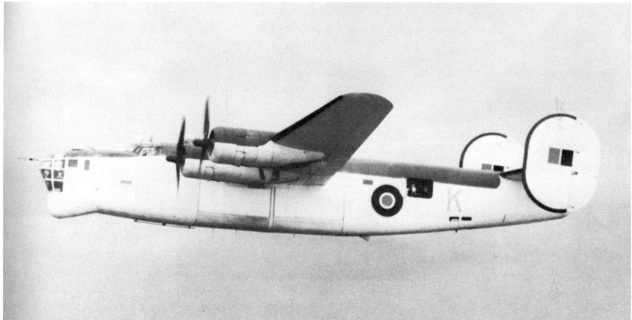

The Consolidated Liberator is famed as a US heavy bomber, but in Canadian service the aircraft was principally used for very long-range coastal patrol work and as a transport. Shown here in the upper view is a Mk III RAF variant and in the lower view is a Mk V ASW and reconnaissance aircraft. (RAF and RCAF Photos)

DETAILS

Model No: B-24J   **Marks:** B. Mk VI, C. Mk VI, C. Mk VII, C. Mk VIII,   **Role:** Patrol, Transport
G.R. Mk V, G.R. Mk VI, G.R. Mk VIT, G.R. Mk VIII

TOS: 1943   **SOS:** 1948   **No:** 148   **Service:** RCAF

SPECIFICATIONS B-24J

Manufacturer:	Consolidated Aircraft and various other American companies under licence
Crew/Passengers:	normal bomber crew of ten
Powerplant:	four 1,200 hp Pratt & Whitney Twin Wasp R-1830-65 14 cylinder radials
Performance:	Max Speed: 290 mph (467 km/h) Cruising Speed: 190 mph (306 km/h)
	Service Ceiling: 28,000 ft (8,534 m) Range: 2,200 miles (3,540 km)
Weights:	Empty: 37,000 lb (16,783 kg) Gross: 65,000 lb (29,484 kg)
Dimensions:	Span: 110 ft 0 in (33.5 m) Length: 67 ft 2 in (20.47 m)
	Height: 18 ft 0 in (5.94 m)
Armament:	Provision for ten 0.50 Browning machine guns in 4 turrets and 2 waist gun positions plus 2 bomb bays for up to 8,000 lbs of bombs or stores
Original Cost:	$336,000 US

Consolidated
CANSO

The Consolidated Catalina and Canso were close cousins. The Canso was the true amphibious version of the design and therefore included a conventional undercarriage to allow for either water or land use. The Canso provided over two decades of valuable service to the RCAF. The Catalina variant came first and was produced beginning in 1935 for the US Navy. The amphibious version, designated PBY-5A, came into service early in 1941 and the RCAF began using the aircraft on anti-submarine patrols that same year. After the Second World War, the RCAF used Cansos for search and rescue, arctic survey and various transport operations.

Preceded by the Consolidated Catalina into service, the Canso versions of the aircraft featured a retractable, wheeled undercarriage, which reduced the aircraft's handling difficulties. More than 700 versions of the Canso rolled off Boeing Canada and Canadian Vickers assembly lines and the RCAF was a prime user of the type. (RCAF Photo)

DETAILS

Designation: PBY-5A	**Model No:** 28-5A	**Role:** Patrol	
TOS: 1941	**SOS:** 1962	**No:** 224	**Service:** RCAF

SPECIFICATIONS PBY-5A

Manufacturer:	Consolidated; also licence-built by Boeing (Canada) Ltd
Crew/Passengers:	Crew of eight or nine
Powerplant:	two 1200 hp (895 kW) Pratt & Whitney R-1830-92 Twin Wasp radials
Performance:	Max Speed: 175 mph (282 km/h) — Cruising Speed: 113 mph (182 km/h)
	Service Ceiling: 13,000 ft (3,960 m) — Range: 2,350 mi (3,782 km)
Weights:	Empty: 20,910 lb (9,485 kg) — Maximum Take-off: 35,420 lb (16,067 kg)
Dimensions:	Span: 104 ft 0 in (31.7 m) — Length: 63 ft 10 in (19.47 m)
	Height: 20 ft 2 in (6.15 m) — Wing Area: 1400 sq ft (130 sq m)
Armament:	one 0.5 in (12.7 mm) machine gun in each blister, one or two 0.3 in (7.62 mm) machine guns in bow turret and one 0.3 (7.62 mm) machine gun in rear ventral hatch. Provisions for up 1,000 lb (454 kg) in bombs or depth charges
Cost:	Unknown

Consolidated
CATALINA

The Consolidated Catalina and Canso were close cousins. The Catalina was the true flying boat version of the design and therefore did not include a conventional undercarriage to allow for either water or land use. The Catalina variant came first and was produced beginning in 1935 for the US Navy. The RCAF began using the aircraft on anti-submarine patrols early in 1941. After the Second World War, the RCAF retired its Catalinas and began using Cansos for search and rescue, arctic survey and various transport operations because of that type's greater flexibility.

Early in the war versions of the Consolidated Catalina were purchased from the US to provide the RCAF Eastern Air Command with modern long-range flying boats. As seen here, the Catalina was a pure flying boat design, requiring beaching dollies or large cranes to remove the aircraft from the water. (Comox Air Force Museum Photos)

DETAILS

Designation:	**Model No:** PBY-5A	**Marks:** Mk IA&B, II, III, IIIA, IV, IVA, VB	**Role:** Patrol
TOS: 1941	**SOS:** 1946	**No:** 30	**Service:** RCAF

SPECIFICATIONS Mark IB

Manufacturer:	Consolidated; also licence-built by Boeing (Canada) Ltd	
Crew/Passengers:	Crew of eight or nine	
Powerplant:	two 1200 hp (895 kW) Pratt & Whitney R-1830 Twin Wasp radials	
Performance:	Max Speed: 190 mph (306 km/h)	Cruising Speed: 179 mph (288 km/h)
	Service Ceiling: 24,000 ft (7,315 m)	Range: 4,000 mi (6,437 km)
Weights:	Empty: 14,240 lb (6,459 kg)	Maximum Take-off: 27,080 lb (12,283 kg)
Dimensions:	Span: 104 ft 0 in (31.70 m)	Length: 65 ft 2 in (19.86 m)
	Height: 17 ft 11 in (5.46 m)	Wing Area: 1,400 sq ft (130.06 sq m)
Armament:	one 0.5 in (12.7 mm) machine gun in each blister, one 0.3 in (7.62 mm) machine gun in bow turret and one 0.3 (7.62 mm) machine gun in rear ventral hatch. Provisions for up 2,000 lb (907 kg) in bombs or depth charges	
Cost:	Unknown	

Consolidated
COURIER

The RCAF took delivery of two Consolidated XO-17A Couriers in February of 1928. The aircraft were flown from Buffalo, New York to Camp Borden north of Toronto. The Courier design originated through a request from the US Navy for a modification of the company's PT-1 biplane design that was ordered into large-scale production for the US Army in 1924. The US Navy ordered modifications, which included the substitution of a 220 hp Wright J-4 (R-790) radial engine and provisions for the installation of a large single float under the fuselage and small stabilizing floats under the wingtips. The fin and rudder were also increased in size for this seaplane configuration. In Canadian service, the aircraft were used for advanced flying training and for air-to-air gunnery practice. The aircraft soldiered on for more than a decade before being scrapped.

A wintry view of a Consolidated Courier in RCAF colours. The aircraft was also flown in RCAF service using floats. (Comox AFM Photo)

DETAILS

Designation: **Model No:** XO-17A   **Role:** Trainer/Float Plane

TOS: 1928   **SOS:** 1941   **No:** 2   **Service:** RCAF

SPECIFICATIONS

Manufacturer:	Consolidated Aircraft Corporation	
Crew/Passengers:	two pilots in tandem	
Powerplant:	one 220 hp Wright J-5 (R-790) radial engine	
Performance:	Max Speed: 102 mph (164 km/h)	Cruising Speed: 81 mph (130 km/h)
	Service Ceiling: 14,500 ft (4,420 m)	Range: 300 mi (483 km)
Weights:	Empty: 1,785 lb (810 kg)	Gross: 2,481 lb (1,125 kg)
Dimensions:	Span: 34 ft 6 in (10.52 m)	Length: 28 ft 1 in (8.56 m)
	Height: 10 ft 3 in (3.12 m)	Wing Area: 300 sq ft (27.87 sq m)
Armament:	Provision for light machine gun	
Cost:	Unknown	

Consolidated
PRIVATEER

A Consolidated C-87 RY-3 Privateer was loaned to the RCAF by the RAF in 1946. The first of the "Rockcliffe Ice Wagons," the aircraft was later replaced by a purpose-modified Canadair North Star. The RY-3 was a military transport version of the PB4Y-2 Privateer which itself was a modified version of the Liberator featuring a single fin and lengthened fuselage. The "Rockcliffe Ice Wagon" was primarily used for in-flight de-icing tests and other cloud seeding experiments.

Here are two views of the original "Rockcliffe Ice Wagon". (LAC Photos # PA-166980, PA-65976)

DETAILS

Designation:	**Model No:** RY-3	**Marks:** Mk IX	**Role:** Test
TOS: 1946	**SOS:** 1949	**No:** 1	**Service:** RCAF

SPECIFICATIONS PB4Y-2

Manufacturer: Consolidated Aircraft Corporation

Crew/Passengers: Crew of eight to eleven, depending on the mission flown

Powerplant:

Performance: Max Speed: 317 mph (510 km/h) Cruising Speed: 210 mph (338 km/h)
Service Ceiling: 36,000 ft (10,973 m) Range: 2630 mi (4,232 km)

Weights: Empty: 37,765 lb (17,232 kg) Gross: 62,000 lb (28,123 kg)

Dimensions: Span: 103 ft 9 in (31.62 m) Length: 73 ft 10 in (22.50 m)
Height: 19 ft 2 in (5.84 m) Wing Area: 1,420 sq ft (131.92 sq m)

Armament: None

Cost: Unknown

Curtiss
H-16

The Curtiss H-16 was a First World War twin-engine flying boat designed to a USN specification for a patrol aircraft. The H-16 was a design improvement of the company's H-12 series flying boat. The H-16 featured a laminated wood veneer hull with sponsons along the lower edges and unequal span biplane wings. The design was further sold to Britain in unassembled kit form. In Britain, the air- craft were assembled by RNAS Felixstowe and were fitted with British engines. The British versions were therefore known as the F.2, F.3 and F.5. Both British and American versions of the aircraft proved to be successful. The Canadian Air Force of the 1920s was also a large user of flying boats. Consequently, two H-16 flying boats were briefly acquired. Their actual service history is sparse.

A Curtiss H-16 flying boat on beaching gear, similar to those used by the RCAF. (LAC # 006393)

DETAILS

Designation: **Model No:**   **Marks:**   **Role:** Flying Boat

TOS: 1922   **SOS:** 1924   **No:** 2   **Service:** RCAF

SPECIFICATIONS

Manufacturer:	Curtiss Aeroplane and Motor Company
Crew/Passengers:	crew of four
Powerplant:	two 400 hp Liberty 12 piston engines

Performance:	Max Speed: 95 mph (153 km/h)	Cruising Speed:
	Service Ceiling: 9,950 ft (3,033 m)	Range: 378 mi (608 km)
Weights:	Empty: 7,400 lb (3,357 kg)	Gross: 10,900 lb (4,944 kg)
Dimensions:	Span: 95 ft ¾ in (28.98 m)	Length: 46 ft 1½ in (14.06 m)
	Height: 17 ft 8⅝ in (5.40 m)	Wing Area: 1,164 sq ft (108.14 sq m)
Armament:	provisions for five Lewis machine guns on flexible mounts plus up to four 230 lb (104 kg) bombs	
Cost:	Unknown	

Curtiss
HS-2L

In the First World War, the HS family of flying boats developed by Curtiss for the USN proved to be highly successful. Following the marriage of the HS-1 hull design and the popular Liberty engine, the HS-1 was ordered into large-scale production as the US Navy's standard coastal patrol flying boat. The design was then further modified with an additional six-foot panel in the centre-wing section increasing the span from 62 to 74 feet. This increase allowed for the carriage of a heavier bomb load and the modification resulted in a new designation of HS-2L. In 1918 in order to combat the growing submarine menace off Canada's east coast, the Royal Navy requested that two air bases be constructed, and the Royal Canadian Naval Air Service thus came into being. Unfortunately, starting with no trained crews or aircraft proved to be a daunting task. Consequently, the US Navy was invited to fill the gap and a detachment of USN personnel arrived in Halifax in August 1918 to begin operations using four HS-2L flying boats. The officer in charge of the USN detachment was Lieutenant Richard E. Byrd, USN(R), who later gained fame both as an aviator and polar explorer. With the Armistice, flying operations quickly wound down. The USN detachment disbanded, leaving behind 12 HS-2Ls as a donation to the Canadian government. These and other aircraft were then used by the RCAF on fishery, anti-rum-running and custom patrols on both the east and west coasts. The type also pioneered bush flying into Canada's wilderness in both military and civilian hands. The HS-2L remained the standard single-engine patrol and training flying boat for the USN in the post-war era as well.

A Curtiss HS-2L flying boat, G-CYAF in post-war RCAF colours is seen here being launched at Victoria Beach, Man., 28 May 1924. (LAC # PA-53337)

DETAILS

Designation: **Model No:** HS-2L **Role:** Patrol Flying Boat

TOS: 1920 **SOS:** 1928 **No:** 30 **Service:** RCAF

SPECIFICATIONS

Manufacturer:	Curtiss Aeroplane Division	
Crew/Passengers:	crew of four or five	
Powerplant:	one 350 hp Liberty 12 piston engine	
Performance:	Max Speed: 83 mph (134 km/h)	Cruising Speed:
	Service Ceiling: 5,200 ft (1,585 m)	Range: 517 mi (832 km)
Weights:	Empty: 4,300 lbs (1,950 kg)	Gross: 6,432 lb (2,918 kg)
Dimensions:	Span: 74 ft 0.5 in (22.58 m)	Length: 39 ft 0 in (11.89 m)
	Height: 14 ft 7 in (4.44 m)	Wing Area: 803 sq ft (74.60 sq m)
Armament:	Provisions for one flexibly mounted 0.30 calibre machine gun in rear cockpit plus two 230 lb bombs or depth charges under the wings	
Cost:	Unknown	

Curtiss
JENNY (CANUCK)

During the First World War, the Royal Flying Corps began setting up flying schools in Canada starting in 1916. The RFC selected the Curtiss JN-3 Jenny as their training aircraft. The type was then manufactured in Canada under licence by Canadian Aeroplanes Limited and the Canadian version was given the designation JN-4 Canuck. The Canuck went on to become numerically the most important trainer of Canadian and British pilots and the design lent itself to a wide variety of training purposes including air-to-air gunnery, photography, and wireless radio training. RFC training schools in both Canada and the USA used the aircraft extensively. After the war, numerous JN-4 Canucks made their way into civilian use. The Canadian government received over 50 JN-4s as part of a post-war Imperial gift but only ten of these aircraft saw active use in the CAF of the 1920s.

A restored museum example of the JN-4 Canuck in original RFC training colours. (CF Photo)

DETAILS

Designation:	**Model No:** JN-4	**Marks:**	**Role:** Trainer
TOS: 1917	**SOS:** 1924	**No:** 2,320	**Service:** RFC/CAF

SPECIFICATIONS

Manufacturer: Canadian Aeroplanes Limited
Crew/Passengers: two pilots in tandem or one pilot plus one passenger
Powerplant: one 90 hp Curtiss OX-2 or OX-5 piston engine
Performance: Max Speed: 74 mph (121 km/h)   Cruising Speed: 60 mph (96.5 km/h)
Service Ceiling: 11,000 ft (3,353 m)   Range:
Weights: Empty: 1,390 lb (631 kg)   Gross: 1,920 lb (872 kg)
Dimensions: Upper Span: 43 ft 7³/₈ in (13.29 m)   Lower Span: 34 ft 8⁵/₁₆ in (10.57 m)
Length: 27 ft 2¹/₂ in (8.29 m)   Height: 9 ft 11 in (3.02 m)
Wing Area: 361 sq ft (33.5 sq m)
Armament: provision for forward firing Vickers machine gun or flexible Scharff-ring mounted machine gun in rear cockpit
Cost: $5,465 US

Curtiss
TOMAHAWK

The Curtiss P-40 was a development of the company's radial engine P-36 and the experimental YP-37 fighters. The P-40 variants became among the most widely used fighters of the Second World War, being employed by over a dozen air forces. An early production variant was known as the Tomahawk. Four overseas RCAF squadrons including No. 400, 403, 414 and 430 Squadron flew Tomahawks on defensive patrols, reconnaissance, army cooperation and training duties while stationed in England. By 1943, however, the Tomahawk was badly outclassed and all of these squadrons had converted to either Spitfires or Mustangs. A small number of Tomahawk aircraft were brought on strength as part of the home war establishment.

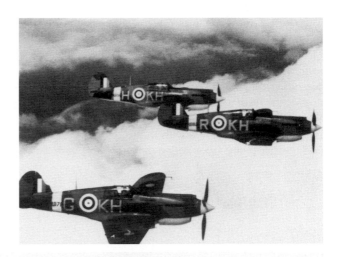

Although not as fast or manoeuvrable as most other contemporary fighters, the P-40 was appreciated for its heavy armament and ability to withstand considerable damage. The Tomahawk was primarily used in North Africa and South East Asia. The above photos are RCAF P-40B aircraft probably while briefly stationed in England. (CF Photo, LAC # PA-136240).

DETAILS

Designation:	**Model No:** P-40A & B	**Marks:** Mk I, II, IIA, IIB	**Role:** Fighter, Advanced Pilot Trainer
TOS: 1943	**SOS:** 1946	**No:** 4	**Service:** RCAF

SPECIFICATIONS Tomahawk IIB

Manufacturer:	Curtiss Wright Aircraft	
Crew/Passengers:	one pilot	
Powerplant:	one 1,090 hp Allison V-1710-C-15 piston engine	
Performance:	Max Speed: 328 mph (528 km/h)	Cruising Speed: 278 mph (447 km/h)
	Service Ceiling: 30,500 ft (9,296 m)	Range: 945 mi (1,521 km)
Weights:	Empty: 5,615 lb (2,546 kg)	Gross: 6,789 lb (3,079 kg)
Dimensions:	Span: 37 ft 4 in (11.38 m)	Length: 31 ft 8 in (9.65 m)
	Height: 10 ft 7 in (3.23 m)	Wing Area: 236 sq ft (21.95 sq m)
Armament:	two 0.50 in (12.7 mm) nose-mounted machine guns and two .303 in (7.7 mm) wing-mounted machine guns	
Cost:	Unknown	

Curtiss
KITTYHAWK

The Curtiss Kittyhawk was a further improved development of the company's successful P-40 fighter. The improvements included a more powerful engine, additional armament, provision for the carriage of bombs plus numerous other design changes. The P-40 variants became among the most widely used fighters of the Second World War, being employed by over a dozen air forces. Kittyhawks came into service with the RCAF in late 1941. In addition to being operated overseas, they were flown by No. 14, 111, 118, 132, 133, and 135 Squadron of the home war establishment. No. 14 and 111 Squadron were deployed and operated in the Aleutian campaign. On 25 September 1942, Squadron Leader K.A. Boomer, Commanding Officer of No 111 Squadron, destroyed a Japanese Zero floatplane during a fighter sortie in a Kittyhawk over Kiska in the Aleutians. This proved to be the first and only RCAF air combat victory over North American soil.

A fine air-to-air view of an RCAF Kittyhawk from No. 118(F) Squadron. (CF Photo)

DETAILS

Designation:	**Model No:** P-40D, E, K, H	**Marks:** Mk I, IA, III, IV	**Role:** Fighter
TOS: 1941	**SOS:** I946	**No:** 143	**Service:** RCAF

SPECIFICATIONS Kittyhawk III

Manufacturer:	Curtiss Wright Aircraft	
Crew/Passengers:	one pilot	
Powerplant:	one 1,600 hp Allison V-1710-81 piston engine	
Performance:	Max Speed: 362 mph (583 km/h)	Cruising Speed:
	Service Ceiling: 30,000 ft (9,144 m)	Range: 1,190 mi (1,915 km)
Weights:	Empty: 6,400 lb (2,903 kg)	Gross: 8,500 lb (3,856 kg)
Dimensions:	Span: 37 ft 4 in (11.38 m)	Length: 31 ft 2 in (9.50 m)
	Height: 10 ft 7 in (3.23 m)	Wing Area: 236 sq ft (21.95 sq m)
Armament:	six 0.5 in (12.7 mm) wing-mounted machine guns plus up to 1,000 lb (454 kg) in bombs	
Cost:	$45,000 US	

Curtiss
SEAMEW

In 1937, the USN drew up a specification for a high-speed scouting monoplane to replace its biplanes aboard the fleet's battleships and cruisers. The resulting competitor from the Curtiss Company was a slender, mid-wing monoplane with a low aspect ratio wing and a large central float along with underwing stabilizers. Test flights on the initial configuration revealed serious stability and control problems, after which upturned wing tips and an enlarged tail fin were introduced. Although designed as a seaplane, the type could also be employed as a landplane. Under the pressure of war, the type was selected by Britain for Royal Navy use and 250 aircraft were subsequently procured under Lend-Lease arrangements. The British aircraft were the S03C-2C variant that featured a 24-volt electrical system, a V-770-8 engine along with improved radios and hydraulic brakes. The type proved to be operationally disappointing and was relegated to training

duties. The RCN consequently acquired a number of the type for its own training purposes in Canada where they were used at the No. 1 Naval Air Gunnery School in Yarmouth, Nova Scotia.

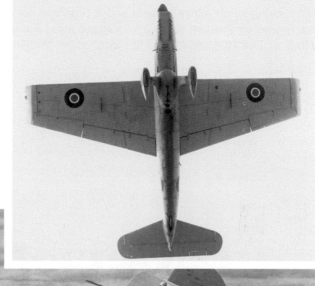

An American Curtiss Seamew and an RCN Seamew flying overhead. (Author's collection)

DETAILS

Designation:	**Model No:** S03C-2C	**Marks:** Mk I	**Role:** Scouting and observation seaplane, trainer
TOS: 1943	**SOS:** 1944	**No:** 82	**Service:** RCN

SPECIFICATIONS

Manufacturer:	Curtiss Aeroplane Division	
Crew/Passengers:	one pilot and one observer in tandem	
Powerplant:	one 600 hp Ranger SGV-770-6 piston engine	
Performance:	Max Speed: 172 mph (279 km/h)	Cruising Speed: 125 mph (201 km/h)
	Service Ceiling: 15,800 ft (4,816 m)	Range: 1,150 mi (1,851 km)
Weights:	Empty: 4,800 lbs (2,177 kg)	Gross: 7,000 lb (3,175 kg)
Dimensions:	Span: 38 ft 0 in (11.55 m)	Length: 35 ft 8 in (10.87 m)
	Height: 14 ft 2 in (4.31 m)	Wing Area: 293 sq ft (27.22 sq m)
Armament:	Provisions for one fixed forward-firing 0.30 calibre machine gun and one flexibly mounted 0.50 calibre machine gun in rear cockpit plus two 100 lb (45 kg) bombs or 325 lb (147 kg) depth charges under the wings and up to 500 lb in stores under the fuselage	
Cost:	Unknown	

Curtiss-Reid
RAMBLER

The Curtiss Aeroplane & Motor Company of the USA had acquired the Canadian-origin Reid Aircraft Company in 1928 and was renamed the Curtiss-Reid Aircraft Company. The Curtiss-Reid Rambler was a Canadian designed and built trainer. It was intended to fill the needs of flying clubs springing up across Canada and it possessed several innovative features. It was a sesquiplane with folding wings to facilitate storage and it incorporated Warren truss bracing that eliminated the need for bracing wires. The interplane struts were streamline tubing. The RCAF evaluated the aircraft type and despite already having a plethora of other trainers, it elected to purchase a small number of the aircraft. The Ramblers enjoyed a relatively productive and lengthy career, lasting well into the Second World War.

The Curtiss-Reid Rambler trainer displayed very clean lines without the more normal bracing wires. (CF Photo)

DETAILS

Designation:	**Model No:**	**Marks:**	**Role:** Trainer
TOS: 1929	**SOS:** 1944	**No:** 9	**Service:** RCAF

SPECIFICATIONS

Manufacturer:	Curtiss-Reid Aircraft Company
Crew/Passengers:	two pilots in tandem
Powerplant:	either one 85/100 hp D.H. Gipsy I , or 120 hp D.H. Gipsy II engine

Performance:
Max Speed: 112 mph (180 km/h)	Cruising Speed: 107 mph (172 km/h)
Service Ceiling: 14,000 ft (4,270 m)	Range:

Weights: Empty: 1,075 lb (488 kg) — Gross: 1,650 lb (749 kg)

Dimensions:
Span: 33 ft 0 in (10.06 m)	Length: 24 ft 0 in (7.31 m)
Height: 8 ft 0 in (2.44 m)	Wing Area: 238 sq ft (22.11 sq m)

Armament: None

Cost: Unknown

Dassault
FALCON/MYSTERE 20

The Dassault Falcon was a short to medium range transport and executive jet, which was also known as the Mystere 20 in civilian service. In CF service, the aircraft began as a VIP executive transport for senior government and defence officials. The aircraft's high performance and robust design also allowed the CF to convert it to an electronic warfare variant. No. 412 Transport Squadron at Uplands, Ottawa, employed the transport versions, while the electronic warfare variants were flown by No. 414 (EW) Squadron. The Falcons were retired in 1988 and many of the ex-CF aircraft continued in the EW training role in private hands.

This view illustrates an electronic warfare/airborne sensor variant of the CC-117 Falcon which was also used in a VIP executive transport version. (CF Photo)

DETAILS

Designation: CC-117, EW-117   **Model No:** 20   **Role:** Transport/Electronic Warfare
TOS: 1967   **SOS:** 1988   **No:** 8   **Service:** RCAF/CF

SPECIFICATIONS

Manufacturer:	Dassault Aircraft	
Crew/Passengers:	two pilots and up to ten passengers	
Powerplant:	two 4,700 lb thrust General Electric CF700-2D-2 turbofan engines	
Performance:	Max Speed: 560 mph (901 km/h)	Cruising Speed: 511 mph (823 km/h)
	Service Ceiling: 42,000 ft (12,802 m)	Range: 964 mi (1,552 km)
Weights:	Empty:	Gross: 28,660 lb (13,000 kg)
Dimensions:	Span:	Length:
	Height:	Wing Area:
Armament:	None	
Cost:	$1,330,000	

De Havilland
D.H.4

Following Canada's contributions to the First World War, in 1919 as part of an Imperial gift 114 aircraft were donated to Canada. These aircraft, along with twelve airships and a vast quantity of other material including hangars and vehicles also included in the gift, were to form the nucleus of Canada's new home-based air force. The Canadian Air Force was authorized on 18 February, 1920 and was to be a non-permanent organization with former officers and men of the RAF and the CAF in England being invited to serve for up to five weeks a year with operations initially centered at Camp Borden, Ontario. Twelve De Havilland D.H.4 aircraft were included in the Imperial Gift. Built in quantity by both the British and the US militaries D.H.4s had already been flown by Canadians in combat serving in both the RFC and RNAS. The type was used on day bombing raids and reconnaissance operations. In the post-war period, the D.H.4 was used by CAF pilots for refresher training, aerial photography and for forestry patrols.

A CAF De Havilland D.H. 4 in early civil air board markings, probably at Camp Borden, being prepared for an early mail-carrying experiment. (RCAF Photo)

DETAILS

Designation:	**Model No:** D.H.4	**Marks:**	**Role:** Utility
TOS: 1920	**SOS:** 1928	**No:** 12	**Service:** RFC/RNAS/CAF/RCAF

SPECIFICATIONS

Manufacturer:	De Havilland Aircraft Co
Crew/Passengers:	one pilot and one bomber/gunner or two pilots
Powerplant:	either one 250 hp Rolls Royce Eagle III or VI (322 hp),VII (325 hp),VIII (375 hp) or 420 hp Liberty engines
Performance:	Max Speed: 119 mph (192 km/h) — Cruising Speed:
	Service Ceiling: 16,000 ft (4,877 m) — Endurance: 3.2 hours
Weights:	Empty: 2,010 lb (912 kg) — Gross: 3,146 lb (1,427 kg)
Dimensions:	Span: 42 ft 5 in (12.93 m) — Length: 30 ft 8 in (9.35 m)
	Height: 10 ft 5 in (3.17 m) — Wing Area: 440 sq ft (40.88 sq m)
Armament:	Provisions for twin synchronized Vickers machine-guns forward and one Lewis machine gun in a flexible mount aft plus up to 450 lbs (204 kg) in light bombs.
Cost:	Imperial gift

De Havilland
D.H.9a

In 1919 as part of an Imperial gift, 114 aircraft were donated to Canada following the country's contributions in the First World War. These aircraft, along with twelve airships and a vast quantity of other material including hangars and vehicles also included in the gift, were to form the nucleus of Canada's new home-based air force. The Canadian Air Force was authorized on 18 February, 1920 and was to be a non-permanent organization with former officers and men of the RAF and the CAF in England being invited to serve for up to five weeks a year. Operations were initially centered at Camp Borden, Ontario. Twelve De Havilland D.H.9a aircraft were included in the Imperial Gift. Built in quantity by both the British and the US militaries, the D.H.9a, popularly known as the "Nine Ack" had already been flown by Canadians in combat serving in the RFC. The type had been used on day bombing raids and reconnaissance operations. In the immediate post-

war period, D.H.9As served with No 2 Squadron of the CAF, which had been formed in England after the Armistice. In the later post-war period, the D.H.9a was used by CAF pilots for refresher training, aerial photography and for forestry patrols. The aircraft's principle fame in this period was in the Air Board's trans-Canada flight of 1920. The purpose of the flight was to draw the attention of the Canadian public to the Air Board and the CAF and the capability of their post-war aircraft for future airmail and passenger operations. The flight was accomplished in relays of crews and aircraft and left Halifax, Nova Scotia on 7 October with a Fairey seaplane. At Winnipeg, Manitoba the seaplanes and flying boats used throughout the eastern leg of the journey were replaced by three D.H.9as, of which only one (G-CYBF) finally made it to Vancouver, British Columbia on 17 October, covering 3,265 miles, after eleven days during which 45 hours were airborne.

This photo illustrates a D.H.9 from the Royal Flying Corps in the First World War. The CAF's De Havilland D.H. 9a carried early Civil Air Board markings similar to the D.H.4 aircraft. (LAC Photo #006370)

DETAILS

Designation:	**Model No:** D.H.9a	**Marks:**	**Role:** Utility
TOS: 1920	**SOS:** 1929	**No:** 12	**Service:** RFC/CAF/RCAF

SPECIFICATIONS

Manufacturer:	De Havilland Aircraft Co	
Crew/Passengers:	one pilot and one bomber/gunner or two pilots	
Powerplant:	either one 230 hp Siddeley Puma or 350 hp Rolls-Royce Eagle or 400 hp Liberty engines	
Performance:	Max Speed: 114 mph (183 km/h)	Cruising Speed:
	Service Ceiling: 16,500 ft (5,029 m)	Endurance: 5.75 hours
Weights:	Empty: 2,800 lb (1,270 kg)	Gross: 4,900 lb (2,223 kg)
Dimensions:	Span: 46 ft 0 in (14.02 m)	Length: 30 ft 0 in (9.14 m)
	Height: 10 ft 9 in (3.28 m)	Wing Area: 488 sq ft (45.36 sq m)
Armament:	Provisions for one synchronized Vickers machine gun forward and one Lewis machine gun in a flexible mount aft plus up to 450 lbs (204 kg) in light bombs.	
Cost:	Imperial gift	

De Havilland
GIPSY MOTH/CIRRUS MOTH/GENET MOTH

In February 1925, a prototype of the De Havilland Moth flew in Britain and was recognized as an outstanding trainer. Quickly put into full production, the aircraft was manufactured with a variety of different engines, the most popular of which being the A.D.C. Cirrus and D.H. Gipsy engines. Depending on the engine installation chosen, the aircraft was then known as either the Gipsy Moth, Cirrus Moth, or Genet Moth. The RCAF initially acquired the Moth as an *ab initio* trainer to replace its Avro 504s. The aircraft proved to be very popular and versatile. It could be flown either on wheels or with floats.

A variety of De Havilland DH-60 Moths served in the RCAF but with airframes containing three different power plants. The upper image is a poor but interesting airborne view of the De Havilland Gipsy Moth in Civil Air Board colours. (CF and Comox Air Force Museum Photos)

DETAILS

Designation:	**Model No:** D.H.60	**Marks:** Mk I, III, V	**Role:** Trainer
TOS: 1928	**SOS:** 1948	**No:** Gipsy (89) Genet (2)	**Service:** RCAF

SPECIFICATIONS

Manufacturer: De Havilland Aircraft Co

Crew/Passengers: two pilots

Powerplant: either one 100 hp D.H. Gipsy I, 120 hp D.H. Gipsy II or 105 hp Cirrus Hermes or 120 hp Gipsy III or 85 hp General Aircraft V4 or 95 hp Genet engines

Performance:
Max Speed: 95 mph (152 km/h)   Cruising Speed: 85 mph (137 km/h)
Service Ceiling: 17,000 ft (5,180 m)   Range:

Weights: Empty: 890 lb (404 kg)   Gross: 1,550 lb (703 kg)

Dimensions:
Span: 30 ft 0 in (9.14 m)   Length: 23 ft 8½ in (7.23 m)
Height: 8 ft 9½ in (2.68 m)   Wing Area: 242 sq ft (22.48 sq m)

Armament: None

Cost: Unknown

De Havilland
HAWK MOTH

The De Havilland D.H.75 Hawk Moth first flew in 1928. It was a four-seat cabin monoplane designed for light transport. It featured composite construction including a welded steel fuselage and tail along with wooden wing sub-structure and all-over fabric covering. The first aircraft was fitted with a new 198 hp De Havilland Ghost engine but it proved to be underpowered and the performance was disappointing. Consequently, the second aircraft was powered by a 240 hp Armstrong Siddeley Lynx engine along with an increased wing span. Redesignated as the D.H.75A, this aircraft was exported to Canada in 1929 and then demonstrated to the RCAF on both wheels and skis. The machine was subsequently purchased for

general transportation duties. Two further examples were also acquired in 1930 for the same purpose. The RCAF's experience with the type was not good. The undercarriage design was flawed and caused several crashes. One aircraft was written off as a result. While operating on wheels and skis, weakness in the wing root attachment fittings necessitated expensive repairs. Attempts to operate the aircraft on floats revealed further structural problems. As well, the aircraft suffered from a limited payload capability. The continuing problems resulted in the type's premature retirement in 1934 and the surviving aircraft were cut up as training aids in 1935.

An RCAF DeHavilland Hawk Moth in floatplane configuration laid up on a beaching dolly. The floatplane configuration revealed structural problems with the design. (LAC Photo #62799)

DETAILS

Designation:	**Model No:** D.H. 75A	**Role:** Utility	
TOS: 1930	**SOS:** 1934	**No:** 3	**Service:** RCAF

SPECIFICATIONS

Manufacturer: De Havilland Aircraft Co

Crew/Passengers: one pilot and up to three passengers. Provisions for dual control

Powerplant: one 240 hp Armstrong Siddeley Lynx Mk VIA piston engine

Performance:
Max Speed: 128 mph (206 km/h) Cruising Speed: 105 mph (169 km/h)
Service Ceiling: 15,500 ft (4,724 m) Range: 560 mi (901 km)

Weights: Empty: 2,380 lb (1,080 kg) Gross: 3,800 lb (1,724 kg)

Dimensions:
Span: 47 ft 0 in (14.33 m) Length: 28 ft 10 in (8.79 m)
Height: 9 ft 0 in (2.74 m) Wing Area: 334 sq ft (31.03 sq m)

Armament: None

Cost: First a/c $24,885, Subsequent a/c $22,410

De Havilland
PUSS MOTH

The wide success of the De Havilland Gipsy Moth led to the development of a faster aircraft with a welded tube fuselage featuring an enclosed cabin for more speed and comfort. The result was a high-wing monoplane known as the Puss Moth, which was essentially a two seat aircraft although three could be carried. The RCAF acquired the Puss Moth for instrument training and as a general communication high-speed touring aircraft. An unusual feature of the aircraft was an air brake provided by turning the undercarriage strut through 90 degrees.

The RCAF Puss Moth clearly displays its distinctive high-wing monoplane configuration but at the same time similarity to other aircraft in the De Havilland lineage in this photograph. (LAC Photo # PA-62938)

DETAILS

Designation:	**Model No:** D.H.80A	**Marks:**	**Role:** Utility
TOS: 1931	**SOS:** 1944	**No:** 19	**Service:** RCAF

SPECIFICATIONS

Manufacturer:	De Havilland Aircraft Co	
Crew/Passengers:	one pilot and up to two passengers	
Powerplant:	one 130 hp D.H. Gipsy Major engine	
Performance:	Max Speed: 128 mph (206 km/h)	Cruising Speed: 105 mph (169 km/h)
	Service Ceiling: 17,500 ft (5,334 m)	Range: 300 mi (483 km)
Weights:	Empty: 1,265 lb (574 kg)	Gross: 2,050 lb (930 kg)
Dimensions:	Span: 36 ft 9 in (11.20 m)	Length: 25 ft 0 in (7.62 m)
	Height: 6 ft 10 in (2.08 m)	Wing Area: 222 sq ft (20.62 sq m)
Armament:	None	
Cost:	Unknown	

De Havilland
TIGER MOTH/MENASCO MOTH

The DH 82 Tiger Moth was the last in a long line of biplanes built by the De Havilland Aircraft Company Ltd. The Tiger Moth first entered service with the Royal Air Force in 1931 and became the standard elementary trainer for the next two decades. The RCAF adopted the type in 1938 and it also became the standard *ab initio* trainer at the Canadian elementary flying training schools under the British Commonwealth Air Training Plan. Canadian production aircraft differed from the British versions and featured a two-piece cowling, heated cockpits, and large sliding canopies. A shortage of the original 145 hp Gipsy Major engines further led to some

Canadian versions being equipped with 160 hp Menasco Pirate engines and this sub-type was often referred to as a Menasco Moth. The type was generally well liked by pilots and could be used for aerobatic training as well as blind flying instruction.

The DH-82C Tiger Moth, in which thousands of Commonwealth pilots trained, was a vital aircraft in the British Commonwealth Air Training Plan. Built by De Havilland Canada in Toronto, over 1500 Tiger Moths equipped many Elementary Flying Schools throughout Canada. Canadian modifications included float and ski fittings, a sliding canopy, a cockpit heater, a redesigned cowling, more powerful engines, and a tailwheel. (CF and RCAF photos)

DETAILS

Designation:	**Model No:** D.H. 82 A&C	**Role:** Trainer	
TOS: 1938	**SOS:** 1947	**No:** 1546	**Service:** RCAF

SPECIFICATIONS

Manufacturer: De Havilland Aircraft Co
Crew/Passengers: Up to two pilots
Powerplant: One 145 hp Gipsy Major or one 160 hp Menasco Pirate in-line piston engine
Performance: Max Speed: 109 mph (175 kph) Cruising Speed: 93 mph (150 kph)
Service Ceiling: 13,600 ft (4,145 m) Range: 302 mi (486 km)
Weights: Empty: 1,115 lb (506 kg) Maximum Take-off: 1,770 lb (813 kg)
Dimensions: Span: 29 ft 4 in (8.94 m) Length: 23 ft 11 in (7.24 m)
Height: 8 ft 9½ in (2.68 m) Wing Area: 239 sq ft (22.20 sq m)
Armament: None
Cost: Unknown

De Havilland
FOX MOTH

The De Havilland Fox Moth was designed in 1932 as a light economical transport and it borrowed heavily from the De Havilland Tiger Moth design, using many of its components. The aircraft featured a welded tube fuselage with an enclosed cabin for speed and comfort. Eight British-built Fox Moths were imported into Canada between 1932 and 1935. The RCAF acquired a single Fox Moth for use during the Second World War but few details are available as to its use.

These are two views of civilian Fox Moths similar to the one used by the RCAF. (CF Photo and Author's Collection)

DETAILS

Designation:	**Model No:** D.H.83	**Marks:**	**Role:** Utility
TOS: 1941	**SOS:** 1945	**No:** 1	**Service:** RCAF

SPECIFICATIONS

Manufacturer: De Havilland Aircraft Co

Crew/Passengers: one pilot and up to 4 passengers or 600 lb (272 kg) of freight

Powerplant: one 130 hp D.H. Gipsy Major engine

Performance:
Max Speed: 110 mph (172 km/h) — Cruising Speed: 96 mph (160 km/h)
Service Ceiling: 10,500 ft (5,334 m) — Range: 415 mi (668 km)

Weights: Empty: 1,219 lb (552 kg) — Gross: 2,100 lb (953 kg)

Dimensions:
Span: 30 ft 10⅝ in (9.41 m) — Length: 25 ft 9 in (7.85 m)
Height: 8 ft 4¾ in (2.56 m) — Wing Area: 247 sq ft (22.9 sq m)

Armament: None

Cost: Unknown

De Havilland
HORNET MOTH

The RCAF purchased a single De Havilland Hornet Moth in the 1930s, as a possible replacement for the successful Gipsy Moth aircraft already in RCAF service. It is likely the aircraft type was intended for instrument training and as a general communication high-speed touring aircraft. However the Hornet Moth was not as economical to operate as the Gipsy Moth and no further purchases were made. Few details of its use are available.

A view of a De Havilland Hornet Moth similar to that used by the RCAF. (Author's collection)

DETAILS

Designation:	**Model No:** D.H.87B	**Marks:**	**Role:** Utility/Trainer
TOS: 193?	**SOS:** 193?	**No:** 1	**Service:** RCAF

SPECIFICATIONS B model

Manufacturer:	De Havilland Aircraft Co	
Crew/Passengers:	one pilot and up to two passengers	
Powerplant:	one 130 hp D.H. Gipsy Major engine	
Performance:	Max Speed: 124 mph (200 km/h)	Cruising Speed: 105 mph (169 km/h)
	Service Ceiling: 14,300 ft (4,359 m)	Range: 623 mi (1,003 km)
Weights:	Empty: 1,192 lb (541 kg)	Gross: 1,925 lb (873 kg)
Dimensions:	Span: 31 ft 4 in (9.55 m)	Length: 24 ft 11½ in (7.61 m)
	Height: 7 ft 2 in (2.18 m)	Wing Area: 220.5 sq ft (20.49 sq m)
Armament:	None	
Cost:	Unknown, but less than £800	

De Havilland
DRAGONFLY

When the Royal Canadian Mounted Police (RCMP) organized its Air Division, it acquired a small fleet of three De Havilland Dragonfly aircraft as its main element of aerial transport. The versatile light twin-engine biplane provided for up to five passengers and crew. An elegant streamlined design, the aircraft featured a plywood fuselage skin and high aspect ratio wings. At the outbreak of the Second World War, the scarcity of suitable aircraft for the RCAF eventually led to the requisitioning of all of the RCMP's Dragonfly aircraft for military use. In addition, a further three Dragonflys were acquired for RCAF use including the De Havilland company demonstrator and two new, unsold aircraft. The RCAF employed the aircraft in light transport and communication roles for the duration of hostilities. Two aircraft were written off in RCAF service and at the war's end, the air force returned the surviving aircraft to civilian use.

A De Havilland Dragonfly in RCAF colours illustrating its sleek lines and highly tapered wings. (RCAF Photo)

DETAILS

Designation:	**Model No:** D.H. 90	**Role:** Utility	
TOS: 1940	**SOS:** 1945	**No:** 6	**Service:** RCAF

SPECIFICATIONS

Manufacturer:	De Havilland Aircraft Co
Crew/Passengers:	one pilot and up to four passengers
Powerplant:	two 130 hp De Havilland Gipsy I piston engines

Performance:

Max Speed: 144 mph (232 km/h)	Cruising Speed: 125 mph (201 km/h)
Service Ceiling: 16,000 ft (4,877 m)	Range: 885 mi (1,424 km)

Weights:

Empty: 2,500 lb (1,134 kg)	Gross: 4,000 lb (1,814 kg)

Dimensions:

Span: Upper 43 ft 0 in (13.11 m)	Lower 38 ft 6 in (11.73 m)
Length: 31 ft 8 in (9.65 m)	Height: 9 ft 2 in (2.79 m)
Wing Area: 256 sq ft (23.78 sq m)	

Armament:	None
Cost:	£2,650

De Havilland
MOSQUITO

The De Havilland Mosquito was called either the "Wooden Wonder" or the "Termite's Dream" because of its unusual plywood construction. Although its construction did provide drawbacks in tropical climates, in the European theatre and in Canada the aircraft proved to be outstandingly successful. Its wooden construction made it one of the first stealthy aircraft in an era of radar. It was probably one of the most versatile aircraft of the Second World War being used in fighter, bomber, reconnaissance, anti-shipping and even in transport roles. Bomber and reconnaissance variants carried no defensive armament relying instead on their high speed for protection. A total of six Canadian squadrons flew Mosquitos in a variety of tasks and roles. No. 400 Squadron flew the aircraft on photographic reconnaissance missions. Four RCAF Night Fighter squadrons (Nos. 406,409,410 and 418) flew Mosquitos on night fighter and intruder operations. During the V-1 pilotless missile blitz attacks of 1944, 409 Squadron Mosquitos destroyed 10 missiles and 418 Squadron shot down a total of 82 V-1s. No. 404 Squadron was also equipped with Mosquitos, employing them on coastal anti-shipping and submarine strikes.

"Mossie" was the nickname for one of the most remarkable combat aircraft of the Second World War, the De Havilland Mosquito. The original all-wood design was intended as a light bomber but quickly proved highly versatile with reconnaissance, fighter-bomber, night fighter and intruder variants being developed. In all, De Havilland Canada built 1,134 Mosquitos before the war's end, of which 444 were on strength with the RCAF from 1 June 1943 to 28 September 1951. (Comox AFM Photo)

DETAILS
Designation: **Model No:** D.H.98   **Marks:** Mk II, Mk XII, FB Mk VI, FB Mk 21, FB Mk 26, FB Mk XXX, B Mk VII, B Mk XX, B Mk 25, NF Mk II, NF Mk XIII, PR Mk VIC, PR Mk XVI, T Mk 27

Role: Bomber, Reconnaissance, Night Fighter, Coastal Strike

TOS: 1943   **SOS:** 1951   **No:** 444   **Service:** RCAF

SPECIFICATIONS Mark II
Manufacturer: De Havilland Aircraft Co
Crew/Passengers: crew of two
Powerplant: two 1,230 hp Rolls Royce Merlin 21 engines
Performance: Max Speed: 380 mph (612 km/h)   Cruising Speed: 300 mph (483 km/h)
Service Ceiling: 36,000 ft (10,973 m)   Range: 1,860 mi (2,990 km)
Weights: Empty: 14,100 lb (6,396 kg)   Gross: 17,500 lb (7,938 kg)
Dimensions: Span: 52 ft 2 in (16.5 m)   Length: 40 ft 6 in (12.34 m)
Height: 15 ft 3½ (4.66 m)   Wing Area:
Armament: For Mark II: none, but provisions for up four 500 lb (227 kg) bombs and in later Marks up to 4,000 lb (1,814 kg). For night fighter variants: armament consisted of four 20 mm Hispano cannon and four .303 in (7.7 mm) Browning machine guns
Cost: Unknown

De Havilland
VAMPIRE

On 20 September 1940, a prototype of the De Havilland Vampire became the third British jet aircraft type to fly. It was fully introduced into service too late however to see active combat during the Second World War. Canada briefly evaluated the second British jet, the Gloster Meteor, and after the acquisition of a sole Mark I De Havilland Vampire eventually selected the Vampire as the first jet-powered aircraft for full scale RCAF service. The first of 85 Mark III aircraft began to arrive in 1948. The aircraft were primarily assigned to RCAF Auxiliary Squadrons. No. 421 Squadron at Chatham, New Brunswick was the only regular force squadron to employ the aircraft. Its unusual design featured a variety of materials. While the aircraft was primarily metal, the cockpit section featured a composite balsa wood construction similar to the De Havilland Mosquito. Vampires were rapidly superceded in the jet age and the last examples were retired in 1958.

The Vampire was the RCAF's first jet fighter to serve in any great number, 86 being flown from 1946 until 1958. The lower view displays a De Havilland Vampire in early RCAF service, while the upper view illustrates a restored example after its arrival at CFB Comox for display at the museum. (CF Photo and Author's collection)

DETAILS

Designation: **Model No:** D.H.100   **Marks:** Mk I, III, V   **Role:** Fighter
TOS: 1946   **SOS:** 1958   **No:** 86   **Service:** RCAF

SPECIFICATIONS Mark III

Manufacturer:	De Havilland Aircraft Co		
Crew/Passengers:	one pilot		
Powerplant:	one 3,100 lb (1,405 kg) thrust De Havilland Goblin 2 jet engine		
Performance:	Max Speed: 531 mph (855 km/h)	Cruising Speed:	
	Service Ceiling: 43,500 ft (13,260 m)	Range:	
Weights:	Empty: 7,134 lb (3,235 kg)	Gross: 11,970 lb (5,430 kg)	
Dimensions:	Span: 40 ft 0 in (12.19 m)	Length: 30 ft 9 in (9.37m)	
	Height: 8 ft 10 in (2.69 m)	Wing Area: 226 sq ft (20.99 sq m)	
Armament:	four 20 mm cannon		
Cost:	Unknown		

De Havilland
COMET

When the De Havilland Comet was introduced into RCAF service in early 1953, it gave the RCAF the distinction of being the first air force in the world to operate jet transports. During their seven years on active duty, the RCAF's two Comets established "firsts" and set records as a matter of routine. On their delivery flights, they established speed records from London to Ottawa. When they went into squadron service, the Comets made the RCAF the first organization to operate scheduled jet transatlantic flights. A series of initially mysterious fatal accidents to commercially operated Comets overseas caused the RCAF Comets to be grounded for safety reasons in 1954. In August 1956, the two aircraft were flown to Britain for modifications (the aircraft were re-designated as Mark IXB following the changes) and the following month, they returned to Canada and resumed operational service. Employed by

412 Squadron, the two Comets flew across Canada and around the world in a wide variety of assignments. The aircraft were also used to test and train NORAD defences by simulating high-speed bomber-like targets. By 1965, after logging more than 5,000 hours each, the airframes were time-expired and both aircraft were retired from further RCAF use.

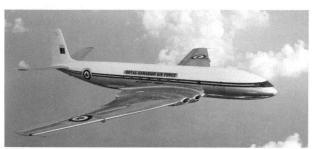

The De Havilland Comet gave the RCAF the distinction of being the first air force in the world to operate jet transports. (CF Photos)

DETAILS

Designation: **Model No:** D.H.106   **Marks:** Mk IA, IXB   **Role:** Transport
TOS: 1953   **SOS:** 1965   **No:** 2   **Service:** RCAF

SPECIFICATIONS

Manufacturer: De Havilland Aircraft Co
Crew/Passengers: forty passengers (up to 12,000 lb (5,443 kg))
Powerplant: four De Havilland Ghost Mark II jet engines at 5,000 lbs thrust each
Performance: Max Speed: Cruising Speed: 460 mph (740 km/h)
Service Ceiling: 40,000 ft (12,192 m)   Range: 2,500 mi (4,024 km)
Weights: Empty: Gross: 117,000 lb (53,071 kg)
Dimensions: Span: 114 ft 9.75 in (34.99 m)   Length: 93 ft 1 in (28.37 m)
Height: 29 ft 4.25 in (8.95 m)   Wing Area:
Armament: None
Cost: Unknown

De Havilland
SEA HORNET

The tremendous wartime success of the De Havilland Mosquito led to the development of a faster aircraft with the same basic features and construction techniques. The resulting design was elegant, streamlined and with a top speed of 488 mph (780 km/h), the Hornet was faster than jet fighters of the day. The De Havilland Hornet in fact became the last piston-engine fighter to serve in the Royal Air Force. Unfortunately, it arrived too late to see active service in the Second World War but the type remained in service well into the 1950s. The Royal Navy was also quick to see the usefulness of the design, and suitable modifications including folding wings, an arrestor hook and other specialized equipment for seaborne use resulted in the F.20 Sea Hornet. The RN deployed one Sea Hornet to Canada for cold weather trials and the RCAF subsequently briefly acquired the aircraft for test purposes.

Several views of the Sea Hornet show off its elegant lines. (RAF Photo and Author's collection)

DETAILS

Designation:	**Model No:** D.H.103	**Marks:** F.20	**Role:** Naval Fighter/Reconnaissance
TOS: 1948	**SOS:** 1948	**No:** 1	**Service:** RCAF

SPECIFICATIONS F.3 (RAF version)

Manufacturer:	De Havilland Aircraft Co	
Crew/Passengers:	one pilot	
Powerplant:	two 2,030 hp Rolls-Royce Merlin 133/134 engines	
Performance:	Max Speed: 488 mph (780 km/h)	Cruising Speed:
	Service Ceiling:37,500 ft (11,430 m)	Range: 2,500 mi (4,022 km)
Weights:	Empty:	Gross: 16,100 lb (7,303 kg)
Dimensions:	Span: 45 ft 0 in (13.71 m)	Length: 36 ft 8 in (11.17 m)
	Height: 14 ft 2 in (4.32 m)	Wing Area: 222 sq ft (20.62 sq m)
Armament:	four 20 mm cannon and provisions for 2,000 lb (907 kg) of bombs	
Cost:	Unknown	

De Havilland (Canada)
CHIPMUNK

The De Havilland-built Chipmunk was an original design and development of De Havilland of Canada Limited. It first came into service as elementary trainer with the RCAF in 1952 and was exported to various other countries as well. The aircraft was a tandem seat, fixed undercarriage, all-metal monoplane designed for use as a primary trainer. Student pilots were given approximately 25 hours on the Chipmunk prior to proceeding onto more advanced trainers. Many thousands of pilot trainees from the RCAF and from other NATO air forces were introduced to the art of flying on the Chipmunk. Fully aerobatic and able to perform precise manoeuvres in tight airspace, the tiny trainer entertained many with its aerial antics at RCAF flying displays across Canada.

A fine air-to-air study of a De Havilland Chipmunk in late RCAF/CAF service. (CF Photo)

DETAILS

Designation: CT-120	**Model No:** D.H.C.1	**Marks:** Mk I, III	**Role:** Trainer
TOS: 1948	**SOS:** 1971	**No:** 100	**Service:** RCAF/CF

SPECIFICATIONS

Manufacturer: De Havilland Canada designed and built
Crew/Passengers: two pilots
Powerplant: one 145 hp De Havilland Gipsy Major 10 piston engine

Performance:	Max Speed: 140 mph (225 km/h)	Cruising Speed: 124 mph (200 km/h)
	Service Ceiling: 17,200 ft (5,240 m)	Range:
Weights:	Empty: 1,199 lb (544 kg)	Gross: 1,930 lb (875 kg)
Dimensions:	Span: 34 ft 4 in (10.46 m)	Length: 25 ft 5 in (7.74 m)
	Height: 7 ft 0 in (2.13 m)	Wing Area: 172.5 sq ft (16.02 sq m)
Armament:	none	
Original Cost:	Unknown	

De Havilland (Canada)
OTTER

The De Havilland-built Otter light transport aircraft was a development of the previous De Havilland Beaver Short Take-Off and Landing (STOL) design. The Otter was in fact originally to be named the King Beaver and it followed its predecessor's configuration very closely. It featured a conventional stressed skin construction and had a braced wing with full-span slotted flaps with the outer portions acting as ailerons. The design proved to be highly versatile and the aircraft could be operated on wheels,

floats or skis. The RCAF initially selected the Otter to re-equip a number of its Auxiliary squadrons for emergency and rescue duties. The aircraft also saw action in an extensive range of UN missions. The Otter also proved popular with other armed forces such as the United States Army and Navy as well as other air forces. The Otter has seen extensive use as a light utility transport in a variety of military and now civilian uses.

The CSR-123 Otter utility transport aircraft. (CF Photo)

DETAILS

Designation: CSR-123   **Model No:** D.H.C.3   **Role:** Utility Transport

TOS: 1953   **SOS:** 1982   **No:** 69   **Service:** RCAF/CF

SPECIFICATIONS

Manufacturer:	De Havilland Canada designed and built	
Crew/Passengers:	two pilots and nine passengers	
Powerplant:	one 600 hp Pratt & Whitney S3HI-G Wasp piston engine	
Performance:	Maximum Speed: 160 mph (257 km/h)	Cruising Speed: 138 mph (222 km/h)
	Service Ceiling: 17,900 ft (5,426 m)	Range:
Weights:	Empty: 5,287 lb (2,398 kg)	Gross: 8,000 lb (3,629 kg)
Dimensions:	Span: 58 ft 0 in (17.7 m)	Length: 41 ft 10 in (12.8 m)
	Height: 13 ft 0 in (3.96 m)	Wing Area: 375 sq ft (34.83 sq m)
Armament:	none	
Original Cost:	$136,800	

De Havilland (Canada)
CARIBOU

The De Havilland-built Caribou transport aircraft was designed with Short Take-Off and Landing (STOL) characteristics. It featured a conventional stressed skin construction and had a cantilever-wing with full-span double-slotted flaps with the outer portions acting as ailerons. It was the first De Havilland Canada aircraft to feature a retractable undercarriage. The RCAF initially selected the Caribou to fulfill UN support duties for the Congo, purchasing four aircraft along with a range of support equipment. The aircraft were never deployed to the Congo but did see action in an extensive range of UN missions. The Caribou also proved popular with other armed forces such as the United States Army and the Royal Australian and Malaysian Air Forces. The Caribou has seen extensive use as a light tactical transport in a variety of military and now civilian uses.

An RCAF CC-108 Caribou transport aircraft painted in UN colours (overall white) and markings flying alongside a sister aircraft, a CSR-123 Otter. (CF Photo)

DETAILS

Designation: CC-108	**Model No:** D.H.C.4	**Marks:** Mk IA, IB	**Role:** Transport
TOS: 1960	**SOS:** 1971	**No:** 9	**Service:** RCAF/CF

SPECIFICATIONS

Manufacturer: De Havilland Canada designed and built

Crew/Passengers: two pilots, one flight engineer and thirty passengers or thirty-two troops

Powerplant: two 1,450 ESHP Pratt & Whitney R2000-7M2 Twin Wasp piston engines

Performance:
Maximum Speed: 214 mph (344 km/h)
Service Ceiling: 27,500 ft (8,381 m)
Cruising Speed: 180 mph (290 km/h)
Range:

Weights:
Empty: 17,630 lb (12,247 kg)
Gross: 28,500 lb (22,317 kg)

Dimensions:
Span: 95 ft 7½ in (29.15 m)
Height: 31 ft 9 in (9.67 m)
Length: 72 ft 7 in (22.12 m)
Wing Area: 912 sq ft (84.7 sq m)

Armament: none

Original Cost: $632,648

De Havilland (Canada)
BUFFALO

The De Havilland-built Buffalo was a new updated version of the De Havilland Caribou aircraft. The aircraft provided enhanced Short Take-Off and Landing (STOL) characteristics over its predecessor while doubling the range and carrying fifty percent more payload. The Buffalo has seen extensive use as a light tactical transport in a variety of military and now civilian uses. In the CF, the aircraft type has progressively converted to SAR duties while retaining a secondary transport role. No. 442 Squadron in 19 Wing Comox is now the last operator of this aircraft type, and employs its excellent mountain flying capabilities in its search and rescue function.

Aircraft 115465 is a CC-115 Buffalo SAR variant from 442 Squadron. The Buffalo aircraft's fine STOL handling qualities are particularly well suited to the rugged terrain found on Canada's west coast (CF Photo)

DETAILS

Designation: CC-115   **Model No:** D.H.C.5   **Role:** Transport/SAR
TOS: 1967   **SOS:** In-service   **No:** 15   **Service:** RCAF/CF

SPECIFICATIONS

Manufacturer: De Havilland Canada designed and built
Crew/Passengers: (SAR Crew) two pilots, one flight engineer, one navigator and two SAR Techs
Powerplant: two 3,060 ESHP General Electric 2CT64-820-3 engines
Performance: Max Speed: 227 kt (421 km/h)
Service Ceiling: 27,500 ft (8,382 m)   Range: 650 nm (1205 km)
Weights: Empty: (Transport) 27,000 lb (12,247 kg)   Gross: 45,000 lb (22,317 kg)
(SAR) 29,500 lbs (13,381 kg)
Dimensions: Span: 96 ft (29.26 m)   Length: 79 ft (24.08 m)
Height: 28 ft 8 in (8.73 m)   Wing Area: 945 sq ft (87.8 sq m)
Armament: none
Original Cost: $1,935,000

De Havilland (Canada)
TWIN OTTER

In the Canadian north, where the weather can change at a moment's notice, the Twin Otter provides short take-off and landing (STOL) capabilities on floats, skis or wheels. It is a highly maneuverable, light, versatile transport aircraft used primarily in northern Canada in support of Rangers and Cadets, and to transport units from southern areas of Canada to the north for exercises. Twin Otters are also used to help support Canadian Forces Station Alert, the northernmost permanent habitation in the world, by ferrying supplies and providing medevac service when needed. As well, the Twin Otter flies Search and Rescue (SAR) missions throughout the north, and generally supports Canadian Forces there. Its ability to transport up to twenty passengers or 2,999 kg of payload and its range of 1,296 km earmark it for use in a part of the country where every distance is measured in hundreds of kilometers.

The CC138 Twin Otter from 440 (T&R) Squadron based in Yellowknife has performed "yeoman service" as a northern utility aircraft for the CF. (CF Photo)

DETAILS

Designation: CC-138	**Model No:** D.H.C.6	**Role:** Utility	
TOS: 1971	**SOS:** In service	**No:** 8	**Service:** CF

SPECIFICATIONS

Manufacturer:	De Havilland Canada
Crew/Passengers:	Up to four crew and twenty passengers
Powerplant:	Two Pratt & Whitney Canada PT6A-27, 620 SHP (434 KW) turboprops
Performance:	Cruising Speed: 145 kts (274 km/h)
	Service Ceiling: 26,700 ft (8,138 m)
	Range: 775 nm (1,435 km) with 2,550 lb (1,156 kg) payload
Weights:	Gross: 12,500 lb (5,670 kg)
Dimensions:	Span: 65 ft 0 in (19.81 m) Length: 49 ft 6 in (15.1 m)
	Height: 18 ft 6 in (5.66 m) Wing Area:
Armament:	None
Cost:	$670,000

De Havilland (Canada)
DASH 7

The Dash 7 was a Canadian designed and built four-engine, medium-range transport aircraft. It was designed to take advantage of De Havilland's STOL expertise. Despite being four-engined, the design was known to be very quiet and it successfully incorporated specific design enhancements to achieve this goal. Two Dash 7 aircraft were acquired for the Canadian Air Mobility Tasking in NATO,

moving personnel and paraphernalia around Europe. The aircraft were purchased with quick-change interiors allowing for the interchange of passengers and freight. In this role the aircraft replaced two aging CC-109 Cosmopolitan transports. During the draw-down of Canadian Forces in Europe, the Dash 7 aircraft were themselves replaced by more economical Dash 8 transports.

An airborne view of the CF version of the Dash 7. (CF Photo)

DETAILS

Designation: CC-132	**Model No:** D.H.C. 7	**Role:** Transport	
TOS: 1979	**SOS:** 1985	**No:** 2	**Service:** CF

SPECIFICATIONS

Manufacturer:	De Havilland Canada
Crew/Passengers:	two pilots and up to fifty passengers and two crew
Powerplant:	four 1,120 shp Pratt & Whitney PT-6A-50 turboprop engines

Performance:	Max Speed: 268 mph (431 km/h)	Cruising Speed: 263 mph (421 km/h)
	Service Ceiling: 20,400 ft (6,222 m)	Range: 1,355 mi (2,180 km)
Weights:	Empty: 27,350 lb (12,406 kg)	Gross: 44,000 lb (19,958 kg)
Dimensions:	Span: 93 ft 0 in (28.35 m)	Length: 80 ft 8 in (24.58 m)
	Height: 26 ft 2 in (7.98 m)	Wing Area: 860 sq ft (79.9 sq m)
Armament:	None	
Cost:	Unknown	

De Havilland (Canada)
DASH 8

The Dash 8 is a Canadian designed and built twin-engine, medium-range transport aircraft. It is a highly successful successor to the company's Dash 7 aircraft and like its predecessor, it was designed to take advantage of De Havilland's STOL expertise. The design is known to be very quiet and it successfully incorporated specific design enhancements to achieve this goal. Two Dash 8 aircraft were acquired for the Canadian Air Mobility Tasking in NATO , moving personnel and paraphernalia around Europe. The aircraft were purchased with quick-change interiors allowing for the interchange of passengers and freight.

In this role the aircraft replaced two Dash 7 aircraft. The success of the original Dash 8 design resulted in its use for various specialized platforms. The need for a navigation trainer in the CF then resulted in the extensive modification of the aircraft for this role. The most prominent external feature was an extended nose section to house radar equipment. Extensive avionics and navigation consoles were also fitted to the interior. These modified aircraft are used primarily as a training tool at the Canadian Forces Air Navigation School (CFANS) at 17 Winnipeg, Manitoba.

This is an airborne view of the standard CF transport version of the Dash 8 in the original European theatre camouflage for its NATO support role. (CF Photo)

DETAILS

Designation: CC-142, CT-142   **Model No:** D.H.C. 8   **Role:** Transport & Navigation Trainer
TOS: 1985   **SOS:** In Service   **No:** 2 x CC-142 & 4 X CT-142   **Service:** CF

SPECIFICATIONS

Manufacturer: De Havilland Canada
Crew/Passengers: two pilots and up to thirty-six passengers
Powerplant: two Pratt & Whitney Canada PW120A turboprop engines
Performance: Max Speed: 309 mph (497 km/h)   Cruising Speed:
Service Ceiling: Range: 1,025 mi (1,650 km)
Weights: Empty: 22,100 lb (10,024 kg)   Max T/O: 34,500 lb (15,650 kg)
Dimensions: Span: 85 ft 0 in (25.91 m)   Length: 73 ft 0 in (22.25 m)
Height: 24 ft 7 in (7.49 m)   Wing Area: 585 sq ft (54.35 sq m)
Armament: None
Cost: CC-142 $8,390,000   CT-142 $14,298,000

Douglas
O-2BS (MO-2B)

The Douglas O-2 biplane family was one of the longest-lived American designs during the inter-war period. Entering service with the US military as early as 1924, some later models were still in service at the outbreak of the Second World War. The O-2 design featured conventional construction for the period with a welded steel tube fuselage and wooden wings. Fuel was carried in extra thick centre section stubs for the lower wings. O-2B models were identical with the original O-2A model series except the former featured dual controls. The RCAF's O-2BS was originally purchased directly from Douglas during O-2 production for the US Army. (In fact the aircraft was delivered factory fresh in a US Army colour scheme.) Mr. J.D. McKee, a wealthy American aviation-enthusiast, acquired it and it was first used in a trans-Canada flight from Montreal to Vancouver in September 1928. Squadron Leader A.E. Godfrey of the RCAF flew the aircraft on this historic trip. After the unfortunate death of Mr. McKee in an aviation accident in Quebec, the RCAF acquired the aircraft.

It was subsequently converted to MO-2B standard and was equipped with a Pratt & Whitney 425 hp Wasp radial engine. It was converted at the same time to a silver colour scheme and carried the G-CYZG registration. The aircraft could carry an extra seat in this configuration and the aircraft was then used for photographic survey work for the rest of its career.

The RCAF's one and only MO-2B, in the upper image, was bought from J. Dalzell McKee in 1927. Refitted with a more powerful radial engine and a third seat, the MO-2B served exclusively in the floatplane configuration until 1930, using the Government registration G-CYZG. (RCAF photo and LAC Photo #PA- 062407)

DETAILS

Designation: | **Model No:** O-2BS (MO-2B) | **Role:** Float Plane
TOS: 1927 | **SOS:** 1930 | **No:** 1 | **Service:** RCAF

SPECIFICATIONS

Manufacturer: Douglas Aircraft Company
Crew/Passengers: (OS-2B) two pilots in tandem (MO-2B) one pilot, one navigator and one photographer
Powerplant: originally one 420 hp Liberty engine and later one 425 hp Wasp radial engine
Performance: Max Speed: 126 mph (203 km/h) — Cruising Speed:
Service Ceiling: 10,000 ft (3,048 m) — Range:
Weights: Empty: 3,027 lb (1,373 kg) — Gross: 4,706 lb (2,135 kg)
Dimensions: Span: 39 ft 8 in (12.09 m) — Length: 29 ft 6 in (8.99 m)
Height: 14 ft 4 in (4.36 m) — Wing Area: 411 sq ft (38.18 sq m)
Armament: None
Cost: Unknown

Douglas
BOSTON (HAVOC)

The Boston medium bomber and its fighter variant, the Havoc, were well familiar to many Canadians both in the RCAF and RAF during the Second World War. No. 418 (RCAF) Squadron used them as night intruders when such operations were still in the experimental stage. No.

418 Squadron operated the type from March 1942 until July 1943, when they were replaced by Mosquito aircraft. Later models had their standard armament supplemented with a tray mounted in the belly containing four 20 mm cannon.

This fine study of a Boston Mk III in flight illustrates an aircraft from 418 (RCAF) Squadron, which flew offensive missions against European targets. (RCAF Photo)

DETAILS

Designation: **Model No:** A20C, J, K/DB-7   **Marks:** Mk III, IIIA, IV, V   **Role:** Bomber

TOS: 1941   **SOS:** 1945   **No:** 3   **Service:** RCAF

SPECIFICATIONS Mark III

Manufacturer:	Douglas Aircraft
Crew/Passengers:	three to five crew
Powerplant:	two 1600 hp (1193 KW) Wright GR-2600-A5B radial engines

Performance:	Max Speed: 304 mph (489 km/h)	Cruising Speed: 250 mph (402 km/h)
	Service Ceiling: 24,250 ft (7,391 m)	Range: 1,020 mi (1,642 km)
Weights:	Empty: 12,200 lb (5,534 kg)	Maximum Take-off: 25,000 lb (11,340 kg)
Dimensions:	Span: 61 ft 4 in (18.69 m)	Length: 47 ft 0 in (14.33 m)
	Height: 15 ft 10 in (4.83 m)	Wing Area: 465 sq ft (43.20 sq m)
Armament:	four fixed forward 0.303 in (7.7 mm) machine guns in nose	
	two 0.303 in (7.7 mm) machine guns in dorsal and ventral positions	
	up to 2000 lb (907 kg) of bombs	
Cost:	$74,000 US	

Douglas
DAKOTA

First flown on 17 December 1933 at Clover Field in Santa Monica, California, the Douglas DC-3 is arguably one of the most successful aircraft ever built. Designated "Dakota" or C-47 by RAF/RCAF, the aircraft was known by a wide variety of different names (Skytrain, Skytrooper, DAK, Goonie Bird) and different designations (DC3, C-47, C-53, R4D) in various services. Highly adaptable, this transport aircraft could be fitted with skis or Jet Assisted Take Off (JATO) bottles. In the RCAF and CF, it served in a wide variety of roles including various training purposes such as navigation, radio and radar training, along with target towing, transport, and search and rescue duties.

The Dakota was one of the longest serving military aircraft ever produced. Above is a nighttime view of a Dakota in RAF WW II service, while the lower photo illustrates two modified CC-129 aircraft from Cold Lake, Alberta, which were originally used for CF-104 radar training in the 1970s and 80s. (RAF & CF Photos)

DETAILS

Designation: CC-129/CT-129   **Model No:** DC-3/C-47   **Marks**: Mk III, Mk IIICSC, F, FP, P, R, S&R, U, and Mk IVM, MF, MFP, P, ST, T

Role: Transport, Training, Target Towing, SAR
TOS: 1943   **SOS:** 1989   **No:** 169   **Service:** RCAF/CF

SPECIFICATIONS

Manufacturer: Douglas Aircraft Corporation
Crew/Passengers: Two pilots and up to three crew or thirty-six passengers
Powerplant: two 1200 hp Pratt & Whitney R-1830-92 radials
Performance: Max Speed: 199 kts (369 km/h)   Cruising Speed: 145 kts (269 km/h)
                     Service Ceiling: 24,100 ft (7,345 m)   Range: 1,300 nm (2,414 km)
Weights: Max Take-Off: 26,000 lbs (11,793 kg)
Dimensions: Span: 95 ft 0 in (28.95 m)   Length: 64 ft 5½ in (19.64 m)
Armament: none
Original Cost: $165,000

Douglas
DIGBY

The Digby, designed for the US Army Air Corps as the B-18, was actually derived from the DC-2 which was in turn the forerunner to the DC-3 Dakota. The Digby had the same wings, engines and tail components as the transport aircraft. With the onset of war, the RCAF quickly acquired twenty Digby aircraft for patrol work. They served with No. 10 and No.161 Bomber Reconnaissance Squadron as patrol bombers and with No. 121, 164 and 167 Transport Squadrons. Squadron Leader C.L. Annis' crew flying a Digby of No. 10 (BR) Squadron on 25 October 1941 carried out the first attack on a U-boat by Eastern Air Command (EAC). Altogether Digbys of EAC carried out 11 attacks on U-boats. U-520 was confirmed sunk by Flying Officer F. Raymes' crew of No 10 (BR) Squadron, on 30 October 1942.

RCAF Digby aircraft, which were derived from a Douglas transport design, were used to patrol Canada's east coast after the outbreak of war.
(LAC Photo # PA-140642)

ETAILS

Designation: B-18	**Model No:** DB-1	**Marks:** Mk I	**Role:** Patrol Bomber/Transport
TOS: 1939	**SOS:** 1946	**No:** 20	**Service:** RCAF

SPECIFICATIONS B-18A Bomber

Manufacturer:	Douglas Aircraft Corporation	
Crew/Passengers:	Crew of six including two gunners, bomb aimer, navigator, and two pilots	
Powerplant:	two 1,000 hp (746 kw) Wright R-1820-53 Cyclone 9 radials	
Performance:	Max Speed: 215 mph (346 km/h)	Cruising Speed: 167 mph (269 km/h)
	Service Ceiling: 16,321 ft (7,403 m)	Range: 1,200 mi (1,931 km)
Weights:	Empty: 16,321 lb (7,403 kg)	Maximum Take-off: 27,673 lb (12,552 kg)
Dimensions:	Span: 89 ft 6 in (27.28 m)	Length: 57 ft 10 in (17.63 m)
	Height: 15 ft 2 in (4.62 m)	Wing Area: 965 sq ft (89.65 sq m)
Armament:	Three .30 in (7.62 mm) machine guns in nose, dorsal and ventral positions plus up to 6,500 lb (2,948 kg) in bombs or depth charges	
Cost:	Unknown	

Fairchild
ARGUS

Less well known than its much larger namesake manufactured in the 1960s by Canadair for ASW patrol, the first Argus in RCAF service was acquired on 17 January 1940. The Fairchild Argus was a four-passenger, general-purpose aircraft. The RCAF acquired two of these light aircraft when an American citizen and a staff member of *Reader's Digest* magazine each donated an Argus to the service. No. 12 Communication Squadron, based at Rockcliffe in Ottawa initially used the aircraft. The aircraft were later used for refresher training. One of the pair was involved in an accident in 1942 and salvaged parts were used to provide spares for the other twin. At the end of the Second World War, the remaining Argus was returned to civilian use.

A trim-looking Fairchild Argus in RCAF service. (RCAF Photo)

DETAILS

Designation:	**Model No:** 24H, 24R	**Role:** Utility Transport	
TOS: 1940	**SOS:** 1945	**No:** 24H (1), 24R (1)	**Service:** RCAF

SPECIFICATIONS

Manufacturer:	Fairchild Aircraft Company
Crew/Passengers:	one pilot and up to three passengers
Powerplant:	one 150 hp Ranger 6-140-BIA piston engine

Performance:	Max Speed: 117 mph (188 km/h)	Cruising Speed: 113 mph (182 km/h)
	Service Ceiling: 14,750 ft (4,496 m)	Range:
Weights:	Empty: 1,467 lb (666 kg)	Gross: 2,400 lb (1,089 kg)
Dimensions:	Span: 35 ft 4 in (10.77 m)	Length: 23 ft 9 in (7.24 m)
	Height: 8 ft 0 in (2.44 m)	Wing Area:
Armament:	None	
Cost:	Unknown	

Fairchild
51

The Fairchild Aircraft Company carried on with progressive development of its FC-2 model aircraft, which first flew in 1926. It was a four-seat cabin monoplane designed for light transport. It featured composite construction including a welded steel fuselage and tail along with a strut-braced wooden wing and all-over fabric covering. The 51 version standardized on four longerons for aft fuselage construction and a 300 hp Wright R-975 radial engine was substituted. This variant was again designed with aerial photography in mind and therefore featured an enclosed and heated cabin with extra windows to allow for an improved downward view. The RCAF again procured the type for this role. In the late 1930s, however, some RCAF Model 51 aircraft had light bomb racks under the fuselage and were used for practice bombing at Camp Borden.

An RCAF Fairchild 51 being pushed by a ground party. Commercial bush plane designs such as this were important to the RCAF's roles and missions during the 1920s and 1930s. (Comox Air Force Museum Photo)

DETAILS

Designation:	**Model No:** 51, 51A	**Role:** Utility		
TOS: 1930	**SOS:** 1946	**No:** 51(6), 51A (9)		**Service:** RCAF

SPECIFICATIONS 51

Manufacturer:	Canadian Vickers under licence from Fairchild	
Crew/Passengers:	one pilot and up to three passengers	
Powerplant:	one 300 hp Wright R-975 radial piston engine	
Performance:	Max Speed: 131 mph (211 km/h)	Cruising Speed: 105 mph (169 km/h)
	Service Ceiling: 15,500 ft (4,724 m)	Range:
Weights:	Empty: 2,256 lb (1,070 kg)	Gross: 4,000 lb (1,816 kg)
Dimensions:	Span: 44 ft 0 in (13.4 m)	Length: 30 ft 10⁹/₁₆ in (9.4 m)
	Height: 9 ft 1 in (2.77 m)	Wing Area: 272 sq ft (25.27 sq m)
Armament:	Provision for light bombs	
Cost:	Unknown	

Fairchild
71

The Fairchild Aircraft Company carried on with progressive development of its FC-2 model aircraft, which first flew in 1926. The FC-2W was a further development featuring a 50 ft span and a doubling of engine power. Further refinements led to yet another model designation for a seven-seat cabin monoplane designed for light transport. The model 71, as it was known, again featured composite construction including a welded steel fuselage and tail along with a strut-braced wooden wing and all-over fabric covering. This variant was again designed with aerial photography in mind and therefore featured a camera bay for vertical photography and low rear-door windows to permit oblique photography. The RCAF found its Fairchild 71 aircraft rugged, reliable and highly useful in the aerial survey role.

An RCAF Fairchild 71 aircraft #633 complete with floats and beaching gear, probably on Canada's west coast. Fairchild 71B 633 (earlier G-CYVX) was one of twelve on strength with the RCAF from 20 May, 1930 to 2 October, 1941 (in addition to eleven 71s), although one (G-CYVE/630) was later converted to a 71C. (CF Photo)

DETAILS

Designation: | **Model No:** 71A, 71B, 71C | **Role:** Utility
TOS: 1929 | **SOS:** 1942 | **No:** 71A(11), 71B(1), 71C(1) | **Service:** RCAF

SPECIFICATIONS 71B

Manufacturer:	Fairchild (Canada)
Crew/Passengers:	one pilot and up to six passengers
Powerplant:	one 420 hp Pratt & Whitney Wasp radial piston engine

Performance: Max Speed: 132 mph (212 km/h) — Cruising Speed: 112 mph (180 km/h)
Service Ceiling: 14,000 ft (4,267 m) — Range: 900 mi (1,448 km)
Weights: Empty: 3,160 lb (1,435 kg) — Gross: 5,500 lb (2,497 kg)
Dimensions: Span: 50 ft 0 in (15.39 m) — Length: 35 ft 10¼ in (10.93 m)
Height: 9 ft 4 in (2.84 m) — Wing Area: 310 sq ft (28.76 sq m)
Armament: None
Cost: Unknown

Fairchild
SUPER 71P

Unlike the Fairchild Aircraft Company's previous designs, which had featured a progressive development of previous models, the Super 71 was an all-new Canadian design despite its model number. The Super 71 was designed for freight transport in the far north. The Super 71 featured a duralumin monocoque-fuselage along with a strut-braced metal wing and tail surfaces. The RCAF was again interested in a variant of the Super 71 for aerial photography. It ordered two modified aircraft for this role under the designation Super 71P. These featured a camera bay for vertical photography. Additional changes included an enclosed cockpit forward of the wing, the wing instead terminated in a hump aft of the cockpit and a more powerful geared Wasp engine was fitted. The RCAF found its 71P aircraft less than satisfactory in the aerial survey role. The aircraft's many flaws, including structural problems with the floats, overheating of the engines, adverse handling on the water and on the ground with brake problems, all contributed to a poor reputation. One aircraft was assigned to RCAF Station Trenton as an air ambulance but little use appears to have been made of the aircraft in this role.

An RCAF Fairchild Super 71P in floatplane configuration with beaching dollies attached. (LAC Photo # PA-63184)

DETAILS

Designation:	**Model No:** Super 71P	**Role:** Utility	
TOS: 1929	**SOS:** 1940	**No:** 2	**Service:** RCAF

SPECIFICATIONS

Manufacturer: Fairchild (Canada)

Crew/Passengers: one pilot and up to eight passengers.

Powerplant: one 600 hp Pratt & Whitney S2H1-G Wasp radial piston engine

Performance: Max Speed: 142 mph (228.5 km/h) Cruising Speed: 119.5 mph (192 km/h)
Service Ceiling: 19,000 ft (5,791 m) Range: 800 mi (1,288 km)

Weights: Empty: 4,682 lb (2,126 kg) Gross: 7,090 lb (3,219 kg)

Dimensions: Span: 58 ft 0 in (17.67 m) Length: 36 ft 2 in (11.02 m)
Height: 10 ft 6 in (3.2 m) Wing Area: 392 sq ft (34.56 sq m)

Armament: None

Cost: Unknown

Fairchild
FLYING BOX CAR

The Fairchild designed C-119's distinctive twin boom layout and box-like cavernous fuselage earned it the name "Flying Box Car". Its rear-opening clamshell doors permitted fast and efficient handling of bulk loads. The type went through a number of redesigns with increases to the fuselage dimensions, more powerful engines and many other changes. The RCAF took delivery of its first aircraft in 1952. No. 435 and 436 Squadron of Air Transport Command used Flying Box Cars extensively throughout the 1950s, including on UN missions. Missions to the Arctic were also routine. The Canadian Army employed RCAF Box Cars for airborne exercises and the type could deploy up to 62 fully equipped paratroops. The Box Cars were originally intended to supersede the RCAF's Dakota aircraft but this was not to be the case. The last Box Cars were retired from RCAF service in July 1965 but Dakotas soldiered on in various roles.

Two examples of the CC-119 Flying Box Car. On the top is an aircraft soon after introduction and on the bottom is another in late service, just before retirement. Note the differences in markings and configuration. (Author's collection)

DETAILS

Designation: CC-119   **Model No:** C-119   **Role:** Tactical troop and cargo transport

TOS: 1952   **SOS:** 1967   **No:** 35   **Service:** RCAF

SPECIFICATIONS

Manufacturer: Fairchild Engine and Airplane Corporation

Crew/Passengers: crew of five and up to 62 troops or 35 stretcher cases or up to 10,000 lb payload

Powerplant: two 3,500 hp Wright R-3350-85 piston engines

Performance: Max Speed: 250 mph (402 km/h)   Cruising Speed: 205 mph (330 km/h)

Service Ceiling: 23,900 ft (7,285 m)   Range: 2,000 mi (3,219 km)

Weights: Empty: 40,000 lbs (18,144 kg)   Gross: 64,000 lb (29,030 kg)

Dimensions: Span: 109 ft 3 in (33.30 m)   Length: 86 ft 6 in (26.37 m)

Height: 26 ft 6 in (8.08 m)   Wing Area: 1,447 sq ft (134.43 sq m)

Armament: None

Cost: $590,000 US

Fairchild
RAZORBACK

The Fairchild FC-2 first flew in 1926. It was a four-seat cabin monoplane designed for light transport. It featured a 220 hp Wright J-5 Whirlwind engine along with composite construction including a welded steel fuselage and tail along with a strut-braced wooden wing and all-over fabric covering. Early production aircraft had only three longerons in the rear fuselage, giving the aircraft a "razorback" appearance and hence its name. Subsequent versions eliminated this distinctive feature with four-longeron construction. The aircraft was designed with aerial photography in mind and therefore featured an enclosed and heated cabin with extra windows to allow for an improved downward view. The RCAF initially procured the type for this role. The RCAF then decided to standardize engine powerplants across a variety of its fleets. Consequently, the design was re-engineered with a 215 hp Armstrong Siddeley Lynx engine. Re-designated as the FC-2L, this aircraft was then demonstrated to and accepted by the RCAF. Another version for the RCAF, known as the FC-2V, was also developed. The design was further evolved into the 51 and 71 models.

A Fairchild Razorback undergoing a ground run-up. (Comox AFM Photo)

DETAILS

Designation:	**Model No:** FC-2, FC-2L, FC-2V	**Role:** Utility	
TOS: 1927	**SOS:** 1938	**No:** FC-2(15), FC-2L (6), FC-2V(6)	**Service:** RCAF

SPECIFICATIONS FC-2L

Manufacturer:	Ottawa Car Company & Canadian Vickers under licence from Fairchild	
Crew/Passengers:	one pilot and up to three passengers.	
Powerplant:	one 215 hp Armstrong Siddeley Lynx G radial piston engine	
Performance:	Max Speed: 105.5 mph (170 km/h)	Cruising Speed: 85 mph (137 km/h)
	Service Ceiling: 13,100 ft (3,993 m)	Range:
Weights:	Empty: 2,749 lb (1,248 kg)	Gross: 4,180 lb (1,898 kg)
Dimensions:	Span: 44 ft 0 in (13.4 m)	Length: 30 ft 11 in (9.43 m)
	Height: 9 ft 1 in (2.77 m)	Wing Area: 272.4 sq ft (25.3 sq m)
Armament:	None	
Cost:	Unknown	

Fairchild
KR-34

The Fairchild KR-34 was a development of the popular Kreider-Reisner Challenger three-place, open-cockpit biplane. Kreider-Reisner Aircraft Co. Inc in Hagarstown, Maryland, which eventually became a division of Fairchild Aircraft, originally manufactured the design. The KR-34 featured plywood and spruce wings plus a chromally welded steel tube fuselage with wooden fairing strips and a fabric covering. There was an entrance door to the front cockpit and a baggage compartment behind the rear cockpit accessible by a door on the left-hand side. The RCAF evaluated the aircraft type and despite already having a plethora of other trainers, it elected to purchase one of these aircraft. Few details are available for the rationale or its actual use.

A view of a Fairchild KR-34 trainer similar to that used by the RCAF. (CF Photo)

DETAILS

Designation:	**Model No:** KR-34	**Marks:**	**Role:** Trainer
TOS: 1930	**SOS:** 1936	**No:** 1	**Service:** RCAF

SPECIFICATIONS

Manufacturer: Fairchild Aircraft Company
Crew/Passengers: two pilots in tandem
Powerplant: 165 hp Wright J-6 radial engine
Performance: Max Speed: 120 mph (193 km/h)   Cruising Speed: 102 mph (164 km/h)
Service Ceiling: 14,100 ft (4,298 m)   Range: 510 mi (821 km)
Weights: Empty: 1,524 lb (691 kg)   Gross: 2,368 lb (1,074 kg)
Dimensions: Upper Span: 30 ft 1 in (9.17 m)   Lower Span: 28 ft 9 in (9.06 m)
Length: 23 ft 2 in (7.06 m)   Height: 9 ft 3 in (2.82 m)
Wing Area: 285 sq ft (26.48 sq m)
Armament: None
Cost: $6,575 US

Fairchild
CORNELL

As the Second World War progressed, the RCAF needed a more advanced trainer for the BCATP. The existing DH 82C Tiger Moths and Fleet 16Bs used for elementary flying training proved to be a significant step down from contemporary service aircraft. In the spring of 1941, the RCAF therefore decided on a development of the Fairchild Aircraft (US) Company's PT-19 trainer design. The RCAF version was to feature an enclosed cockpit, an improved heating system, and equipment changes including a Ranger piston engine. This modified version was to be known as the Fairchild Cornell in Canada. It rapidly entered production and found favour at elementary flying schools across Canada beginning in 1943. Although it had some in-service problems, the Cornell provided reliable service in its intended role until after the war.

The photo above is a nice colour view of the RCAF Fairchild Cornell trainer. This particular aircraft is now part of the Canadian Aviation Museum collection. (CF Photo)

DETAILS

Designation:	**Model No:** PT-26, PT-26A, PT-26B	**Marks:** Mk I, II, III	**Role:** Trainer
TOS: 1943	**SOS:** 1948	**No:** 1,553	**Service:** RCAF

SPECIFICATIONS PT-26A

Manufacturer:	Fleet Aircraft Limited (Canada)	
Crew/Passengers:	two pilots in tandem	
Powerplant:	one 200 hp Ranger 6-440-C5 piston engine	
Performance:	Max Speed: 122 mph (195 km/h)	Cruising Speed: 101 mph (162.5 km/h)
	Service Ceiling: 13,200 ft (4,023 m)	Range: 420 mi (676 km)
Weights:	Empty: 2,022 lb (918 kg)	Gross: 2,736 lb (1,242 kg)
Dimensions:	Span: 36 ft 11 in (11.2 m)	Length: 28 ft 8 in (8.43 m)
	Height: 7 ft 7½ in (2.32 m)	Wing Area: 200 sq ft (18.6 sq m)
Armament:	None	
Cost:	Unknown	

Fairey
IIIC

The Fairey IIIC arrived virtually too late to see active service in the First World War. Several Fairey IIC aircraft did however see service with the Royal Air Force during operations against the Bolsheviks in Northern Russia in 1919. In Canada, during this same period, a Fairey IIIC was being modified for a possible transatlantic crossing. These preparations came to naught with the successful transatlantic crossing by Alcock and Brown in a modified Vickers Vimy aircraft. The Fairey IIIC aircraft's principle fame in this period for the CAF was in the Air Board's trans-Canada flight of 1920. The purpose of the flight was to draw the attention of the Canadian public to the Air Board and the CAF, and the capability of their post-war aircraft for future airmail and passenger operations. The flight was accomplished in relays of crews and aircraft and commenced in Halifax, Nova Scotia on 7 October with the Fairey IIIC seaplane. Unfortunately, this aircraft's participation was cut short by a crash approximately 20 miles north of Saint John, New Brunswick. The remainder of the journey was completed by other flying boats and by three D.H.9as of which only one D.H.9 (G-CYBF) finally made it to Vancouver, British Columbia on 17 October, after eleven days with 45 hours airborne and covering 3,265 miles.

The Fairey IIIC floatplane depicted here is similar to that used by the Canadian Air Force. (LAC Photo # PA-006752)

DETAILS

Designation:	Model No: IIIC	Marks:	Role: Reconnaissance Floatplane
TOS: 1920	SOS: 1920	No: 1	Service: CAF

SPECIFICATIONS

Manufacturer:	Fairey Aircraft Co	
Crew/Passengers:	one pilot and one observer/gunner	
Powerplant:	one 375 hp Rolls-Royce Eagle VIII engine	
Performance:	Max Speed: 110 mph (177 km/h)	Landing Speed: 44 mph (71 km/h)
	Service Ceiling: 15,000 ft (4,572 m)	Range:
Weights:	Empty: 3,392 lb (1,539 kg)	Gross: 4,800 lb (2,177 kg)
Dimensions:	Span: 46 ft 1¼ in (14.05 m)	Length: 36 ft 0 in (10.97 m)
	Height: 12 ft 2 in (3.71 m)	Wing Area: 476 sq ft (44.22 sq m)
Armament:	Provisions for one synchronized Vickers machine gun forward and one Lewis machine gun in a flexible mount aft plus light bombs	
Cost:	Unknown	

Fairey
ALBACORE

The Fairey Albacore had been designed to replace the Fairey Swordfish biplane on Royal Navy carriers but in the end the "Stringbag" outlived its proposed successor. Albacores did, however, serve with distinction in several actions, particularly in the Mediterranean. In RCAF service, the Albacore must be credited with two distinctions; it was the last operational biplane to be used by the RCAF and the only one ever to see action. In November 1943, "A" flight of No. 415 (RCAF) Squadron was equipped with Albacores for use in coastal operations. The aircraft usually operated at night and on anti-shipping patrols car-

ried a crew of two and armament consisting of six 250 lb bombs in lieu of a torpedo. Highlights of 415's operations included the sinking of the German torpedo boat *Grief* on 24 May 1944 and the suppression of enemy E-boats, which attempted to interfere with Allied shipping following the invasion of Normandy. When No. 415 Squadron was transferred from Coastal to Bomber Command, its Albacores and most of the aircrews who were nearing the end of their tours were then sent to No. 119 (RAF) Squadron.

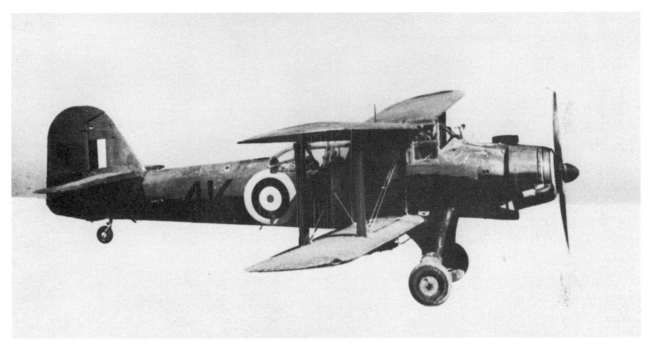

The Fairey Albacore was designed to replace the Fairey Swordfish. In the end, the latter outlasted its successor in British wartime service. (CF Photo)

DETAILS

Designation:	**Model No:**	**Marks:** Mk I	**Role:** Torpedo Bomber
TOS: 1943	**SOS:** 1949	**No:** 6	**Service:** RCAF

SPECIFICATIONS

Manufacturer:	Fairey Aircraft Company
Crew/Passengers:	Two or three
Powerplant:	one 1,130 hp (843 KW) Bristol Taurus XII radial engine
Performance:	Max Speed: 161 mph (259 km/h) — Cruising Speed: 116 mph (187 km/h)
	Service Ceiling: 20,700 ft (6,310 m) — Range: 930 mi (1,497 km)
Weights:	Empty: 7,250 lb (3,289 kg) — Maximum Take-off: 10,460 lb (4,745 kg)
Dimensions:	Span: 50 ft 0 in (15.24 m) — Length: 39 ft 10 in (12.14 m)
	Height: 14 ft 2 in (4.32 m) — Wing Area: 623 sq ft (57.88 sq m)
Armament:	one forward firing .303 in (7.7 mm) machine gun and twin Vickers "K" guns in rear cockpit plus provisions for one 1,610 lb (730 kg) torpedo or six 250 lb (113 kg) or four 500 lb (227 kg) bombs
Cost:	Unknown

Fairey
BATTLE

First flown in March 1936, the Fairey Battle was operationally obsolete by 1939 when it was scheduled for active service as a front line combat aircraft. Following a gallant but hopeless exposure in France at the beginning of the war, the type was relegated to training duties, in which it contributed far more to the war effort than it had as an operational asset. The RCAF had received its first Battles in August 1939 when eight were shipped by rail to Camp Borden. More were sent from England and large numbers were eventually to be employed as dual control trainers, target tugs and gunnery trainers in the many Bombing and Gunnery Schools of the BCATP. With the introduction of Bolingbrokes and Harvards, the numbers of Battles in RCAF use declined, but they still continued in service until the end of hostilities. No.111 and 122 Squadron of the RCAF also flew Battles.

A fine study of the Fairey Battle aircraft, in this case a colourfully marked target towing aircraft with yellow and black stripes. (Comox AFM Photo)

DETAILS

Designation:	**Model No:**	**Marks:** Mk I, IT, IIT	**Role:** Trainer
TOS: 1939	**SOS:** 1946	**No:** 740	**Service:** RCAF

SPECIFICATIONS Mark I

Manufacturer:	Fairey Aircraft Company
Crew/Passengers:	crew of three
Powerplant:	one 1,030 hp (768 kW) Rolls Royce Merlin engine

Performance:	Max Speed: 257 mph (414 km/h)	Cruising Speed: 210 mph (338 km/h)
	Service Ceiling: 25,000 ft (7,620 m)	Range: 1,000 mi (1,609 km)
Weights:	Empty: 6,647 lb (3,015 kg)	Maximum Take-off: 10,792 lb (4,895 kg)
Dimensions:	Span: 54 ft 0 in (16.46 m)	Length: 42 ft 4 in (12.90 m)
	Height: 15 ft 6 in (4.72 m)	Wing Area: 422 sq ft (39.20 sq m)
Armament:	one .303 in (7.7 mm) machine gun in starboard wing and one Vickers "K" gun in rear cockpit plus provisions for up 1,000 lb (454 kg) of bombs	
Cost:	Unknown	

Fairey
FIREFLY

The Fairey Firefly first saw active service in the Second World War. Canadian aircrews flew early model Fairey Firefly aircraft onboard RN fleet carriers, primarily in the Pacific theatre. Despite the Firefly's unenviable task as a flak suppression and support aircraft, it proved itself to be a formidable all-weather strike aircraft. It was "pleasant" to fly but not for the observer who had an extremely cramped, rear cockpit. In the post-war period, the RCN obtained the loan of two light fleet carriers. Fairey Fireflys made up part of the aircraft complement for both HMCS *Warrior* and HMCS *Magnificent*. Progressively improved models were flown in RCN service with the final variant the FR V (A/S) model being optimized for the anti-submarine warfare role that became the RCN's principle focus. The last RCN Fireflys were struck off strength in 1954.

Two "frosty" views of a Fairey Firefly being tested by the Winter Experimental Establishment. (Author's collection)

DETAILS

Designation:	**Model No:**	**Marks:** FR I, FR IV, FR V(A/S), T1, T2
Role: Naval Strike Fighter/ASW/Reconnaissance		
TOS: 1947	**SOS:** 1954	**No:** 12 FR IV, 4 TI, 2 T2 **Service:** RCN

SPECIFICATIONS FR IV

Manufacturer:	Fairey Aircraft Company
Crew/Passengers:	one pilot and one observer/gunner
Powerplant:	one 2,250 hp Rolls-Royce Griffon 74 piston engine
Performance:	Max Speed: 386 mph (621 km/h) Cruising Speed: 220 mph (354 km/h)
	Service Ceiling: 28,400 ft (8,656 m) Range: 1,300 mi (2,092 km)
Weights:	Empty: 9,674 lb (4,388 kg) Gross: 16,096 lb (7,301 kg)
Dimensions:	Span: 41 ft 2 in (12.55 m) Length: 27 ft 11 in (8.51 m)
	Height: 14 ft 4 in (4.37 m) Wing Area: 330 sq ft (30.66 sq m)
Armament:	Four fixed 20 mm guns in wings plus provisions for eight 60 lb (27 kg) unguided rockets or two 1,000 (454 kg) bombs on under-wing racks.
Cost:	Unknown

Fairey
SWORDFISH

First appearing in 1933, the open-cockpit biplane Fairey Swordfish was used by the Royal Navy as a torpedo bomber throughout the Second World War. The type primarily operated from aircraft carriers but was also flown from land bases in cross-Channel actions. Although seemingly antiquated in comparison to other Second World aircraft types, the Swordfish gave a good account of itself in several major battles, including the sinking of the German battleship *Bismark* and the raid on the Italian port of Taranto. The aircraft type was progressively used as a torpedo bomber, as a shore based mine layer, as a convoy ASW protection aircraft flown from escort carriers, as a night-time flare dispenser, and as a rocket armed anti-shipping strike aircraft as well as for various other training and utility purposes. However, the Swordfish only entered Canadian service in 1943, and was primarily used by the Royal Canadian Navy as a training aircraft. In deference to Canadian winters, some of these latter aircraft were fitted with an enclosed cockpit.

A Fairey Swordfish torpedo plane with what appears to be an all female torpedo loading crew passing in front. (Comox AFM Photo)

DETAILS

Designation:	**Model No:** T.S.R.II	**Marks:** Mk II, III, IV	**Role:** Torpedo Bomber
TOS: 1943	**SOS:** 1947	**No:** 105	**Service:** RCN

SPECIFICATIONS Mark II (land plane version)

Manufacturer:	Fairey Aircraft Company	
Crew/Passengers:	one pilot and one or two observer/gunners	
Powerplant:	one 750 hp Bristol Pegasus XXX radial piston engine	
Performance:	Max Speed: 138 mph (222 km/h)	Cruising Speed: 120 mph (193 km/h)
	Service Ceiling: 10,700 ft (3,260 m)	Range: 1,030 mi (1,658 km)
Weights:	Empty: 4,700 lb (2,132 kg)	Gross: 7,510 lb (3,406kg)
Dimensions:	Span: 45 ft 6 in (13.87 m)	Length: 35 ft 8 in (10.87 m)
	Height: 12 ft 4 in (3.76 m)	Wing Area: 607 sq ft (56.39 sq m)
Armament:	Provisions for one synchronized .303 in (7.7 mm) machine gun forward and one Lewis machine gun in a flexible mount aft plus provisions for one 1,610 lb (730 kg) torpedo, up to 1,500 lb (680 kg) light bombs or up to eight 60 lb (27 kg) unguided rockets on under wing racks.	
Cost:	Unknown	

Felixstowe
F.3

The Felixstowe F.3 was a First World War British twin-engine flying boat designed by the commander of RNAS *Felixstowe*, and generally based on American Curtiss designs. The F.3 was a design improvement of the F.1 and F.2 series flying boat by the same designer. Similar to contemporary Curtiss designs, the F.3 featured a laminated wood veneer hull with sponsons along the lower edges and unequal span biplane wings. These aircraft were often flown on North Sea patrols by Canadian aircrew serving with the Royal Naval Air Service. Later Canadian use of the F.3 Felixstowe was prompted by the delivery of eleven aircraft as part of an Imperial gift to Canada. The Canadian Air Force of the 1920s frequently used flying boats. Consequently, the donated F.3 flying boats were put to good use. One aircraft was used by the Air Board for the first trans-Canada flight in 1920, for the Rivière du Loup, Quebec, to Winnipeg, Manitoba segment.

In 1920 the Canadian Air Board sponsored a project to conduct the first ever trans-Canada flight. The leg from Rivière du Loup to Winnipeg was flown by Lieutenant Colonel Leckie and Major Hobbs in a Felixstowe F.3 to determine the feasibility of such flights for future air mail and passenger service. (CF Photo)

DETAILS

Designation:	**Model No:** F.3	**Marks:**	**Role:** Flying Boat
TOS: 1921	**SOS:** 1923	**No:** 11	**Service:** CAF

SPECIFICATIONS

Manufacturer:	Felixstowe
Crew/Passengers:	crew of four
Powerplant:	two 345 hp Rolls Royce Eagle VIII piston engines
Performance:	Max Speed: 93 mph (150 km/h) — Cruising Speed:
	Service Ceiling: 8,000 ft (2,438 m) — Range: 270 mi (450 km)
Weights:	Empty: 7,958 lb (3,609 kg) — Gross: 12,235 lb (5,550 kg)
Dimensions:	Upper Span: 102 ft 0 in (31.09 m) — Lower Span: 74 ft 2 in (22.61 m)
	Length: 49 ft 3 in (15.01 m) — Height: 18 ft 8 in (5.69 m)
	Wing Area: 1,432 sq ft (133.03 sq m)
Armament:	provisions for four Lewis machine guns on flexible mounts plus up to four 230 lb (104 kg) bombs
Cost:	Unknown

Fleet
Fawn

The Fleet Fawn was originally designed by the American Consolidated Aircraft Limited. The company then acquired Fleet Aircraft. The Fawn had conventional construction methods of the period, with a welded steel-tube fuselage and composite metal, wood and fabric design features. The RCAF acquired the aircraft type as an elementary trainer. In service, the aircraft went through progressive updates and enhancements. A variety of engines were fitted, and a fuselage belly tank and fixed cockpit enclosure or "coupe top" with hinged sides were optional features. In the late 1930s a sliding cockpit enclosure was developed and this became a standard feature on all RCAF aircraft. The aircraft could also be flown on wheels, floats and skis. The Fleet Fawn was a rugged and successful elementary trainer that served the RCAF well. The last aircraft were struck off strength in 1947.

The diminutive Fleet Fawn aircraft served as a basic flying trainer. (CF Photo)

DETAILS

Designation:	**Model No:** Model 7B, C, G	**Marks:** Mk I, II	**Role:** Trainer
TOS: 1931	**SOS:** 1947	**No:** 51	**Service:** RCAF

SPECIFICATIONS 7B

Manufacturer:	Fleet Aircraft of Canada	
Crew/Passengers:	two pilots in tandem	
Powerplant:	one 125 hp Kinner B-5 radial piston engine	
Performance:	Max Speed: 112 mph (180 km/h)	Cruising Speed: 87 mph (140 km/h)
	Service Ceiling: 15,500 ft (4,724 m)	Range: 320 mi (515 km)
Weights:	Empty: 1,130 lb (513 kg)	Gross: 1,860 lb (844 kg)
Dimensions:	Span: 28 ft 0 in (8.5 m)	Length: 21 ft 6 in (6.5 m)
	Height: 7 ft 10 in (2.4 m)	Wing Area: 194 sq ft (18.06 sq m)
Armament:	None	
Cost:	Unknown	

Fleet
Finch

The Fleet Finch was essentially a further development of the company's Fawn design. The RCAF had evaluated the Fleet 10D, which was a development of its Fleet Model 7 aircraft. The RCAF then requested further modifications to the design of the aircraft to make it fully aerobatic, along with other equipment changes. This revised design was then designated as the Model 16 or Finch in RCAF service. The aircraft had conventional construction for the period with a welded steel-tube fuselage and composite metal, wood and fabric design features. The RCAF acquired the aircraft type as an elementary trainer. In service, a sliding cockpit enclosure was developed and this became a standard feature on all RCAF aircraft. The Fleet Finch, like its predecessor the Fleet Fawn, was a rugged and successful elementary trainer that served the RCAF well. The last aircraft were struck off strength in 1947.

A Fleet Finch trainer aircraft in standard BCATP colours. (CF Photo)

DETAILS

Designation:	**Model No:** Model 16B, R	**Marks:** Mk I, II	**Role:** Trainer
TOS: 1939	**SOS:** 1947	**No:** 431	**Service:** RCAF

SPECIFICATIONS 16B

Manufacturer:	Fleet Aircraft of Canada	
Crew/Passengers:	two pilots in tandem	
Powerplant:	one 125 hp Kinner B-5 radial piston engine	
Performance:	Max Speed: 104 mph (167 km/h)	Cruising Speed: 85 mph (137 km/h)
	Service Ceiling: 10,500 ft (3,200 m)	Range: 320 mi (515 km)
Weights:	Empty: 1,122 lb (509 kg)	Gross: 2,000 lb (908 kg)
Dimensions:	Span: 28 ft 0 in (8.5 m)	Length: 21 ft 8 in (6.6 m)
	Height: 7 ft 9 in (2.36 m)	Wing Area: 194 sq ft (18.06 sq m)
Armament:	None	
Cost:	Unknown	

Fleet
FORT

The Fleet Fort was originally designed in Canada as an "advanced flying trainer" and orders for 200 were placed in 1940 as part of the British Commonwealth Air Training Plan. Full-scale production was not able to commence immediately and the first model was not flying until April 1941. By then the availability of the Fairchild Cornell trainer and a change in what constituted an "advanced trainer" led to the contract being cut back sharply and only 101 Forts were delivered between June 1941 and June 1942. The Fleet 60 was designed as a monoplane with a low elliptical wing and a raised rear cockpit. An unusual feature was the fixed undercarriage. Although fixed, the undercarriage was fitted with a retractable fairing. This feature was intended to familiarize student pilots with an undercarriage retraction mechanism but without causing any damage should the student forget. The Forts were used primarily at No. 2 Wireless School, Calgary, and No. 3 Wireless School, Winnipeg, for training of radio operators. The last Forts saw active service in 1944 and they were completely retired from use by 1945.

This frontal view depicts the unusual looking Fleet Fort. Note the externally braced wings. (LAC Photo # PA-64009)

DETAILS

Designation:	**Model No:** 60	**Role:** Trainer	
TOS: 1941	**SOS:** 1945	**No:** 101	**Service:** RCAF

SPECIFICATIONS

Manufacturer:	Fleet Aircraft of Canada	
Crew/Passengers:	one pilot and one wireless operator trainee	
Powerplant:	one 250 hp or one 330 hp Jacobs radial piston engine	
Performance:	Max Speed: 162 mph (261 km/h)	Cruising Speed: 135 mph (217 km/h)
	Service Ceiling: 15,000 ft (4,572 m)	Range:
Weights:	Empty: 2,530 lb (1,149 kg)	Gross: 3,500 lb (1,589 kg)
Dimensions:	Span: 36 ft 0 in (10.97 m)	Length: 26 ft 10 in (8.18 m)
	Height: 8 ft 3 in (2.51 m)	Wing Area: 216 sq ft (20.07 sq m)
Armament:	None	
Cost:	Unknown	

Fleet
Freighter

The Fleet Freighter was a twin-engine aircraft designed for cargo operations in the rugged bush country. The fuselage was of welded steel-tube construction with aluminum fairing strips and a fabric covering, but with a semi-monocoque nose of aluminum. The inboard wing sections were of metal stressed-skin construction and the outer wing sections were of composite construction with wooden spars, duralumin ribs and fabric covering. For freight handling there were large doors in the fuselage along a hatch in the front cabin floor. The RCAF ordered two Fleet Freighters originally for paratroop training. The aircraft were never used in this role however and were instead used for freighting and air ambulance duties.

Images of the Fleet Freighter in RCAF service are difficult to find. This photo illustrates the aircraft type in prominent RCAF colours. (M. McIntyre Collection)

DETAILS

Designation:	**Model No:** 50K	**Marks:**	**Role:** Utility
TOS: 1942	**SOS:** 1944	**No:** 2	**Service:** RCAF

SPECIFICATIONS 50K

Manufacturer:	Fleet Aircraft of Canada	
Crew/Passengers:	two pilots plus up to twelve passengers	
Powerplant:	two 330 hp Jacobs L-6MB radial piston engines	
Performance:	Max Speed: 150 mph (241 km/h)	Cruising Speed: 132 mph (212 km/h)
	Service Ceiling: 15,000 ft (4,572 m)	Range:
Weights:	Empty: 4,600 lb (2,088 kg)	Gross: 8,326 lb (3,780 kg)
Dimensions:	Upper Span: 45 ft 0 in (13.7 m)	Lower Span: 43 ft 4 in (13.21 m)
	Length: 36 ft 0 in (10.97 m)	Height: 13 ft 1 in (3.99 m)
	Wing Area: 528 sq ft (49.0 sq m)	
Armament:	None	
Cost:	Unknown	

Fokker
D VII

The Fokker D VII was a highly successful German single-seat biplane fighter that entered into large-scale service late in the First World War. The D VII had a fuselage of welded steel tube covered with aluminum and fabric combined with thick-section wings covered in both plywood and fabric. The D VII's performance was excellent and some 700 D VIIs were in service at the time of the Armistice. The type was the only aeroplane specifically mentioned in the Treaty of Versailles for surrender to the Allies. Several captured examples were then acquired and flown by members of the CAF in England before disbandment. At least 24 of these WW I trophies appear to have been shipped to Canada in the post-war period. Air Force pilots then flew a number of these Fokker D VII aircraft in the summer and fall of 1919. At least four D VIIs were flown in daily flying exhibitions at the Canadian National Exhibition in 1919 in a team lead by Canadian ace, Colonel W. G. Barker, as the first Canadian Air Force air display team. Col Barker also flew a D VII aircraft in the New York–Toronto air race in August 1919. In 1920, the surviving aircraft were shipped to Camp Borden and some were sent to various other institutions and cities. Shortly after this period, the surviving aircraft in Air Force hands were ordered destroyed. Several other types of German "war trophies" such as the Junkers J.1, Pfalz D XII, Roland D VIb and Rumpler CVII were also shipped to Canada but there is no record of these aircraft types being regularly flown by Air Force pilots.

An interesting view of one of the Canadian Fokker D VII "war trophies" on display, possibly in Camp Borden. (CF Photo)

DETAILS

Designation:	**Model No:** DVII	**Marks:**	**Role:** Fighter
TOS: 1919	**SOS:** 192?	**No:** undetermined	**Service:** CAF

SPECIFICATIONS D VII

Manufacturer:	Fokker, or Albatros under license		
Crew/Passengers:	one pilot		
Powerplant:	one 185 hp BMW IIIa in-line piston engine		
Performance:	Max Speed: 117 mph (187 km/h)	Cruising Speed:	
	Service Ceiling: 22,965 ft (7,000 m)	Range:	
Weights:	Empty: 1,477 lb (670 kg)	Gross: 2,112lb (960 kg)	
Dimensions:	Span: 29 ft 3½ in (8.90 m)	Length: 22 ft 11½ in (6.95 m)	
	Height: 9 ft 2¼ in (2.75 m)	Wing Area: 221.4 sq ft (20.50 sq m)	
Armament:	Twin 0.312 in (7.92 mm) machine guns		
Cost:	Unknown		

Fokker
Super Universal

The Fokker Super Universal was a further development of the company's Universal design. This revised design was built using typical Fokker methods with a fabric-covered welded steel-tube fuselage and empennage plus a plywood-covered, wood cantilever wing with a thick high lift wing section. Canadian built aircraft featured a greater capacity electrical system and larger fuel tanks in the wings. The RCAF acquired the aircraft type exclu-sively for an expedition to explore the Hudson Strait. In service, the aircraft were employed as float planes and wore civilian markings exclusively. The Fokker Super Universal, like its predecessor, was a rugged and successful bush transport that served the RCAF well during the Hudson Strait survey. The aircraft were however struck off strength following the expedition.

The Fokker Super Universal aircraft shown here, G-CAHE, has been re-assembled from packing crates for use by the RCAF during a survey of Hudson Strait. (CF Photo)

DETAILS

Designation:	**Model No:**	**Role:** Utility Transport	
TOS: 1927	**SOS:** 1929	**No:** 6	**Service:** RCAF

SPECIFICATIONS Float plane

Manufacturer: Canadian Vickers Ltd under license from Fokker
Crew/Passengers: two pilots side by side plus up to six passengers
Powerplant: one 400 hp Pratt & Whitney Wasp A radial piston engine
Performance: Max Speed: 138 mph (222 km/h) Cruising Speed: 118 mph (190 km/h)
Service Ceiling: 18,000 ft (5,486 m) Range: 700 mi (1,127 km)
Weights: Empty: 3,550 lb (1,610 kg) Gross: 5,150 lb (2,336 kg)
Dimensions: Span: 50 ft 8 in (15.44 m) Length: 36 ft 7 in (11.15 m)
Height: 9 ft 5 in (2.87 m) Wing Area: 387 sq ft (35.95 sq m)
Armament: None
Cost: $21,900

Ford
TRI-MOTOR

The Ford Tri-Motor design was one of the most successful early transports. It was one of the largest all-metal aircraft built in America up to that time and it featured corrugated aluminum covering on the fuselage, wings, tail and on the internally braced cantilever wing. The aircraft had gained quick acceptance from airlines and other services for its advanced features. The RCAF acquired its single example in 1929. The aircraft was purchased initially as a replacement for the RCAF's one and only Keystone Puffer aircraft which had been used in experimental crop/forest dusting. The RCAF's Tri-motor therefore holds the distinction of being one of the first and largest crop dusting aircraft. The aircraft carried the registration G-CYWZ and the last two "WZ" call letters were prominently displayed on the fuselage. The aircraft was often referred to by this shortened designation. The Tri-motor was also used to transport the servicing personnel for the RCAF's aerobatic team, the Siskins, on their Trans-Canada Air Pageant of 1931. In addition, it was used for radio-range calibration along with a myriad of other duties. The aircraft proved to be very versatile and operated on wheels, skis and floats during its service life. Sold in 1937, the aircraft was ironically destroyed in 1939 on the ground in Vancouver, after an RCAF Hurricane fighter swerved off the runway and collided with the parked Tri-motor.

The RCAF's only Ford Trimotor (G-CYWZ) was acquired in June 1929, for agricultural and forestry spray experiments. It served in these and other roles until early 1937. Even by this late date, it was still the RCAF's largest aircraft on inventory. (Comox AFM Photo)

DETAILS

Designation:	**Model No:** 4-AT	**Role:** Transport	
TOS: 1929	**SOS:** 1937	**No:** 1	**Service:** RCAF

SPECIFICATIONS

Manufacturer:	Ford Motor Company, Aircraft Division
Crew/Passengers:	crew of two pilots and up to fifteen passengers or 1,200 lbs (544 kg) of cargo or insecticide
Powerplant:	three 300 hp Wright Whirlwind J-6R75A piston engines
Performance:	Max Speed: 152 mph (245 km/h) Cruising Speed: 122 mph (196 km/h)
	Service Ceiling: 19,000 ft (5,791 m) Range: 515 mi (829 km)
Weights:	Empty: 7,500 lbs (3,402 kg) Gross: 12,500 lb (5,670 kg)
Dimensions:	Span: 77 ft 10 in (23.72 m) Length: 49 ft 3 in (15.01 m)
	Height: Wing Area: 835 sq ft (77.57 sq m)
Armament:	None
Cost:	Unknown

General Aircraft
HOTSPUR

The General Aircraft Hotspur was initially designed as a combat assault glider. It featured all-wood construction with plywood skins. Although it was a successful design, only 20 Hotspurs were ever used operationally during the Second World War. However over one thousand Mk II and Mk III versions were used by various glider training schools. The Mk II had a reduced wing span (reduced by 16 ft (4.88 m)) and featured dual controls and modified flaps and ailerons. Canada acquired 22 examples for training purposes.

This is an idyllic in-flight view of the General Aircraft Hotspur glider. The type was primarily used as a training aircraft for glider ops familiarization. (RCAF photo)

DETAILS

Designation:	**Model No:**	**Marks:** Mk II	**Role:** Glider
TOS: 1942	**SOS:** 1945	**No:** 22	**Service:** RCAF

SPECIFICATIONS

Manufacturer: General Aircraft Company
Crew/Passengers: two pilots and up to six troops or a variety of stores
Powerplant: None
Performance: Max Speed: 130 mph (209 km/h) — Landing Speed: 56 mph (90 km/h)
Service Ceiling: 10,000 ft (3,345 m) — Range: Tow plane dependent
Weights: Empty: 1,661 lb (753 kg) — Gross: 3,598 lb (1,632 kg)
Dimensions: Span: 61 ft 11 in (18.87 m) — Length: 39 ft 4 in (11.99 m)
Height: 10 ft 10 in (3.30 m) — Wing Area: 272 sq ft (25.27 sq m)
Armament: None
Cost: Unknown

Gloster
METEOR

The Gloster Meteor was the first operational jet fighter to be introduced into Allied service during the Second World War. It entered active service with the RAF in the summer of 1944 and many of its first missions were flown to counter the "Buzz Bomb" V-1 attacks being launched against Britain. Two Canadian pilots flying Meteors scored victories in this campaign. Flying Officer W. McKenzie, while flying with No. 616 (RAF) Squadron shot down a V-1 "Doodlebug" on 8 August 1944, while Flying Officer J. Ritch scored yet another the next day. In the post-war period of 1945, the RAF shipped a Meteor Mk III to Canada for test and evaluation purposes. A further three

Meteor aircraft were to arrive for similar purposes. The experience of the Canadian "jet" pilots in the Meteors helped solidify the early procurement of the De Havilland Vampire as Canada's first operational jet fighter in 1948. However, the RCAF was not yet finished with the Meteor. In June 1950, the Minister of National Defence confirmed the re-deployment of 421 Squadron back overseas "in order to acquire experience in the latest technique of air operations." No. 421 Squadron was subsequently equipped with (RAF-owned) Meteor Mk 7 aircraft for these operations in England.

A nice view of one the RAF Gloster Meteor jet fighter aircraft used for post-war cold-weather evaluations. (CF Photo)

DETAILS

Designation:	**Model No:** G41.D	**Marks:** F Mk III, F Mk IV, T Mk 7	**Role:** Fighter, Test/Evaluation
TOS: 1945	**SOS:** 1948	**No:** 4	**Service:** RCAF

SPECIFICATIONS F Mk III

Manufacturer:	Gloster Aircraft
Crew/Passengers:	one pilot
Powerplant:	two 2,000 lb thrust Rolls-Royce Derwent 1 centrifugal turbojet engines
Performance:	Max Speed: 410 mph (660 km/h) Cruising Speed:
	Service Ceiling: 44,000 ft (13,410 m) Range: 1,000 mi (1,610 km)
Weights:	Empty: 8,140 lb (3,693 kg) Gross: 13,800 lb (6,260 kg)
Dimensions:	Span: 43 ft 0 in (13.11 m) Length: 41 ft 4 in (12.60 m)
	Height: 13 ft 0 in (3.96 m) Wing Area:
Armament:	four 20 mm Hispano cannon
Cost:	Unknown

Grumman
ALBATROSS

In the RCAF, the Grumman Albatross was selected to replace the Second World War Canso amphibian employed on post-war Search and Rescue duties. It filled similar roles for the United States Air Force, Navy and Coast Guard as well as other western nations. Designed as an amphibian, the aircraft could operate from land, water or unprepared snow and ice surfaces by using removable skid and ski gear. Reversible propellers gave it manouevrability on the water and shortened the landing run while JATO (Jet Assisted Take-Off) bottles could be used to get the aircraft airborne quickly under adverse take-off conditions. The aircraft type was last operated in Comox by 442 Squadron and was replaced by the CC115 Buffalo aircraft.

The Albatross SAR aircraft proved to be highly versatile, operating from land, water or ice. (RCAF Photo)

DETAILS

Designation: CSR-110   **Model No:**   **Role:** Amphibian, SAR, Transport
TOS: 1960   **SOS:** 1970   **No:** 10   **Service:** RCAF

SPECIFICATIONS

Manufacturer:	Grumman Aircraft Corporation	
Crew/Passengers:	two pilots with eight to twelve passengers	
Powerplant:	two 1425 hp Wright R1820-82 radial engines	
Performance:	Max Speed: 185 kts (343 km/h)	Cruising Speed: 155 kts (287 km/h)
	Service Ceiling: 22,000 ft (6,705 m)	Range: 2,849 nm (5,280 km) with drop tanks
Weights:	Empty: 22,883 lbs (10,379 kg)	Maximum Take-off: 35,500 lbs (16,100 kg)
Dimensions:	Span: 96 ft 8 in (29.46 m)	Length: 63 ft 7 in (19.38 m)
	Height: 25 ft 10 in (7.87 m)	Wing Area: 1,035 sq ft (96.15 sq m)
Armament:	none	
Original Cost:	$1,026,155	

Grumman
AVENGER

The Grumman Avenger made a major contribution to the outcome of the Second World War as a carrier-based naval aircraft. Procured in large numbers, the type saw action with Allied Forces in virtually all theatres of operation. Robust and reliable, the Avenger survived in large numbers into the post-war period and was adapted to a wide variety of uses. In 1951, the Royal Canadian Navy's anti-submarine 880 and 881 Squadrons were re-equipped with wartime Avengers which had been overhauled, modified and brought up to date. The RCN Avengers were fitted with the Magnetic Anomaly Detection (MAD) boom for submarine detection, the first fleet in Canadian service to be so modified. Other visible fittings included the UPD 501 (fitted below the engine cowling and above the MAD boom) to pick up radar signals and allow direction finding, and four zero-length rocket rails on the lower surface of the wing. In 1955, a further 8 TBM-3W2 AEW aircraft were acquired with extensive modifications fitted, including a rotating radar receiver-transmitter housed in a large bulbous under-fuselage radome. These "Guppy" aircraft made up the AEW Flight of 880 Squadron, providing long range "look-out" for the fleet. In addition to ASW and AEW duties, Avenger squadrons also provided aircraft for the Observer School, target towing, pilot proficiency, and miscellaneous fleet duties.

The RCN Avenger from HMCS *Shearwater*, Nova Scotia, shown here is an AS3 variant similar to the USN's TBM-3E. (CF Photo)

DETAILS

Designation: TBF/TBM   **Model No:** TBM-3E   **Marks:** Mk AS3, AS3M, AS3M2, TBM–3W2
Role: Fleet ASW, AEW, Utility
TOS: 1951   **SOS:** 1960   **No:** 125 (total) TBM-3W2 (8)   **Service:** RCN

SPECIFICATIONS Mk AS3

Manufacturer:	Grumman Aircraft; Canadian modifications by Fairey Aviation Company Ltd
Crew/Passengers:	one pilot, two crew
Powerplant:	one 1,750 hp Wright Cyclone GR-2600-20 radial piston engine

Performance:	Max Speed: 259 mph (417 km/h)	Cruising Speed: 171 mph (275 km/h)
	Service Ceiling: 23,000 ft (7,010 m)	Range: 1,020 mi (1,642 km)
Weights:	Empty: 10,600 lb (4,808 kg)	Gross: 16,300 lb (7,394 kg)
Dimensions:	Span: 54 ft 2 in (16.50 m)	Length: 40 ft 0 in (12.19 m)
	Height: 15 ft 8 in (4.78 m)	Wing Area: 490 sq ft (45.52 m)
Armament:	Provisions for two fixed 0.50 cal (12.7 mm) machine guns in the wings and two machine guns in dorsal and ventral positions plus provisions for up to 2,000 lbs (907 kgs) of bombs, depth charges, rockets or fuel tanks	
Cost:	Unknown	

Grumman
GOBLIN

The G-23 Goblin was based on the Grumman FF-1 two-seat naval biplane fighter. In 1937 the Canadian Car and Foundry Company acquired a license to build the Grumman FF-1 aircraft, known as the Goblin, and subsequently manufactured 57 of these aircraft. The majority of these aircraft were exported and although the type had been offered to the RCAF, it was not originally considered suitable. The aircraft had been assessed as too slow and obsolete. The advent of war gradually changed this bleak assessment and the RCAF acquired the final batch of 15 aircraft. In December of 1940, "A" Flight of No.

118 Squadron was equipped with Goblins at Rockcliffe in Ottawa, and subsequently became No. 118 (Fighter) Squadron. Later the unit moved to Dartmouth, Nova Scotia where the Squadron's aircraft for a time constituted the sole fighter force on the east coast. Late in 1941 the Goblins were supplemented by more modern P-40 Kittyhawks but they were not completely replaced until May 1942. No. 123 (Army Co-operation) Squadron also flew five Goblins for a brief time but had disposed of them by the end of March 1942.

An interesting formation of RCAF Goblins. Note the differences in canopies. (CF Photo)

DETAILS

Designation:	**Model No:** G-23	**Marks:** Mk I	**Role:** Fighter
TOS: 1940	**SOS:** 1942	**No:** 15	**Service:** RCAF

SPECIFICATIONS

Manufacturer:	Canadian Car and Foundry Company under license from Grumman
Crew/Passengers:	one pilot and one observer
Powerplant:	one 745 hp Wright R-1820-F53 Cyclone radial
Performance:	Max Speed: 223 mph (359 km/h) Cruising Speed:
	Service Ceiling: 29,400 ft (8,960 m) Range:
Weights:	Empty: 3,279 lb (1,488 kg) Gross: 4,728 lb (2,146 kg)
Dimensions:	Upper Span: 34 ft 6 in (10.51 m) Length: 24 ft 6 in (7.47 m)
	Height: 11 ft 1 in (3.78 m) Wing Area: 310 sq ft (28.80 sq m)
Armament:	Two forward firing .30 Browning machine guns and one flexible mount for the observer
Cost:	Unknown

Grumman
GOOSE

The Grumman Goose was a twin-engine amphibian designed primarily for the civil market. The eight-seat design first flew on 29 May 1937. However, its modern design quickly garnered the attention of various militaries. The RCAF acquired the first example for use in 1938 and it was employed on communication and light transportation duties. During the Second World War, further aircraft were acquired and the design's versatility and ruggedness saw it through the conflict and well into the post-war era.

This view shows a pristine-looking RCAF Grumman Goose aircraft on the tarmac. Although some aircraft could be found in camouflage colours, many aircraft in service were finished similar to the plain silver paint scheme illustrated here. (RCAF Photo)

DETAILS

Designation:	**Model No:** G-21A	**Marks:** Mk II	**Role:** Amphibian, Transport
TOS: 1938	**SOS:** 1956	**No:** 31	**Service:** RCAF

SPECIFICATIONS

Manufacturer:	Grumman Aircraft
Crew/Passengers:	two crew and five to seven passengers
Powerplant:	two 450 hp Pratt & Whitney Wasp Jr R-985-AN-6 radials
Performance:	Max Speed: 201 mph (323 km/h) Cruising Speed: 191 mph (307 km/h)
	Service Ceiling: 21,300 ft (6,492 m) Range: 640 miles (1,030 km)
Weights:	Empty: 5,425 lbs (2,461 kg) Maximum Take-off: 8,000 lbs (3,629 kg)
Dimensions:	Span: 49 ft 0 in (14.95 m) Length: 38 ft 6 in (11.73 m)
	Height: 16 ft 2 in (4.93 m) Wing Area: 375 sq ft (34.84 sq m)
Armament:	none
Original Cost:	unknown

Grumman
TRACKER (DeHavilland)

The Grumman Tracker was Canadian built by DeHavilland under license from Grumman aircraft for use as an ASW aircraft in the Royal Canadian Navy. The Tracker was built to be flown hard. Originally used for anti-submarine warfare work off HMCS *Bonaventure*, the Canadian Tracker was built 18 inches shorter than its American counterpart to allow it to fit in the *Bonnie's* hangar. This carrier-borne aircraft was a state-of-the art, all-weather ASW platform carrying the latest electronic gear. For such a compact airframe, the Tracker boasted a respectable amount of equipment to fulfil its duties, including a Magnetic Anomaly Detector (MAD) boom, surface-search radar, internal bomb bay for bombs, depth charges or torpedoes, spotlight, sonobuoy dispensers and wing pylons for bombs or rockets. With integration of the CF, the aircraft type was then land-based and used for

coastal patrol and maritime surveillance work until it was retired. In service from 1956 until 1989, the Tracker was one of the longest-serving piston-engine aircraft in the Canadian Forces inventory.

Two late-model CP-121 Trackers, as evidenced by the low-visibility paint schemes. The photo on the bottom illustrates some of the armament the aircraft could carry, in this case six LAU-5002 rocket pods with their CRV7 rockets. (Author's collection & CF Photo)

DETAILS

Designation: CP-121	**Model No:** S-2, CS2F-1, CS2F-2	**Role:** ASW, Patrol	
TOS: 1956	**SOS:** 1989	**No:** 101	**Service:** RCN, CF

SPECIFICATIONS

Manufacturer:	DeHavilland Canada license-built version of the Grumman design
Crew/Passengers:	two pilots and two crew
Powerplant:	two 1525 hp Wright R-1820-82 engines
Performance:	Max Speed: 287 kts (532 km/h) — Cruising Speed: 130 kts (240.9 km/h)
	Service Ceiling: 10,000 ft (305 m) — Range: 1200 nm (2,228 km)
Weights:	Empty: 17,500 lb (7,945 kg) — Gross: 24,193 lb (10,984 kg)
Dimensions:	Span: 69 ft 8 in (21.23 m) — Length: 42 ft 3 in (12.88 m)
	Height: 16 ft 3½ in (4.96 m) — Wing Area: 485 sq ft (45.1 sq m)
Armament:	Provision for six Mk 43 torpedoes and/or CRV7 rockets in bomb bays or underwing pylons
Original Cost:	$1,100,000

Handley Page
HALIFAX

Names painted on the sides of RCAF Halifax bombers, like "Willy the Wolf," "The Champ," "Big Chief Wa-Hoo," and "Vicky the Vicious Virgin" reflected the affection that Canadian wartime crews felt for the big four-engine bombers. They could absorb tremendous punishment and still fly home. One Halifax aircraft, named "Friday the Thirteenth," survived 128 sorties. The Halifax was perhaps overshadowed by its larger cousin in Bomber Command, the Avro Lancaster, but many Canadian crews were more than satisfied with the aircraft type and it was perhaps Canada's most important bomber in the Second World War. Apart from the bomber offensive, the Halifax was also used in Coastal Command to hunt submarines, and for special operations such as towing gliders or making parachute drops of supplies and agents in occupied territories.

"O" for Oscar, a Halifax bomber from 424 "Tiger" Squadron is shown here taxing for take off. During its career with the Tigers, it completed 62 sorties on enemy targets. This Halifax III is equipped with Bristol Hercules radial engines but other versions used the more well known Rolls-Royce Merlin engines (top right). (RCAF Photos)

DETAILS
Model No: HP 56, 57, 58, 59, 60, 61, 62, 63   **Marks:** Mk I, II, III, IV, V, VI, VII
Role: Bomber, ASW, Transport and Glider Tug
TOS: 1940   **SOS:** 1945   **No:** 84 Mk I, 1,977 Mk II, 2,091 Mk III
Service: RAF/RCAF 904 Mk V, 467 Mk VI, 35 Mk VII

SPECIFICATIONS Mk III
Manufacturer:	Handley Page Aircraft Ltd designed and built
Crew/Passengers:	seven crew (pilot, navigator, bomb aimer, radio operator, gunners)
Powerplant:	Four Rolls Royce Merlin or Bristol Hercules XVI radial engines at 1,615 hp
Performance:	Max Speed: 280 mph (450 km/h) at 13,500 ft
	Service Ceiling: 41,000 ft (12,496 m) Range: 3,000 m (4,830 km)
Weights:	Empty: 36,000 lbs (16,320 kg) Gross: 65,000 lbs (29,450 kg)
Dimensions:	Span: 98 ft 10 in (30.2 m) Length: 70 ft 1 in (21.4 m)
	Wing Area: 1,200 sq ft (111.5 sq m)
Armament:	Nine Browning .303 calibre machine guns plus provisions for 13,000 lbs (5,900 kg) of bombs or stores
Original Cost:	Unknown

Handley Page
HAMPDEN

Known as the "Flying Suitcase," the Hampden was one of three bomber types (including the Wellington and Whitley) that formed the backbone of the RAF's Bomber Command in 1939. Armed originally with only three machine guns and used in daylight bombing raids, increasing losses forced an increase in armament and a switch to night ops. The Hampden served operationally in Bomber Command until September 1942 and then soldiered in Coastal Command as a torpedo bomber and minelayer until December 1943. Two RCAF bomber squadrons, No. 408 and 420 Squadron, and one RCAF torpedo bomber squadron, No. 415 Squadron, used this aircraft type in overseas operations. After they were withdrawn from active service, Hampdens still carried on in the training role. Some 200 of these aircraft were flown to Canada where they were used for bombing and gunnery training. There were 160 Hampdens built in Canada during the war.

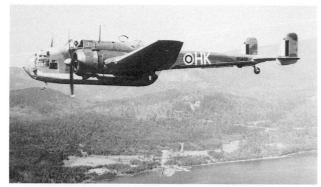
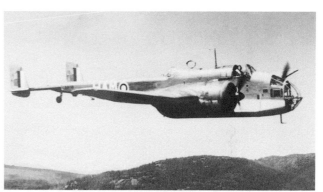
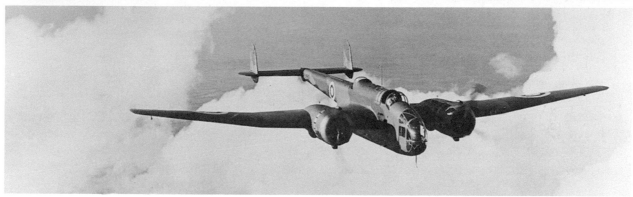

On the home front, Handley Page Hampdens were primarily seen on Canada's west coast where they were used by an operational training unit. (CF Photos)

DETAILS

Designation:	**Model No:** HP52	**Marks:** B Mk I, TB Mk I	**Role:** Bomber, Torpedo Bomber, Trainer
TOS: 1941	**SOS:** 1944	**No:** 96	**Service:** RCAF

SPECIFICATIONS Mark I

Manufacturer:	Handley Page Aircraft Ltd	
Crew/Passengers:	crew of four	
Powerplant:	two 1,000 hp (746 kW) Bristol Pegasus XVII radial engines	
Performance:	Max Speed: 254 mph (409 km/h)	Cruising Speed: 167 mph (269 km/h)
	Service Ceiling: 19,000 ft (5,791 m)	Range: 1,885 ft (3,034 m)
Weights:	Empty: 11,780 lb (5.343 kg)	Maximum Take-off: 18,756 lb (8,508 kg)
Dimensions:	Span: 69 ft 2 in (21.08 m)	Length: 53 ft 7 in (16.33 m)
	Height: 14 ft 11 in (4.55 m)	Wing Area: 668 sq ft (62.06 sq m)
Armament:	two forward firing and twin .303 in (7.7 mm) machine guns, the latter in dorsal and ventral positions plus provisions for up to 4,000 lb (1,814 kg) in bombs or torpedoes	
Cost:	Unknown	

Handley Page
HARROW

Originally designed as a bomber, the Handley-Page Harrow was already obsolete at the outbreak of the Second World War. Consequently, it saw far more use as a transport. Prior to war, a British civilian company brought two Harrows to Newfoundland in preparation for a projected trans-Atlantic aerial refuelling service. Britain had been a pioneer in experiments of this nature prior to the war. With hostilities commenced, the RCAF then acquired both Harrow aircraft for transport use. It appears, however, that only one of these aircraft was flown in active service during a brief one-year period.

A Handley Page Harrow transport on the tarmac in Nova Scotia shown in its original civilian markings. (Comox AFM Photo)

DETAILS

Designation:	**Model No:** HP 54	**Marks:** Mk II	**Role:** Transport
TOS: 1940	**SOS:** 1941	**No:** 2	**Service:** RCAF

SPECIFICATIONS Mk II

Manufacturer:	Handley Page Aircraft Company	
Crew/Passengers:	crew of five plus provision for twenty passengers	
Powerplant:	two 925 hp (690 kW) Bristol Pegasus XX radial engines	
Performance:	Max Speed: 200 mph (322 km/h)	Cruising Speed: 163 mph (262 km/h)
	Service Ceiling: 22,800 ft (6,949 m)	Range: 1,250 mi (2,012 km)
Weights:	Empty: 13,600 lbs (6,169 kg)	Gross: 23,000 lbs (10,433 kg)
Dimensions:	Span: 88 ft 5 in (26.95 m)	Length: 82 ft 2 in (25.04 m)
	Height: 19 ft 11 in (6.07 m)	Wing Area: 1,090 sq ft (101.26 sq m)
Armament:	none, but provision for four 0.303 in (7.7 mm) machine guns	
Original Cost:	Unknown	

Hawker
AUDAX

The Hawker Hart light day-bomber entered service with the RAF in 1930. Its exceptional speed and performance prompted a number of variants for specific roles, such as the Audax, Demon, Hind, and Osprey. The Audax also saw RCAF service. The Audax was an army cooperation variant featuring the Hart's engine and armament but with lengthened exhaust manifolds and a message pick-up hook mounted on an undercarriage spreader bar. The design was intended to replace the Armstrong Whitworth Atlas, and which the RCAF employed in this same role. Their actual use is unclear, but it is likely that the aircraft were used as instructional training aids prior to their withdrawal from service in 1943.

A wintry view of the streamlined Hawker Audax on skis showing the extended exhaust and the pick-up hook underneath the fuselage. (LAC Photo #62981)

DETAILS

Designation:	Model No:	Marks:	Role: Utility
TOS: 1933	SOS: 1943	No: 6	Service: RCAF

SPECIFICATIONS

Manufacturer:	Hawker Aircraft Company	
Crew/Passengers:	one pilot and one observer/gunner	
Powerplant:	one 525 hp (391 kW) Rolls-Royce Kestrel IB engine	
Performance:	Max Speed: 172 mph (275 km/h)	Cruising Speed:
	Service Ceiling: 26,400 ft (8,047 m)	Range: 430 mi (692 km)
Weights:	Empty: 3,251 lbs (1,475 kg)	Gross: 4,381 lbs (1,987 kg)
Dimensions:	Span: 37 ft 3 in (11.35 m)	Length: 29 ft 7 in (9.02 m)
	Height: 10 ft 7 in (3.23 m)	Wing Area: 348 sq ft (32.33 sq m)
Armament:	provisions for one forward firing 0.303 in (7.7 mm) machine gun and one 0.303 in (7.7 mm) flexible mount Lewis gun in rear cockpit plus up to 500 lb (227 kg) in light bombs	
Original Cost:	Unknown	

Hawker
HART

Designed as a light day-bomber, the Hawker Hart entered service with the RAF in 1930. At the time, it was one of the fastest aircraft, out-performing other bombers and even front-line fighters. The exceptional performance of the design then prompted a number of variants for specific roles. These other variants such as the Audax, Demon, Hind, and Osprey were similar in overall appearance but differed in mission and equipment fit. The Audax and Hind also saw RCAF service. By 1937, however, even the Hart itself was being badly outclassed by contemporary designs. Nevertheless the RCAF acquired a few examples

in that year. Their actual role is unclear, but it is likely that the aircraft served as instructional training aids prior to their withdrawal from use in 1943.

Two views of the Hawker Hart light bomber, which had outclassed contemporary fighter designs in terms of its overall performance. (Author's Collection)

DETAILS

Designation:	**Model No:**	**Marks:**	**Role:** Utility
TOS: 1937	**SOS:** 1943	**No:** 3	**Service:** RCAF

SPECIFICATIONS Hind data

Manufacturer:	Hawker Aircraft Company
Crew/Passengers:	one pilot and one observer/gunner
Powerplant:	one 525 hp (391 kW) Rolls-Royce Kestrel IB engine
Performance:	Max Speed: 186 mph (299 km/h) Cruising Speed:
	Service Ceiling: 26,400 ft (8,047 m) Range: 430 mi (692 km)
Weights:	Empty: 3,251 lbs (1,475 kg) Gross: 5,298 lbs (2,403 kg)
Dimensions:	Span: 37 ft 3 in (11.35 m) Length: 29 ft 4 in (8.94 m)
	Height: 10 ft 7 in (3.23 m) Wing Area: 348 sq ft (32.33 sq m)
Armament:	provisions for one forward firing 0.303 in (7.7 mm) machine gun and one 0.303 in (7.7 mm) flexible mount Lewis gun in rear cockpit plus up to 500 lb (227 kg) in light bombs
Original Cost:	Unknown

Hawker
HIND

The Hawker Hart entered service with the RAF in 1930. The Hind was an improved version of the Hart featuring a more powerful Rolls-Royce Kestrel engine, a tail wheel vice tail skid, a cut-down rear fuselage to improve the field of fire, and an improved prone position for bomb aiming. The Hind briefly saw RCAF service commencing in 1942. By 1942, however, the Hind was being badly outclassed by contemporary designs. It is likely that the aircraft were used as instructional training aids prior to their withdrawal from use in 1943.

This streamlined Hawker Hind is a restored example belonging to the Canadian Aviation Museum. (APP Photo)

DETAILS

Designation:	**Model No:**	**Marks:**	**Role:** Utility
TOS: 1942	**SOS:** 1943	**No:** 4	**Service:** RCAF

SPECIFICATIONS

Manufacturer: Hawker Aircraft Company
Crew/Passengers: one pilot and one observer/gunner
Powerplant: one 640 hp (477 kW) Rolls-Royce Kestrel V piston engine
Performance: Max Speed: 186 mph (299 km/h)   Cruising Speed:
Service Ceiling: 26,400 ft (8,047 m)   Range: 430 mi (692 km)
Weights: Empty: 3,251 lbs (1,475 kg)   Gross: 5,298 lbs (2,403 kg)
Dimensions: Span: 37 ft 3 in (11.35 m)   Length: 29 ft 7 in (9.02 m)
Height: 10 ft 7 in (3.23 m)   Wing Area: 348 sq ft (32.33 sq m)
Armament: provisions for one forward firing 0.303 in (7.7 mm) machine gun and one 0.303 in (7.7 mm) flexible mount Lewis gun in rear cockpit plus up to 510 lb (230 kg) in light bombs
Original Cost: Unknown

Hawker
HURRICANE

First flown in 1935, the Hurricane served throughout the Second World War in virtually every theatre of operations. The RCAF received its first Hurricanes in February 1939. The first RCAF squadron to fire its guns in anger, No. 401 Squadron, flew Hurricanes in the Battle of Britain. Two other RCAF squadrons, No. 402 and 417 Squadron, flew the type in overseas operations, while a further ten squadrons operated the aircraft in Canada.

The Canadian Car and Foundry Company began Canadian production in January 1940 at Fort William. A total of 1,451 Hurricanes were built in this country. While not so graceful or well known as its fighting mate, the Spitfire, the Hurricane proved to be rugged in service and highly adaptable, and was used in a wide variety of roles carrying diverse types of weapons and armament.

The Hawker Hurricane was the RAF's premiere fighter at the beginning of the Second World War. At the outbreak of hostilities, it was also the RCAF's only modern fighter. This RCAF Hurricane has been preserved by the Canada Aviation Museum. (CF Photo)

DETAILS

Designation:	**Model No:**	**Marks:** Mk I, IIA, IIB, IIC, IV, XII, XIIA	**Role:** Fighter
TOS: 1939	**SOS:** 1948	**No:** 503	**Service:** RCAF

SPECIFICATIONS Mark I

Manufacturer: Built by Canadian Car & Foundry Company under license from Hawker
Crew/Passengers: one pilot
Powerplant: one 1,300 hp (768 kW) Rolls Royce Merlin II or III engine
Performance: Max Speed: 318 mph (512 km/h) Cruising Speed:
Service Ceiling: 33,400 ft (10,180 m) Range: 440 mi (708 km)
Weights: Empty: 4,670 lb (2,118 kg) Gross: 6,600 lb (2,994 kg)
Dimensions: Span: 40 ft 0 in (12.14 m) Length: 31 ft 5 in (9.58 m)
Height: 13 ft 1 in (3.99 m) Wing Area: 258 sq ft (23.97 sq m)
Armament: eight .303 in (7.7 mm) Browning machine guns
Cost: $50,000

Hawker
SEA FURY

The Hawker Sea Fury was a single-seat carrier borne fighter-bomber. It was one of the longest lived of all Hawker designs; conceived in 1942, the type was still in production and for sale as late as 1960. It even saw combat action with the RN in Korea. The RCN equipped No. 803 and 883 Squadron (later designated VF-870 and VF-871) with the type and these squadrons flew 75 Sea Furies from February, 1948 to April, 1957 operating from both HMCS *Magnificent* and its replacement, HMCS *Bonaventure*. One of the Sea Furys acquired was

a Mk.10 while the other 74 were F.B. Mk.11s. These were both single seat fighters and fighter-bombers, and were similar except that the Mk 11s were equipped to carry the 100/1,000 pound jettisonable wing bomb carriers. The outer portions of the wings of both models could be folded upwards hydraulically to facilitate stowage below decks on an aircraft carrier. The RCN Sea Fury aircraft were replaced by the RCN's first jet fighter, the McDonnell F2H3 Banshee.

This view of an RCN Sea Fury illustrates its full naval heritage with the folded wings. This aircraft is now part of the Canada Aviation Museum collection (CF Photo)

DETAILS

Designation:	**Model No:**	**Marks:** FB X, XI	**Role:** Fighter Bomber
TOS: 1948	**SOS:** 1957	**No:** 75	**Service:** RCN

SPECIFICATIONS FB XI

Manufacturer:	Hawker Aircraft Company	
Crew/Passengers:	one pilot	
Powerplant:	one 2,480 hp Bristol Centaurus 18 radial engine	
Performance:	Max Speed: 460 mph (740 km/h)	Cruising Speed: 270 mph (435 km/h)
	Service Ceiling: 36,000 ft (10,970 m)	Range: 1,250 mi (2,012 km)
Weights:	Empty: 12,500 lbs (5,670 kg)	Gross: 21,000 lbs (9,525 kg)
Dimensions:	Span: 38 ft 4½ in (11.71 m)	Length: 34 ft 8 in (10.56 m)
	Height: 15 ft 10½ in (4.82 m)	Wing Area: 280 sq ft (26.01 sq m)
Armament:	four 20mm cannon plus provisions for 12 x 60 lb (27 kg) rockets or two 1,000 lb (454 kg) bombs	
Original Cost:	Unknown	

Hawker
TEMPEST

The Hawker Tempest was one of the finest fighters of the Second World War. A successor to the Hawker Typhoon, the Tempest was rushed into service and to a large extent helped diffuse the V-1 flying rocket attacks on southern England in 1944. The aircraft's outstanding performance allowed it to catch up to and destroy many of these vengeance weapons. As with the Typhoon, many RCAF pilots flew the Tempest while being posted to RAF Squadrons. The aircraft also performed well against superior German jet aircraft such as the Me-262, and an RCAF pilot scored the first such victory while flying a Tempest. The Tempest continued in operation until the end of the war in Europe. Despite being well liked, however, the type was replaced by jet-powered Meteors and Vampires in the post-war period. The RCAF only "officially" brought one aircraft, a Mk VI (number NV999), on strength in this post-war period, for one year, from February 1946 to February 1947, for trials purposes.

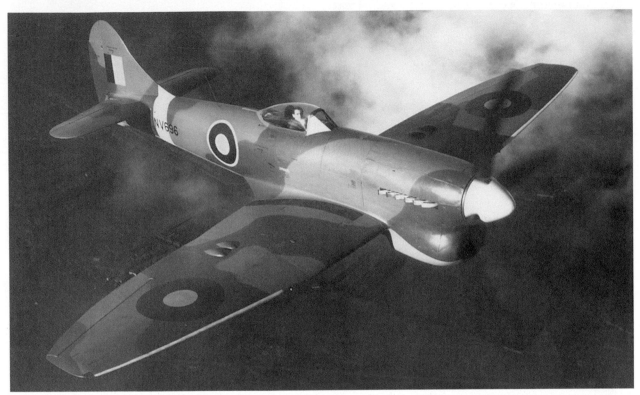

A nice view of the Hawker Tempest clearly illustrating its Typhoon predecessor's heritage with its distinctive "blown" Plexiglas canopy and nose (chin) mounted radiator. (RAF Photo)

DETAILS
Designation: | **Model No:** | **Marks:** Mk VI | **Role:** Fighter/Fighter Bomber
TOS: 1946 | **SOS:** 1947 | **No:** 1 | **Service:** RCAF

SPECIFICATIONS Mk V
Manufacturer: Hawker Aircraft Company
Crew/Passengers: one pilot
Powerplant: one 2,180 hp Napier Sabre IIA in-line piston engine
Performance: Max Speed: 426 mph (686 km/h) | Cruising Speed:
Service Ceiling: 36,500 ft (11,125 m | Range: 1,530 mi (2,462 km)
Weights: Empty: 9,000 lbs (4,082 kg) | Gross: 13,540 lbs (6,142 kg)
Dimensions: Span: 41 ft 0 in (12.50 m) | Length: 33 ft 8 in (10.26 m)
Height: 16 ft 1 in (4.90 m) | Wing Area: 302 sq ft (28.06 sq m)
Armament: four 20mm cannon plus provisions for 12 x 60 lb (27 kg) rockets or two 1,000 lb (454 kg) bombs
Original Cost: Unknown

Hawker
TOMTIT

The Hawker Tomtit was designed as a two-seat elementary trainer of all metal construction with fabric covering. Designed to replace long serving Avro 504 trainers in the RAF, it proved to have delightful flying qualities, and it possessed two features not previously seen on an elementary trainer: Handley Page type automatic slots fitted to the upper wings, and full provision for blind-flying instruction was made in the rear cockpit. In addition, the arrangement of the cockpits well clear of the main plane facilitated a rapid exit in the event of emergencies.

However, exactly why the Tomtit was acquired for RCAF use remains somewhat unclear. The RCAF already had three other trainers in service including the Avro Tutor, De Havilland Gipsy Moth and Fleet Fawn. The RCAF therefore only acquired two Hawker Tomtits, numbers 139 and 140, but they remained in service from May 1930 to July 1943. They belonged to No. 7 (General Purpose) Squadron and later to No. 12 (Communications) Squadron, both located at RCAF Station Rockcliffe.

The attractive-looking Hawker Tomtit possessed several features not previously seen on an elementary trainer. (Author's Collection)

DETAILS

Designation: N/A   **Model No:** 621   **Role:** Trainer

TOS: 1930   **SOS:** 1943   **No:** 2   **Service:** RCAF

SPECIFICATIONS

Manufacturer:	HG Hawker Aircraft Engineering Co Ltd
Crew/Passengers:	two pilots
Powerplant:	one 150 hp Amstrong Siddeley Mongoose IIIC radial engine

Performance:	Max Speed: 124 mph (200 km/h)	Cruising Speed: 102 mph (164 km/h)
	Service Ceiling: 19,500 ft (5,944 m)	Range: 350 mi (563 km)
Weights:	Empty: 1,100 lb (499 kg)	Gross: 1,750 lb (794 kg)
Dimensions:	Span: 28 ft 6 in (8.69 m)	Length: 23 ft 8 in (7.21 m)
	Height: 8 ft 4 in (2.54 m)	Wing Area: 238 sq ft (22.11 sq m)
Armament:	None	
Cost:	Unknown	

Hiller
NOMAD

The Hiller Nomad initially served as a light reconnaissance helicopter with the Canadian Army. It was used primarily for aerial observation and brigade liaison duties. Although nominally capable of carrying three personnel, the cramped bubble cockpit was more suited to just two. Optional litters could be strapped to the sides on top of the landing skids. Like many early helicopter designs, the Nomad was perhaps underpowered; its piston engine developed just 305 hp at mean sea level. With the integration of the Canadian Armed Forces, the type became the joint training helicopter for the service first at Rivers, Manitoba and then at CFB Portage La Prairie. The Nomad was a particularly difficult aircraft on which to learn to fly because of its peculiar cyclic actuation system. Two pedals were moved by the cyclic which in turn tilted the rotor blades. Unfortunately, this design also produced a lag in actuation and this lag could be particularly difficult for student pilots to master. In 1972, the Nomad was superseded in the training role by the Bell CH-136 Kiowa.

The CH-112 Hiller Nomad was initially used as a reconnaissance helicopter for the Canadian Army and then transitioned to the training role. (CF Photo)

DETAILS

Designation: CH-112   **Model No:** UH-12E/OH-53D   **Marks:**   **Role:** Light Reconnaissance/Training Helicopter
TOS: 1961   **SOS:** 1972   **No:** 27   **Service:** RCA/RCAF

SPECIFICATIONS

Manufacturer: Hiller
Crew/Passengers: two pilots and one passenger
Powerplant: one six-cylinder Lycoming VO-540-B1D piston engine producing 305 horsepower
Performance: Max Speed: 96 mph (155 km/h)   Cruising Speed: 82 mph (132 km/h)
Service Ceiling: 15,500 ft (4,724m)   Range:
Weights: Empty: 1,896 lb (860 kg)   Gross: 2,750 lb (1,247 kg)
Dimensions: Rotor Diameter: 35 ft 0 in (10.67 m)   Length: 40 ft 8½ in (12.41 m)
Height: 10 ft 1½ in (3.09 m)   Width: 10 ft 0 in (3.05 m)
Armament: none
Cost: $75,021

Keystone
PUFFER

The RCAF acquired two Keystone Puffer aircraft for experimental crop/forest dusting. Starting in 1921, the RCAF and its predecessor, the Canadian Air Board, had been helping the Department of Agriculture in its investigations into forest and crop disease response. After some initial cooperative ventures, in 1927 the Agriculture Department again asked for RCAF assistance. Two pilots were sent to the United States for training in aerial dusting. At the same time, a contract was placed with Keystone Aircraft Corporation of Bristol Pennsylvania for two Huff-Duland aircraft, which had been specifically designed for crop-dusting. One of the aircraft was to be equipped with the standard wheel undercarriage while the other was to be delivered as a float plane. The Huff-Duland aircraft were then re-designated as Keystone Puffers. The aircraft were used for a variety of crop dusting experiments for control of such problems as forest pests, wheat rust and mosquito larvae. The experiments also revealed the hazards of flying a relatively large, heavily laden single-engine aircraft at tree top heights. This drawback led to the purchase of a multi-engine Ford Tri-Motor for increased reliability along with an increased hopper capacity. The Puffer aircraft remained on strength until late 1934 when they were declared obsolete.

Shown here is one of the RCAF's two Keystone Puffers. Note the staining on the lower fuselage from the crop dusting spray. (RCAF Photo)

DETAILS

Designation:	**Model No:**	**Role:** crop dusting wheel or float plane	
TOS: 1927	**SOS:** 1934	**No:** 2	**Service:** RCAF

SPECIFICATIONS

Manufacturer: Keystone Aircraft Corporation
Crew/Passengers: one pilot and up to 1,500 lbs (680 kg) of insecticide
Powerplant: one 200 hp Wright Whirlwind J-4 or J-5C radial piston engine
Performance: Max Speed: 109 mph (175 km/h)   Cruising Speed:
Service Ceiling: 15,250 ft (4,648 m)   Range:
Weights: Empty: 3,140 lbs (1,424 kg)   Gross: 5,500 lb (2,945 kg)
Dimensions: Span: 50 ft 0 in (15.24 m)   Length: 38 ft 3 in (11.65 m)
Height: 14 ft 3 in (4.34 m)   Wing Area:
Armament: None
Cost: Unknown

Lockheed
212

The Lockheed Model 212 was a small, low-winged, twin engine monoplane of all-metal construction. Essentially the design was a further development of the earlier "Model 12" Electra Junior also used by the RCAF. Designated Model 212, this was the military variant of the design proposed by Lockheed in 1938. It was fitted with a dorsal turret having a .303 in machine gun plus a fixed forward weapon of similar calibre and under-fuselage racks for up to eight 100 lb bombs. With no formal or-

ders pending, however, this experimental machine was subsequently brought back to model 12-A standard and delivered to the RCAF in June 1940. Normally, the Model 212 carried two pilots and up to six passengers, but decreasing the passenger complement benefited its range through increased fuel capacity. The RCAF acquired the prototype Model 212, in addition to its ten Electra Juniors, for use as a high-speed executive transport.

The sole RCAF Model 212, shown here, was virtually identical to the more numerous Model 12 Electra Juniors also used by the RCAF. A Noorduyn Norseman can be seen in the background. (LAC Photo #PA-64052)

DETAILS

Designation:	**Model No:** 212	**Role:** Transport	
TOS: 1940	**SOS:** 1945	**No:** 1	**Service:** RCAF

SPECIFICATIONS

Manufacturer:	Lockheed Aircraft Corporation
Crew/Passengers:	two pilots and up to six passengers of
Powerplant:	two Wasp Jr SB engines rated at 400 hp (450 hp for take-off)
Performance:	Max Speed: 225 mph (362 km/h) — Cruising Speed: 213 mph (342 km/h)
	Service Ceiling: 22,900 ft (6,980 m) — Range: 800 mi (1,290 km)
Weights:	Empty: 5,690 lb (2,703 kg) — Gross: 8,650 lb (3,883 kg)
Dimensions:	Span: 49 ft 6 in (15.09 m) — Length: 36 ft 4 in (11.07 m)
	Height: 9 ft 9 in (2.97 m) — Wing Area: 352 sq ft (32.70 sq m)
Armament:	Original provisions for a dorsal turret having a .303 in machine gun plus a fixed forward weapon of similar calibre and under-fuselage racks for up to eight 100 lb (45 kg) bombs
Cost:	Unknown

Lockheed
AURORA

The CP140 Aurora is a four-engine turboprop, long-range maritime patrol aircraft built for the Canadian Forces by Lockeed Corporation. The aircraft type entered service in 1980 to replace the Canadair Argus. The Aurora is a successful marriage of the Lockheed P-3 Orion airframe with then-modern avionics similar to the S-3 Viking carrier-borne aircraft. The aircraft's sensors are primarily intended for antisubmarine work but are also capable of maritime surveillance, counter-drug and search and rescue missions. The P-3 airframe is a variant of the much older Lockheed Electra airliner originally proposed to the United States Navy as a patrol bomber in 1957. In 1976, the Aurora variant won the Canadian Long-Range Patrol Aircraft competition to replace the Argus, and 18 aircraft were delivered commencing in 1980. A further three aircraft with significantly different mission avionics were acquired in the early 1990s for non-ASW roles. These later variants were named Arcturus in CF service. The P-3 airframe currently forms the maritime patrol "backbone" for many nations including the United States, Australia, New Zealand, Japan, Norway, Spain, and Portugal among others.

The CP-140 Aurora maritime patrol aircraft in two different (early & later) colour schemes: In the earlier gray and white scheme, the aircraft is dropping a SKAD (Survival Kit Air Droppable). The fleet was later repainted in a low observable all-grey paint scheme with toned-down markings. (CF Photos)

DETAILS

Designation: CP-140 **Model No:** P-3 **Role:** ASW

TOS: 1980 **SOS:** In service **No:** 18 **Service:** CF

SPECIFICATIONS

Manufacturer: Lockheed Aircraft Corporation

Crew/Passengers: two pilots, one flight engineer, four navigators, four AESOPs

Powerplant: four Allison T-56-A-14 turbine engines

Performance: Max Speed: 405 kts (750 km/h) Cruising Speed: 350 kts (648 km/h)

Service Ceiling: 35,000 ft (10,668 m) Range: 5,000 nm (9,266 km) Endurance: 17 hrs

Weights: Empty: 61,491 lb (27,892 kg) Gross: 142,000 lb (64,410 kg)

Dimensions: Span: 99 ft 8 in (30.37 m) Length: 116 ft 10 in (35.61 m)

Height: 33 ft 9 in (10.30 m) Wing Area: 1,300 sq ft (120.7 sq m)

Armament: provisions for eight Mk 46 torpedoes, depth charges, mines, etc

Original Cost: $24,905,000

Lockheed
ARCTURUS

The CP140 Arcturus is a further development of the four-engine turboprop, long-range maritime patrol CP-140 Aurora aircraft built for the Canadian Forces by Lockeed Corporation. In 1976, the Aurora variant won the Canadian Long-Range Patrol Aircraft competition to replace the Argus, and 18 aircraft were delivered commencing in 1980. Options for a further six CP-140 Aurora aircraft were never initiated. Eventually, however, the need for additional airframes, particularly for flight crew training sorties that caused fatigue damage, was recognized. A further three aircraft (P-3C airframes) with significantly different mission avionics were therefore acquired in the early 1990s for non-antisubmarine warfare roles including marine surface surveillance, Search and Rescue, drug interdiction, and pilot training. These later variants were named Arcturus in CF service. In essence the Arcturus are assigned all the roles of the Aurora, except that of ASW. There are no significant external differences between the CP-140A and CP-140 aircraft, although some minor changes were made to the fuselage structure.

Principal mission systems include the AN/APS-507 surveillance radar. The CP-140A can carry and deploy two SKADs (Survival Kit Air Dropable) and can carry weapons in the internal weapons bay. The latter case is only for transport purposes. There are no underwing attachment points and the sonobuoy tubes are not wired for use. The aircraft does have the tail boom extension but the associated Magnetic Anomaly Detection (MAD) equipment is not fitted. Similarly, the aircraft do not have the belly-mounted vertical camera system. The principle visible external difference is the lack of the wingtip-mounted ESM equipment fitted to the CP-140 aircraft. The CP-140As have four observer stations with bubble windows and the auxiliary escape hatch behind the pilot's seat has an optical window for handheld photography. The three Arcturus aircraft have met their original mandate of reducing wear and tear on the Aurora fleet and provided a vital boost in both maritime and Arctic surveillance capabilities.

CP-140A Arcturus aircraft were purchased principally to relieve the Aurora fleet in demanding pilot proficiency missions. Take-offs, landings and circuit work are hard on the fatigue life of a patrol airframe. (CF Photo)

DETAILS
Designation: CP-140A | **Model No:** P-3 | **Role:** ASW
TOS: 1993 | **SOS:** In service | **No:** 3 | **Service:** CF

SPECIFICATIONS
Manufacturer: Lockheed Aircraft Corporation
Crew/Passengers: two pilots, one flight engineer, and up to fifteen crew/sensor operators
Powerplant: four Allison T-56-A-14 turbine engines
Performance: Max Speed: 405 kts (750 km/h)   Cruising Speed: 350 kts (648 km/h)
Service Ceiling: 35,000 ft (10,668 m)   Range: 5,000 nm (9,266 km) Endurance: 17 hrs
Weights: Empty: 61,491 lb (27,892 kg)   Gross: 142,000 lb (64,410 kg)
Dimensions: Span: 99 ft 8 in (30.37 m)   Length: 116 ft 10 in (35.61 m)
Height: 33 ft 9 in (10.30 m)   Wing Area: 1,300 sq ft (120.7 sq m)
Armament: none but provisions for two SKADs
Original Cost: Unknown

Lockheed
HERCULES

The Hercules, considered to be one of the most versatile heavy-lift planes in the Canadian fleet, is used in the transport of equipment and cargo, in Search and Rescue (SAR) operations and in air-to-air refuelling of fighters. The Hercules can be loaded and unloaded quickly, with little equipment, and is especially useful in delivering supplies because it does not need a lot of room to land. The plane can also be easily re-configured to carry fuel. During Operation Boxtop, the restocking of Canadian Forces Station Alert, the northernmost permanent habitation in the world, the aircraft are fitted with large fuel tanks to transport more than 100 planeloads of fuel. Since entering the fleet in 1960, the Hercules has also delivered humanitarian aid to many trouble spots around the world.

The CC-130 Hercules aircraft is the most versatile aircraft in the CF transport fleet (CF Photo)

DETAILS

Designation: CC-130   **Model No:** H-73, H-80, H-90   **Marks:** C-130 B, E, H, H(T)   **Role:** Transport/AAR Refueller
TOS: 1960   **SOS:** In service   **No:** 44   **Service:** RCAF/CF

SPECIFICATIONS H-Model

Manufacturer:	Lockheed Aircraft Corporation
Crew/Passengers:	Crew: two pilots, one navigator, one flight engineer, and one loadmaster
Troops:	up to ninety, or Paratroops: sixty-four, or Litters: seventy-four plus two attendants
Powerplant:	Four Allison T-54-A-15 turboprop engines with 4,910 EHP (3,661 KW)

Performance:	Max Speed: 368 mph (621 km/h)	Cruising Speed: 355 mph (571 km/h)
	Service Ceiling: 42,900 mph (13,075 km/h)	Range: 5,465 mi (8,795 km)
Weights:	Empty: 76,780 lb (34,827 kg)	Maximum Take-off: 175,000 lb (79,379 kg)
Dimensions:	Span: 132 ft 7 in (40.41 m)	Length: 97 ft 10 in (29.81) m
	Height: 38 ft 1 in (11.61 m)	Wing Area: 1,745.5 sq ft (162.16 sq m)
Armament:	None, but provision for chaff and flare dispensers	
Cost:	CC130B $2,141,440 CC130H(73) $4,973,000 CC130H(84) $22,415,000	

Lockheed
HUDSON

The Lockheed Hudson was developed from the Lockheed Model 14 transport design and became a familiar sight to many members of the RAF, RCAF, RAAF and USAF. The Hudson was used originally for bombing but gained a more prominent niche in anti-shipping and anti-submarine patrol work along with air-sea rescue and meteorological missions. Overseas, No. 407 Squadron flew Hudsons on anti-shipping operations from September 1941 until January 1943. They attacked enemy convoys at mast-height level and bombed more than 400,000 tons of enemy shipping. In Canada, the RCAF flew a total of 243 Hudsons with Nos 11, 113, 119, 120, and 145 Bomber-Reconnaissance Squadrons. No. 11 Squadron formed on the type on 3 November 1939, becoming the first RCAF unit to use the aircraft. The first U-boats sunk by Eastern Air Command (EAC) aircraft were victims of Hudson aircraft flown by No. 113 Squadron (31 July

1942) and No. 145 Squadron (30 October 1942). In all EAC Hudsons made 28 attacks on German submarines. No. 11 Squadron converted to Liberators in August 1944, but Hudsons continued to fly with operational training squadrons, at Nos. 121 and 167 (Composite) Squadrons and with No. 168 (Heavy Transport) Squadron until after the war.

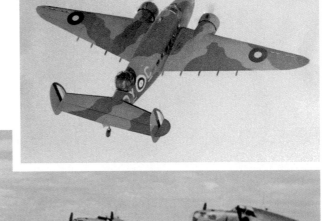

The overhead view of an RCAF Lockheed Hudson Mk I shown here illustrates the wartime camouflage finish and clearly showing the dorsal turret. This Hudson belonged to No. 11 (Bombing & Reconnaissance) Squadron, based at RCAF Station Dartmouth, NS. Developed from a pre-war transport design, the Hudson was a numerically important light bomber in RAF and RCAF service. (Comox AFM and CF Photos)

DETAILS

Designation:	**Model No:** 214, 414	**Marks:** BMk I, II, III, V, VI	**Role:** Patrol
TOS: 1938	**SOS:** 1948	**No:** 247	**Service:** RCAF

SPECIFICATIONS Mk VI

Manufacturer:	Lockheed Aircraft Company
Crew/Passengers:	crew of five
Powerplant:	two 1,200 hp (895 kw) Pratt & Whitney Twin Wasp R-1830-S3C4-G radial engines
Performance:	Max Speed: 261 mph (420 km/h) — Cruising Speed:
	Service Ceiling: 21,000 ft (8,230 m) — Range: 1,160 mi (3,476 km)
Weights:	Empty: 12,929 lbs (5,864 kg) — Gross: 18,500 lbs (8,391 kg)
Dimensions:	Span: 65 ft 6 in (19.96 m) — Length: 44 ft 4 in (13.51 m)
	Height: 11ft 11 in (3.63 m) — Wing Area: 551 sq ft (51.19 sq m)
Armament:	twin .303 in (7.7 mm) machine guns in fixed forward nose position and in dorsal turret position, one .303 in machine gun in ventral position plus an internal bomb bay and underwing pylons for up to 1,000 lbs (227 kg) in bombs, depth charges or fuel tanks
Original Cost:	Unknown

Lockheed
LODESTAR

The Lockheed Lodestar transport design drew heavily from the company's Hudson bomber and earlier transport designs. Lockheed's Model 18 initially combined a new, lengthened fuselage with the Model 14 wings, tail unit and engines. The RCAF acquired a small number of Lodestar aircraft for transport duties. Starting in 1943,

No. 164 Squadron flew Lodestar aircraft on a run from Moncton, NB to Goose Bay, Labrador, transporting essential freight, equipment and personnel during the construction of RCAF Station Goose Bay. The type was also flown by the US Army Air Corps and US Navy.

A fully camouflaged RCAF Lockheed Lodestar VIP transport is shown here on the tarmac. Towards the end of the war, aircraft such as these were stripped of the paint to save both weight and fuel. (LAC Photo # PA-64763)

DETAILS

Designation: 60A	**Model No:** 18	**Marks:** Mk II	**Role:** Transport
TOS: 1943	**SOS:** 1948	**No:** 18	**Service:** RCAF

SPECIFICATIONS

Manufacturer:	Lockheed Aircraft Company	
Crew/Passengers:	crew of three plus provision for fourteen passengers	
Powerplant:	two 1,200 hp Wright Cyclone R-4-1820-87 radial engines	
Performance:	Max Speed: 266 mph (428 km/h)	Cruising Speed: 200 mph (322 km/h)
	Service Ceiling: 30,100 ft (7,620 m)	Range: 2,500 mi (4,023 km)
Weights:	Empty: 12,500 lbs (5,670 kg)	Gross: 21,000 lbs (9,525 kg)
Dimensions:	Span: 65 ft 6 in (19.96 m)	Length: 49 ft 10 in (15.19 m)
	Height: 11 ft 11 in (3.63 m)	Wing Area: 551 sq ft (51.19 sq m)
Armament:	none	
Original Cost:	Unknown	

Lockheed
NEPTUNE

The Neptune was a medium range maritime reconnaissance aircraft originally designed for and equipped with reciprocating engines. In 1952, the Lockheed Aircraft Company developed an improved version of the Neptune, known to the US Navy as the P2V-7, which satisfactorily met RCAF requirements for a medium range reconnaissance aircraft to partially replace the Lancaster in that role. This improved variant was scheduled to come off the production line staring in 1954. In 1957, the decision was made to provide the aircraft with jet thrust augmentation by installing two Westinghouse jet engine pods. The additional thrust improved take-off, increased endurance by allowing higher weights of fuel and generally improved the overall performance of the aircraft.

These two of views of the Lockheed Neptune in Canadian service illustrate the original midnight blue paint scheme and the more standard overall grey and white scheme introduced later in its service career. The J-34 jet-engine pods are clearly visible on the outboard wings. (CF Photos)

DETAILS
Designation: CP-122   **Model No:** P2V-7   **Role:** ASW

TOS: 1955   **SOS:** 1968   **No:** 25   **Service:** RCAF

SPECIFICATIONS
Manufacturer:	Lockheed Aircraft Company
Crew/Passengers	crew of ten
Powerplant:	two Wright R3350-32W Piston engines plus two J34 Westinghouse podded jet engines each with 3,400 lbs thrust

Performance:	Max Speed: 356 mph (572 km/h)	Cruising Speed: 207 mph (333 km/h)
	Service Ceiling: 22,000 ft (6,706 m)	Range: 2,200 mi (3,540 km)
Weights:	Empty: 49,935 lb (22,651 kg)	Maximum Take-off: 79,895 lb (36,240 kg)
Dimensions:	Span: 103 ft 10 in (31.65 m)	Length: 91 ft 8 in (27.94m)
	Height: 29 ft 4 in (8.94 m)	Wing Area: 1,000 sq ft (92.90 sq m)
Armament:	Provision for two torpedoes, mines, depth charges, bombs internally plus rockets externally	
Original Cost:	$1,284,400	

Lockheed
SILVER STAR

The Silver Star is more often referred to as the T-33 or T-Bird. The CT-133 Silver Star has a long and distinguished history with the Canadian Forces. The world's first purpose-built jet trainer, the T-33 evolved from America's first successful jet fighter, the Lockheed P-80 Shooting Star that briefly flew operationally during the Second World War. Initially known as the P-80C, the trainer variant flew better than its single seat cousins. Powered by an Allison J33-35 single-shaft, turbojet engine with a thrust rating of 5,200 lbs, the improvements to the trainer meant it climbed faster, cruised better and overall was slightly faster than the fighter version. In May 1949, the designation for the aircraft was officially switched to T-33. The RCAF's first introduction to the aircraft followed two years later, when the first of twenty Lockheed built T-33As were delivered on loan. The aircraft

were known to the RCAF as the Silver Star Mk 1. This first group was followed by a second loan of ten more aircraft. On 13 September 1951, Canadair signed a licence agreement with Lockheed to build T-33 aircraft for the RCAF. The Canadair built version known internally as the CL-30 (and as the T-33ANX by Lockheed and the USAF) was to be powered by an uprated Nene-10 engine licensed by Rolls Royce and supplied by Orenda Ltd. Once in production, the RCAF designated the new aircraft as the Mk 3 and the original Lockheed aircraft were eventually returned.

The original Lockheed-produced T-33 Silver Stars were externally distinguished by the original F-80-style underwing drop tanks. (RCAF and LAC Photo # PA-67567)

DETAILS

Designation: CT-133	**Model No:** T-33A	**Marks:** Mk I, II	**Role:** Trainer
TOS: 1951	**SOS:** 1966	**No:** 31	**Service:** RCAF/RCN

SPECIFICATIONS Mk I

Manufacturer:	Lockheed Aircraft	
Crew/Passengers:	two crew in ejection seats	
Powerplant:	one Allison J33-A-35 single-shaft, turbojet engine with a thrust rating of 5,200 lbs	
Performance:	Max Speed: 600 mph (965 km/h)	Cruising Speed: 455 mph (732 km/h)
	Service Ceiling: 47,000 ft (14,325 m)	Range: 1,025 mi (1,650 km) with tip tanks
Weights:	Empty: 8,365 lbs (3,794 kg)	Gross: 12,071 lbs (5,475 kg)
Dimensions:	Span: 38 ft 10½ in (11.85 m)	Length: 37 ft 8½ in (11.49 m)
	Height: 11 ft 8 in (3.6 m)	Wing Area: 234.8 sq ft (21.81 sq m)
Armament:	none, but provisions for two 0.50 cal Browning machine guns and underwing pylons	
Original Cost:	Unknown	

Lockheed
STARFIGHTER

Late in 1959, Canadair was selected to produce 200 strike, reconnaissance versions of the Lockheed designed F-104 Starfighter, designated as the CF-104, to replace the F-86 Sabres being flown by the RCAF in NATO. The aircraft was known by a wide variety of nicknames, some flattering and some not so flattering (i.e. the "missile with a man in it" referred to the design while "flying lawn dart" and "widow-maker" referred to the high number crashes the type suffered in the early years). Prior to the delivery of Canadair-built versions of the Starfighter, however, the RCAF acquired a number of Lockheed-built aircraft.

The first was a single-seat variant used for test and evaluation purposes. Subsequently, Lockheed also provided an additional 39 dual aircraft. The Mk. I duals were Dual Training Aircraft, and were intended for use in Canada with the Operational Training Unit (OTU), and therefore were not equipped to carry a bomb dispenser. The OTU was No. 6 Strike/Reconnaissance Operational Training Unit and was later re-designated as 417 Strike/Reconnaissance Operational Training Squadron at RCAF Station/ CFB Cold Lake, Alberta. The CF-104 was replaced in service by the CF-18 Hornet.

A trio of F-104 Starfighters for Germany, Canada and Japan are shown here above Palmdale, California where Lockheed manufactured and tested the aircraft. Later versions of the CF-104 Starfighter were license-built by Canadair (RCAF Photo)

DETAILS

Designation: CF-104 A/D   **Model No:** F-104G   **Marks:** Mk I (A), Mk I (Dual)   **Role:** Fighter/Strike/Dual Trainer

CF104A   **TOS:** 1963   **SOS:** 1969   **No:** 1

CF104D   **TOS:** 1963   **SOS:** 1984   **No:** 39   **Service:** RCAF, CF

SPECIFICATIONS

Manufacturer:	Lockheed Aircraft Corporation
Crew/Passengers:	one or two pilots in ejection seats
Powerplant:	one General Electric (Orenda) J-79-OEL-7 turbojet with afterburning (10,000 lbst to 15,800 lbst in afterburner)
Performance:	Max Speed: Mach 2.2, 1,450 mph (2,334 km/h) Cruising Speed: Mach 1.2, 915 mph
	Service Ceiling: 58,000 ft (17,660 m) Range: 2,180 miles (3,510 km)
Weights:	Empty: 14,082 lb (6,387 kg) Gross: 28,779 lbs (13,510 kg)
Dimensions:	Span: 21 ft 11 in (6.68 m) w/o tip tanks Length: 54 ft 9 in (16.69 m)
	Height: 13 ft 6 in (4.11 m) Wing area: 196 sq ft (18.21 sq m)
Armament:	Provision for one 20 mm M61A-1 cannon, plus bombs, rockets, or tanks on underwing or fuselage pylons
Original Cost:	$1,200,000 single, $1,400,000 dual

Lockheed
VENTURA

The Lockheed Ventura was a military development of the Lockheed Lodestar transport design and both drew heavily from the company's earlier Hudson bomber design. The Lockheed-Vega V-146 Ventura was in use by the RCAF from 16 June 1942 to 18 April 1947 in the home defence coastal patrol role in both Eastern and Western Air Command. They were flown by 8, 113, 115, 145, and 149 Squadrons, as well as by 1 Central Flying School, Trenton, Ontario, and by No. 34 Operational Training Unit, at Penfield Ridge, New Brunswick. A total of 21 Mk. I, 108 Mk. II, and 157 G.R. Mk. V were in service during this period, for a total of 286 aircraft.

Several late model RCAF GR Mk V Venturas are shown here on the tarmac in various locations on Canada's west coast (note the difference in camouflage finishes) (Comox AFM Photos)

DETAILS

Designation: PV-1, PV-2, B-34	**Model No:** V-146	**Marks:** BMk I, II, GR. MkV	**Role:** Patrol
TOS: 1942	**SOS:** 1957	**No:** 286	**Service:** RCAF

SPECIFICATIONS Mk I

Manufacturer:	Lockheed Aircraft Company	
Crew/Passengers:	crew of five	
Powerplant:	two 2,000 hp Pratt & Whitney Double Wasp R-2800-1 radial engines	
Performance:	Max Speed: 300 mph (483 km/h)	Cruising Speed: 260 mph (418 km/h)
	Service Ceiling: 25,000 ft (7,620 m)	Range: 950 mi (1,529 km)
Weights:	Empty: 17,250 lbs (7,824 kg)	Gross: 26,000 lbs (11,793 kg)
Dimensions:	Span: 65 ft 6 in (19.96 m)	Length: 51 ft 3 in (15.62 m)
	Height: 11ft 11 in (3.63 m)	Wing Area: 551 sq ft (51.19 sq m)
Armament:	provisions for up to five 0.50 cal Browning machine guns, an internal bomb bay and underwing pylons for up to 500 lbs (227 kg) in bombs, depth charges or fuel tanks	
Original Cost:	Unknown	

Martin
BALTIMORE

The Martin Baltimore was developed from its predecessor, the Martin Maryland that had been pressed into service at the beginning of the Second World War. The Baltimore was developed in response to a British specification and provided for greater power and a deepened fuselage to allow crew members to move around. The prototype entered service in 1942 and was used by the RAF exclusively in the Mediterranean theatre. RAF Ferry Command loaned a single Baltimore to the RCAF for "special" project duties for a short period in 1942. In all likelihood, these special project duties included spraying gases for various experimental trials.

A view of the sole RCAF Martin Baltimore. (RCAF photo)

DETAILS

Designation:	**Model No:** A-30	**Marks:** Mk III	**Role:** Bomber
TOS: 1942	**SOS:** 1942	**No:** 1	**Service:** RCAF

SPECIFICATIONS Mk III

Manufacturer:	Martin	
Crew/Passengers:	one pilot and three crew	
Powerplant:	two 1,660 hp Wright Cyclone GR-2600-A5B radial engines	
Performance:	Max Speed: 302 mph (486 km/h)	Cruising Speed:
	Service Ceiling: 24,000 ft (7,315 m)	Range: 950 mi (1,529 km)
Weights:	Empty: 10,204 lb (4,629 kg)	Gross: 23,000 lb (10,433 kg)
Dimensions:	Span: 61 ft 4 in (18.69 m)	Length: 48 ft 5¾ in (14.77 m)
	Height: 17 ft 9 in (5.41 m)	Wing Area: 539 sq ft (50.07 sq ft)
Armament:	Provision for eight to ten 0.303 in (7.7 mm) machine guns and 2,000 lb (907 kg) of bombs	
Cost:	Unknown	

Martinsyde
F.6

The Martinsyde Aircraft Company was actively engaged in the construction of a transatlantic monoplane at the outbreak of the First World War. The war years saw the company focus on fighter production although their effective designs never achieved large-scale production. Immediately after the war the company tried to re-enter the civilian market with new long-range designs, primarily intended for mail carriage. The company also returned to its previous transatlantic design interests. While successful transatlantic attempts failed to materialize using Martinsyde aircraft, the design spawned several civil models including a Type A Mk I with two open cockpits and a Type A Mk II with an enclosed cabin for four passengers. The Air Board acquired a Martinsyde F.6, which was a two-seat development of the F.4 design, in 1920 for testing and evaluation purposes. It was transferred for RCAF use in 1922. The aircraft apparently had a brief career in the Air Force, flying primarily from Camp Borden.

A Martinsyde Type A Mk II shown here on floats was very similar in overall lines to the little known Martinsyde F.6. (CF Photo)

DETAILS

Designation:	**Model No:** F.6	**Role:** Utility	
TOS: 1922	**SOS:** 1925	**No:** 1	**Service:** CAF/RCAF

SPECIFICATIONS

Manufacturer:	Martinsyde Aircraft Company		
Crew/Passengers:	two pilots or one pilot and observer		
Powerplant:	one 300 hp Hispano-Suiza piston engine		
Performance:	Max Speed: 145 mph (233 km/h)	Cruising Speed:	
	Service Ceiling:	Range:	
Weights:	Empty: 1,810 lb (821 kg)	Gross:	
Dimensions:	Span: 32 ft 9½ in (9.99 m)	Length: 25 ft 5½ in (7.76 m)	
	Height: 10 ft 4 in (3.15 m)	Wing Area:	
Armament:	None		
Cost:	Unknown		

McDonnell
BANSHEE

Procured second-hand from the USN, the McDonnell F2H-3 Banshee was the only carrier-based air defence jet fighter used by the RCN from 1955 to 1962. Until the CF-18 Hornet, the Banshee, also nicknamed the "Banjo," was the only Canadian military aircraft armed with AIM-9 Sidewinder missiles. The Banshee was a rugged and reliable, all weather, fleet defence and ground attack fighter. In Canadian Navy operational service, all 39 Banshee aircraft were based in Shearwater, NS and flew with VF870 and VF871 Squadrons, until the two were amalgamated as VF870 in 1959. VX10 Experimental Squadron also flew the Banshee in order to do acceptance evaluations. Squadrons were deployed aboard Canada's sole aircraft carrier of the period, HMCS *Bonaventure*. The Banshee was well liked by pilots because of its good performance on the deck and in the air, as well as its all-weather capability, 800-mile tactical radius, and Mach 0.8 speed capability. The aircraft also formed the basis of the RCN's premiere aerobatic team known as the "Grey Ghosts." The four-ship formation team participated in many air shows.

The RCN's only jet fighters were the McDonnell F2H-3 Banshees, which were procured used from the US Navy. (CF Photo)

DETAILS

Designation:	**Model No:** F2H-3	**Marks:**	**Role:** Trainer
TOS: 1955	**SOS:** 1962	**No:** 39	**Service:** RCN

SPECIFICATIONS

Manufacturer:	McDonnell Aircraft Corporation
Crew/Passengers:	one pilot in an ejection seat
Powerplant:	Two Westinghouse J34-WE-34 turbojet engines with a thrust rating of 3,250 lbs
Performance:	Max Speed: 479 mph (771 km/h) Cruising Speed: 248 mph (399 km/h)
	Service Ceiling: 41,100 ft (12,527 m) Range: 1,170 mi (1,882 km)
Weights:	Empty: 6,683 lbs (3,031 kg) Gross: 12,035 lbs (5,459 kg)
Dimensions:	Span: 40 ft 9 in (12.42 m) Length: 38 ft 9 in (11.81 m)
	Height: 14 ft 2 in (4.32 m) Wing Area:
Armament:	four 20mm cannons, plus provisions for two Sidewinders, sixteen rockets, or six 500-lb (227 kg) bombs
Original Cost:	Unknown

McDonnell
VOODOO

A formidable fighter aircraft, the McDonnell F-101 Voodoo was acquired by the RCAF, under some controversy, as a replacement for the CF-100 fleet in Air Defence Command. After the dramatic cancellation of the Canadian designed CF-105 Arrow aircraft just two years before, the nuclear-capable CF-101 Voodoo and the Bomarc missile were acquired by the RCAF in a deal with the United States. As a supersonic, all-weather interceptor, the twin-engine, two-seat Voodoo provided high speed, excellent climb performance and a very good combat radius and ceiling plus additional flexibility in replacing the CF-100. Used almost exclusively in the NORAD defence role, the aircraft type proved to be a safe and reliable weapons platform until replaced by the McDonnell Douglas CF-18 Hornet in the mid-eighties.

This pair of CF101 Voodoos, in late CF service as evidenced by the colour scheme, belonged to 407 (Nighthawks) Squadron based in CFB Comox. (CF Photo)

DETAILS

Designation: CF-101   **Model No:** F-101B/F   **Role:** Fighter Interceptor

TOS: 1961   **SOS:** 1984   **No:** 132   **Service:** RCAF/CF

SPECIFICATIONS

Manufacturer:	McDonnell Aircraft Corporation	
Crew/Passengers:	two crew (pilot/navigator) in ejection seats	
Powerplant:	two Pratt & Whitney J-57-P53/55 Turbojets with 11,990 lbs thrust and 14,990 lbs (A/B)	
Performance:	Max Speed: 1,220 kts (1,963 km/h)	Cruising Speed:
	Service Ceiling: 51,000 ft (15,545 m)	Range: 1,550 m (2,494 km)
Weights:	Empty:	Gross: 39,900 lbs (18,097 m)
	Maximum Take-off: 46,673 lbs (21,171 kg)	
Dimensions:	Span: 39 ft 8 in (12.09 m)	Length: 67 ft 5 in (20.55 m)
	Height: 18 ft 0 in (5.49 m)	Wing Area: 368 sq ft (34.18 sq m)
Armament:	Two AIR-2A Genie nuclear tipped rockets and two AIM-4D Falcon missiles	
Original Cost:	$1,590,000	

McDonnell-Douglas (Boeing)
HORNET

In the 1970s, the Air Force decided that a single multi-role fighter type would replace its CF-101 Voodoos, CF-104 Starfighters and CF-116 Freedom Fighters. The resulting New Fighter Aircraft competition culminated in the selection of the McDonnell-Douglas F/A-18 Hornet. Canada became the first export customer for the type in a contract worth $2.34 billion (Cdn). A number of solely Canadian modifications were incorporated into the aircraft design. These included changes for Canadian unique weapons, a 600,000 candle power searchlight in the starboard nose for night intercepts, a modified survival kit and a land based ILS system replacing the USN automatic carrier landing system. Deployed to Canadian air defence (NORAD) and NATO squadrons, the CF-18 Hornet lived up to all expectations. The multi-role capability of the

Hornet has been repeatedly proven in CF use and the aircraft have been operationally employed in the Gulf War and more recently, in the NATO campaign over Kosovo. In the Gulf War, the aircraft were employed in both CAP and conventional strikes. Flying from Aviano, Italy, in the skies over Kosovo and Serbia, the aircraft was primarily employed in the attack role, dropping both conventional and precision-guided munitions.

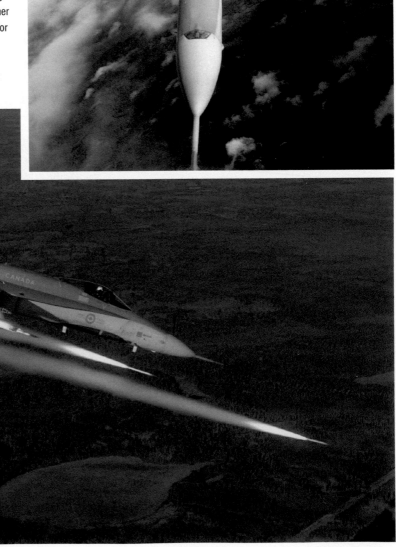

A view of a CF-18 Hornet from the Aerospace Engineering Test Establishment (AETE) firing CRV7 rockets and another view of an AETE aircraft carrying BL-755 cluster bombs for test purposes. Overleaf: Individual examples of the CF-18 Hornet have been regularly painted with various special and colourful designs when employed in the solo aircraft demonstration role. (CF Photos)

DETAILS

Designation: CF-188A/B   **Model No:** F/A-18A/B   **Role:** Fighter

TOS: 1982   **SOS:** In service   **No:** 138 (98 single, 40 dual)   **Service:** CF

SPECIFICATIONS

Manufacturer:	McDonnell-Douglas Aircraft Corporation
Crew/Passengers:	one pilot (CF-18A) or two pilots (CF-18B)
Powerplant:	2 x General Electric F404-GE-400 low-bypass turbofans at 16,000 lb (7,258 kg) thrust

Performance:	Max Speed: Mach 1.8	Cruising Speed:
	Service Ceiling: 49,000 ft (15,000 m)	Unrefuelled Range: 2,300 mi (3,704 km)
		(retractable air-to-air refuelling probe fitted)
Weights:	Empty: 23,400 lb (10,614 kg)	Gross: 37,000 lb (16,783 kg)
	Maximum Take-off: 49,355 lb (22,387 kg)	
Dimensions:	Unfolded Span: 40 ft 5 in (12.32 m) (with missiles)	Folded Span: 27 ft 6 in (8.38 m)
	Length: 56 ft 0 in (17.07 m)	Height: 15 ft 3 in (4.66 m)
	Wing Area: 400 sq ft (37.16 sq m)	

Armament:	Internally mounted M61A1 20mm cannon and provisions for AIM9 Sidewinder and AIM7 Sparrow air-to-air missiles, Maverick air-to-ground missiles, conventional bombs and precision-guided bombs, unguided CRV7 rockets, fuel tanks etc
Cost:	Approximately $24 M (Cdn) per aircraft

Noorduyn
NORSEMAN

The Noorduyn Norseman ranks as probably one of the most important designs in Canadian aviation history. An eight-seat general-purpose "bush" aircraft, it was the first Canadian designed and built aircraft to see worldwide use. Designed by Mr. R.B.C. Noorduyn, the design incorporated the specific requests and suggestions of Canadian bush pilots in which good performance on wheels, floats and skis was considered a prerequisite. First flown in 1935, the type gained rapid acceptance. At the outbreak of war, the RCAF placed orders which eventually totaled 99 aircraft of various models. The US government was by far the largest customer, however, purchasing over 800 Norseman aircraft for military use. The utility of the design ensured its use post-war. The last RCAF example was retired in 1957, although numerous civilian examples soldiered on long after this date.

The Noorduyn Norseman floatplane was a rugged and highly dependable bush plane design. Used by the RCAF throughout the Second World War, in the immediate post-war period, the later model Norseman, as seen here, formed the backbone of the RCAF's search and rescue units. (RCAF Photo)

DETAILS

Designation:	**Model No:** C-64	**Marks:** Mks I, II, III, IV, V	**Role:** Utility Transport/Float plane
TOS: 1940	**SOS:** 1957	**No:** 100	**Service:** RCAF

SPECIFICATIONS Wheeled version

Manufacturer: Noorduyn Aviation Limited and Canadian Car & Foundry
Crew/Passengers: one pilot and up to seven passengers
Powerplant: one 600 hp Pratt & Whitney Wasp Jr radial piston engine
Performance: Max Speed: 155 mph (249 km/h)   Cruising Speed: 141 mph (227 km/h)
Service Ceiling: 17,000 ft (5,182 m)   Range: 464 mi (745 km)
Weights: Empty: 4,250 lb (1,928 kg)   Gross: 7,400 lb (3,357 kg)
Dimensions: Span: 51 ft 8 in (15.75 m)   Length: 32 ft 4 in (9.86 m)
Height: 10 ft 3 in (3.12 m)   Wing Area: 325 sq ft (30.19 sq m)
Armament: None
Cost: Unknown

North American
NA-26

Developed from the NA-16 series of trainer aircraft in the US, the sole NA-26 was in fact a civilian, company demonstrator aircraft. Prior the development of the NA-26, all the NA-16 series of aircraft had been equipped with fixed undercarriages and mechanical flap systems. The NA-26 incorporated a hydraulic system to allow for retraction of the undercarriage and for the extension and retraction of the flaps. The NA-26 was essentially the immediate forerunner of the very famous Harvard or Texan training aircraft. The NA-26 was serialled in the US as NX18990 and was widely used as a company demonstrator. By 1940, the success of the later improved models made NX18990 surplus to company requirements. It was then sold to the RCAF and officially became #3345. It was first retrofitted with a canopy from a later model AT-6 variant and used alongside other Harvard aircraft at No. 2 Flying Training School at Uplands in Ottawa. The aircraft was subsequently upgraded to Harvard Mk II standard. It was eventually written off in a crash in 1942.

The sole NA-26 demonstrator in RCAF service was hard to distinguish from the far more numerous Harvard aircraft. Note the lack of a full rear canopy in this view. (M. McIntyre Collection)

DETAILS

Designation:	**Model No:** NA.26	**Marks:** Mk I, II	**Role:** Trainer
Service: RCAF			

SPECIFICATIONS

Manufacturer:	North American Aircraft	
Crew/Passengers	crew of two	
Powerplant:	one 550 hp Pratt & Whitney Wasp R-1340 radial piston engine	
Performance:	Max Speed: 205 mph (330 km/h)	Cruising Speed: 170 mph (274 km/h)
	Service Ceiling: 23,000 ft (7,010 m)	Range: 750 mi (1,207 km)
Weights:	Empty: 4,158 lb (1,886 kg)	Maximum Take-off: 5,250 lb (2,381 kg)
Dimensions:	Span: 42 ft 10 in (13.06 m)	Length: 29 ft 0 in (8.84 m)
	Height: 11 ft 8 in (3.56 m)	Wing Area: 253 sq ft (23.50 sq m)
Armament:	None	
Cost:	Unknown	

North American
NA-44

The NA-44 was the second North American company demonstrator aircraft acquired by the RCAF. Unlike the NA-26, the NA-44 was not intended as a training aircraft and instead was marketed as a combat aircraft. The NA-44 was serialled in the US as NX18981 and it was equipped to take four fixed .30 calibre Colt machine guns and one rear, flexible mount gun of the same type. Underwing and centre-section bomb racks were also installed. In order to provide a useful warload capacity, a more powerful R-1830-F52 Wright Cyclone radial piston engine was fitted. This engine provided 60 percent more horsepower than the comparable engine in the Harvard. By 1940, after some successful South American sales of the NA-44 variants, NX18981 became surplus to company requirements. It was then sold to the RCAF and officially became #3344. Stripped of its armament, its powerful engine made the aircraft a sprightly performer. Consequently the "Jeep," as the aircraft became known, was "commandeered" by senior officers at its base in Trenton. The aircraft survived wartime duties to eventually be struck off charge in 1947 when it was sold for civilian use.

This view of the sole NA-44 demonstrator aircraft illustrates the distinctive light blue and yellow paint scheme originally applied to the aircraft, which was later reversed. (RCAF Photo)

DETAILS
Designation: **Model No:** NA.26?????   **Marks:** Mk I, II   **Role:** Trainer
Service: RCAF

SPECIFICATIONS
Manufacturer: North American Aircraft
Crew/Passengers: crew of two
Powerplant: one 890 hp Wright Cyclone R-1820 radial piston engine
Performance: Max Speed: 205 mph (330 km/h)   Cruising Speed: 170 mph (274 km/h)
                        Service Ceiling: 23,000 ft (7,010 m)   Range: 750 mi (1,207 km)
Weights: Empty: 4,158 lb (1,886 kg)   Max T/O: 5,250 lb (2,381 kg)
Dimensions: Span: 42 ft 10 in (13.06 m)   Length: 29 ft 0 in (8.84 m)
                        Height: 11 ft 8 in (3.56 m)   Wing Area: 253 sq ft (23.50 sq m)
Armament: None
Cost: $17,000 US

North American
MITCHELL

The B-25 Mitchell was a highly successful American-designed medium bomber of the Second World War. The type was widely exported, and six Royal Air Force squadrons in the 2nd Tactical Air Force flew B-25 Mitchells in various theatres of operation. Many RCAF officers and men were attached to the RAF units that operated

the type. Following the war, the Mitchell was supplied in quantity to RCAF Auxiliary Squadrons along with various other units. It was used primarily as a pilot, navigational or radar trainer and also as a high-speed transport until its retirement in the spring of 1962.

These two views of RCAF B-25 Mitchell bombers depict operational (upper) and training (lower) aircraft. In the post-war era, all of the aircraft had their paint stripped and were retained in various roles in this overall bare-metal finish. (RCAF and Comox AFM Photos)

DETAILS

Designation:	**Model No:** B-25B, D, J	**Marks:** Mk I, II, III	**Role:** Bomber
TOS: 1942	**SOS:** 1962	**No:** 164	**Service:** RCAF

SPECIFICATIONS

Crew/Passengers:	two pilots and up to three additional crew depending on mission	
Powerplant:	two 1,700 hp Wright Cyclone R-2600-13 radial engines	
Performance:	Max Speed: 272 mph (438 km/h)	Cruising Speed: 230 mph (370 km/h)
	Service Ceiling: 24,200 ft (7,380 m)	Range: 1,350 mi (2,173 km)
Weights:	Empty: 19,418 lb (8,808 kg)	Gross: 35,000 lb (15,876 kg)
Dimensions:	Span: 67 ft 7 in (20.60 m)	Length: 52 ft 11 in (16,13 m)
	Height: 16 ft 4 in (4.98 m)	Wing Area: 610 sq ft (56.67 sq ft)
Armament:	Provision for eight 0.5 in (12.7 mm) machine guns and 3,000 lb (1,361 kg) of bombs	
Cost:	Unknown	

North American
MUSTANG

The North American Mustang was first flown in 1940 and eventually became one of the finest long-range fighters of the Second World War. Early versions, fitted with Allison engines, initially lacked high altitude performance and were therefore used by both the RAF and RCAF for low-level reconnaissance and ground attack duties. Further modifications to the design resulted in the marriage of the Rolls-Royce Merlin engine to a redesigned airframe. This latter combination, known as the Mark IV in RAF and RCAF service, proved to be outstanding. Three RCAF Squadrons (No. 400, 414 and 430) used early model Mustangs in the reconnaissance role and No. 441 and 442 Squadron converted to the Mk IV in 1945 for long-range escort duties. In the post-war period, the RCAF acquired a further 88 Mustang IV aircraft for use by both regular and auxiliary squadrons. The aircraft survived in this latter role until 1961.

The North American Mustang Mk IV entered Canadian service in 1947 and this aircraft # CB 569 belonged to Central Air Command Composite Flight located at RCAF Station Trenton. In this post-war period, the Mustang Mk IV was used to equip RCAF auxiliary squadrons until the late 1950s. (CF Photo)

DETAILS

Designation: P-51 or F-51 **Model No:** P-51A, B, C, D **Marks:** Mk I, II, III, IV **Role:** Fighter, Fighter-Reconnaissance
TOS: 1947 **SOS:** 1961 **No:** 130 **Service:** RCAF

SPECIFICATIONS P-51D

Manufacturer:	North American Aircraft
Crew/Passengers:	one pilot
Powerplant:	one 1,590 hp Packard (license-built) V-1650-7 Merlin piston engine

Performance:	Max Speed: 448 mph (721 km/h)	Cruising Speed: 360 mph (579 km/h)
	Service Ceiling: 41,900 ft (12,771 m)	Range: 1,300 mi (2,092 km)
Weights:	Empty: 7,125 lb (3,232 kg)	Gross: 11,600 lb (5,262 kg)
Dimensions:	Span: 37 ft 1 in (11.29 m)	Length: 32 ft 3 in (9.83 m)
	Height: 13 ft 8 in (4.17 m)	Wing Area: 235 sq ft (21.83 sq m)
Armament:	six 0.5 in (12.7 mm) machine guns plus provisions for two 500 lb (227 kg) bombs, eight rockets or two drop tanks	
Cost:	$54,000 US	

North American
HARVARD

The North American Harvard is another famous and highly successful design. Also known by a wide variety of other names (Harvard, Texan, Yellow Peril) or designations (AT-6, T-6, etc), the aircraft was heavily used by the RAF/RCAF during the British Commonwealth Air Training Plan in the Second World War and subsequently for NATO pilot training in the post-war era. Approximately 11,000 Canadians and 8,000 Allied airmen received pilot training on Harvards in Canada during the war. The aircraft could also be modified as an armament trainer capable of carrying either machine guns, rockets or practice bombs.

The North American Harvard served as the RCAF's mainstay flying training aircraft for over two decades. Nicknamed the "Yellow Peril", the Harvard was one of the most reliable training aircraft ever produced. It realistically bridged the gap between the initial trainers and more advanced aircraft. Above is a nice aerial view of a late-model Harvard in post-war RCAF service. (CF Photo)

DETAILS

Designation:	**Model No:** NA-66/76, T-6	**Marks:** Mk I, IIA, IIB, III, IV	**Role:** Trainer
TOS: 1939	**SOS:** 1965	**No:** 2258	**Service:** RCAF/RCN

SPECIFICATIONS Mk IV

Manufacturer:	Canadian Car & Foundry Ltd under license from North American Aircraft
Crew/Passengers:	two pilots
Powerplant:	one 600 hp Pratt & Whitney R-1340-AN-1 Wasp radial engine

Performance:	Max Speed: 180 mph (290 km/h)	Cruising Speed: 140 mph (225 km/h)
	Service Ceiling: 22,400 ft (6,827 m)	Range: 750 miles
Weights:	Empty: 3,995 lb (1,814 kg)	Gross: 5,235 lb (2,376 kg)
Dimensions:	Span: 42 ft (12.81 m)	Length: 28 ft 11 in (8.8 m)
	Height: 11 ft 8½ in (3.55 m)	Wing Area: 253.7 sq ft (23.57 sq m)
Armament:	Provision for machine guns, rockets and practice bombs	
Original Cost:	$27,000 US	

North American
YALE

The North American Yale was the forerunner to the highly successful Harvard design by the same company. With the outbreak of the Second World War, the RCAF eventually acquired a total of 119 Yale aircraft between 23 August 1940 and 25 September 1946. Assembly of the Yale in Canada was licenced to Norduyn in addition to their production of the Harvard and Norseman. The North American Yale was very similar to the Harvard, the most obvious difference being fixed landing gear as opposed to the retractable undercarriage found on the Harvard. Originally ordered in quantity by the French,

the first Yales were diverted to the RCAF after the fall of France. The Yale aircraft instruments were consequently annotated in French and calibrated in the metric system so all were placarded with conversion tables. Other differences and limitations found in this design included engine and propeller controls, which worked in opposite directions to standard practice. Electric starters were not included so the engines had to be hand cranked, and the aircraft were chronically underpowered. Nevertheless, the aircraft provided valuable service for aircrew training at the outbreak of war.

Seen here reflected in melted snow waters at Camp Borden, the North American Yale was very similar to the Harvard, the most obvious difference being fixed landing gear as opposed to the retractable undercarriage found on the Harvard. (CF Photo)

DETAILS

Designation:	**Model No:** NA-64	**Marks:**	**Role:** Trainer
TOS: 1940	**SOS:** 1946	**No:** 119	**Service:** RCAF

SPECIFICATIONS

Manufacturer:	Norduyn Aircraft Ltd under license from North American Aircraft
Crew/Passengers:	two pilots
Powerplant:	one 420 hp Wright Whirlwind R-975-E3 radial engine
Performance:	Max Speed: 200 mph (322 km/h) Cruising Speed: 145 mph (233 km/h)
	Service Ceiling: 16,500 ft (5,035 m) Range: 750 mi (1,208 km)
Weights:	Empty: 3,324 lb (1,057 kg) Gross: 4,500 lb (2,040 kg)
Dimensions:	Span: 41 ft 0 in (12.57 m) Length: 28 ft 8 in (8.70 m)
	Height: 8 ft 10½ in (2.70 m) Wing Area: 246 sq ft (33 sq m)
Armament:	None
Original Cost:	Unknown

Northrop
DELTA

In 1935, when the RCAF wanted a high performance photographic aircraft, it considered the Northrop Gamma but instead settled on Northrop's transport version of the same aircraft, the Northrop Delta. Canadian Vickers was commissioned to build an initial four aircraft under license and these were the first all-metal stressed-skin aircraft to be built in Canada. The Delta used the same wing as the Gamma, had split flaps and a non-retractable undercarriage like its predecessors. The larger fuselage accommodated up to eight passengers. For RCAF use, the design was modified to accept three Fairchild A-3 cameras at the rear of the cabin. The cabin floor was strengthened to accept freight loads and a large upward opening freight door was installed on the port side. Two Deltas were armed with a defensive machine gun fitted in an open hatch in the roof. A plexiglass fairing provided protection from the slipstream. This particular installation was not very satisfactory, causing buffeting and a marked decrease in performance.

An RCAF Northrop Delta #676 from No. 8 Squadron is seen here preparing for a flight from Rockcliffe, Ont. to Sydney, N.S. on 26 August 1939. Note the powered launch belonging to the RCAF Marine Service. (CF Photo)

DETAILS

Designation:	**Model No:**	**Marks:** Mk I, II	**Role:** Transport
TOS: 1936	**SOS:** 1945	**No:** 20	**Service:** RCAF

SPECIFICATIONS

Manufacturer:	Canadian Vickers under license from Northrop	
Crew/Passengers:	two pilots and up to eight passengers	
Powerplant:	one 775 hp Wright SR-1820 F-52 Cyclone engine	
Performance:	Max Speed: 205 mph (329.8 km/h)	Cruising Speed: 170 mph (273 km/h)
	Service Ceiling: 22,000 ft (6.705 m)	Range:
Weights:	Empty: 4,566 lbs (2,073 kg)	Gross: 7,350 lbs (3,337 kg)
Dimensions:	Span: 48 ft (14.63 m)	Length: 33 ft 2 in (10.11 m)
	Height: 10 ft 6 in (3.2 m)	Wing Area: 363 sq ft (33.72 sq m)
Armament:	Provisions for one machine gun in dorsal rear open hatch and up to 250 lb (113.5 kg) in bombs under the wings	
Cost:	Unknown	

Northrop
NOMAD

The Northrop A-17A was a military development of the commercially successful Northrop Gamma. First delivered in 1935 to the US Army Air Corps as a two-seat, light attack bomber, the Northrop A-17A was essentially obsolete by the time the Second World War erupted. Notwithstanding this fact, in June 1940, the Royal Air Force purchased 93 surplus A-17As for various training roles. The RCAF consequently acquired a small number of Nomads, as they became known in British service, exclusively for training purposes as part of the British Commonwealth Air Training Plan. They were never used operationally overseas. Initially, the aircraft were used at Camp Borden to check out qualified civilian pilots who were offering their services to the air force. In 1941, the aircraft were modified to a target-towing configuration to allow for air-to-air gunnery training at various schools in Quebec and Ontario. In addition to their use by the RCAF in Canada, the Royal Norwegian Air Force trained some aircrew in exile on the A-17A at airports in Toronto and Muskoka. The RCAF Nomads were retired with the cessation of hostilities. The Nomads were not particularly outstanding aircraft, but they did provide reliable training service, logging an average of approximately 3,000 flying hours each in their four and a half years of service.

An RCAF Northrop Nomad is shown here with, surprisingly, no markings visible. The aircraft may have been in the midst of repainting. (CF Photo)

DETAILS

Designation:	**Model No:** A-17A	**Marks:** Mk I	**Role:** Trainer
TOS: 1940	**SOS:** 1945	**No:** 32	**Service:** RCAF

SPECIFICATIONS

Manufacturer:	Northrop
Crew/Passengers:	crew of two: pilot & observer in tandem
Powerplant:	one 825 hp Pratt & Whitney Twin Wasp Junior R-1535-13 radial engine
Performance:	Max Speed: 220 mph (354 km/h) — Cruising Speed:
	Service Ceiling: 19,400 ft (5,915 kg) — Range: 730 mi (1,175 km)
Weights:	Empty: 5,106 lb (2,316 kg) — Maximum Take-Off: 7,543 lb (3,421 kg)
Dimensions:	Span: 47 ft 9 in (14.55 m) — Length: 31 ft 8 in (9.65 m)
	Height: 12 ft 0 in (3.66 m) — Wing Area: 362 sq ft (33.63 sq m)
Armament:	Provisions for five 0.30 cal machine guns (four in the wings and one on a flexible mount in the rear cockpit) plus four 100 lb (45 kg) bombs
Cost:	Unknown

Percival
PRENTICE

The Percival Prentice was designed as a basic trainer and served as the RAF's main basic trainer between 1948 and 1953. It was an all-metal, low-wing monoplane with fixed landing gear. The enclosed cockpit was a marked departure from typical RAF predecessors such as the Tiger Moth. It incorporated many new features based upon the experiences of training wartime pilots. Up-turned wing tips were an identifying feature. The RCAF acquired one example in 1948, possibly for evaluation purposes. Few details of the type in RCAF service are available and it lasted only one year. The De Havilland Chipmunk eventually became the RCAF's standard elementary trainer.

The RAF Percival Prentice aircraft shown here is similar to the sole example acquired by the RCAF. (Comox AFM Photo)

DETAILS

Designation:	**Model No:** P.40	**Marks:** Mk I	**Role:** Trainer
TOS: 1948	**SOS:** 1948	**No:** 1	**Service:** RCN

SPECIFICATIONS

Manufacturer:	Percival Aircraft Ltd
Crew/Passengers:	one pilot and one student pilot side-by-side and provisions for a 2nd student
Powerplant:	one 251 hp De Havilland Gipsy Queen 32 piston engine
Performance:	Max Speed: 143 mph (230 km/h) Cruising Speed: 136 mph (219 km/h)
	Service Ceiling: 18,000 ft (5,486 m) Range: 396 mi (637 km)
Weights:	Empty: 3,232 lbs (1,466 kg) Gross: 4,200 lb (1,905 kg)
Dimensions:	Span: 46 ft 0 in (14.02 m) Length: 31 ft 3 in (9.53 m)
	Height: 12 ft 10½ in (3.92 m) Wing Area: 305 sq ft (28.33 sq m)
Armament:	None
Cost:	Unknown

Sikorsky
S-51

The Sikorsky S-51 design followed the now classic helicopter configuration, with a single main rotor and an anti-torque tail rotor. It first flew in February 1946 and was the first Sikorsky helicopter to receive approval for civil use. Most S-51 helicopters however went into military service where they were often known under the designation H-5. It was the first of the early helicopters with adequate lifting capacity and cabin space to permit transport and air-sea rescue duties. The aircraft proved to be very popular and was selected by the RCAF for training as well as rescue purposes. Seven were taken on strength in 1947 and were the first

RCAF helicopters. The first experience with RCAF H-5s provided valuable exposure to rotary wing operations and solidified the helicopter's reputation for versatility and valuable service.

RCAF H-5s were used for basic search and rescue operations and all were painted in a high visibility overall yellow paint scheme as a result.
(Author's collection and CF Photo)

DETAILS

Designation: H-5	**Model No:** S-51	**Role:** Utility Helicopter	
TOS: 1947	**SOS:** 1965	**No:** 7	**Service:** RCAF

SPECIFICATIONS

Manufacturer:	Sikorsky Aircraft Division	
Crew/Passengers:	one pilot and up to three passengers	
Powerplant:	one 450 hp Pratt & Whitney R-985-AN-5 Wasp Jr radial piston engine	
Performance:	Max Speed: 103 mph (166 km/h)	Cruising Speed: 85 mph (137 km/h)
	Service Ceiling: 13,500 ft (4,115 m)	Range: 280 mi (451 km)
Weights:	Empty: 3,810 lb (1,728 kg)	Gross: 5,500 lb (2,494 kg)
Dimensions:	Rotor Diameter: 49 ft 0 in (14.94 m)	Length: 44 ft 11½ in (13.70 m)
	Height: 12 ft 11 in (3.9 m)	
Armament:	None	
Cost:	Unknown	

Sikorsky
S-55

The Sikorsky S-55 design followed what became the classic helicopter configuration with a single main rotor and an anti-torque tail rotor. It was the first of the early helicopters with adequate lifting capacity and cabin space to permit troop or cargo transport along with air-sea rescue duties. The aircraft proved to be very popular and was selected by both the RCAF and RCN for slightly different purposes. The Royal Canadian Navy version of the S-55 was designated as the HO4S. The main role for the HO4S version was Search and Rescue standby (referred to as "plane guard" duties) on the carriers HMCS *Magnificent* and *Bonaventure*. The helos were to be ready to assist in the event of a crash or a ditching. On 21 September 1953, the first such rescue was made when a Sea Fury pilot was picked up 32 seconds after having to ditch alongside the carrier.

Two RCAF S-55s shown here with an S-58 and H-21 hovering in the background. (CF Photo)

DETAILS

Designation: **Model No:** H-19, S-55, HO4S-3   **Role:** Utility Helicopter

TOS: 1950   **SOS:** 1966   **No:** 15   **Service:** RCAF, RCN

SPECIFICATIONS

Manufacturer:	Sikorsky Aircraft Division	
Crew/Passengers:	one pilot and up to eight passengers	
Powerplant:	one 550 hp Wright R-1340 radial piston engine	
Performance:	Max Speed: 101 mph (163 km/h)	Cruising Speed: 85 mph (137 km/h)
	Service Ceiling: 10,500 ft (3,200 m)	Range: 370 mi (595 km)
Weights:	Empty: 4,590 lb (2,082 kg)	Gross: 7,900 lb (3,583 kg)
Dimensions:	Rotor Diameter: 53 ft 0 in (16.15 m)	Length: 42 ft 2 in (12.85 m)
	Height: 13 ft 4 in (4.06 m)	
Armament:	None	
Cost:	Unknown	

Sikorsky
S-58

The S-58 made its first flight on 8 March 1954. This Sikorsky design closely resembled the company's previous S-55 design. The engine was a more powerful 1,525 hp Wright R-1820 radial engine still obliquely located in the nose so that the transmission shaft ran at right angles to the engine straight into the gearbox beneath the rotor hub. However, unlike the S-55 with its nose wheel landing gear, the S-58 instead featured a tail wheel design plus folding main rotor blades, and the entire rear fuselage and tail rotor could be folded forward. The RCAF acquired a small number of S-58 helicopters. They were used initially during the construction of the Mid-Canada radar chain. In addition, they were also used for search and rescue, pilot training and range patrol operations, primarily at CFB Cold Lake, Alberta.

An RCAF S-58 utility helicopter is shown here in a rare colour view and in this case undergoing routine maintenance. Easy access to the radial piston engine was afforded by the large clamshell nose doors. (CF Photo)

DETAILS

Designation: CH-126 **Model No:** S-58, H-34 **Role:** Utility Helicopter
TOS: 1955 **SOS:** 1971 **No:** 6 **Service:** RCAF

SPECIFICATIONS

Manufacturer: Sikorsky Aircraft Division
Crew/Passengers: two pilots and one loadmaster crewman plus up to twelve passengers or 4,200 lbs (1,905 kg) cargo
Powerplant: one 1,525 hp Wright R-1820-84 piston engine
Performance: Max Speed: 123 mph (198 km/h) Cruising Speed: 98 mph (158 km/h)
Service Ceiling: 9,500 ft (2,896 m) Range: 182 mi (293 km)
Weights: Empty: 7,900 lb (3,583 kg) Gross: 14,000 lb (6,350 kg)
Dimensions: Rotor Diameter: 56 ft 0 in (17.07 m) Length: 46 ft 9 in (14.25 m)
Height: 15 ft 11 in (4.85 m)
Armament: None
Cost: Unknown

Sikorsky
SEA KING

The Sea King, first introduced in 1961, was initially acquired by the air element of the Royal Canadian Navy as an anti-submarine warfare helicopter for Canadian ships. Space aboard naval vessels is always at a premium, and the Sea King, with its fold-up rotor and tail, fitted perfectly on the smallest deck. To further enhance this capability a Canadian developed and manufactured Helicopter Haul-down Rapid Securing Device (HHRSD) was installed on board purpose-designed destroyers. Better known as the "Bear-Trap" system, it stabilized the helicopter in the hover over the deck by means of a cable and helped center the helo over a small opening in the landing pad. Once landed and secured, the system was then used to tow the aircraft into a hangar. The system enabled Sea Kings to land on destroyers rolling plus or minus 31 degrees, pitching nine degrees and heaving up to 20 feet per second. With both day and night flight capabilities the Sea King has been carried aboard many Maritime Command destroyers, frigates and replenishment ships.

Over the years, submarine hunting has become less of a priority and the Sea King has been adapted to other roles. Domestically, Sea Kings have increasingly become responsible for search and rescue operations, disaster relief, fisheries patrols, environmental surveillance and drug interdiction. They have also been instrumental in international operations of peacekeeping and humanitarian assistance. Sea King helicopter air detachments, known as HELAIRDETS, are provided to Canadian ships on east and west coasts as an integral part of the ships' surface and sub-surface surveillance and weapons systems.

HELAIRDETS are embarked whenever their respective ship is deployed. They frequently participate in international operations with allied forces, combined operations with either Naval or Army elements of the CF and national operations with other Canadian governmental agencies. Six of the original Sea Kings were extensively modified, incorp rating an acoustic system that used sonobuoys instead of a dipping sonar, a magnetic anomaly detector (MAD), and a new tactical navigation system. This equipment enabled crews to localize and track underwater contacts without being detected. A standard Sea King crew comprised two pilots, a tactical coordinator (TACCO) and an airborne electronic sensor operator (AES Op) or sensor operator (SENSO) depending on the missions or type of aircraft. For some operational missions, an extra TACCO or AES Op was added to assist with operations in the back-end of the helicopter. After four plus decades of service, the age of Canada's only ship-borne helicopter makes it increasingly difficult to perform its many roles and consequently on-going upgrades have included new uprated engines and main gearboxes.

Primarily an ASW design, the CH-124 Sea King helicopter has faithfully served both the RCN and the CF in a variety of roles. These views illustrate later model variants of the aircraft. (CF Photos and Author's collection)

DETAILS

Designation: CHSS-2, CH-124   **Model No:** S-61, SH-3D   **Role:** ASW Helicopter

TOS: 1961   **SOS:** In Service   **No:** 41   **Service:** RCN/CF

SPECIFICATIONS

Manufacturer:	United Aircraft of Canada (Sikorsky Helicopters)	
Crew/Passengers:	two pilots, one navigator, one airborne electronic sensor operator	
Powerplant:	Two 1,500 hp General Electric T-58-GE-8F turboshaft engines	
Performance:	Max Speed: 166 mph (267 km/h)	Cruising Speed: 104 mph (167 km/h)
	Service Ceiling: 14,700 ft (4,480m)	Range: 991 mi (616 km)
Weights:	Empty: 11,865 lb (5,382 kg)	Maximum T/O: 20,542 lb (9,318 kg)
Dimensions:	Rotor span: 62 ft 0 in (18.90 m)	Length: 72 ft 8 in (22.15 m)
	Height: 16 ft 10 in (5.13 m)	Main Rotor Disc Area: 3,019 sq ft (280.5 sq m)
Armament:	Mk 46 Mod V homing torpedoes up to 840 lb (381 kg), plus provision for self-defence machine gun	
Cost:	$1,390,000	

Sopwith
CAMEL

The Sopwith Camel became the most successful British fighter of the First World War. The Sopwith F.1 and 2F.1 Camel first went into operations on the Western Front in 1917 and then served in virtually every theatre of RFC, RNAS and RAF service. Several Canadian aces used the Camel as their mount. Very maneuverable, it could be tricky to fly in the hands of a novice pilot. For experienced pilots, however, the aircraft proved to be a superb fighter. The guns were mounted on the forward fuselage with their breeches enclosed in a faired metal cowling;

a "hump" that gave the Camel its name. Several Camels were shipped to Canada in the post-war period as part of an Imperial gift. Three registered Sopwith F.1 Camels then entered service with the RCAF at Camp Borden in 1924. The following year, the RCAF purchased seven additional aircraft to provide further spares for the active aircraft. These latter aircraft were in fact 2F.1 models that had been navalized variants. Used primarily by wartime experienced fighter pilots for refresher training, the Camels lasted another five years before being scrapped.

The Sopwith Camel is arguably the most famous British fighter of the First World War and many Canadian pilots achieved the status of ace while using this type as their mount. This colour view illustrates a restored example belonging to the Canada Aviation Museum. (CF Photo)

DETAILS

Designation:	**Model No:** F.1, 2F.1	**Marks:**	**Role:** Fighter
TOS: 1924	**SOS:** 1929	**No:** 10	**Service:** RFC, RCAF

SPECIFICATIONS 2F.1

Manufacturer:	Sopwith Aviation Company	
Crew/Passengers:	one pilot	
Powerplant:	one 130 hp Clerget, 110 hp Le Rhone, 100 hp Gnome Monosoupape or 150 hp Bentley B.R.1 radial piston engines	
Performance:	Max Speed: 115 mph (185 km/h)	Cruising Speed:
	Service Ceiling: 19,000 ft (5,791 m)	Range:
Weights:	Empty: 929 lb (421 kg)	Gross: 1,453 lb (659 kg)
Dimensions:	Span: 28 ft 0 in (8.53 m)	Length: 18 ft 9 in (5.72 m)
	Height: 8 ft 6 in (4.17 m)	Wing Area:
Armament:	Twin 0.303 calibre Vickers machine guns plus provisions for two 50 lb (22.7 kg) bombs	
Cost:	Unknown	

Sopwith
DOLPHIN

The Sopwith Dolphin fighter entered RFC service in 1918. The unusual negative or back-staggered equal span wings caused some initial pilot distrust but the excellent qualities of the fighter quickly overcame any concerns. The design of the upper wings meant that the pilot's head projected through the upper centre section. The Dolphin's firepower was increased with the addition of a pair of Lewis guns mounted in the centre section on each side of the pilot to fire forward and upwards at 45 degrees. These features all combined to give the Dolphin an unusual appearance. On 05 August 1918, the first two all Canadian RAF Squadrons were formed in England. By November, No. 1 Fighter Squadron of the Canadian Air Force was formed. This unit was equipped with Sopwith Dolphins on 20 November 1918. With the disbandment of the Canadian Air Force in England in 1919, the Dolphins were retired from Canadian service.

A view of a Sopwith Dolphin similar to those used by No. 1 Fighter Squadron of the short-lived Canadian Air Force in England in December 1918. (CF Photo)

DETAILS

Designation: | **Model No:** | **Marks:** | **Role:** Fighter
TOS: 1918 | **SOS:** 1919 | **No:** 18 | **Service:** CAF

SPECIFICATIONS

Manufacturer: Sopwith Aviation Co. Ltd.
Crew/Passengers: one pilot
Powerplant: one 200 Hispano-Suiza piston engine
Performance: Max Speed: 131 mph (211 km/h) Cruising Speed:
Service Ceiling: 21,000 ft (6,401 m) Range:
Weights: Empty: 1,391 lb (631 kg) Gross: 2,008 lb (911 kg)
Dimensions: Span: 32 ft 6 in (9.91 m) Length: 22 ft 3 in (6.78 m)
Height: 8 ft 6 in (2.59 m) Wing Area:
Armament: provisions for two forward-firing Vickers machine guns plus a pair of Lewis guns mounted in the centre section on each side of the pilot to fire forward and upwards at 45 degrees.
Cost: Unknown

Sopwith
SNIPE

The Sopwith Snipe was the last British fighter to enter full-scale squadron service in the First World War. Originally intended as a replacement for the Sopwith Camel, both aircraft types nevertheless saw the Armistice and only three squadrons were fully equipped with the Snipe. In Canadian history, the Snipe is firmly associated with one of Canada's greatest aces, Major William Barker. While flying the Snipe, Major Barker was awarded the Victoria Cross after a deliberate single-handed encounter with large numbers of enemy aircraft. Desperately outnumbered, he shot down several aircraft and although wounded and having crashed, he survived to become one of the post-war leaders of the RCAF. The Snipe aircraft soldiered on well into the 1920's in both the RAF and RCAF. The RCAF acquired a handful of the type as part a Commonwealth gift of aircraft to Canada. These aircraft saw service in Camp Borden, primarily for fighter pilot proficiency training, before being finally retired in 1923.

The Sopwith Snipe was an advanced fighter design for its day. This restored example of the Sopwith Snipe at the Canada Aviation Museum is preserved in the personal colours of the WWI Canadian ace Major William Barker. (CF Photo)

DETAILS

Designation:	**Model No:** 7F.1	**Marks:**	**Role:** Fighter
TOS: 1919	**SOS:** 1923	**No:** 3	**Service:** RCAF

SPECIFICATIONS

Manufacturer:	Sopwith Aircraft Company	
Crew/Passengers:	one pilot	
Powerplant:	one 230 hp Bentley BR2 radial piston engine	
Performance:	Max Speed: 121 mph (195 km/h)	Cruising Speed:
	Service Ceiling: 19,500 ft (5,940 m)	Range: 363 mi (584 km)
Weights:	Empty: 1,312 lb (595 kg)	Gross: 2,020 lb (916 kg)
Dimensions:	Span: 31 ft 1 in (9.47 m)	Length: 19 ft 10 in (6.05 m)
	Height: 9 ft 6 in (2.90 m)	Wing Area: 271 sq ft (25.18 sq m)
Armament:	two machine guns and provisions for light bombs	
Cost:	Unknown	

Stearman (Boeing)
KAYDET

The Stearman Aircraft Company, eventually a Boeing Company subsidiary, was the principle manufacturer of the famous series of "ab-initio" trainers collectively called the PT-13, PT-17 and PT-27 Kaydet, used by the US Armed Forces during the Second World War. With the demand for training aircraft in Canada necessitated by the British Commonwealth Air Training Plan, arrangements were made in late 1941 to procure 300 Kaydets for the RCAF under Lend-Lease arrangements. The aircraft were to be modified to PT-27 standard to suit the Canadian conditions and RCAF requirements. These modifications included equipment changes for night flying plus an improved cockpit heating system and canopy for winter flying conditions. Production

delays for these modifications, however, resulted in virtually all the aircraft being produced to the US military's basic PT-17 model standard. Although the aircraft were reluctantly accepted by the RCAF and introduced into service, the lack of the necessary modifications quickly resulted in complications and dissatisfaction for the basic flying training program then underway. Despite being sturdy, reliable aircraft, in November 1942, the decision was therefore made to withdraw the type from use and substitute an equivalent number of Fairchild Cornells on existing production contracts. The Kaydets were then returned to the US over a period of six months in 1943, for use by the US Navy and US Army Air Corps.

An RCAF Stearman Kaydet flies overhead. (RCAF Photo)

DETAILS

Designation: PT-17, PT-27 **Model No:** **Role:** Trainer

TOS: 1942 **SOS:** 1943 **No:** 301 **Service:** RCAF

SPECIFICATIONS

Manufacturer:	Stearman Aircraft Company
Crew/Passengers:	two pilots in tandem
Powerplant:	one 200 hp Wright Whirlwind radial engine

Performance:	Max Speed: 122 mph (196 km/h)	Cruising Speed: 107 mph (172 km/h)
	Service Ceiling: 11,700 ft (3,566 m)	Range: 400 mi (644 km)
Weights:	Empty:	Gross: 2,810 lb (1,275 kg)
Dimensions:	Span: 32 ft 0 in (9.73 m)	Length: 25 ft ¼ in (7.63 m)
	Height: 9 ft 2 in (2.79 m)	Wing Area: 298 sq ft (27.69 m)
Armament:	None	
Cost:	$11,000 US	

Stinson
SENTINEL

The use of light aircraft for liaison, communication and various training duties was well established in the RCAF in the 1920s and 1930s. With the outbreak of the Second World War, the RCAF impressed several examples of the Stinson Model 105 Voyager, which was then in production as a three seat commercial light aircraft. The Stinson Sentinel was a military version of the same aircraft produced for the US Army featuring a larger fuselage. Additionally, a further modification to the fuselage incorporating an upward-hinged hatch aft of the cabin allowed for the provision of a stretcher. This latter feature made the aircraft useful as a front line ambulance and the design was used to good effect by both British and American forces in both the Pacific theatre and later in the Korean conflict. The RCAF eventually acquired 26 examples of the Voyageur or Sentinel. In RCAF service, the aircraft was also used in the training of wireless operators at Prince Albert, Saskatchewan.

This particular RCAF Sentinel had been impressed into service from civilian use which explains the aircraft's colour scheme. (LAC Photo # PA145833)

DETAILS

Designation: L-5	**Model No:** HV-75 / 105	**Marks:**	**Role:** Utility Transport
TOS: 1940	**SOS:** 1946	**No:** 26	**Service:** RCAF

SPECIFICATIONS L-5

Manufacturer:	Stinson Aircraft Division of Consolidated Vultee Aircraft Corporation	
Crew/Passengers:	one pilot and one passenger	
Powerplant:	one 185 hp Lycoming O-435-1 piston engine	
Performance:	Max Speed: 130 mph (209 km/h)	Cruising Speed:
	Service Ceiling: 15,800 ft (4,816 m)	Range: 420 mi (676 km)
Weights:	Empty: 1,550 lb (703 kg)	Gross: 2,020 lb (916 kg)
Dimensions:	Span: 34 ft 0 in (10.36 m)	Length: 24 ft 1 in (7.34 m)
	Height: 7 ft 11 in (2.41 m)	Wing Area: 155 sq ft (14.40 sq m)
Armament:	None	
Cost:	$10,000 US	

Supermarine
SPITFIRE

First flown in 1936, the Spitfire would become famous as the leading British fighter of the Second World War. A total of 20,351 Spitfires (excluding naval variants) were built which was more than any other British warplane. No. 403 Squadron first flew the Spitfire on Canadian operations in March 1941 and a total of 14 RCAF squadrons eventually flew this type of aircraft. Of these squadrons, ten were fighter or fighter-bomber squadrons in Europe, three formed an RCAF fighter-reconnaissance wing, and one squadron, No. 417 Squadron, flew fighter-bombers in North Africa, Sicily, and Italy. The first enemy jet fighter, a German Me 262, to be shot down fell to a Spitfire from No. 401 Squadron. Interestingly, despite the large number of Spitfires flown operationally by Canadians, the RCAF only had a handful of Spitfires on official establishment strength throughout the war. These aircraft were primarily unarmed reconnaissance variants used for various test and photographic missions. The first Spitfire in Canada, on loan from the RAF, was used in 1940 to test the first "G" suit, which also was invented in Canada.

An unarmed home-war establishment Spitfire Mk V used for high altitude testing is shown here (CF Photo)

DETAILS
Designation: **Model No:** 300, 329, 331, 359, 360, 361, 365, 379, 380   **Marks:** Mk IA, II, IIA, IIB, VA, VB, VC, VIII, IXB, IXC, IXE, XI, XV, XIV, XIVE, XVIE

Role: Fighter
TOS: 1940   **SOS:** 1950   **No:** 8   **Service:** RCAF

SPECIFICATIONS Mk I
Manufacturer: Supermarine Aircraft
Crew/Passengers: one pilot
Powerplant: one 1,030 hp (768 kW) Rolls Royce Merlin II piston engine
Performance: Max Speed: 364 mph (586 km/h)   Cruising Speed:
Service Ceiling: 31,500 ft (9,601 m)   Range: 395 mi (636 km)
Weights: Empty: 4,341 lb (1,969 kg)   Gross: 5,800 lb (2,631 kg)
Dimensions: Span: 36 ft 10 in (11.23 m)   Length: 29 ft 11 in (9.10 m)
Height: 11 ft 5 in (3.48 m)   Wing Area: 242 sq ft (22.48 m)
Armament: eight .303 in (7.7 mm) machine guns in the wings
Cost: Unknown

Supermarine
SEAFIRE

First flown in 1936, the Spitfire would become famous as the leading British fighter of World War II. The Supermarine Seafire was a derivative of this famous Spitfire fighter. Developed for carrier use, the Seafire incorporated changes such as a tail hook, attachments for catapult use, and in later variants, folding wings. The first Seafires (converted Spitfires) entered service in 1942 and they served with distinction in all theatres of operation. In the immediate post-war period, Canada acquired

Seafires to equip its front line naval air squadrons. Naval Air Squadrons No. 803 and 883 operated Seafire Mk XV aircraft from Canada's first official aircraft carrier, HMCS *Warrior*, from 1946 to 1948. Seafires also made up the RCN's first aerobatic formation team, popularly known as Watson's Flying Circus, named after the Squadron CO. The Hawker Sea Fury eventually superseded the Seafire aircraft in RCN service.

An RCN Mk XV Seafire (externally very similar to the Spitfire V) is shown here in the earliest post-war colour scheme used by the Navy. (CF Photo)

DETAILS

Designation:	**Model No:** 377	**Marks:** Mk XV	**Role:** Fighter, Light Attack, Fighter Reconnaissance
TOS: 1946	**SOS:** 1954	**No:** 35	**Service:** RCN

SPECIFICATIONS Mk XV

Manufacturer:	Supermarine Aircraft Ltd	
Crew/Passengers:	one pilot	
Powerplant:	one 1,850 hp Rolls Royce Griffon VI piston engine	
Performance:	Max Speed: 383 mph (616 km/h)	Cruising Speed:
	Service Ceiling: 35,000 ft (10,668 m)	Range:
Weights:	Empty: 6,200 lb (2,812 kg)	Gross: 8,000 lb (3,629 kg)
Dimensions:	Span: 36 ft 10 in (11.23 m)	Length: 32 ft 3 in (9.82 m)
	Height: 10 ft 8 in (3.25 m)	Wing Area: 242 sq ft (22.48 m)
Armament:	Two 20 mm cannon and four .303 in (7.7 mm) machine guns in the wings plus provisions for light bombs or fuel tanks	
Cost:	Unknown	

Supermarine
STRANRAER

With the threat of the Second World War approaching, in 1936 the RCAF began searching for a coastal patrol aircraft. It looked to the RAF for suggestions and selected the Supermarine Stranraer and then placed an order for the type for license manufacture by Canadian Vickers. The Stranraer featured a hull manufactured from anodized Alclad sheeting with wings and tail surfaces manufactured from duralumin and covered with fabric. The Canadian prototype aircraft was delivered in 1938 and with the outbreak of war additional aircraft were ordered into production. The Stranraers served faithfully on both coasts during the early part of the war. They proved to be good

seaworthy aircraft but their antiquated biplane design eventually led to their being relegated to training duties. By 1944, some had even been declared surplus and sold into civilian use.

The Stranraer provided vital long-range patrol capabilities throughout the Second World War. Two views of the Stranraer in its element. (RCAF Photos via Comox AFM)

DETAILS

Designation:	**Model No:**	**Marks:**	**Role:** Amphibian
TOS: 1938	**SOS:** 1946	**No:** 40	**Service:** RCAF

SPECIFICATIONS

Manufacturer: Canadian Vickers

Crew/Passengers: Crew of five: pilot, navigator, radio operator and two gunners

Powerplant: two 810 hp Bristol Pegasus X radial engines

Performance: Max Speed: 165 mph (265 km/h)   Cruising Speed: 110 mph (177 km/h)
Service Ceiling: 20,000 ft (6,096 m)   Range: 1,140 mi (1,834 km) or 1,750 mi (2,816 km) with 130 Imp gal (591 l) external tanks

Weights: Empty: 12,534 lb (5,690 kg)   Gross: 19,900 lb (9,035 kg)

Dimensions: Span: 85 ft 0 in (25.81 m)   Length: 54 ft 6 in (16.61 m)
Height: 21 ft 9 in (7.64 m)   Wing Area: 1,457 sq ft (135.35 sq m)

Armament: three .303 cal flexible mount machine guns in nose, midship and tail positions plus 1,260 lb (572 kg) bombs or depth charges or 130 Imp gallon (591 l) fuel tanks on external racks

Cost: Unknown

Supermarine
WALRUS

The Supermarine Walrus did not equip any official RCAF Squadrons but it was flown in small numbers within Canada and by some RCAF/RCN personnel on overseas missions. The Walrus, affectionately known as the "Shagbat" in RCN and RAF parlance, was a rather ungainly looking aircraft from the same designer of the elegant Spitfire, R.J. Mitchell. Designed originally for catapult launched fleet reconnaissance and spotting duties,

the "Shagbat" also provided the RAF with a valuable air-sea rescue capability starting in 1941. Rescue missions within close proximity to enemy coastlines were the routine. Despite its appearance, the Walrus established a solid reputation for reliability and ability to withstand damage. Eight Walrus aircraft were also used in Canada by the RCAF and for the No. 1 Naval Air Gunners School in Yarmouth, NS.

A Supermarine Walrus seaplane is shown here being hoisted aboard ship. (LAC Photo # PA-116626)

DETAILS

Designation:	**Model No:**	**Marks:** Mk I, II	**Role:** Amphibian
TOS: 1943	**SOS:** 1947	**No:** 8	**Service:** RCN/RCAF

SPECIFICATIONS Mk II

Manufacturer:	Supermarine Aircraft	
Crew/Passengers:	crew of three or four	
Powerplant:	one 775 hp Bristol Pegasus VI radial engine	
Performance:	Max Speed: 135 mph (217 km/h)	Cruising Speed: 95 mph (153 km/h)
	Service Ceiling: 18,500 ft (5,640 mi)	Range: 600 miles (966 km)
Weights:	Empty: 4,900 lb (2,223 kg)	Maximum Take-off: 7,200 lb (3,266 kg)
Dimensions:	Span: 45 ft 10 in (13.97 m)	Length: 37 ft 3 in (11.35 m)
	Height: 15 ft 3 in (4.65 m)	Wing Area: 610 sq ft (56.67 sq m)
Armament:	provisions for one Vickers gun in bow and two amidships, 760 lb (345 kg) light bombs below wings	
Cost:	Unknown	

Vickers
VIKING

The Vickers Viking was a single engine flying boat purchased in 1923 to meet a CAF tender for an aircraft suitable to replace the wartime-vintage Curtiss HS-2L flying boats. Canadian Vickers had proposed its parent company's Vickers Viking IV. The mahogany wood hull of the aircraft gave them a rich appearance. The aircraft was in fact almost exclusively of wood construction except for tubular engine mounts supporting the Rolls Royce Eagle engines. The CAF's selection of this engine left the aircraft considerably underpowered and this deficiency remained through the type's entire career. Although seating for five was possible, the aircraft were usually limited to only three personnel because of the performance limitations. The aircraft were also found to have poor characteristics while taxiing in the water. Nevertheless, they were pressed into service and used at a number of bases but primarily in the province of Manitoba, mostly for survey or transport work. The aircraft were amphibious-capable, having wheels fitted but water borne landings were the normal activity and the gear served as a convenient beaching capability. In 1924, an RCAF pilot flew a Viking aircraft 900 miles in twelve days delivering treaty payments to Indian reservations across Northern Ontario. This extended duration flight was considered a rare accomplishment in the period.

The Viking IV was chosen by the Canadian Air Force as a replacement for the Curtiss HS-2L. The crew was housed in open cockpits and an additional camera position in the nose was specified by the RCAF. The Rolls-Royce engine version of the aircraft was chosen, primarily for reasons of economy, but this caused the Viking IV to be considerably underpowered for an aircraft of its size and weight. (RCAF Photo)

DETAILS

Designation:	**Model No:**	**Marks:** Mk IV	**Role:** Flying Boat
TOS: 1923	**SOS:** 1931	**No:** 8	**Service:** RCAF

SPECIFICATIONS

Manufacturer:	Canadian Vickers	
Crew/Passengers:	crew of three: one pilot and two passengers	
Powerplant:	one 360 hp Rolls Royce Eagle VIII or IX pusher engine	
Performance:	Max Speed: 102 mph (164 km/h)	Cruising Speed: 80 mph (128 km/h)
	Service Ceiling: 9,000 ft (2,743 m)	Range:
Weights:	Empty: 3,750 lb (1,701 kg)	Gross: 5,600 lb (2,541 kg)
Dimensions:	Span: 50 ft 0 in (15.24 m)	Length: 34 ft 0 in (10.36 m)
	Height: 15 ft 1 in (4.6 m)	Wing Area: 594 sq ft (55.2 sq m)
Armament:	None	
Cost:	Unknown	

Waco
AQC-6

The WACO AQC-6 was a "Custom Cabin" biplane built by Waco in 1936. The design incorporated a wide variety of engines of seven different types. With each of the engine types, the aircraft received a slightly different designation and model number. Each of these models was like a different aircraft because of the varying degrees of performance. The "Custom Cabin" design was plush and comfortable and was intended for sportsmen and businessmen, being lavishly equipped for its day. With the Jacobs L-6 engine installed providing 330 hp, the model became known as the AQC-6. This improved engine and extra horsepower combined with a controllable pitch propeller meant the aircraft provided excellent service. The ACQ-6 was capable of being operated year-round, operating comfortably on wheels, skis or floats.

The handsome Waco AQC-6 floatplane depicted here is similar to the sole example used by the RCAF. (LAC Photo # PA-RD001071)

DETAILS

Designation:	**Model No:** AQC-6	**Marks:**	**Role:** Utility Transport
TOS: 1942	**SOS:** 1942	**No:** 1	**Service:** RCAF

SPECIFICATIONS

Manufacturer:	Waco Aircraft Company	
Crew/Passengers:	one pilot and up to four passengers	
Powerplant:	Jacobs L-6 providing 300 hp (330 hp for take-off)	
Performance:	Max Speed: 170 mph (274 km/h)	Cruising Speed: 155 mph (249 km/h)
	Service Ceiling: 18,500 ft (5,638 m)	Range: 550 mi (885 km)
Weights:	Empty: 2,313 lbs (1,049 kg)	Gross: 3,650 lbs (1,656 kg)
Dimensions:	Span: 35 ft 0 in (10.67 m)	Length: 26 ft 8 in (8.13 m)
	Height: 8 ft 8 in (2.64 m)	Wing Area: 244 sq ft (22.67 sq m)
Armament:	None	
Cost:	$8,975 US	

Waco
CG-15

The Waco CG-15 was a development of the successful Waco CG-4 Hadrian standard glider. Waco had essentially developed an improved version of the CG-4A. Interestingly, the changes consisted of a reduction in the wingspan from 83 ft 8 in to 62 ft 2 in, elimination of the wing spoilers, a revised nose shape, improved cantilever undercarriage and numerous internal fitment changes. The changes increased the normal gross weight by 500 lbs (227 kg) and the towing speed increased to 180 mph (290 km/h). Originally 427 CG-15 gliders were delivered to the US military. Canada acquired a single example for evaluation purposes.

This wintry view of the American CG-15 glider acquired by Canada for test purposes illustrates the revised wing-span among other improvements made to original Waco design. (LAC Photo # PA-65385)

DETAILS

Designation: | **Model No:** CG-15 | **Marks:** | **Role:** Glider
TOS: 1946 | **SOS:** 1950 | **No:** 1 | **Service:** RCAF

SPECIFICATIONS

Manufacturer: Waco Aircraft Company
Crew/Passengers: two pilots and up to thirteen troops or a variety of stores
Powerplant: None
Performance: Max Speed: 180 mph (290 km/h) — Stalling Speed:
Service Ceiling: 10,000 ft (3,345 m) — Range: Tow plane dependent
Weights: Empty: — Gross:
Dimensions: Span: 62 ft 2 in (25.50 m) — Length: 48 ft 4 in (14.73 m)
Height: 12 ft 7 in (3.84 m) — Wing Area:
Armament: None
Cost: Unknown

Waco
PG-2A

The Waco PG-2A was a unique powered development of the successful Waco CG-4 Hadrian standard glider. In 1943, the US military had originally developed a prototype powered version of the Hadrian with two Franklin flat-four piston engines in nacelles beneath the wings. The object of this conversion was to allow the glider to return under its own power after completing a mission.

After tests with this prototype, a further ten conversions of the aircraft were ordered with Ranger L-440-7 piston engines. These production versions were then known by the PG-2A designation. The service trials were apparently of interest to the RCAF and one PG-2A was briefly trialed here in Canada during the immediate post-war period.

A view of the sole Waco PG-2A glider in RCAF colours. (J McNulty photo)

DETAILS

Designation:	**Model No:** PG-2A	**Marks:**	**Role:** Powered Glider
TOS: 1946	**SOS:** 1947	**No:** 1	**Service:** RCAF

SPECIFICATIONS

Manufacturer:	Waco Aircraft Company	
Crew/Passengers:	two pilots and up to thirteen troops	
Powerplant:	two Ranger L-440-7 piston engines	
Performance:	Max Speed:	Cruising Speed:
	Service Ceiling:	Range:
Weights:	Empty:	Gross:
Dimensions:	Span: 83 ft 8 in (25.50 m)	Length: 48 ft 4 in (14.73 m)
	Height: 12 ft 7 in (3.84 m)	Wing Area: 852 sq ft (79.15 sq m)
Armament:	None	
Cost:	Unknown	

Waco
HADRIAN (HAIG)

The Hadrian was the first and most widely used troop glider employed by the Allies during the Second World War. It was a mixture of wood, fabric and metal construction and featured an upward-hinged nose section that permitted direct loading of vehicles into the box-section fuselage. In addition to heavy regular usage the type was also committed to unique experiments such as a successful transatlantic crossing under tow involving Canadian crews. In post-war Canada, a small number of gliders were also retained in service for experimentation and trials.

A view of the Waco CG-4A glider in RCAF colours while in Rivers, Manitoba showing the wing profile to good effect. (RCAF Photo)

DETAILS

Designation:	**Model No:** CG-4A	**Marks:**	**Role:** Glider
TOS: 1944	**SOS:** 1955	**No:** 32	**Service:** RCAF

SPECIFICATIONS

Manufacturer: Waco Aircraft Company

Crew/Passengers: two pilots and up to thirteen fully-equipped troops or a variety of stores

Powerplant: None

Performance: Max Speed: 150 mph (241 km/h) Stalling Speed: 44 mph (71 km/h)
Service Ceiling: 10,000 ft (3,345 m) Range: tow plane dependent

Weights: Empty: 3,700 lb (1,678 kg) Gross: 7,500 lb (3,402 kg)

Dimensions: Span: 83 ft 8 in (25.50 m) Length: 48 ft 4 in (14.73 m)
Height: 12 ft 7 in (3.84 m) Wing Area: 852 sq ft (79.15 sq m)

Armament: None

Cost: $24,000 US

Westland
LYSANDER

Designed and built by Westland Aircraft Ltd. as an Army co-operation aircraft, the Lysander first entered RCAF service in 1939. No. 110 (later 400) Squadron was the first RCAF unit to be sent overseas and was equipped with Lysanders, as was No. 112 Squadron, the second squadron, which followed in June 1940. Four squadrons used the "Lizzie" in Canada for artillery spotting, drogue towing, reconnaissance and close support training. The aircraft type also won fame later in the war by transporting agents into enemy occupied territories.

The RCAF Lysander aircraft shown here in Canada likely in 1939 displays a bare metal / silver finish which was quickly replaced by standard RAF camouflage scheme with the outbreak of hostilities. (Comox AFM Photo)

DETAILS

Designation:	Model No:	Marks: Mk II, IITT, III, IIIA, IIIT	Role: Utility Transport
TOS: 1939	SOS: 1946	No: 329	Service: RCAF

SPECIFICATIONS Mk IIITT

Manufacturer:	Westland Aircraft Ltd
Crew/Passengers:	crew of two: pilot and crewman
Powerplant:	one 870 hp Bristol Mercury XX or XXX radial
Performance:	Max Speed: 217 mph (349 km/h) Cruising Speed: 170 mph (273.5 km/h)
	Service Ceiling: 23,850 ft (7,269 m)
Weights:	Empty: 4,840 lb (2,197 kg) Gross: 6,000 lb (2,724 kg)
Dimensions:	Span: 50 ft (15.24 m) Length: 30 ft 6 in (9.3 m)
	Height: 11 ft 6 in (3.5 m) Wing Area: 260 sq ft (24.15 sq m)
Armament:	Provision for two forward fixed plus one rear mounted flexible .303 machine guns and provisions for light practice bombs on stub wings attached to wheel spats
Original Cost:	Unknown

CANADIAN FORCES AIRCRAFT ANNOUNCED OR CONTRACTED FOR BUT NOT YET IN USE OR DELIVERED

CH-148 Cyclone (Sikorsky).

Boeing
GLOBEMASTER

The C-17 was derived from a McDonnell Douglas mid-1970s YC-15 design intended to replace the Hercules. In the 1980s this design was resurrected to answer a new USAF CX (Cargo Experimental) requirement. Re-engined and enlarged, the redesigned C-17 was meant to supply the USAF with a strategic airlifter which could carry more than a C-141Starlifter but also had tactical capabilities that were lacking in the C-5 Galaxy transport. The C-17 is powered by a military version of the high-bypass turbofan engine used by the Boeing 757 jetliner. The designers at McDonnell Douglas also incorporated some systems from the DC-10 commercial aircraft to try to curb costs. Four C-17s have been ordered for Canadian use.

The C-17 Globemaster aircraft will be the largest aircraft in the CF transport fleet. (USAF photos)

DETAILS

Designation: CC-???   **Model No:** C-17   **Marks:**   **Role:** Transport

TOS: Ordered   **SOS:**   **No:** 4   **Service:** CF

SPECIFICATIONS

Manufacturer:	Boeing
Crew/Passengers:	Crew: two pilots, one tech crewman, and one or two loadmasters
	Troops: up to 144 or Litters: 36 plus 102 ambulatory
Powerplant:	Four Pratt & Whitney PW 2040 (F117-PW-100) turbofan engines each with 40,440 lbs thrust
Performance:	Max Speed: 403 mph (648 km/h)
	Service Ceiling: 45,000 ft (13,715 m)
Weights:	Empty: 227,000 lb (25,645 kg)
Dimensions:	Span: 169 ft 9 in (51.74 m)
	Height: 55 ft 1 in (16.79 m)
Armament:	None but provision for chaff and flare dispensers
Cost:	

Cruising Speed:

Range: 5063 mi (8,148 km)

Maximum Take-off: 585,000 lb (265,350 kg)

Length: 174 ft 0 in (53.04) m

Wing Area: 3,800 sq ft (353.03 sq m)

Boeing
CHINOOK

The Boeing CH-47F+ Chinook is a special uprated variant of the heavy-lift tandem-rotor helicopter first acquired by the CF in 1974. The CF intends to order 16 of these much improved versions for use in heavy lift operations.

The CH-47F Chinook is a much improved variant of the standard heavy-lift workhorse design. Canadian aircraft will likely be a further improved development of the F model with long-range internal fuel tanks. This photo illustrates the original CH-147 (CH-47C) after slinging a CT-133 Silver Star in Moose Jaw. The inset shows the first flight of the CH-47F model design. (CF and Boeing Photos)

DETAILS

Designation: CH-147   **Model No:** CH-47F   **Role:** Transport Helicopter

TOS: Ordered   **SOS:**   **No:** 16   **Service:** CF

SPECIFICATIONS CH-47F

Manufacturer:	Boeing
Crew/Passengers:	four: two pilots, one flight engineer and one loadmaster plus up to forty-four passengers, thirty-three troops or up 28,000 lb (12,700 kg) external loads
Powerplant:	two Honeywell 4,075 shp (3,039 kW) T55-GA-714A turboshaft engines

Performance: Max Speed: 177 mph (285 km/h)   Cruising Speed: 161 mph (259 km/h)
Hover Ceiling: 9,800 ft (2,985 m)   Range: 115 mi (185 km)

Weights: Empty: 25,463 lb (11,550 kg)   Maximum Takeoff: 54,000 lbs (24,494 kg)

Dimensions: Rotor Diameter: 60 ft 0 in (18.29 m)   Length: 98 ft 10½ in (30.14 m)
Height: 22 ft 6 in (6.86 m)

Armament: None

Original Cost: Unknown

Lockheed Martin
HERCULES

The latest version of the C1-30 Hercules, the J model, has the unofficial nickname of Super Hercules. It is the most advanced version of the aircraft and it features numerous technological improvements that add to operational capability while at the same time reducing operating and maintenance costs. Essentially, all that stays is the basic airframe shape. Composite materials have replaced metal components to make the aircraft lighter. The propulsion system has been redesigned and features four Rolls Royce AE2100D3 engines (4,591 SHP each). Dowty R391 all-composite, six-blade propellers generate 29 percent more thrust while increasing fuel efficiency. The under-wing, external fuel tanks that are such a familiar feature of previous C-130 models are consequently no longer necessary on the C-130J. The J model's two-person, state-of-the-art cockpit is fully digital and includes four multifunctional LCD displays, two holographic Head-Up Displays, and electronic, digital readouts for aircraft flight controls and operating and navigating systems. The displays and general aircraft lighting are Night Vision System compatible. A 1553 data bus, two mission computers, and two back-up bus interface units provide dual system redundancy. In addition, the computers provide for an integrated diagnostics system that monitors and records the status of the aircraft's structure and systems. The cargo area has also been improved with the addition of an Enhanced Cargo Handling System, decreasing loadmaster workload, reducing times for configuration changes, and allowing for very precise airdrops.

The CC-130J Hercules is a significantly redesigned aircraft with only a small percentage in common with the other Hercules in the CF transport fleet. Externally almost identical to its older cousins (except for 6-bladed propellers), internally it is virtually completely redesigned with all new avionics, fly-by-wire and redesigned cockpit controls. (Lockheed Martin Photo)

DETAILS

Designation: CC-130   **Model No:** C130J   **Marks:** C-130J   **Role:** Transport
TOS: Ordered   **SOS:**   **No:** 16-   **Service:** CF

SPECIFICATIONS J-Model

Manufacturer:	Lockheed Martin Aircraft Corporation
Crew/Passengers:	Crew: two pilots, one tech crewman and one or two loadmasters
	Troops: up to 128 or Paratroops: 92 or Litters: 74 plus two attendants
Powerplant:	Four Allison AE2100D3 turboprop engines with 4,591 EHP (3,425 KW)

Performance:

Max Speed: 435 mph (700 km/h)	Cruising Speed: 400 mph (645 km/h)
Service Ceiling: 42,900 mph (13,075 km/h)	Range: 5,465 mi (8,795 km)

Weights:

Empty: 75,562 lb (34,274 kg)	Maximum Take-off: 155,000 lb (70,305 kg)

Dimensions:

Span: 132 ft 7 in (40.41 m)	Length: 97 ft 9 in (29.79) m
Height: 38 ft 10 in (11.84 m)	Wing Area: 1,745 sq ft (162.12 sq m)

Armament: None but provision for chaff & flare dispensers
Cost:

Lockheed Martin
JOINT STRIKE FIGHTER (JSF)

Lockheed Martin's Joint Strike Fighter (JSF) concept is a family of aircraft that meets multi-service needs while accommodating unique service requirements including low observability (stealth). Three variants share a highly common structure, including the same fuselage and internal weapons bay. The aircraft employs a derivative of the Pratt & Whitney F119 engine that powers the F-22 stealth fighter. The JSF offers conventional take-off and landing (CTOL) capability for the Air Force, carrier suitability for the Navy, and short takeoff/vertical landing (STOVL) capability for the Marine Corps, Royal Navy and Royal Air Force. Lockheed Martin received one of two JSF Concept Demonstration contracts awarded by the US government in November 1996 (Boeing offered a competing design). The program included development, manufacture and flight test of two demonstrator aircraft by each team; a number of concurrent technology

demonstration programs for critical risk reduction; and design trade studies to refine the Preferred Weapons System Concept for the operational JSF version. The Lockheed Martin design was selected as the winner and is now proceeding through an Engineering and Manufacturing Development phase, followed by production. Approximately 3,000 JSF aircraft were originally planned for the US Air Force, Navy, Marine Corps, and the UK Royal Navy and Royal Air Force, replacing several current aircraft types. Other international governments have expressed interest in Lockheed Martin's JSF program, including current participants Denmark, the Netherlands, Norway, Italy, Canada, Singapore, Turkey and Israel. Canadian participation has included limited partner status throughout the program and guarantees an option to purchase.

Two views of the prototypes for the X-35 JSF design. (Lockheed Martin Photos)

DETAILS
Designation: X-35 A, B, C **Model No:** 220 A, B, C **Marks:** **Role:** Fighter/Strike aircraft
Service: Under Development for USAF, USN, USMC and RN plus others

SPECIFICATIONS
Manufacturer: Lockheed Martin Aircraft Corporation
Crew/Passengers: one or two pilots in ejection seats
Powerplant: one Pratt & Whitney JSF119-PW-611 turbofan with optional shaft-driven lift fan engine for STOVL capability
Performance: Max Speed: Mach 1.8   Cruising Speed: Mach 1.2
Combat Radius: X-35A: 703 nm   X-35B: 496 nm   X-35C: 799 nm
Weights: Empty: X35A: 26,717 lb (12,119 kg)   X35B: 29,735 lb (13,488 kg)   X35C: 30,049 lb (13,630 kg)
Dimensions: X35A, B: Length: 50 ft 6 in (15.47 m);   X35C: 50 ft 10 in (15.48 m)
X35A, B: Span: 35 ft 0 in (10.67 m)   Wing area: 406 sq ft (37.72 sq m)
X35C: Span: 43 ft 0 in (13.11 m)   Wing area: 620 sq ft (57.60 sq m)
Armament: Provision for one 27 mm BK27 cannon, two AIM-120 AMRAAMs, two 2,000 lb munitions internally plus bombs, rockets, or tanks on underwing pylons
Original Cost: Projected to be less than $40M (2001 US)

Sikorsky
CYCLONE

The Westland-Augusta EH-101 had originally been chosen as Canada's new Anti-Submarine Warfare (ASW) helicopter to replace the Sea King helicopter. The ASW variant was to be known as the CH-148 Petrol and the SAR variant was to be designated the CH-149 Chimo. The first of 50 EH-101s was to be delivered in 1993. Unfortunately, after considerable development effort, a new Canadian government elected to cancel the delivery of the helicopters as part of cost cutting measures, terminating the program. The SAR competition was eventually won by a civilianized variant of the EH-101 known as the CH-149 Cormorant. In 2004, the Canadian gov-

ernment decided to purchase of 28 of the Sikorsky-designed Superhawk (to be known in Canadian service as the Cyclone) helicopters to replace the CH124 Sea Kings. The Cyclone, as the aircraft is to be called, will assume all the roles of the Sea King, including anti-submarine warfare, beyond-visual identification, search and rescue, as well as ship to shore delivery. The Cyclone was the result of a prolonged procurement process that lasted over 20 years. Ironically, the Cyclone beat out another version of the CH-149 Cormorant. The Canadian Forces will be the first military customer for the S-92 aircraft and the first to use it as a shipborne aircraft.

Two views of the S-92 prototype, which will eventually become the CH148 Cyclone. (Sikorsky Photos)

DETAILS

Designation: CH-148   **Model No:** S-92   **Marks:**   **Role:** ASW/Utility Helicopter

TOS: Not yet in service   **SOS:** Not yet determined   **No:** 28   **Service:** CF

SPECIFICATIONS   S-92 data

Manufacturer:	Sikorsky
Crew/Passengers:	two pilots, a flight engineer and a weapons systems officer plus provisions for rescue hoists, 10,000 lb/4,535 kg external cargo
Powerplant:	two General Electric CT7-8A engines, each producing a maximum of 2,520 shaft horsepower

Performance:

Max Speed: 155 kts (290 km/h)	Cruising Speed: 140 kts (260 km/h)
Service Ceiling: 11,500 ft (3,500 m)	Range: 490 nm (910 km)

Weights:

Empty: 15,200 lb (6,893 kg)	Gross: 26,500 lb (12,018 kg)

Dimensions:

Rotor Diameter: 56 ft 4 in (17.17 m)	Length: 68 ft 5 in (20.85 m)
Height: 21 ft 2 in (6.45 m)	

Armament: Torpedoes, self-defence guns

Cost: $13.5M

NON-CANADIAN FORCES (IE CIVILIAN LEASED, ETC) AIRCRAFT FLOWN BY CF PERSONNEL DURING TRAINING, TEST OR OTHER MILITARY MISSIONS

CT-155 Hawk (CF CK2004-0065-18d).

Avro (Canada)
ARROW

One of the most famous aircraft in Canadian history, the CF-105 Arrow never made it into operational use with the RCAF. The CF-105 Arrow was a supersonic all-weather two-seat interceptor designed and produced by Avro Aircraft Limited in Malton, Ontario. Avro had avoided the normal prototype stage and launched directly into manufacture of production aircraft. Five pre-production standard aircraft were outfitted with J-57 engines and flight test systems. The sixth aircraft was equipped with the full production Orenda Iroquois engines but this aircraft never flew prior to program cancellation. A total of 31 more aircraft were also in production when the entire effort was terminated by the federal government on 20 February 1959.

The legendary CF105 Arrow Mk I supersonic fighter was test-flown by RCAF pilots and operational implementation plans were well underway before the overall program was cancelled. (CF Photo)

DETAILS

Designation: CF-105	**Model No:**	**Marks:** Mk I, II	**Role:** Fighter
TOS: 1958	**SOS:** 1959	**No:** 5	**Service:** ordered by RCAF

SPECIFICATIONS Mark 1

Manufacturer:	Avro Canada
Crew/Passengers:	Two (pilot and navigator / weapons officer)
Powerplant:	2 Pratt & Whitney J-57 P5 turbojet engines each with 12,500 lbs thrust or (18,000 lbs in A/B)
Performance:	Max Speed: Mach 2.0 or 700 kts (1,297 km/h)
	Service Ceiling: 53,000 ft (15,240 m) Combat Radius: 300 mi (483 km)
Weights:	Empty: 48,923 lb (22,211 kg) Gross: 57,000 lb (25,855 kg)
	Maximum Take-off: 68,600 lb (31,144 kg)
Dimensions:	Span: 50 ft (15.24 m) Length: 77 ft 10 in (23.71 m)
	Height: 21 ft 3 in (6.48 m) Wing Area: 1,225 sq ft (113.8 sq m)
Armament:	Provisions for internal carriage of up to four AIM-4 Falcon or Sparrow 2 missiles
Cost:	Unknown

Beech
KING AIR

The King Air is a highly successful executive turbine transport design that proved to be very popular, with over 2,000 models sold and in service. The design was constantly evolved and improved in service and the Super King Air represented the ultimate in this line. The CF was faced with a requirement to teach multi-engine turboprop handling to those pilots graduating from a piston and jet training program. Consequently, the CF acquired three Super King Air aircraft for this purpose. These aircraft were retired in 1995 following the conversion of the entire training program to a civilian-run and organized program. The requirement for the aircraft was not eliminated but the civilian contractor supplied their own C90A King Airs (as opposed to Super King Airs) for this purpose. Eight Beech King Airs were therefore provided to the military under contract by their owner, Bombardier, and used for multi-engine training of military pilots by military instructors. These aircraft were subsequently replaced by seven C90B King Airs owned by the Allied Wings consortium that took over the Southport contract.

The King Air aircraft seen here on the flight line at Southport, Manitoba (formerly CFB Portage la Prairie) display the Bombardier insignia on their tails. (CF Photo)

DETAILS

Designation: CT-145 **Model No:** C90A , C90B **Role:** Trainer

TOS: 1995 **SOS:** In-Service **No:** 8 C90A, 7 C90B **Service:** Contractor Provided

SPECIFICATIONS

Manufacturer:	Beech Aircraft Corporation
Crew/Passengers:	crew of two with provisions for eight passengers
Powerplant:	two 550 eshp Pratt & Whitney PT-6A-21 turboprop engines

Performance:	Max Speed: 284 mph (457 km/h)	Cruising Speed:
	Service Ceiling: 28,100 ft (8,565 m)	Range: 1,243 mi (2,001 km)
Weights:	Empty: 5,765 lb (2,615 kg)	Maximum Take-off: 9,650 lb (4,377 kg)
Dimensions:	Span: 50 ft 3 in (15.32 m)	Length: 35 ft 6 in (10.82 m)
	Height: 14 ft 3 in (4.34 m)	Wing Area: 293.94 sq ft (27.31 sq m)
Armament:	None	
Cost:	Unknown	

Beech
SUPER KING AIR

The Super King Air was a highly successful executive turbine transport design that proved to be very popular, with over 2,000 models sold and in service. The design was constantly evolved and improved in service and the Super King Air represented the ultimate in this line. The CF was faced with a requirement to teach multiengine turboprop handling to those pilots graduating from a piston and jet training program. Consequently, the CF leased three Super King Air aircraft for this purpose. These aircraft were returned in 1995 following the conversion of the entire training program to a civilianrun and organized program. The requirement for these aircraft was not eliminated, but the civilian contractor supplied their own King Airs for this purpose.

A Super King Air on the ramp, similar those CT-145 aircraft leased by the CF. (Bill Knight/Eagle 19 Photo)

DETAILS

Designation: CT-145   **Model No:** B200   **Role:** Trainer

TOS: 1990   **SOS:** 1995   **No:** 3   **Service:** CF

SPECIFICATIONS

Manufacturer: Beech Aircraft Corporation

Crew/Passengers: crew of two with provisions for thirteen passengers

Powerplant: two 850 eshp Pratt & Whitney PT-6A-42 turboprop engines

Performance: Max Speed: 338 mph (544 km/h)   Cruising Speed: 325 mph (523 km/h)

Service Ceiling: 35,000 ft (10,668 m)   Range: 2,272 mi (3,656 km)

Weights: Empty: 8,060 lb (3,656 kg)   Gross: 12,500 lb (5,670 kg)

Dimensions: Span: 54 ft 6 in (16.64 m)   Length: 43 ft 9 in (13.38 m)

Height: 15 ft 0 in (4.57 m)   Wing Area: 303 sq ft (28.15 sq m)

Armament: None

Cost: Unknown

Bell
JET RANGER

Following successful experience with the Bell Kiowa, the CF selected the Bell 206 BIII Jet Ranger improved commercial derivative for basic helicopter training duties. The Jet Rangers were essentially purchased "off the shelf" for delivery to the military. Primarily employed in this role at CFB Portage La Prairie in Manitoba, the Jet Rangers possessed more powerful engines and consequently better "hot and high" performance than their operational cousins. The performance of the helicopters spawned a helicopter display team flown by instructors who were known as The Dragonflies. As result of a UN mission to Central America requiring this better performance, some of the Jet Rangers were rapidly modified for operational UN use and actively deployed. The entire Jet Ranger fleet was officially retired from the CF in 1992, only to re-emerge as contractor flown and maintained training aircraft in a now civilianized primary flying training facility in support of the CF program.

The CH-139 Jet Ranger training helicopter in a high visibility training colour scheme. (CF Photo)

DETAILS

Manufacturer: Bell   **Designation:** CH-139   **Model No:** 206 BIII   **Role:** Training Helicopter

TOS: 1992   **SOS:** In Service   **No:** 14   **Service:** Leased from Bombardier and Allied Wings contractors

SPECIFICATIONS

Manufacturer: Bell Textron Helicopters

Crew/Passengers: two pilots plus up to three passengers

Powerplant: one 420 SHP Allison 205-C20B turboshaft engine

Performance: Max Speed: 140 mph (225 km/h)   Cruising Speed: 133 mph (214 km/h)

Hover Ceiling: 13,200 ft (4,025 m)   Range: 430 mi (692 km)

Weights: Empty: 1,702 lb (722 kg)   Gross: 3,200 lbs (1,452 kg)

Dimensions: Rotor Diameter: 33 ft 4 in (10.16 m)   Length: 38 ft 9½ in (11.82 m)

Height: 9 ft 6 in (2.89 m)   Rotor Disc Area: 872.7 sq ft (81.07 sq m)

Armament: None

Original Cost: Unknown

Boeing
B-47 STRATOJET

The Boeing B-47 Stratojet was the first swept-wing bomber built in any quantity in the world. Initial design work began in 1943 and with the end of the war, the final design benefited from results obtained from German research. The first prototype was ready to fly in 1947. The B-47 went on to achieve quantity production for the USAF and became the mainstay of the Strategic Air Command. By comparison the RCAF did not pursue any bomber force in the post-war period. The RCAF, however, did acquire one B-47 Stratojet (USAF B-47 No. 51-2051) for test and evaluation purposes. Ironically this bomber was acquired to facilitate the test of a fighter engine for the new Avro Arrow interceptor then under development. The B-47 became a flying test bed for Orenda's Iroquois engine trials in

which the test engine was mounted in a nacelle on the rear fuselage. In doing so, it became the only seven-engined B-47. Besides adding this engine pylon and nacelle, the extensive structural modifications included double skinning the rear fuselage, strengthening bulkheads and adding bulkheads and longerons. The co-pilot's station was modified into a flight test engineer's station, test instrumentation was installed in the bomb bay and 8,000 lb (3,600 kg) of ballast was installed in the nose to counter the weight of the Iroquois engine. In subsequent test flights, the B-47 had its primary engines shut down and the aircraft was able to fly powered solely by the Iroquois. With the termination of the Arrow/Iroquois program, the aircraft was returned to the United States.

The sole B-47 Stratojet in RCAF colours. The Iroquois engine test pod is visible at the rear of the aircraft. (Avro Photo)

DETAILS

Designation:	**Model No:** B-47B	**Role:** Test and Evaluation	
TOS: 1955	**SOS:** 1959	**No:** 1	**Service:** RCAF

SPECIFICATIONS

Manufacturer: Boeing Airplane Company
Crew/Passengers: two pilots and one navigator
Powerplant: six 6,000 lb thrust GE J-47 turbojet engines plus one Iroquois test engine
Performance: Max Speed: 606 mph (975 km/h) — Cruising Speed: 557 mph (896 km/h)
Service Ceiling: 40,500 ft (12,344 m) — Range: 4,000 mi (6,438 km)
Weights: Empty: 80,756 lb (36,631 kg) — Gross: 206,700 lb (93,759 kg)
Dimensions: Span: 116 ft 0 in (35.36 m) — Length: 109 ft 10 in (33.48 m)
Height: 27 ft 11 in (8.51 m) — Wing Area: 1,428 sq ft (132.67 sq m)
Armament: None
Cost: $1,888,000 US

BAE Systems
HAWK

Student pilots in the NATO Flying Training in Canada (NFTC) program who are selected for jet training will transit from the CT-156 Harvard II to the CT-155 Hawk, and will continue to train at 15 Wing Moose Jaw. In addition, the Hawk will be used at 4 Wing Cold Lake during the fourth phase of jet pilot training. The BAE Systems Hawk 115 was selected for its similarities to sophisticated front-line fighter aircraft. Its principle features include: an advanced glass cockpit with a Heads Up Display (HUD); a multi-function display, hands-on throttle and stick controls; integrated navigation and weapon aiming systems;

and a high-powered turbofan engine. It is considered one of the most advanced trainers ever built. With its advanced technology, the Hawk is capable of performing a wide range of combat missions, translating into a cost-effective bottom line for pilot training In Canada. Student pilots will spend 80 hours training on the Hawk in Moose Jaw, followed by an additional 45 hours in the Fighter Lead-In program in Cold Lake. At this stage, pilots will be ready to join 410 Squadron, the Operational Training Unit, which flies CF-18 Hornets.

A pair of BAE Systems CT-155 Hawk aircraft are shown here in standard NFTC colours. (CF Photo)

DETAILS

Designation: CT-155	**Model No:** 115	**Marks:**	**Role:** Advanced Jet Trainer
TOS: 2000	**SOS:** In Service	**No:** 15	**Service:** Leased from Bombardier

SPECIFICATIONS Hawk 100 Series

Manufacturer:	British Aerospace Systems		
Crew/Passengers:	two pilots in tandem		
Powerplant:	one 5,900 lb Rolls-Royce Mk 871 Adour turbofan engine		
Performance:	Max Speed: 1,609 mph (1,000 km/h)	Cruising Speed:	
	Service Ceiling: 46,000 ft (14,021 m)	Range:	
Weights:	Empty: 9,700 lb (4,400 kg)	Gross: 20,062 lb (9,100 kg)	
Dimensions:	Span: 32 ft 7 in (9.94 m)	Length: 40 ft 7 in (12.43 m)	
	Height: 13 ft 1 in (3.98 m)	Wing Area: 180 sq ft (16.69 sq m)	
Armament:	none but provisions for under-wing drop tanks, rockets, missiles, practice bombs and under-fuselage gun pod		
Cost:	Leased from Bombardier		

Canadair
CL-84 DYNAVERT TILTROTOR

The unique Canadair CL-84 Dynavert was started as a company private venture in response to NATO specification. The NATO requirement called for a transport, reconnaissance, SAR and ground support aircraft that could take-off vertically, and perform short take-offs and landings (STOL). Canadair's response was a relatively conventional design in appearance, which featured a wing that could be tilted upward through 100 degrees, complete with turboshaft engines powering large 14 ft (4.3 m) diameter rotors. The tailplane and twin vertical stabilizers also pivoted and the most unconventional fea-tures were horizontally mounted contra-rotating tail rotors. This overall unique design foreshadowed the much later successful "tiltrotor" designs by Bell / Boeing. However, despite successful VTOL demonstrations by the prototype and by three subsequently improved trial aircraft, the Canadair Dynavert never entered production. The aircraft had been accepted by the Canadian Armed Forces for the trials and were also subject to extensive tests by the US Navy and Marine Corps. The Canadair aircraft helped pioneer the feasibility of the "tiltrotor" concept but unfortunately proved to be ahead of its time.

The Canadair CL-84 Dynavert in a later CAF paint scheme demonstrating its tiltrotor configuration. (Canadair Photo)

DETAILS

Designation: CX-131	**Model No:** CL-84 and CL-84-1	**Role:** Test and Evaluation	
TOS: 1969	**SOS:** 1971	**No:** 4 CL-84 (1), CL-84-1 (3)	**Service:** CF

SPECIFICATIONS

Manufacturer:	Canadair Aircraft Ltd	
Crew/Passengers:	two pilots in ejection seats	
Powerplant:	two 1,500 hp Lycoming T-53 turboshaft engines	
Performance:	Max Speed: 321 mph (517 km/h)	Cruising Speed: 309 mph (497 km/h)
	Service Ceiling: 10,000 ft (3,050 m)	VTOL Range: 420 mi (677 km)
Weights:	Empty: 8,775 lb (3,980 kg)	Gross VTOL: 12,600 lb (5,714 kg)
	Gross STOL: 14,500 lb (6,577 kg)	
Dimensions:	Span: 34 ft 8 in (10.56 m)	Length: 53 ft 7½ in (16.34 m)
	Height (wing at 90 deg): 17 ft 1½ in (5.22 m)	Wing Area: 233 sq ft (21.67 sq m)
Armament:	None but provisions for two 100-gallon (455-litre) drop tanks	
Cost:	Unknown	

Grob
G120A

First flown in 1999, the Grob 120A is a development of the company's G 115 trainer series and is designed to meet modern airline pilot and military pilot training requirements. The ultra-modern all-composite design incorporates numerous advanced features including EFIS, a retractable landing gear and a 194 kW (260 hp) Textron Lycoming AEIO-540 flat-six engine. The aircraft replaces the Slingsby Firefly (which in turn replaced the CT-134 Musketeer) as the Air Force's *ab-initio* pilot trainer. It is a modern lightweight composite civilian design adapted for military training, including aerobatic training. These aircraft do not actually belong to the military, but rather are owned by the Allied Wings consortium led by Kelowna Flightcraft. The training location is still familiar to many military-trained pilots, as the Southport, Manitoba training area was originally known as CFB Portage la Prairie during the time when the military maintained its own facilities for pilot training there.

The Grob 120A aircraft will be employed at Southport, Manitoba (formerly CFB Portage la Prairie) for pilot ab-initio training. (Photo courtesy of Grob Aircraft)

DETAILS

Designation: CT-120?   **Model No:** G120A   **Role:** Trainer
TOS: 2006   **SOS:** In-Service   **No:** 9   **Service:** Contractor Provided

SPECIFICATIONS

Manufacturer: Burkhart Grob Luft-und Raumfahrt GmbH & Co KG
Crew/Passengers: crew of two; instructor and student side by side
Powerplant: one 260 hp Textron Lycoming AEIO-540 flat-six engine
Performance: Max Speed: 264 mph (426 km/h)   Cruising Speed: 191 mph (307 km/h)
   Service Ceiling: 18,000 ft (5,490 m)   Range: 955 mi (1,537 km)
Weights: Empty: 2,116 lb (960 kg)   Max: 3,174 lb (1,440 kg)
Dimensions: Span: 33 ft 5¼ in (10.19 m)   Length: 26 ft 5½ in (8.07 m)
   Height: 8 ft 5¼ in (2.57 m)   Wing Area: 143.16 sq ft (13.3 sq m)
Armament: None
Cost: Unknown

MBB
BK 117

The BK-117 was a civilian rigid-rotor light helicopter man-ufactured by MBB (now Eurocopter) in Germany. Because of the lack of availability of a CH-124 Sea King and a lack of cabin space in unit CH-135 Twin Huey aircraft, the sole BK-117A3 was leased by AETE for a test program (used to evaluate Helicopter Integrated Navigation System (HINS) equipment proposed for inclusion in the ill-fated New Shipborne Aircraft (NSA) program which was sub-sequently cancelled by the government). The BK-117 of-fered plenty of room for test equipment and two pallets were installed along with various antennas, receivers and test instrumentation. The serial number was CH143106.

The test flights for the HINS evaluation were flown by AETE crews in the vicinity of Holloman and Vandenberg AFBs in the US. The aircraft was returned to MBB Canada for civilian use following termination of the program.

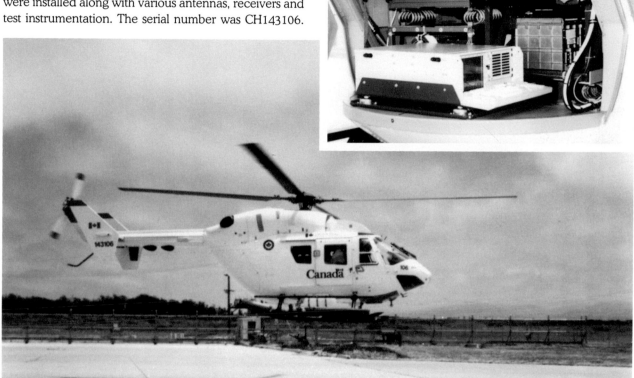

The sole CH-143 BK-117, seen here in the test role. (CF Photo)

DETAILS

Designation: CH-143	**Model No:** BK 117 A-3D	**Marks:**	**Role:** Light Reconnaissance Helicopter
TOS: 1990	**SOS:** 1990	**No:** 1	**Service:** CF

SPECIFICATIONS

Manufacturer: MBB (Eurocopter)
Crew/Passengers: two pilots and up to ten passengers
Powerplant: 2 x 770 hp SNECMA Turbomeca Arriel 1E2 turboshaft engines
Performance: Max Speed: 163 mph (262 km/h)   Cruising Speed:
Hover Ceiling: 8,300 ft (2,530 m)   Range: 336 mi (541 km)
Weights: Empty: 3,891 lb (1,765 kg)   Gross: 7,385 lb (3,350 kg)
Dimensions: Rotor Diameter: 36 ft 1 in (11.00 m)   Length: 42 ft 8 in (13.01 m)
Height: 12 ft 7 in (3.84 m)   Width:
Armament: none
Cost: Leased from MBB Canada

Raytheon
HARVARD II

The Raytheon Harvard II is an export version of the Raytheon Texan II aircraft currently in USAF and USN service. The Raytheon design is in fact a further enhanced development of the Pilatus-designed PC-9 trainer aircraft. Although based on the PC-9, the Raytheon Joint Primary Aircraft Training System (JPATS) submission for the US forces required extensive changes including cockpit pressurization, improved bird-strike protection, zero-zero ejection seats and a single-point pressure refueling capability. The Harvard IIs are, in turn, identical to the Texan II aircraft except for the addition an automatic direction finder, a second VOR, propeller de-icing system, standby VHF transceiver and an approach chart holder installed on the cockpit glare shield. Student pilots chosen to attend NATO Flying Training in Canada (NFTC) complete their basic flight training in Moose Jaw, Saskatchewan on the Raytheon CT-156 Harvard II aircraft. Canadian military pilots training on the Harvard II have arrived at Moose Jaw after initial screening at Portage La Prairie on contractor-leased Slingsby Firefly aircraft. They then spend 95 hours on the Harvard II, at which point they are streamed into the fighter, multi-engine or helicopter programs for further advanced training.

The Raytheon CT-156 Harvard II aircraft in NFTC colours. (CF Photo)

DETAILS

Designation: CT-156	**Model No:** T-6A-1	**Marks:** II	**Role:** Trainer
TOS: 2000	**SOS:** In Service	**No:** 20	**Service:** Leased from Bombardier

SPECIFICATIONS Harvard II

Manufacturer:	Raytheon
Crew/Passengers:	two pilots in tandem
Powerplant:	one 1,700 shp Pratt & Whitney PT-6A-68 *Adour* turboprop engine derated to 1,100 shp driving a four-blade Hartzell variable pitch propeller
Performance:	Max Speed: 448 mph (500 km/h) — Cruising Speed:
	Service Ceiling: 35,000 ft (10,668 m) — Range: 2,736 mi (1,700 km)
Weights:	Empty: 4,600 lb (2,087 kg) — Gross: 6,300 lb (2,857 kg)
Dimensions:	Span: 32 ft 2½ in (10.13 m) — Length: 33 ft 3¼ in (10.14 m)
	Height: 10 ft 8½ in (3.26 m) — Wing Area: 176 sq ft (16.29 sq m)
Armament:	none
Cost:	Leased from Bombardier

A.E.A.
SILVER DART

The original Silver Dart was the result of a combined effort by men whose names have since earned a prominent place in Canadian and American aviation. They were Dr. Alexander Graham Bell, inventor of the telephone and long a believer in powered flight; J.A.D. McCurdy whose pioneer work in aviation won him international acclaim; and Glen H. Curtiss, whose name became a byword in American aviation. In 1907, they formed the Aerial Experiment Association, together with F.W. "Casey" Baldwin and Lieutenant Selfridge of the US Army. Built by members of the Aerial Experiment Association, the Silver Dart was the first fixed-wing powered aircraft flown in Canada. It made its first flight on 23 February 1909 and J.A.D. McCurdy made history when he

flew the Silver Dart from Bras d'Or Lake at Baddeck, Nova Scotia. The Silver Dart only flew a half-mile, but it was the first heavier-than-air machine to fly in Canada or in the British Empire. After 300 flights, the Silver Dart and an improved version known as the Baddeck No. 1 were demonstrated to the Canadian Army. Ultimately the Silver Dart crashed and was written off while under trial. While not selected for service, the Silver Dart represents the first experiment in aviation by the Canadian military. In 1959, the RCAF decided to commemorate the fiftieth anniversary of powered flight in Canada by building and flying an exact replica. This Silver Dart replica is now on display at the National Aviation Museum in Ottawa.

The Silver Dart shown here, along with members of the Aerial Experiment Association, was demonstrated for the Canadian military in Petawawa, Ontario. (CF Photo)

DETAILS

Designation: **Model No:**   **Role:** Experimental

TOS: 1909   **SOS:** 02 Aug 1909   **No:** 1   **Service:** Aerial Experiment Association

SPECIFICATIONS

Manufacturer: Aerial Experiment Association

Crew/Passengers: one pilot and one passenger in tandem

Powerplant: one 50 hp 8 cylinder water-cooled Curtiss piston engine

Performance: Max Speed: 50 mph (80 km/h)   Cruising Speed:

Service Ceiling: 50 ft (15.24 m)   Range: 20 mi (32 km)

Weights: Empty: 345 lb (156 kg)   Gross: 860 lb (390 kg)

Dimensions: Span: 49 ft 0 in (14.96 m)   Length: 32 ft 0 in (9.75 m)

Height: 10 ft 0 in (3.05 m)   Wing Area: 420 sq ft (39.02 sq m)

Armament: None

Cost: Unknown

Slingsby
FIREFLY

Commonly known as "the Slingsby," the Slingsby Firefly replaced the Musketeer as the Air Force's *ab-initio* pilot trainer. It was a modern, lightweight, composite civilian design adapted for military training including aerobatic training. These aircraft did not actually belong to the military, but rather to a consortium led by Bombardier (Canadair) and the instructors were civilian employees of the contractor. (Canadair logos were displayed on the side of the fuselage and the Bombardier insignia was placed on the tail.) The Southport, Manitoba training area was known as CFB Portage la Prairie when the military maintained its own facilities for pilot training there.

A Slingsby Firefly aircraft seen here in the vicinity of Southport, Manitoba displays the Bombardier insignia on its tail. (CF Photo)

DETAILS

Designation: CT-111 **Model No:** T67C3 **Role:** Trainer
TOS: 1995 **SOS:** 2005 **No:** **Service:** Contractor Provided

SPECIFICATIONS

Manufacturer: Slingsby Aviation Limited
Crew/Passengers: crew of two; instructor and student side by side
Powerplant: one 160 hp Textron Lycoming AEIO 320-D2A "flat-four" piston engine
Performance: Max Speed: 153 mph (246 km/h) Cruising Speed: 144 mph (231 km/h)
Service Ceiling: 12,000 ft (3,660 m) Range: 650 mi (1,046 km)
Weights: Empty: 1,450 lb (658 kg) Gross: 2,100 lb (952 kg)
Dimensions: Span: 34 ft 9 in (10.59 m) Length: 24 ft¼ in (7.32 m)
Height: 7 ft 9 in (2.36 m) Wing Area: 136.0 sq ft (12.63 sq m)
Armament: None
Cost: Unknown

Various Unmanned Air Vehicles

The Canadian Forces, through the Canadian Forces Experimentation Centre (CFEC) at Shirley's Bay, Ontario, has been investigating the use of various types of UAVs to address a recognized capability deficiency in the areas of Intelligence, Surveillance and Reconnaissance (ISR), and Command and Control (C2). In support of this goal CFEC, through a series of synthetic and live experiments conducted since 2001 and by using leased UAV systems, has been obtaining data and knowledge to determine how UAVs can be used to resolve this deficiency. The CFEC also began 'Concept Development and Experimentation' on UAVs at CFB Suffield, AB in April 2002. Three different models of aircraft were leased from their manufacturers for the duration of the trials.

The three types tested also represented distinct classes of UAV. Smallest of the three was the hand-launched Pointer designed to provide the army with "eyes to see over the next hill." More sophisticated was the light airplane-sized I-GNAT, which requires a conventional runway. Finally, the most unusual was the Canadian-built CL-327 Guardian. This Bombardier product with its contra-rotating

propellers and hourglass shape is also nicknamed "the Peanut." The CF has also purchased the small modular UAV known as the Silver Fox from ACR (Advanced Ceramics Research) of Tuscon Arizona. This drone is larger than the hand-launched FQM-151A Pointer previously tested by the CF at Suffield but still weighs just 10kg due to its construction of plastic, foam, fibreglass, and advanced ceramic materials. The airframe disassembles into components small enough to fit into a container the size of a golf bag. When assembled, the Silver Fox is under 2m long with a wingspan of around 2.5m. The various UAVs used for the different trials have each received temporary Canadian markings and designations.

The photos above illustrate the Altair CU-163301, a medium-altitude, long-endurance Uninhabited Aerial Vehicle (UAV) at 5 Wing Goose Bay in August 2004. The Canadian Forces leased the Altair, designed by General Atomics Aeronautical Systems Incorporated, for an experiment. The Atlantic Littoral Intelligence Surveillance Reconnaissance ISR Experiment (ALIX) experiment conducted by the Canadian Forces Experimentation Center (CFEC), involved various UAVs and their potential for military applications. The UAVs were used to conduct Intelligence Surveillance Reconnaissance (ISR) activities over Baffin Island and Atlantic Canada. (CF Photos)

DETAILS

Designation: CU-XXX | **Model No:** | **Marks:** | **Role:** Target Acquisition and Surveillance Drones
TOS: Various | **SOS:** Various | **No:** Various | **Service:** CF

SPECIFICATIONS Various

Westland
PETROL/CHIMO

The Westland-Agusta EH-101 had originally been chosen as Canada's new Antisubmarine Warfare and Search and Rescue helicopter. The primary platform would have been identical with the original design but the mission equipment to be fitted would have been considerably different. They would have replaced the CH-124 Sea King helicopter in the antisubmarine role and the CH-113 Labrador helicopter in the search and rescue role. The antisubmarine variant was to be known as the CH-148 Petrol and the SAR variant was to be designated the CH-149 Chimo. The first of 50 EH-101s was to be delivered in 1993. Unfortunately, after considerable development effort, a new Canadian government elected to cancel the delivery of the helicopters, terminating the program as part of cost cutting measures. Ironically, the SAR competition was eventually won by a civilianized variant of the EH-101 known as the CH-149 Cormorant.

The original EH-101 prototype shown here was used for various manufacturers' tests. This photo shows it at CFB Shearwater undergoing icing trials. (Author's collection)

DETAILS

Designation: CH-148/CH149   **Model No:** EH-101   **Marks:**   **Role:** ASW/SAR Helicopter
TOS: 1993   **SOS:** Cancelled   **No:** CH-148 (35)   CH-149 (15)   **Service:** CF

SPECIFICATIONS Cormorant data

Manufacturer: Westland-Augusta
Crew/Passengers: two pilots, flight engineer and SAR Techs plus up to thirty passengers, plus provisions for two 223 kg rescue hoists, 3,732 kg external cargo and up to twelve stretchers
Powerplant: three General Electric T700/CT7-6 engines, each producing 1,920 shaft horsepower
Performance: Max Speed: 173 mph (278 km/h)   Cruising Speed:
                    Service Ceiling: Range: 633 mi (1,018 km)
Weights: Empty: 4,600 lb (2,087 kg)   Max T/O: 6,300 lb (11,943 kg)
Dimensions: Rotor Diameter: 60 ft 8 in (18.5 m)   Length: 74 ft 10 in (22.8 m)
                    Height: 21 ft 4 in (6.5 m)
Armament: none
Cost: Unknown

NON-CANADIAN AIRCRAFT FLOWN BY CANADIANS IN OPERATIONS OR COMBAT MISSIONS WHILE ON EXCHANGE TO OTHER AIRFORCES IE RAF, NATO, USAF, USN, ETC- OR MISC TYPES

CU-161 Sperwer (Sagem).

Armstrong Whitworth
F.K.8

The Armstrong Whitworth F.K.8 was a two-seat reconnaissance and light bomber that went into action on the Western Front with the RFC commencing in January 1917. The aircraft proved to be popular and well liked by crews who nicknamed it the "Big Ack." The F.K.8 provided excellent service, particularly in the roles of artillery spotting and in day/night bombing. Perhaps just as important, the type was able to hold its own against contemporary enemy fighters. On 27 March 1918, Canadian 2nd Lt Alan A. McLeod of No. 2 Squadron (RFC)

won the coveted Victoria Cross while flying in an F.K.8. Attacked by enemy fighters, 2nd Lt McLeod and his observer, Lt A.W. Hammond, fought back valiantly but both men were wounded and their aircraft was set on fire. Despite his wounds and being forced out of the cockpit onto the wing by the ensuing flames, Lt McLeod still managed to sideslip the aircraft to a successful crash landing in No Man's Land. He then proceeded to rescue his wounded observer from the wreckage, dragging him to eventual safety.

The Armstrong Whitworth F.K.8 shown here is similar to that flown by Canadian Victoria Cross winner, 2nd Lieutenant A.A. McLeod. (LAC Photo # PA-000297)

DETAILS

Designation: **Model No:** F.K.8   **Marks:**   **Role:** two-seat reconnaissance/light bomber aircraft
Service: RFC

SPECIFICATIONS

Manufacturer:	Armstrong Whitworth & Company Ltd	
Crew/Passengers:	crew of two: pilot and observer/gunner	
Powerplant:	one 160 hp Beadmore or 150 hp RAF 4a piston engine	
Performance:	Max Speed: 90 mph (144 km/h)	Cruising Speed:
	Service Ceiling: 13,000 ft (3,692 m)	Range:
Weights:	Empty: 1,980 lb (898 kg)	Gross: 2,287 lb (1,037 kg)
Dimensions:	Span: 43 ft 6 in (13.26 m)	Length: 31 ft 0 in (9.44 m)
	Height: 10 ft 11 in (3.33 m)	Wing Area:
Armament:	one fixed forward Vickers machine gun and one flexible Lewis machine gun on a Scarff ring and up to 160 lb (73 kg) of bombs	
Cost:	Unknown	

Armstrong Whitworth
ALBEMARLE

Originally designed as a bomber, the Armstrong Whitworth Albermarle was already obsolete at the outbreak of the Second World War. Consequently, it saw exclusive use as a transport and as a glider tug, where it proved to be well suited. The aircraft type was used a pathfinder on D-Day for dropping paratroops of the 6th Airborne Division over Normandy. In the glider tug role, four squadrons of Albemarles were used to tow Airspeed Horsa gliders in support of ground operations in France in 1944 and two squadrons also participated in the ill-fated Arnhem airborne operation. The aircraft featured a mixed steel and wood construction and all versions used the Bristol Hercules XI radial engines. A number of RCAF aircrew flew the Albermarle in the operations described above.

An Armstrong Whitworth Albemarle transport on the tarmac. (DND Photo)

DETAILS

Designation: **Model No:** AW 41   **Marks:** Mk I, II, IV, V, VI   **Role:** Transport, Glider Tug
Service: RAF

SPECIFICATIONS Mk VI

Manufacturer:	Armstrong Whitworth Aircraft Company
Crew/Passengers:	crew of five
Powerplant:	two 1,590 hp (1,186 kW) Bristol Hercules XI radial engines

Performance:	Max Speed: 265 mph (426 km/h)	Cruising Speed: 170 mph (274 km/h)
	Service Ceiling: 18,000 ft (5,485 m)	Range: 1,300 mi (2,092 km)
Weights:	Empty:	Maximum Take-off: 22,600 lbs (10,251 kg)
Dimensions:	Span: 77 ft 0 in (23.47 m)	Length: 59 ft 11 in (18.26 m)
	Height: 15 ft 7 in (4.75 m)	Wing Area: 803.5 sq ft (74.65 sq m)

Armament:	Twin Vickers 0.303 in (7.7 mm) "K" machine guns in dorsal position
Original Cost:	Unknown

Armstrong Whitworth
WHITLEY

The twin-engined Armstrong-Whitworth Whitley originally came into service with the RAF in March 1937, as a heavy bomber. In the early months of the war it was used by the RAF Bomber Command on pamphlet-dropping sorties and in night bombing. In June 1940, Whitleys became the first British bombers to attack targets in Italy when they were used on a raid on Turin and Genoa over the Alps, landing in the Channel Islands to refuel. By April 1942, Whitleys had been withdrawn from first-line use in Bomber Command in favour of Wellingtons, Hampdens and newer four-engine heavy-bombers such as the Stirling and Halifax. Whitleys remained in use, however, in Operational Training Units of Bomber Command, and the type was still widely used until the end of the war in paratroop training and on airborne operations as a troop-carrier and glider tug. Canadian crews saw service with Whitleys while attached to RAF squadrons.

The Armstrong Whitworth Whitley saw service in a number of roles throughout the Second World War. (RAF Photo)

DETAILS
Model No: AW.38   **Marks:** Mk I, II, III, IV, V   **Role:** Bomber
Service: RAF

SPECIFICATIONS   Mk V

Manufacturer:	Armstrong Whitworth Aircraft	
Crew/Passengers:	crew of five	
Powerplant:	two 1,145 hp Rolls Royce Merlin X in-line piston engines	
Performance:	Max Speed: 230 mph (370 km/h)	Cruising Speed: 210 mph (338 km/h)
	Service Ceiling: 26,000 ft (7,925 m)	Range: 1,500 mi (2,414 km)
Weights:	Empty: 19,350 lb (8,777 kg)	Max T/O: 33,500 lb (15,195 kg)
Dimensions:	Span: 84 ft 0 in (25.60 m)	Length: 70 ft 6 in (21.49 m)
	Height: 15 ft 0 in (4.57 m)	Wing Area: 1,137 sq ft (105.63 sq m)
Armament:	4 x .303 in (7.7 mm) machine guns in powered nose and tail turrets plus provisions for up to 7,000 lb (3,175 kg) in bombs	

Avro
MANCHESTER

The Avro Manchester had a relatively brief service career, from November 1940 to June 1942, largely because of problems associated with the unreliability and eventual lack of power of the Rolls-Royce Vulture I engines with which it was fitted. The bomber could, however, maintain height on one engine, and in one case an aircraft flew 600 miles from Berlin to its base in England after its engine was knocked out by gunfire, in addition to other extensive damage. In addition to a 10,350 pound bomb load in a cavernous bomb bay nearly half the length of the fuselage, the armament consisted of eight .303-inch machine-guns: two in the nose, two in a dorsal turret, and four in a turret in the tail. Though unsuccessful, the Avro Manchester design demonstrated sufficient promise to warrant further modification. The decision was therefore made in late 1940 to replace the two Rolls Royce Vulture engines of the Manchester with four of the more reliable Rolls Royce Merlin (in Canada, Packard Merlin) engines, which had a proven record in the Hurricane and Spitfire fighter designs. The revised design was an immediate success, and the Manchester went on to carry the heaviest individual bomb loads of the Second World War.

A photo of an Avro 679 Manchester B Mk. IA, one of 200 whose type served with eleven RAF night bomber squadrons. Canadian aircrew flew the aircraft while in RAF service. (Author's collection)

DETAILS

Designation: N/A   **Model No:** 679   **Marks:** B.I, B.IA   **Role:** Bomber
Service: RAF

SPECIFICATIONS Mk B.IA

Manufacturer:	Avro Aircraft	
Crew/Passengers:	one pilot and up to six crew	
Powerplant:	two 1,760 hp Rolls-Royce Vulture engines	
Performance:	Max Speed: 265 mph (426 km/h)	Cruising Speed: 185 mph (298 km/h)
	Service Ceiling: 19,200 ft (5,850 m)	Range: 1,630 mi (2,623 km)
Weights:	Empty: 29,432 lb (13,350 kg)	Gross: 56,000 lb (25,401 kg)
Dimensions:	Span: 90 ft 1 in (27.46 m)	Length: 69 ft 4 in (21.13 m)
	Height: 19 ft 6 in (5.94 m)	Wing Area: 1,131 sq ft (105.63 sq m)
Armament:	Provision for three gun turrets each with two or four .303 (7.7mm) calibre machine guns and a 10,350 lb (4,695 kg) bomb load	
Original Cost:	Unknown	

Bellanca
SCOUT

The Bellanca Scout is used as a glider tow plane for the Royal Canadian Air Cadet program. The Scout had its origins in the Aeronca 7 Champion developed in the post Second World War era. Aeronca sold the rights for the Champion design to the Champion Aircraft Company in 1951, who developed the Model 7 Traveller and the Challenger. The Citabria aircraft, based on the Challenger, first flew in May 1964. Bellanca took over production of the Model 7 ECA Citabria in 1970. They developed an improved version of the Citabria known as the 7CGBC Citabria 150S, with increased wingspan and trailing edge flaps. In 1971, Bellanca marketed a utility version, known as the 8GCBC Scout, which could be fitted with floats or skis. The 180 horsepower engine installation on these latter aircraft also made them excellent glider tow plane aircraft.

A Bellanca Scout tow plane in Royal Canadian Air Cadet colours, taken at 16 Wing, Borden. (Author's collection)

DETAILS

Designation: | **Model No:** 8GCBC | **Role:** Glider Towing
TOS: | **SOS:** | **No:** | **Service:** Royal Canadian Air Cadets

SPECIFICATIONS

Manufacturer:	Bellanca Aircraft	
Crew/Passengers:	Pilot and observer	
Powerplant:	one 180 hp Lycoming O-360-C2E engine	
Performance:	Max Speed:	Cruising Speed: 106 knots (208 km/h)
	Service Ceiling: 17,000 ft (5,182 m)	
Weights:	Empty: 1,315 lb (596.5 kg)	Gross: 2,150 lb (975 kg)
Dimensions:	Span: 36 ft 2 in (11.02 m)	Length: 23 ft 10 in (7.27 m)
	Height: 8 ft 8 in (2.64 m)	Wing Area:
Armament:	None	
Original Cost:	Unknown	

Bleriot Experimental
B.E.2C

The B.E. 2 (Bleriot Experimental), designed and built by the Royal Aircraft Factory, was one the first British military aircraft used operationally in 1914. The most important innovation in the B.E.2C was the use of staggered wings and the installation of true ailerons on both the upper and the lower wings. The ailerons replaced the earlier wing warping controls used on the B.E.2A and B.E.2B. The B.E.2C also differed from earlier variants in that it had a triangular vertical fin added ahead of the rudder, and the rounded horizontal stabilizer was replaced with a rectangular tailplane. The best-known variant of the B.E.2 series and the one produced in the greatest numbers had the envisioned role of visual reconnaissance and as a camera platform. Although never intended to carry weapons, the model 2C carried a variety of machine guns and bombs, and eventually even rockets when actively in service with either the Royal Flying Corps or the Royal Naval Air Service. The design was progressively developed and further modified into the model B.E.12 and B.E.12(a). Many of the aircrew who flew B.E.2C were Canadians who enrolled in either the RFC or RNAS.

B.E.2 C #8293 carried the subcontractor's trademarks in the center of each interplane strut, and the propeller carried the trademark of the Integral company on each blade. Other than the under-nose bomb rack, this aircraft is unarmed and carries no gun mounts. (CF Photo)

DETAILS

Designation: **Model No:** B.E.2C   **Role:** two-seat reconnaissance/observation aircraft
Service: RFC, RNAS

SPECIFICATIONS

Manufacturer: Royal Aircraft Factory
Crew/Passengers: crew of two: pilot and observer/gunner
Powerplant: one 70 hp Renault or 90 hp Curtiss OX-5 piston engine
Performance: Max Speed: 94 mph (145 km/h)   Cruising Speed:
Service Ceiling: 12,500 ft (3,810 m)   Endurance: 4 hrs
Weights: Empty: 1,370 lb (621 kg)   Gross: 2,142 lb (972 kg)
Dimensions: Span: 37 ft 0 in (11.27 m)   Length: 27 ft 3 in (8.31 m)
Height: 11 ft 1½ in (3.39 m)   Wing Area:
Armament: various arrangements of machine gun(s), rifles, pistols, light bombs and rockets
Cost: Unknown

Bleriot Experimental
B.E.12

The B.E. 12 was a further update of the original B.E. 2 model designed and built by the Royal Aircraft Factory, which was one the first British military aircraft used operationally in 1914. The intent was to create a single fighter by suitably modifying the original design. The original 90 hp engine was removed and the fuselage was modified to accept a larger 150 hp RAF 4a engine. The front cockpit area was faired over and further improvements were made to the fuel and exhaust systems and the tail surfaces. The armament initially consisted of one or two Lewis machine guns splayed outward to clear the propeller disk (which necessitated flying the aircraft crabwise to successfully aim) although this was eventually followed by a crude interrupter gear to allow for true forward firing. The addition of a more powerful engine and armament unfortunately did little to improve the fighter qualities of the design and the overall performance of the type was less than satisfactory. Many of the aircrew who flew B.E.12s were Canadians who enrolled in either the RFC or RNAS.

The B.E.12 was essentially a single-seat fighter variant of the original B.E.2 design. (LAC Photo # PA- 006358)

DETAILS
Designation: **Model No:** B.E.12a, b   **Role:** single seat fighter
Service: RFC, RNAS

SPECIFICATIONS
Manufacturer:	Royal Aircraft Factory	
Crew/Passengers:	one pilot	
Powerplant:	one 150 hp RAF 4a piston engine	
Performance:	Max Speed: 102 mph (164 km/h)	Cruising Speed:
	Service Ceiling: 12,500 ft (3,810 m)	Endurance: 4 hrs
Weights:	Empty: 1,370 lb (621 kg)	Gross: 2,142 lb (972 kg)
Dimensions:	Span: 37 ft 0 in (11.27 m)	Length: 27 ft 3 in (8.31 m)
	Height: 11 ft 1½ in (3.39 m)	Wing Area:
Armament:	various arrangements of Lewis machine gun(s)	
Cost:	Unknown	

Blackburn
SKUA

The Blackburn Skua was the first British monoplane specifically designed for dive-bombing. The crew of a Skua off the coast of Norway shot down the first enemy aircraft claimed by Britain in the Second World War, on 25 September 1939. As a fighter, however, the design was already obsolete and losses were heavy. As a dive-bomber, the type scored some early successes, sinking the German cruiser *Konigsberg* in its Bergen harbour. By 1941, the design was relegated to target towing and advanced training duties and it had been superceded by the Fairey Fulmar in the combat role. Canadian naval pilots attached to the RN saw action in Skuas in both the Norwegian and Mediterranean theatres.

The Blackburn Skua was a compromise design intended to meet a RN specification for both a fighter and dive-bomber. In combat, its design shortcomings became apparent and Fulmars or Sea Hurricanes quickly replaced the type in regular service. (Comox AFM Photo)

DETAILS

Model No: B.24   **Marks:** Mk I, II   **Role:** Fighter/Dive Bomber
Service: RN/FAA

SPECIFICATIONS Mk II

Crew/Passengers:	Pilot and observer in tandem	
Powerplant:	one 890 hp Bristol Perseus XII radial piston engine	
Performance:	Max Speed: 225 mph (362 km/h)	Cruising Speed: 165 mph (266 km/h)
	Service Ceiling: 20,200 ft (6,160 m)	Range: 760 mi (1,223 km)
Weights:	Empty: 5,490 lb (2,490 kg)	Maximum Take-off: 8,228 lb (3,732 kg)
Dimensions:	Span: 46 ft 2 in (14.07 m)	Length: 35 ft 7 in (10.85 m)
	Height: 12 ft 6 in (3.81 m)	Wing Area: 312 sq ft (28.98 sq m)
Armament:	four 0.303 in (7.7 mm) forward-firing machine guns in the wings and one flexible Lewis gun in the rear cockpit with provisions for up to eight 30 lb (14 kg) bombs on underwing racks	

Blackburn
ROC

The Blackburn Roc was a further derivative of the Blackburn Skua. The redesign was very similar in concept to the Boulton Paul Defiant, featuring a rear firing, four-gun powered turret. However, once the aircraft's weaknesses and relatively poor performance were identified, the design was quickly relegated to target towing and advanced training duties. It was superceded by the Fairey Fulmar in the combat role. A few Canadian naval aircrews attached to the RN saw action in Rocs early in the Second World War.

A Blackburn Roc was a development of the Skua and very similar to the Boulton Paul Defiant in concept. In service both the Defiant and the Roc suffered from a lack of performance and agility. (Comox AFM Photo)

DETAILS
Model No: B.25   **Marks:**   **Role:** Fighter/Target Tug
Service: RN / FAA

SPECIFICATIONS
Manufacturer:	Blackburn Aircraft	
Crew/Passengers:	Pilot and gunner in tandem	
Powerplant:	one 905 hp Bristol Perseus XII radial piston engine	
Performance:	Max Speed: 223 mph (359 km/h)	Cruising Speed: 135 mph (217 km/h)
	Service Ceiling: 18,000 ft (5,485 m)	Range: 810 mi (1,304 km)
Weights:	Empty: 6,124 lb (2,778 kg)	Maximum Take-off: 7,950 lb (3,606 kg)
Dimensions:	Span: 46 ft 0 in (14.02 m)	Length: 35 ft 7 in (10.85 m)
	Height: 12 ft 1 in (3.68 m)	Wing Area: 310 sq ft (28.80 sq m)
Armament:	four 0.303 in (7.7 mm) machine guns in power-operated dorsal turret	

Boeing
E-3 SENTRY

The Boeing 707 was the most successful and versatile of the early jet airliners. This versatility led to a wide variety of subsequent military roles. The USAF first used the type as the basis for an Airborne Warning and Control (AWACS) platform designated E-3 Sentry. The E-3 Sentry is a modified Boeing 707/320 commercial airframe with a distinctive rotating radar dome. The dome is 30 feet (9.1 meters) in diameter, six feet (1.8 meters) thick, and is held 11 feet (3.3 meters) above the fuselage by two struts. It contains a radar subsystem that permits all-weather surveillance over a range of more than 200 miles (320 kilometers) for low-flying targets and farther for aerospace vehicles flying at medium to high altitudes. The radar combined with

an identification friend or foe (IFF) subsystem can look down to detect, identify and track enemy and friendly low-flying aircraft by eliminating ground clutter returns that confuse other radar systems. Canadian crews are integrated into USAF E-3 Sentry operations within North America as part of Canada's contribution to NORAD. NATO subsequently acquired a fleet of eighteen Sentry aircraft to provide airborne surveillance, command, control and communication for NATO air operations. Home based in Geilenkirchen, Germany, NATO aircraft are routinely forward deployed and Canadian military personnel serving with NATO also make up part of the associated air and ground crews.

The NATO versions of the E-3 Sentry aircraft, as shown here, are regularly crewed by CF personnel. The NATO aircraft are registered in Luxembourg, which explains the registration on the tail. (CF Photo)

DETAILS

Designation: E-3A   **Model No:** 707-320C   **Role:** Airborne Warning and Control
Service: NATO/USAF

SPECIFICATIONS

Manufacturer: Boeing Aircraft Corporation
Crew/Passengers: two pilots, one navigator, one flight engineer and up to thirteen mission specialists
Powerplant: four Pratt & Whitney 20,500 lb thrust TF-33 100A turbofan engines
Performance: Max Speed: 530 mph (853 km/h)   Cruising Speed:
Service Ceiling: 39,000 ft (11,887 m)   Range: 1,000 mi (1,610 km)
Weights: Empty: Gross: 326,000 lb (147,429 kg)
Dimensions: Span: 145 ft 9 in (44.45 m)   Length: 152 ft 11 in (46.68 m)
Height: 41 ft 9 in (12.70 m)   Wing Area:
Armament: None
Cost: $70M (US)

Boeing Vertol
CHINOOK

The Boeing Vertol CH-47D Chinook was a further up-rated variant of the heavy-lift tandem-rotor helicopter acquired by the CF in 1974 and used primarily for Mobile Command operations. The aircraft type continued to be used extensively by other nations in transport duties despite being retired from the CF for economic reasons. The principle users were the RAF and US Army, who used them for airlift requirements including the transport of troops, rations, military supplies, cargo transport and weapons for mobility operations. Consequently, during the first Gulf War, the Chinook featured prominently in the high mobility ground campaign and in special operations. CF exchange officers flew combat missions in the Chinook during the campaign.

An interesting night vision lens view of a US Army CH-47D in Afghanistan. (CF Photo)

DETAILS
Designation: **Model No:** CH-47D   **Role:** Transport Helicopter
Service: US Army, RAF

SPECIFICATIONS (CH-47D)
Manufacturer: Boeing Vertol
Crew/Passengers: four: two pilots, one flight engineer and one loadmaster plus up to forty-four passengers, thirty-three troops or up 28,000 lb (12,700 kg) external loads
Powerplant: two AVCO Lycoming T55-L-712 turboshaft engines
Performance: Max Speed: 181 mph (291 km/h)   Cruising Speed: 160 mph (257 km/h)
Hover Ceiling: 9,200 ft (2,804 m)   Range: 115 mi (185 km)
Weights: Empty: 22,452 lb (10,175 kg)   Maximum Take-off: 50,000 lbs (22,680 kg)
Dimensions: Rotor Diameter: 60 ft 0 in (18.29 m)   Length: 99 ft 0 in (30.18 m)
Height: 22 ft 6 in (6.86 m)
Armament: None
Original Cost: Unknown

Boulton Paul
DEFIANT

First flown in August 1937, the Boulton Paul Defiant did not participate in operations until 12 May 1940 during the Battle of Britain. An unusual design, the initial surprise afforded by a rear-firing four gun powered turret accounted for 65 enemy aircraft. However, once the aircraft's weaknesses were identified, by August 1940, losses of Defiants were so great that they were withdrawn from front-line duties and transferred to night fighting duties. In this latter role, two RCAF squadrons were equipped with Defiants. No. 409 and 410 Squadron both used the aircraft type briefly but without any success.

An interesting formation view of several Boulton Paul Defiant Mk I aircraft. After a disappointing experience in daylight combat, the type was switched to a night-fighting role. (Comox AFM Photo)

DETAILS

Model No: P.82   **Marks:** Mk I, II   **Role:** Fighter
Service: RAF

SPECIFICATIONS Mk II

Manufacturer:	Boulton Paul Aircraft	
Crew/Passengers:	pilot and gunner in tandem	
Powerplant:	one 1,280 hp Rolls-Royce Merlin XX piston engine	
Performance:	Max Speed: 313 mph (504 km/h)	Cruising Speed: 260 mph (418 km/h)
	Service Ceiling: 30,350 ft (9,250 m)	Range: 465 mi (748 km)
Weights:	Empty: 6,282 lb (2,849 kg)	Maximum Take-off: 8,424 lb (3,821 kg)
Dimensions:	Span: 39 ft 4 in (11.99m)	Length: 35 ft 4 in (10.77 m)
	Height: 11 ft 4 in (3.45 m)	Wing Area: 250 sq ft (23.23 m)
Armament:	four 0.303 in (7.7 mm) machine guns in power operated dorsal turret	

Brewster
BUFFALO

The Brewster F2A-1 Buffalo was test-flown in January 1938, and was the first monoplane fighter used by the US Navy. Finland, Belgium and England purchased improved versions, including the F2A-2, -3, designated as Buffaloes starting in 1940. The British Purchasing Commission ordered a total of 170 Model 339Es in two separate contracts under the British designation Buffalo Mk. I. A number of changes were made to bring the aircraft up to then-current European combat standards: a British-built reflector gunsight replaced the original ring & bead arrangement, armor plate was provided for the pilot, and armored glass was added to the windscreen. The original Curtiss Electric propeller was also replaced with a 10-foot Hamilton Standard propeller. The 339E model was the only Buffalo variant to feature an internal gun camera. A larger fixed tail wheel also replaced the small retractable naval-type tail wheel. These changes brought the gross weight to 6500 pounds, almost a thousand pounds heavier than the standard F2A-2. The maximum speed was lowered to 330 mph and the rate of climb was lowered to only 2600 feet per minute. In addition, the added weight increased the landing speed, and adversely affected the maneuverability. Consequently, the RAF found that the Buffalo with its large, rotund fuselage and underpowered engine had many operational limitations, and was unsuitable for the European war theatre. As a result, the Buffaloes were quickly transferred to the Far East to serve with units in Malaya, Singapore and Burma.

The first Buffaloes arrived in Singapore in the spring of 1941. On the outbreak of Japanese hostilities, the RAAF, RAF, and RNZAF Buffaloes, supported by Dutch Buffaloes, fought gallantly but were badly outclassed and outnumbered by opposing Japanese Zeros. In an attempt to improve the Buffalo's performance, ground crews removed all unnecessary equipment to lower the weight, sometimes replacing the 0.50-inch machine guns with lighter 0.303-inch guns and reducing the ammunition and fuel load. However, these modifications did not even come close to closing the performance gap between the Buffalo and the Zero. The situation in Malaya rapidly deteriorated as the Japanese advance gained momentum, and Commonwealth squadrons were forced to withdraw to Singapore Island. Attrition and combat losses took their toll, and by February of 1942 there were only a few airworthy Buffaloes left. These were withdrawn to the nearby islands of the Netherlands East Indies. When the British evacuated the aircrews to Australia, the remaining Buffaloes were turned over to Dutch squadrons. Royal Canadian Air Force pilots flew the type while assigned to RAF squadrons.

One of the lesser known fighters in RAF service was the American designed Brewster Buffalo. (Comox AFM Photo)

DETAILS
Designation: F2A—3   **Model No:** 339E   **Marks:** Mk I   **Role:** Fighter
Service: RAF

SPECIFICATIONS
Manufacturer:	Brewster Aeronautical Corporation	
Crew/Passengers:	pilot	
Powerplant:	one 1,100 hp Wright Cyclone GR-1820-G 105A radial piston engine	
Performance:	Max Speed: 292 mph (470 km/h)	Cruising Speed: 255 mph (410 km/h)
	Service Ceiling: 30,500 ft (9,296 m)	Range: 650 mi (1,046 km)
Weights:	Empty: 4,479 lb (2,032 kg)	Maximum Take-off: 6,840 lb (3,101 kg)
Dimensions:	Span: 35 ft 0 in (10.67 m)	Length: 26 ft 0 in (7.92 m)
	Height: 12 ft 1 in (3.68 m)	Wing Area: 209 sq ft (19.42 sq m)
Armament:	Two .50 calibre machine guns (fuselage) and two 0.303 calibre guns (wings)	
Cost:	Unknown	

British Aerospace
TORNADO

The Tornado Multi-Role Combat Aircraft was designed by Panavia, a European manufacturing consortium, and became a key operational aircraft for the Royal Air Force. The first variant (G.R . Mk 1) was designed to replace the RAF's Vulcan and Buccaneer squadrons in land strike, maritime strike and reconnaissance missions. A second variant (F.2) was also developed to serve in the air defence interceptor role as a replacement. The Tornado was the first aircraft with a variable-geometry (swing-wing) design. The design has proven successful in both roles and the Tornado has also seen service with the German, Italian and Saudi Arabian Air Forces. During the first Gulf War, the RAF deployed both the G.R.1 and F.2 variants to the region. Canadian Air Force exchange officers on strength with RAF Squadrons flew the F.2 variant during combat missions.

An RAF G.R.4 Tornado fighter-bomber touches down in 4 Wing Cold Lake during a Maple Flag exercise. Canadian officers flew the F.2 interceptor variant of the type during the first Gulf War. (CF Photo)

DETAILS

Designation: **Model No:**   **Marks:** G.R.1, F.2   **Role:** fighter interceptor/bomber   **Service:** RAF

SPECIFICATIONS

Manufacturer:	British Aerospace (Panavia)	
Crew/Passengers:	crew of two: pilot and navigator	
Powerplant:	two 15,000 lb thrust Turbo-Union RB 199-34R turbofan jet engines	
Performance:	Max Speed: Mach 2.2	Cruising Speed:
	Service Ceiling: 50,000+ ft (15,240 m)	Range: 750 mi (1,207 km)
Weights:	Empty: 28,000 lb (12,701 kg)	Gross: 35,000 lb (15,876 kg)
Dimensions:	Span (Extended): 45 ft 8 in (13.92 m)	Span (Swept): 28 ft 3 in (8.61 m)
	Length: 54 ft 9½ in (16.70 m)	Height: 18 ft 8½ in (5.70 m)
	Wing Area: 323 sq ft (30.01 sq m)	
Armament:	two 27 mm Mauser cannon internally plus various stores externally including tanks, missiles, bombs up to 17,000 lb (7,712 kg)	
Cost:	Unknown	

Bristol
BEAUFIGHTER

With a speed of 330 mph, air intercept radar and a one-two punch of cannons and machine guns (or torpedoes or rocket projectiles when engaged in anti-surface duties), the Bristol Beaufighter was one of the Second World War's most formidable night fighters, as well as being the backbone of Coastal Command's anti-shipping war. Beaufighters were used to attack enemy shipping in the North Sea, the English Channel and in the Mediterranean. Beaufighters were flown in both roles by many Canadians while in RAF service and specifically by No. 404, 406, 409, and 410 Squadron in the RCAF. Despite this use, the type was never officially "on strength" with the RCAF.

Complete with D-Day invasion markings, a Bristol Beaufighter TF MkX (# NE365) shown here is armed with cannon and rockets from No. 404 (RCAF) Squadron while based at Strubby, England in 1944. (CF Photo)

DETAILS

Designation: **Model No:** 156   **Marks:** Mk II, VI, X, XI   **Role:** Night Fighter/Strike Fighter
Service: RCAF/RAF

SPECIFICATIONS Mark X

Manufacturer:	Bristol Aircraft Company
Crew/Passengers:	crew of two or three
Powerplant:	two 1,770 hp (1,320 kW) Bristol Hercules XVIII radial engines

Performance: Max Speed: 303 mph (488 km/h)   Cruising Speed: 249 mph (401 km/h)
                     Service Ceiling: 15,000 ft (4,570 m)   Range: 1,470 mi (2,366 km)

Weights: Empty: 15,600 lb (7,076 kg)   Maximum Take-off: 25,200 lb (11,431 kg)

Dimensions: Span: 57 ft 10 in (17.63 m)   Length: 41 ft 8 in (12.70 m)
                     Height: 15 ft 10 in (4.83 m)   Wing Area: 503 sq ft (46.73 sq m)

Armament: four .20 mm cannon and six .303 (7.7 mm) machine guns, each in nose with one .303 (7.7 mm)
                     "k" gun in ventral position. Provisions for up to two 250 lb (113 kg) bombs, eight 90 lb (41 kg)
                     rocket projectiles or one 1,605 lb (728 kg) torpedo

Cost: Unknown

Bristol
BOMBAY

The Bristol Bombay was a transport/bomber created by Bristol aircraft for the RAF. First flown in 1935, the stress-skin all-metal design was relatively advanced for its day. Special features included a door arrangement with a built-in gantry allowing the loading of heavy freight and the fitment of power-operated gun turrets of Bristol design. Its fixed undercarriage was a distinctive feature. By the onset of war, the type was already obsolete, but the lack of suitable transport ensured that production and service of the Bombay was continued. The aircraft consequently gave valuable service throughout the war years. Canadian crews flew missions in Bombays while attached to RAF squadrons.

The Bristol Bombay was originally designed as a bomber. Obsolete by the start of war, the type soldiered on in the transport role primarily in the Middle East (Comox AFM Photo)

DETAILS
Model No: 130   **Marks:** Mk I   **Role:** Transport   **Service:** RAF

SPECIFICATIONS
Manufacturer: Bristol Aircraft Company
Crew/Passengers: crew of three and seating for twenty-four fully-equipped soldiers or up to 5,000 lbs
Powerplant: two 1,010 hp Bristol Pegasus XXII radial piston engines
Performance: Max Speed: 192 mph (309 km/h)   Cruising Speed:
                      Service Ceiling: 22,500 ft (7,620 m)   Range:
Weights: Empty: 13,800 lb (6,260 kg)   Maximum Take-off: 20,000 lb (9,072 kg)
Dimensions: Span: 95 ft 9 in (29.7 m)   Length: 69 ft 3 in (21.1 m)
                      Height: 19 ft 6 in (5.9 m)   Wing Area: 1,340 sq ft (124 sq m)
Armament: .303 in (7.7 mm) machine guns in powered turrets in the nose and tail plus provisions for light bombs on external racks

Bristol
M.1C

The Bristol M.1C monoplane was an ultra-modern design that was truly ahead of its time. Unfortunately, precisely because of its design, it was relegated to obscurity and it served only in small numbers in the Macedonian and Middle East theatres, where its excellent performance remained relatively unnoticed. The prototype M.1A was completed in the summer of 1916 and quickly demonstrated that it was highly manoeuvrable and possessed first class handling characteristics. An impressive top speed of 132 mph, an excellent climb rate of in excess of 1,000 ft per minute plus an operational ceiling of 20,000 ft, coupled with overall excellent pilot visibility all should have ensured its rapid introduction into service on the Western Front. Instead, the "radical" monoplane design was saddled with an officially stated assessment that the landing speed of 49 mph was too high, and this ensured that only 125 were produced for service in less vital theatres. The Royal Flying Corps was the sole user of the type and Canadian pilots saw service in them while attached with the RFC in the Middle East.

This frontal view of the Bristol M1.C monoplane illustrates its radical (for 1916) but clearly ultra-modern design, including its streamlined propeller/nose fairing. (LAC Photo # PA-006365)

DETAILS

Designation: **Model No:** M.1C **Marks:** **Role:** single seat fighter **Service:** RFC

SPECIFICATIONS

Manufacturer:	Bristol (British & Colonial Aeroplane Co.)	
Crew/Passengers:	one pilot	
Powerplant:	one 110 hp Le Rhone 9-cylinder rotary piston engine	
Performance:	Max Speed: 130 mph (200 km/h)	Cruising Speed:
	Service Ceiling: 20,000 ft (6,096 m)	Endurance: 1 hr 45 min
Weights:	Empty: 900 lb (408 kg)	Gross: 1,348 lb (611.5 kg)
Dimensions:	Span: 30 ft 9 in (9.37 m)	Length: 20 ft 5½ in (6.24 m)
	Height: 7 ft 9½ in (2.37 m)	Wing Area:
Armament:	one fixed forward Vickers machine gun	
Cost:	Unknown	

Bristol
SCOUT

The Bristol Scout was truly ahead of its time. Based upon a pre-war racing design, the Bristol Scout became one of the first scout aircraft to be produced in large numbers. Initially unarmed, the design became a true fighter when an aircraft was eventually modified with a Vickers machine gun mounted at an angle to clear the propeller arc. In March 1916, the D model of the Scout became the first British fighter to be armed with a synchronized machine gun. By this time, however, the design was being outdated by more modern designs and the Scout was withdrawn from active service and put to use in training roles. The Scout served with both the Royal Flying Corps and the Royal Naval Air Service, where Canadian pilots saw service in the type.

This unfortunately was a typical fate of many early fighters and trainers. The Bristol Scout, shown here, has nosed over in a landing accident but with relatively little apparent damage. (LAC Photo # PA-125919)

DETAILS

Designation: **Model No:**   **Marks:**   **Role:** single seat fighter
Service: RFC/RNAS

SPECIFICATIONS

Manufacturer: Bristol (British & Colonial Aeroplane Co.)
Crew/Passengers: one pilot
Powerplant: one 80 hp Le Rhone 9-cylinder rotary piston engine
Performance: Max Speed: 100 mph (161 km/h)   Cruising Speed
        Service Ceiling: 16,000 ft (4,877 m)   Endurance: 2½ hrs
Weights: Empty: 760 lb (345 kg)   Gross: 1,250 lb (567 kg)
Dimensions: Span: 24 ft 7 in (7.49 m)   Length: 20 ft 8 in (6.30 m)
        Height: 8 ft 6 in (2.59 m)   Wing Area: 198 sq ft (18.39 sq m)
Armament: one fixed forward Vickers machine gun
Cost: Unknown

Curtiss
H.12

The Curtiss H.12 was a First World War, American designed twin-engine flying boat, which was adopted by the RNAS. The successful qualities of the design led to further improvements and modifications and spawned the British-made Felixstowe series of flying boats. The H.12 model was itself derived from the H.4 Small America design and was essentially a larger and more powerful development. The H.12 featured a laminated wood veneer hull with sponsons along the lower edges and unequal span biplane wings. In RNAS service, the H.12 operated from flying boat stations, and like the F.2 flying boats, were involved in long-range anti-submarine and anti-Zeppelin patrols over the North Sea. H.12 aircraft were often flown on North Sea patrols by Canadian aircrew serving with the RNAS.

Two RNAS Curtiss flying boats are shown here at anchor. (LAC Photo # PA-006392)

DETAILS
Designation: **Model No:** H.12   **Marks:**   **Role:** Flying Boat
Service: RNAS

SPECIFICATIONS

Manufacturer:	Curtiss Aircraft Company	
Crew/Passengers:	crew of four	
Powerplant:	two 275 hp Rolls Royce Eagle I piston engines	
Performance:	Max Speed: 85 mph (150 km/h)	Cruising Speed:
	Service Ceiling: 10,800 ft (2,438 m)	Endurance: 6 hrs
Weights:	Empty: 7,293 lb (3,609 kg)	Gross: 10,650 lb (5,550 kg)
Dimensions:	Upper Span: 92 ft 8½ in (31.09 m)	Length: 46 ft 6 in (15.01 m)
	Height: 16 ft 6 in (5.69 m)	Wing Area: 1,216 sq ft (133.03 sq m)
Armament:	provisions for four Lewis machine guns on flexible mounts plus up to four 230 lb (104 kg) bombs	
Cost:	Unknown	

Curtiss
MOHAWK

The Curtiss P-36 was the first of the new generation of monoplane fighters to enter service with the US Army Air Corps. It was a contemporary of other Second World War fighters such as the Spitfire, the Hurricane, and the Messerschmitt Bf 109, all of which were introduced within a few months of each other in the mid 1930s. Even though the P-36 owed very little to the previous Curtiss "Hawk" series of pursuit biplanes, the name Hawk was still applied to this latest aircraft. With the onset of war, considerable interest in the Hawk had been aroused in Britain as a result of a test flight carried out with an Armée de l'Air Hawk by an RAF pilot in France. The Hawk 75A possessed good performance and manoeuvrability.

At the end of 1939, the Royal Aircraft Establishment arranged for a loan of a Curtiss Hawk from France. Based on these trials, the British government initially considered ordering the Hawk for the RAF. However, the fall of France in June 1940 caused a large number of aircraft to be diverted to Britain (including those Hawk 75As which had not yet been delivered to France before the surrender,

plus those whose pilots had flown them to England to escape the German occupation). The aircraft were taken over by the RAF and given the name Mohawk. The RAF impressed a total of 229 Mohawks. Most of them were former French machines, but a few former Persian Hawks and even some Indian-built machines were included in the Mohawk total as well. Mohawks taken on strength by the Royal Air Force were refitted with British equipment, including 0.303-calibre Browning machine guns. The French throttles were replaced by throttles which operated in the "British fashion" (i.e., pushed forward to increase the power). The RAF eventually decided that Mohawks were not suitable for the European theatre, and sent 72 of them to the South African Air Force. Others were flown by No. 5 and No.155 (RAF) Squadron based in India. At one point, eight Mohawks provided the sole fighter defense of northeast India, and the fighter remained operational on the Burma front until finally replaced by more modern types in December 1943.

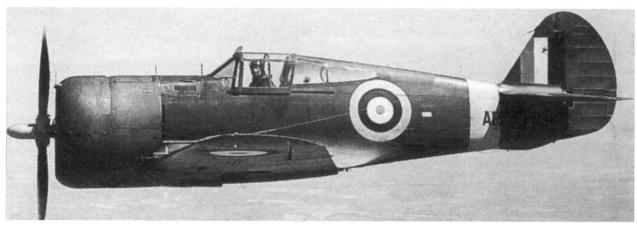

The Curtiss Model 75 was known as the Mohawk in RAF service and it served primarily in India and Burma during World War II (RAF Photo)

DETAILS
Designation: P-36 **Model No:** 75 **Marks:** Mk I, II, III, IV **Role:** fighter
Service: RAF

SPECIFICATIONS
Manufacturer:	Curtiss Aircraft Company	
Crew/Passengers:	pilot	
Powerplant:	one 1050 hp Pratt & Whitney R-1830 piston engine	
Performance:	Max Speed: 313 mph (504 km/h)	Cruising Speed: 250 mph (402 km/h)
	Service Ceiling: 37,200 ft (11,338 m)	Range: 830 mi (1,336 km)
Weights:	Empty: 4,541 lb (2,060 kg)	Gross: 5,650 lb (2,563 kg)
Dimensions:	Span: 37 ft 4 in (11.38 m)	Length: 28 ft 6 in (8.69 m)
	Height: 8 ft 5 in (2.57 m)	Wing Area:
Armament:	one .50 cal machine gun and three .30 cal machine guns and provisions for light bombs	
Cost:	Unknown	

De Havilland
D.H.2

The D.H.2 was the second design by Geoffrey De Havilland for the Aircraft Manufacturing Company and the Royal Flying Corps. Introduced in 1916, the unusual pusher configuration was necessitated by the lack of a suitable interrupter gear to permit a machine gun to fire through the propeller disc. Mounting the engine to the rear of the fuselage permitted the use of a fixed forward machine gun. At that point in the First World War, the German Fokker E.III fighter, which featured a synchronized machine gun, had previously been introduced and it was sweeping the skies of Allied aircraft. The D.H.2 design was relatively clean and sturdy. It featured good manoeuvrability and an excellent rate of climb. Consequently, the D.H.2 design helped end the "Fokker Scourge." Canadian aircrew and groundcrews supported combat action with the D.H.2 while attached to RFC Squadrons.

The distinctive D.H.2 with its "pusher" configuration was a surprisingly good compromise fighter design that easily allowed for forward firing armament. (LAC Photo # PA-006636)

DETAILS

Designation: **Model No:** D.H.2   **Marks:**   **Role:** single seat fighter
Service: RFC

SPECIFICATIONS

Manufacturer:	Aircraft Manufacturing Company (AIRCO) Ltd De Havilland Aircraft
Crew/Passengers:	one pilot
Powerplant:	one 100 hp Gnome 9 cylinder rotary engine

Performance: Max Speed: 93 mph (150 km/h)   Cruising Speed:
Service Ceiling: 14,000 ft (4,267 m)   Endurance: 2 hr 45 min
Weights: Empty: Gross: 1,441 lb (654 kg)
Dimensions: Span: 28 ft 3 in (8.61 m)   Length: 25 ft 2½ in (7.68 m)
Height: 9 ft 6½ in (2.91 m)   Wing Area:
Armament: one fixed forward Lewis machine gun
Cost: Unknown

De Havilland
D.H.6

The De Havilland D.H.6 was designed at the outset as a two-seat elementary trainer. It was also designed with simple features and lines for rapid production. (The type acquired an unusually high number of nicknames including "the Sky Hook," the Crab," the Clutching Hand," "the Flying Coffin," "the Dung Hunter" and "the Sixty.") In addition to training duties the RNAS also pressed the design into service as an anti-submarine patrol aircraft. The

D.H.6 also became the first British aircraft design to be license-built in Canada, when a single example was built for the commanding officer of the RFC in Canada. The D.H.6 was rapidly replaced by the more popular Avro 504 design in the elementary training role. Canadian crews came into contact with the D.H.6 while serving with either the Royal Flying Corps or the Royal Naval Air Service.

A De Havilland D.H.6 trainer belonging to the RFC is illustrated above. A sole example was manufactured in Canada. (LAC Photo # PA-006368)

DETAILS
Designation: **Model No:** D.H.6   **Marks:**   **Role:** two seat trainer/observation aircraft
Service: RFC, RNAS

SPECIFICATIONS
Manufacturer:	De Havilland Aircraft Company	
Crew/Passengers:	crew of two: pilot and observer/student	
Powerplant:	one 90 hp RAF 1a or Curtiss OX-5 piston engine	
Performance:	Max Speed: 75 mph (121 km/h)	Cruising Speed:
	Service Ceiling: 6,100 ft (1,859 m)	Range:
Weights:	Empty: 1,530 lb (695 kg)	Gross: 1,926 lb (874 kg)
Dimensions:	Span: 35 ft 11 in (10.95 m)	Length: 27 ft 11 in (8.51 m)
	Height: 10 ft 9½ in (3.29 m)	Wing Area: 436 sq ft (40.53 sq m)
Armament:	provisions for up to 100 lb (45 kg) of bombs	
Cost:	Unknown	

Douglas
D.C.2

The Douglas D.C.2 was designed in response to a Trans World Airlines (TWA) specification for an all-metal, three-engine airliner capable of carrying twelve passengers. Douglas Aircraft instead responded with a twin-engine design, which in prototype form was known as the D.C.1. The production (D.C.2) version featured more powerful engines and a lengthened fuselage to accommodate 14 passengers. The D.C.2 was in fact the predecessor to the much more famous D.C.3 airliner/transport which itself was basically a stretched and widened version of the D.C.2. With the outbreak of the Second World War, the lack of suitable transport resulted in numerous civilian aircraft being impressed into military service. The RAF acquired a small number of D.C.2 transports and Canadian crews flew the type while attached to RAF units.

A view of a US Army Air Corps Douglas D.C.2 similar to those impressed for use by the RAF. The similarity to the more common D.C.3 is clearly apparent. (USAF Photo)

DETAILS

Designation: **Model No:** D.C.2   **Marks:**   **Role:** Transport
Service: RAF

SPECIFICATIONS

Manufacturer:	Douglas Aircraft
Crew/Passengers:	crew of two and up to fourteen passengers
Powerplant:	two 825 hp SGR-1820-F52 Wright Cyclone radial piston engines

Performance:	Max Speed:	Cruising Speed: 180 mph (290 km/h)
	Service Ceiling: 23,200 ft (7,070 m)	Range: 1,300 mi (2,100 km)
Weights:	Empty:	Gross: 18,560 lb (8,419 kg)
Dimensions:	Span: 95 ft 0 in (28.96 m)	Length: 64 ft 6 in (19.65 m)
	Height: 16 ft 11 in (5.15 m)	Wing Area:
Armament:	None	
Cost:	Unknown	

Fairey
BARRACUDA

First flown in December 1940, the Fairey Barracuda torpedo bomber was designed to replace the obsolete Fairey Swordfish and Albacore biplanes as a front-line combat aircraft. Production and other delays however meant the aircraft type did not begin to see widespread service until 1943. The Barracuda then served in a wide variety of capacities until VJ Day. The design achieved prominence in 1944 when forty Barracudas took off in two waves to successfully attack the German pocket battleship *Tirpitz* anchored in a Norwegian fiord. Several Canadian pilots were involved in this famous attack. The Barracuda also saw numerous actions with the British fleet in the Pacific. Despite its ungainly appearance, the aircraft could carry out a wide variety of missions and was progressively modified to carry bombs, mines, torpedoes, depth charges, rockets, radar masts and radomes, lifeboats and even containers under the wings for dropping agents into occupied territories. Two Royal Canadian Navy squadrons, No. 825 and 826, were initially equipped with Barracudas when they were formed in 1945.

A view of several of the ungainly looking Fairey Barracuda torpedo bombers which featured unusual shouldered-mounted wings with large flaps as seen here (LAC Photo # PA-146652)

DETAILS
Designation: **Model No:**   **Marks:** MkI, II, III, V   **Role:** Torpedo Bomber
Service: RN

SPECIFICATIONS Mark II
Manufacturer:	Fairey Aircraft Company
Crew/Passengers:	crew of three
Powerplant:	one 1,640 hp (1,223 kW) Rolls Royce Merlin 32 engine

Performance:	Max Speed: 240 mph (386 km/h)	Cruising Speed: 205 mph (330 km/h)
	Service Ceiling: 16,600 ft (5,060 m)	Range: 1,150 mi (1,851 km)
Weights:	Empty: 10,818 lb (4,907 kg)	Maximum Take-off: 14,250 lb (6,464 kg)
Dimensions:	Span: 49 ft 2 in (14.99 m)	Length: 39 ft 9 in (12.12 m)
	Height: 12 ft 3 in (3.73 m)	Wing Area: 414 sq ft (38.46 sq m)
Armament:	two .303 in (7.7 mm) Vickers "K" machine guns in rear cockpit plus provisions for up 1,640 lb (744 kg) of torpedoes, bombs, depth charges, mines	
Cost:	Unknown	

Fairey
FULMAR

First flown in March 1937, the Fairey Fulmar was a large two-seat naval fighter used by the Royal Navy's Fleet Air Arm. Perhaps outclassed by contemporary land-based fighters, the Fulmar was nevertheless an advance over the naval types it replaced. It had the eight-gun armament of the Hurricane and Spitfire but carried twice the ammunition. It possessed an endurance time of 5 hours and reasonable overall performance. It could out-climb navalized variants of the Hurricane and featured folding wings, while those on the Hurricanes were fixed. Consequently the design saw wide and varied service (including night fighter, intruder, reconnaissance and patrol duties) in the FAA and lasted until the cessation of hostilities. Canadian naval aircrew saw action in Fulmars while attached to the Royal Navy.

The Fairey Fulmar played a vital and successful role in Royal Navy operations early in the war. Its two-seat configuration, however, imposed a performance penalty. (Comox AFM Photo)

DETAILS
Designation: **Model No:** P.4/34   **Marks:** Mk I, II   **Role:** Two seat naval fighter
Service: RN/FAA

SPECIFICATIONS Mark I
Manufacturer:	Fairey Aircraft Company
Crew/Passengers:	crew of two
Powerplant:	one 1,080 hp (768 kW) Rolls Royce Merlin VIII engine

Performance:	Max Speed: 280 mph (451 km/h)	Cruising Speed: 235 mph (378 km/h)
	Service Ceiling: 21,500 ft (6,555 m)	Range: 800 mi (,288 km)
Weights:	Empty: 8,720 lb (3,955 kg)	Maximum Take-off: 10,700 lb (4,853 kg)
Dimensions:	Span: 46 ft 5 in (14.15 m)	Length: 40 ft 2 in (2.24 m)
	Height: 14 ft 0 in (4.27 m)	Wing Area: 342 sq ft (31.77 sq m)
Armament:	eight .303 in (7.7 mm) machine guns in the wings	
Cost:	Unknown	

Felixstowe
F.2

The Felixstowe F.2 was a British First World War twin-engine flying boat designed by the commander of RNAS *Felixstowe* and generally based on American Curtiss designs. The F.2 was a design improvement of the original F.1 series flying boat by the same designer. Similar to contemporary Curtiss designs, the F.2 featured a laminated wood veneer hull with sponsons along the lower edges and unequal span biplane wings. In service, the F.2 operated from almost every flying boat station of the RNAS and the type bore the brunt of long-range antisub-marine and anti-Zeppelin patrols over the North Sea. Air-to-air combat with Zeppelins or German Branden-burg seaplanes was a common occurrence. The potential for aircraft to be forced down in these circumstances led to the introduction of high visibility paint schemes to facilitate search and rescue operations. The resulting "dazzle" schemes were highly diverse and sometimes gaudy. The F.2 aircraft were often flown on North Sea patrols by Canadian aircrew serving with the RNAS.

RNAS Felixstowe F.2 flying boat dazzle painted in accordance with late-war practice. (RCAF Photo)

DETAILS

Designation: **Model No:** F.2   **Marks:**   **Role:** Flying Boat
Service: RNAS

SPECIFICATIONS

Manufacturer:	Felixstowe	
Crew/Passengers:	crew of four	
Powerplant:	two 345 hp Rolls Royce Eagle VIII piston engines	
Performance:	Max Speed: 93 mph (150 km/h)	Cruising Speed:
	Service Ceiling: 8,000 ft (2,438 m)	Range: 270 mi (450 km)
Weights:	Empty: 7,958 lb (3,609 kg)	Gross: 12,235 lb (5,550 kg)
Dimensions:	Upper Span: 102 ft 0 in (31.09 m)	Lower Span: 74 ft 2 in (22.61 m)
	Length: 49 ft 3 in (15.01 m)	Height: 18 ft 8 in (5.69 m)
	Wing Area: 1,432 sq ft (133.03 sq m)	
Armament:	provisions for four Lewis machine guns on flexible mounts plus up to four 230 lb (104 kg) bombs	
Cost:	Unknown	

Gloster
GLADIATOR

The Gloster Gladiator was the last of a long line of bi-plane fighters to be used by the RAF. First flown in 1934, the design featured a metal structure with fabric covering and an enclosed cockpit. Despite becoming rapidly obsolete, Gladiators were pressed into combat service with the outbreak of the Second World War and saw action in the initial campaigns in Norway, and early actions in Greece and the Western Desert. The Gladiator design was also modified and adapted for use by the Fleet Air Arm, where it was named the Sea Gladiator. Three Sea Gladiators borrowed and manned by the RAF and nick-named "Faith, Hope and Charity" rose to prominence in the desperate defence of the island of Malta. Canadian aircrew flew both Gladiators and Sea Gladiators while attached to British squadrons and units.

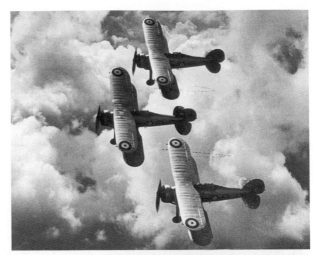

Obsolete by the start of the Second World War, the Gloster Gladiator was nevertheless pressed into combat service by the Royal Air Force and Royal Navy. The photos above illustrate RAF variants. (RAF Photo)

DETAILS
Designation: SS.37   **Model No:**   **Marks:** Mk I, II   **Role:** Fighter
Service: RAF, RN

SPECIFICATIONS
Manufacturer:	Gloster Aircraft Company
Crew/Passengers:	one pilot
Powerplant:	one 830 hp (619 kW) Bristol Mercury IX radial piston engine

Performance:	Max Speed: 257 mph (414 km/h)	Cruising Speed: 212 mph (341 km/h)
	Service Ceiling: 33,500 ft (10,211 m)	Range: 440 mi (708 km)
Weights:	Empty: 3,444 lbs (1,562 kg)	Gross: 4,864 lbs (2,206 kg)
Dimensions:	Span: 32 ft 3 in (9.83 m)	Length: 27 ft 5 in (8.36 m)
	Height: 11 ft 7 in (3.53 m)	Wing Area: 323 sq ft (30.01 sq m)
Armament:	four forward firing 0.303 in (7.7 mm) machine guns; two mounted in the wings and two in the fuselage	
Original Cost:	Unknown	

Grumman
HELLCAT

The Grumman Hellcat was the replacement for the Grumman Wildcat (or Martlet in RN/AA service) and they were supplied to the Royal Navy under Lend-Lease arrangements. The larger, more advanced design was well liked by aircrew and was very robust. Like the Wildcat, the Hellcat too was progressively improved throughout its service. Later variants included a night fighter version with a small radar set mounted under the starboard wing. Hellcats first saw operational service with the Royal Navy during anti-shipping strikes off the coast of Norway; however they were primarily used in the Far East in strikes and missions against Japanese targets. Canadian naval pilots flew the aircraft type on combat missions while attached to the RN.

Arguably one of the most successful naval fighter designs of the Second World War, Grumman Hellcats were pressed into Royal Navy service under lend-lease arrangements with the US. Here Royal Navy Hellcats are being loaded on deck with rocket projectiles. (Comox AFM Photo)

DETAILS

Designation: G-36A, B   **Model No:** F6F-3, -4, -5, -5N   **Marks:** Mk I, II
Role: Fighter, Fighter Bomber, Night Fighter   **Service:** RN

SPECIFICATIONS Mk II

Manufacturer: Grumman Aircraft Ltd
Crew/Passengers: one pilot
Powerplant: one 2,000 hp Pratt & Whitney R-2800-10W Double Wasp radial piston engine
Performance: Max Speed: 371 mph (597 km/h)   Cruising Speed:
                   Service Ceiling: 36,700 ft (11,186 m)   Range: 1,040 mi (1,674 km)
Weights: Empty: 9,212 lb (4,178 kg)   Maximum Take-off: 13,753 lb (6,238 kg)
Dimensions: Span: 42 ft 10 in (13.06 m)   Length: 33 ft 7 in (10.24 m)
                   Height: 14 ft 5 in (4.39 m)   Wing Area: 334 sq ft (31.03 m)
Armament: Six 0.5 in (12.7 mm) machine guns in the wings plus provisions for two 1,000 lb (454 kg) bombs, six 60 lb (27 kg) rockets or fuel tanks
Cost: Unknown

Grumman
MARTLET (WILDCAT)

The Grumman Wildcat (or Martlet in RN/AA service) was the first modern (single-seat monoplane) American naval fighter of the Second World War. First flown in 1937, the Wildcat was characterized by its slightly portly design and fuselage mounted retractable undercarriage. The success of the design ensured orders from both the RN's Fleet Air Arm and the French equivalent. It was progressively modernized and updated throughout the war. The Martlet was the first American-built aircraft in service with the Royal Navy to down a German aircraft (a JU-88 bomber in 1940) during the war. The Royal Navy flew Martlets in virtually all theatres of operation. Canadian naval aircrew flew the aircraft type on combat missions including from small escort carriers on the difficult Arctic convoys to supply Russia.

A view of a US Navy Grumman Wildcat, virtually identical in appearance to the Martlet in Royal Navy service. (Comox AFM Photo)

DETAILS
Designation: G-36A, B   **Model No:** F4F-3, F4F-4   **Marks:** Mk I, II, III, IV, V   **Role:** Fighter
Service: RN

SPECIFICATIONS Mk II
Manufacturer:	Grumman Aircraft Ltd
Crew/Passengers:	one pilot
Powerplant:	one 1,200 hp Pratt & Whitney R-1830-S3C4-G Twin Wasp radial piston engine

Performance:	Max Speed: 315 mph (507 km/h)	Cruising Speed: 260 mph (418 km/h)
	Service Ceiling: 28,000 ft (8,534 m)	Range: 1,150 mi (1,851 km)
Weights:	Empty: 4,649 lb (2,109 kg)	Maximum Take-off: 8,152 lb (3,698 kg)
Dimensions:	Span: 38 ft 0 in (11.58 m)	Length: 28 ft 9 in (8.76 m)
	Height: 9 ft 3 in (2.82 m)	Wing Area: 260 sq ft (24.15 m)
Armament:	Six 0.5 in (12.7 mm) machine guns in the wings plus provisions for bombs, rockets or fuel tanks	
Cost:	Unknown	

Grumman
PANTHER

The Grumman Panther, a carrier-based fighter-bomber, first flew on 24 November 1947. The Pratt & Whitney J-42 jet engine that powered it was a license-built version of the Rolls-Royce Nene engine that would also power Canadair-built versions of the T-33 Silver Star. The Panther was the first US Navy jet fighter to be used in combat when the F9F-2 models flew into action against North Korea. Panther aircraft from the USS *Valley Forge* took part in this inaugural strike on 3 July 1950. An F9F-2 was also the first US Navy aircraft to shoot down a MIG-15 jet fighter. Grumman Panthers went on to fly more than 78,000 sorties throughout the Korean War and accounted for a further fourteen MIG-15 aircraft without loss.

Although the achievements of Canadian Air Force exchange officers flying USAF F-86 Sabres in the Korean conflict are relatively well documented, it is not well known that a Canadian naval pilot also participated in the conflict. Lt Cdr J.J. MacBrien, RCN, was an exchange pilot flying a Panther aircraft from the American carrier, USS *Oriskany*. He was subsequently awarded the Distinguished Flying Cross. Leading a flight on an interdiction mission against supply and storage targets near Pukchong on 1 February 1953, he was cited for "extraordinary achievement" in accomplishing the mission. "Despite marginal flying weather, heavy anti-aircraft fire, he displayed courageous leadership and outstanding pilot skill . . . in the highest traditions of the United States Naval Service."[1]

1. Kealy, J.D.F. and Russell, E.C., *A History of Canadian Naval Aviation, 1918–1962*, Ottawa: Queen's Printer, 1965. P 124.

A view of a restored F9F-2 Panther aircraft similar to that flown by Lt Cdr MacBrien (RCN) during the Korean conflict. (Bill Knight/Eagle 19 Photo)

DETAILS

Designation: **Model No:** F9F-2 **Marks:** **Role:** fighter/bomber
Service: USN

SPECIFICATIONS

Manufacturer:	Grumman Aircraft Ltd		
Crew/Passengers:	one pilot in ejection seat		
Powerplant:	one 5,000 lb (2,270 kg) thrust Pratt & Whitney J-42-2 centrifugal-flow jet engine		
Performance:	Max Speed: 526 mph (849 km/h)	Cruising Speed: 487 mph (784 km/h)	
	Service Ceiling: 44,600 ft (13,060 m)	Range: 1,353 mi (2,178 km)	
Weights:	Empty: 9,303 lb (4,220 kg)	Gross: 16,450 lb (7,461 kg)	
Dimensions:	Span: 38 ft 0 in (1.58 m)	Length: 37 ft 3 in (11.35 m)	
	Height: 11 ft 4 in (3.45 m)	Wing Area: 250 sq ft (23.23 sq m)	
Armament:	four 20 mm cannon and underwing pylons for up to 2,000 lb (907 kg) of bombs		
Cost:	Unknown		

Handley Page
V-0/100, 0/400

The Handley Page V-0/100 was the first practical heavy bomber to go into service with the Royal Flying Corps. Originally developed to meet an Admiralty specification, the V-0/100 had a very large wing span of 100 feet. The design's construction was conventional, if massive, for the day. The maximum bomb load was 1,792 lb (813 kg). A distinctive feature was the large main undercarriage consisting of two steel tube structures supporting two pairs of large wheels each with its own shock absorber. In addition, a surprising feature for such a large aircraft was folding wings, which enabled the bombers to be stowed in the standard canvas Bessonneau field hangars of that time. The first V-0/100s entered service in 1916. The V-0/400 series of aircraft was yet a further improvement of the design. The principle change involved a complete redesign of the fuel system, which also allowed changes to the engine nacelles. The V-0/400 model is noted for delivering large 1,650 lb "Blockbuster" bombs. Canadian crews flew both variants in First World War combat missions.

The Handley Page V-0/400A shown here was one of the RFC's first real heavy bombers of the First World War. (LAC Photo # PA-006401)

DETAILS

Designation:	**Model No:** 0/100, 0/400	**Marks:**	**Role:** Bomber
Service: RFC			

SPECIFICATIONS 0/400

Manufacturer:	Handley Page Aircraft	
Crew/Passengers:	crew of four	
Powerplant:	two 250 hp Rolls Royce Eagle II twelve cylinder engines	
Performance:	Max Speed: 85 mph (137 km/h)	Cruising Speed:
	Service Ceiling: 7,000 ft (2,134 m)	Endurance: 8 hrs
Weights:	Empty:	Maximum Take-off: 14,020 lb (6,359 kg)
Dimensions:	Span: 100 ft 0 in (30.48 m)	Length: 62 ft 10 in (19.15 m)
	Height: 22 ft 0 in (6.71 m)	Wing Area:
Armament:	4 or 5 flexible Lewis machine guns including one mounted on a Scarff ring and up to 1,792 lb (813 kg) of bombs	
Cost:	Unknown	

Handley Page
V-0/1500

The Handley Page V-0/1500 was essentially a larger development of the first practical heavy bomber to go into service with the Royal Flying Corps, the V-0/100, designed by the same manufacturer. Originally the V-0/100 had a wing span of 100 feet while the V-0/1500 featured an even larger wing span of 126 feet. The design's construction was again conventional, if massive, for the day. The maximum bomb load was 7,500 lb (3,402 kg). A distinctive feature was the large main undercarriage consisting of two steel tube structures supporting two pairs of large wheels each with its own shock absorber. In addition, a surprising feature for such a large aircraft was folding wings, which enabled the bombers to be stowed in the standard canvas Bessonneau field hangars of that time. The first V-0/1500s entered service in 1918. Canadian crews flew the bomber in late First World War combat missions.

This view of one of the largest of the First World War RFC bombers, the Handley Page V-0/1500, illustrates its folding wing capability. (RAF Photo)

DETAILS

Designation: **Model No:** 0/1500   **Marks:**   **Role:** Bomber
Service: RFC

SPECIFICATIONS 0/400

Manufacturer:	Handley Page Aircraft	
Crew/Passengers:	crew of four	
Powerplant:	four 375 hp Rolls Royce Eagle VIII twelve cylinder engines	
Performance:	Max Speed: 97 mph (156 km/h)	Cruising Speed:
	Service Ceiling: 10,000 ft (3,048 m)	Endurance: 6 hrs
Weights:	Empty:	Gross: 24,700 lb (11,204 kg)
Dimensions:	Span: 126 ft 0 in (38.41 m)	Length: 62 ft 0 in (18.90 m)
	Height: 23 ft 0 in (7.01 m)	Wing Area:
Armament:	4 or 5 flexible Lewis machine guns including one nose mounted on a Scarff ring and up to 7,500 lb (3,402 kg) of bombs	
Cost:	Unknown	

Hawker
TYPHOON

The Hawker Typhoon was originally designed as interceptor but suffered from teething problems with its Napier Sabre engine, which proved to be unreliable and suffered from poor high-altitude performance. However, at low level, the Typhoon was a superb aircraft. Its strength and firepower made it an ideal fighter-bomber and it soon became the standard ground support aircraft of the RAF's 2nd Tactical Air Force (2 TAF). Three RCAF Squadrons, No. 438, 439 and 440 Squadron, flew the Hawker Typhoon in 2 TAF during the Second World War. In Canadian service, it was renowned for its ground-attack abilities. Usually armed with 4 Hispano 20mm cannons and either bombs or rockets, with either 60 lb (27 kg) high-explosive or 25 lb (11 kg) armour-piercing warheads, the Typhoon could destroy any armoured vehicle on the battlefield. The three RCAF squadrons helped wreck the German Panzer divisions at Caen, Falaise and all over North-West Europe. They also attacked and destroyed V-1 rocket sites, radar stations, bridges, gun emplacements and lines of communication. The Typhoons were subsequently replaced by an improved Hawker design known as the Tempest.

Top left An unidentified Typhoon at a forward operating location is shown being readied for a sortie. Note the rockets under each wing.
Bottom A Typhoon of 439 (RCAF) Squadron lands at its newly acquired base in Belgium. This aircraft, RB402, was the fourth Typhoon to wear the coding "5V P". The first three were either shot down or replaced by newer models. (Comox AFM & CF Photos)

DETAILS
Designation: **Model No:** **Marks:** Mk IB **Role:** Fighter/Fighter Bomber
Service: RAF

SPECIFICATIONS Mk IB
Manufacturer:	Hawker Aircraft Company
Crew/Passengers:	one pilot
Powerplant:	one 2,180 hp (1,626 kW) Napier Sabre IIA in-line piston engine

Performance:	Max Speed: 405 mph (652 km/h)	Cruising Speed: 254 mph (409 km/h)
	Service Ceiling: 34,000 ft (10,363 m)	Range: 510 mi (821 km) with weapons load
Weights:	Empty: 8,800 lbs (3,992 kg)	Gross: 11,400 lbs (5,171 kg)
Dimensions:	Span: 41 ft 7 in (12.67 m)	Length: 31 ft 11 in (9.73 m)
	Height: 15 ft 4 in (4.67 m)	Wing Area: 279 sq ft (25.92 sq m)
Armament:	four 20mm cannons plus provisions for 8 x 60 lb (27 kg) rockets or two 1,000 lb (454 kg) bombs	
Original Cost:	Unknown	

Lockheed
STARLIFTER

Developed as a long-range strategic transport for the USAF, the Lockheed-designed C-141A Starlifter first flew operationally in April 1965. The C-141 became the first jet transport from which US paratroopers jumped and the first jet transport to land in Antarctica. The transport was designed with a changeable cargo compartment for palletized cargo or vehicles and with interchangeable seating arrangements. The C-141B is a stretched variant of the initial model. The B model was lengthened by 23 ft 4 in (7.11 m), which increased the cargo capacity by one third. At the same time, the installation of an in-flight refuelling receptacle was also completed. The first C-141B was received by the Air Force in December 1979 and the entire fleet was converted by 1982. C-141B Starlifter

transports played an integral role in the first Gulf War campaign, and Canadian exchange officers serving with the USAF saw active service on the aircraft type.

The Lockheed C-141 Starlifter is a strategic transport of the United States Air Force, that was employed during the Gulf War campaign and flown by Canadian pilots on exchange at that time. (USAF Photos)

DETAILS
Designation: C-141   **Model No:**   **Marks:** A, B   **Role:** Strategic Cargo or Troop Transport
Service: USAF

SPECIFICATIONS
Manufacturer: Lockheed Aircraft
Crew/Passengers: crew of five or six plus up to 200 troops or 68,725 lb (31,239 kg) cargo
Powerplant: four Pratt & Whitney TF-33-P-7 turbofan engines
Performance: Max Speed: 500 mph (348 km/h)   Cruising Speed:
Service Ceiling: 41,000 ft (12,496 m)   Range:
Weights: Empty: Maximum Take-off: 323,100 lb (146,863 kg)
Dimensions: Span: 160 ft 0 in (48.77 m)   Length: 168 ft 4 in (51.31 m)
Height: 39 ft 3 in (11.96 m)   Wing Area:
Armament: none
Cost: $42.3M (US)

Martin
MARAUDER

The Martin B-26 Marauder was one of the most controversial American combat aircraft of the Second World War. It was numerically the most important US medium bomber used in the European theatre. At one time, however, the B-26 was considered so dangerous an aircraft that aircrews tried to avoid getting assigned to Marauder-equipped units and some crews actually refused to fly B-26s. The Marauder could be safely flown however, if crews were adequately trained. It demanded a higher standard of training from its crews than did its stablemate, the B-25 Mitchell. However, once mastered, the B-26 offered a level of operational safety to its crews unmatched by any other aircraft in its class. Despite its high landing speed of 130 mph, the Marauder had no vicious flying characteristics and its single-engine performance was good. A Martin-designed dorsal turret located behind the bomb bay just ahead of the tail was the first power-operated turret to be fitted to an American bomber.

There were two bomb bays, fore and aft. The unusual bomb bay doors were split in tandem, the forward pair folding in half when opened and the aft set being hinged normally to open outward. Two 2000 lb bombs could be carried in the main forward bomb bay, but up to 4800 pounds of smaller bombs could be carried if the aft bay was used as well. 52 B-26As were delivered to the Royal Air Force under the name Marauder Mk I. Most of them went to the Middle East in 1942 for service in Egypt to defend the Suez Canal against the advance of the Afrika Korps. The RAF was the first service to introduce the Marauder into action in the Mediterranean (predominately where it served) with the first operational mission by Marauders being flown on 28 October 1942. Additional improved aircraft were subsequently delivered to the RAF and helped support Allied forces during the invasion of Italy. Canadian crews saw combat action in Marauders while attached to RAF units.

The controversial Martin Marauder had an ill-deserved reputation. Shown here is a Mk III variant in RAF service. (RAF Photo)

DETAILS

Model No: 179   **Designation:** B-26   **Marks:** Mks I, II, III   **Role:** Bomber   **Service:** RAF

SPECIFICATIONS Mk III

Manufacturer:	Martin Aircraft
Crew/Passengers:	crew of six
Powerplant:	two 2,000 hp Pratt & Whitney R-2800-43 Double Wasp radial piston engines

Performance:	Max Speed: 305 mph (491 km/h)	Cruising Speed: 274 mph (441 km/h)
	Service Ceiling: 28,000 ft (8,543 m)	Range: 1,200 mi (1,931 km)
Weights:	Empty: 24,000 lb (10,886 kg)	Gross: 37,000 lb (16,783 kg)
Dimensions:	Span: 71 ft 0 in (21.64 m)	Length: 57 ft 6 in (17.53 m)
	Height: 20 ft 0 in (6.10 m)	Wing Area: 664 sq ft (61.69 sq m)
Armament:	0.50 cal (12.7 mm) machine guns in nose, dorsal and tail turrets plus provisions for four additional nose-mounted fixed machine guns and up to 4,000 lb (1,814 kg) in bombs	

Martin
MARYLAND

The US designed Martin (Model 167) Maryland was never ordered into service by the US Army Air Corps, but it was to serve in substantial numbers with both the French and British air arms. On January 26, 1939, the French government placed a contract for 115 aircraft. After the German invasion of May 10, 1940, the French Armée de l'Air aircraft were pressed into combat, flying 418 combat sorties from May 22 to June 24; 18 aircraft were lost in action. After the Armistice, most Martin aircraft ended up with the Vichy Air Force, but several managed to escape to England. After the Armistice of June 1940, the British government took over the last 50 Model 167s of a French order, along with a further 75 built under a direct RAF contract which was completed in July of 1940. They were officially named Maryland Mk I in RAF service. Between December 1940 and April 1941, an additional 150 Maryland Mk IIs were delivered to the RAF with R-1830-S3C4-G Twin Wasp engines, each rated at 1000 hp. RAF Marylands served with a general reconnaissance unit in Malta in 1940, and in 1941 with one British and three South African squadrons in northwest Africa. The surviving Model 167s serving with the Vichy Air Force were also used to attack Allied forces in Syria in June of 1941 and American forces near Casablanca in November 1942, making the type an aircraft design which fought on both sides in the Second World War. Canadian crews saw combat action in Marylands while attached to RAF units.

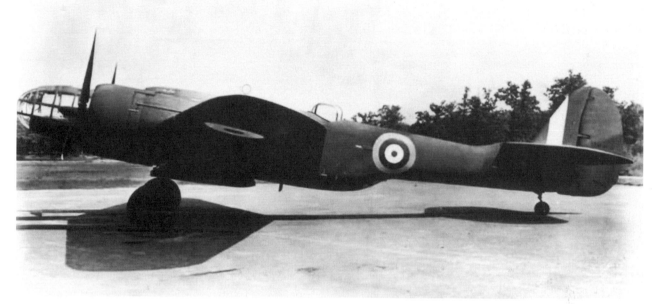

This image illustrates the unusual-looking Martin Maryland as used by the RAF and which served it well as a long-range reconnaissance and light-bomber aircraft. (Comox AFM Photo)

DETAILS

Model No: 167   **Marks:** Mk I, II   **Role:** Bomber   **Service:** RAF

SPECIFICATIONS Mk II

Manufacturer:	Martin Aircraft
Crew/Passengers:	crew of four
Powerplant:	two 1,200 hp R-1830-S3C4-G Twin Wasp radial piston engines

Performance:

Max Speed: 278 mph (447 km/h)	Cruising Speed:
Service Ceiling: 31,000 ft (9,449 m)	Range: 1,800 mi (2,897 km)

Weights: Empty: 11,213 lb (5,086 kg) — Gross: 16,809 lb (7,624 kg)

Dimensions: Span: 61 ft 4 in (18.69 m) — Length: 46 ft 8 in (14.22 m)

Height: 15 ft 0 in (4.57 m) — Wing Area: 539 sq ft (50.07 sq m)

Armament: four .303 in (7.7 mm) machine guns in wings plus single .303 in machine guns in dorsal and ventral positions plus provision for up to 2,000 lb (907 kg) in bombs

Maurice-Farman
SHORTHORN

A biplane "pusher" developed by the French, the Maurice-Farman S.11, more commonly known as the Shorthorn, lacked the characteristic forward elevator of the Maurice-Farman Longhorn. With the nacelle positioned halfway up the interplane struts, the pilot was seated well ahead of the wings and the aircraft was ideally suited to its initial role as a reconnaissance bomber. Adopted by most of the Allied air services, the Shorthorn was often equipped with dual controls and widely used as a trainer throughout much of the war. Canadian pilots attached to the RFC flew Shorthorn aircraft while in training.

Many Canadian pilots, while in England, flew the Maurice Farman S.11 Shorthorn for training. At least two flew them on operational missions. A restored example can be found in the Canada Aviation Museum. (CF Photo)

DETAILS
Designation:	**Model No:** S.11	**Marks:**	**Role:** two seat reconnaissance/trainer aircraft
Service: RFC			

SPECIFICATIONS
Manufacturer: Maurice-Farman Aircraft
Crew/Passengers: crew of two
Powerplant: one 80 hp air-cooled Renault eight cylinder engine
Performance: Max Speed: 72 mph (116 km/h)   Cruising Speed:
Service Ceiling: Range:
Weights: Empty: 1,442 lb (654 kg)   Gross: 2,046 lb (928 kg)
Dimensions: Span: 39 ft 3 in (11.96 m)   Length: 25 ft 9 in (7.85 m)
Height: 10 ft 4 in (3.15 m)   Wing Area:
Armament: none
Cost: Unknown

Miles
MAGISTER

In 1936, after satisfactory results were obtained with Miles Hawk trainers at elementary flying schools operated by civilian contractors, the Hawk trainer was ordered into production for the RAF as an elementary trainer. Changes to the basic design of the Hawk trainer included larger cockpits and provisions for blind flying equipment. It is the first low-wing monoplane to be adopted as a military trainer, where it was known as the Magister. It was also a departure from then RAF policy that only metal aircraft would be accepted for use. In RAF service, the Magister proved to be an excellent trainer. Magisters consequently served in most elementary flying schools and in all RAF command; the type also saw service with the British Army and the Fleet Air Arm. Many Magisters were also used as squadron "hacks" for miscellaneous communication duties and most fighter squadrons each had a Magister on strength. It is therefore no surprise that Canadian pilots flew the type while on training or while attached to RAF or FAA squadrons.

The diminutive RAF elementary trainer, the Miles Magister, shown here in wartime camouflage, could be found in more peaceful days in overall silver or yellow finishes. (LAC Photo # C81438)

DETAILS
Designation: **Model No:** M.14   **Marks:** Mk I, II, III   **Role:** Trainer
Service: RAF, FAA

SPECIFICATIONS Mk III
Manufacturer: Miles Aircraft
Crew/Passengers: crew of two; student and instructor in tandem
Powerplant: one 130 hp De Havilland Gipsy Major piston engine
Performance: Max Speed: 140 mph (225 km/h)   Cruising Speed: 122 mph (196 km/h)
       Service Ceiling: 16,500 ft (5,029 m)   Range: 367 mi (591 km)
Weights: Empty: 1,286 lb (583 kg)   Max T/O: 1,845 lb (837 kg)
Dimensions: Span: 33 ft 10 in (10.31 m)   Length: 24 ft 7½ in (7.51 m)
       Height: 6 ft 8 in (2.03 m)   Wing Area: 176 sq ft (16.35 sq m)
Armament: None
Cost: Unknown

Miles
MASTER

By the mid-1930s, the Royal Air Force had begun to take delivery of high performance monoplane fighters and bombers. Consequently, there was a need for an advanced trainer to introduce students to this high performance regime. Reversing the trend of the time to metal construction, the Miles Master trainer was entirely constructed of wood, and was a very clean low-wing monoplane design. The initial versions were powered by in-line Kestrel piston engines. Problems with the Kestrel engine, however, prompted a redesign for alternative powerplants. Radial engines including the Bristol Mercury and Pratt & Whitney Wasp Junior were then substituted. All variants of the Master had an instructor's seat in the rear cockpit that could be raised to provide a better view for take-off and landing. Many Canadian pilots received their advanced or refresher training on Miles Master aircraft.

This view depicts the Kestrel engine version of the Miles Master Mk IA trainer as used by the RAF for advanced training. (Comox AFM Photo)

DETAILS
Model No: M9   **Marks:** Mk I, IA, II, III   **Roles:** Trainer, Tow Target, Tow plane
Service: RAF

SPECIFICATIONS Mk II
Manufacturer:	Miles Aircraft	
Crew/Passengers:	crew of two; student and pilot in tandem	
Powerplant:	870 hp Bristol Mercury XX radial piston engine	
Performance:	Max Speed: 242 mph (389 km/h)	Cruising Speed:
	Service Ceiling: 25,100 ft (7,650 m)	Range: 393 mi (632 km)
Weights:	Empty: 4,293 lb (1,947 kg)	Maximum Take-off: 5,573 lb (2,528 kg)
Dimensions:	Span: 39 ft 0 in (11.89 m)	Length: 29 ft 6 in (8.99 m)
	Height: 9 ft 3 in (2.82 m)	Wing Area: 235 sq ft (21.83 sq m)
Armament:	provisions for one fixed forward Vickers .303 (7.7mm) machine gun and practice bombs	

Miles
MESSENGER

The Miles Messenger was developed to meet a requirement for an air observation post (AOP). The resulting design was very clean; it featured a one-piece wing with non-retractable external aerofoil flaps, a stocky fixed landing gear and a distinctive triple tail unit. The aircraft was eventually ordered in limited production, primarily to be used as a VIP communications aircraft. It performed successfully in this role until the end of the war.

The delicate-looking Miles Messenger successfully served in the RAF as a VIP communications and liaison aircraft. (RAF Photo)

DETAILS

Designation: **Model No:** M.38   **Marks:**   **Role:** AOP, Liaison and VIP communications
Service: British Army, RAF

SPECIFICATIONS

Manufacturer: Miles Aircraft
Crew/Passengers: pilot and up to three passengers
Powerplant: one 140 hp De Havilland Gipsy Major piston engine
Performance: Max Speed: 116 mph (187 km/h)   Cruising Speed: 95 mph (153 km/h)
                      Service Ceiling: 14,000 ft (4,267 m) Range: 260 mi (418 km)
Weights: Empty: 1,518 lb (689 kg)   Maximum Take-off: 1,900 lb (862 kg)
Dimensions: Span: 36 ft 2 in (11.02 m)   Length: 24 ft 0 in (7.32 m)
                      Height: 9 ft 6 in (2.90 m)   Wing Area: 191 sq ft (17.74 sq m)
Armament: None
Cost: 2,500 (Br) pounds

Morane-Saulnier
PARASOL

A "parasol" monoplane, the Morane-Saulnier Type L was a one or two-seat fighter reconnaissance aircraft. It was the first aircraft armed with a fixed machine gun that fired through the propeller arc. Any bullets that struck the propeller were deflected by steel plates. Armed with a Hotchkiss machine gun firing 8 mm solid copper bullets, the famous ace, Roland Garros tested the design in April 1915. He proceeded to score three victories in three suc-cessive weeks before the Germans captured the aircraft. On 19 December 1915, Captain M. Bell-Irving of Van-couver, BC flying a Parasol from No. 1 (RFC) Squadron engaged three enemy aircraft, destroying one and driving off the others. He evaded others and pressed home fur-ther attacks and was wounded in the process. He was subsequently awarded the Distinguished Service Order, the first decoration won by a Canadian in the RFC.

The Morane Saulnier Type L Parasol fighers, shown here in RFC colours, were serving France at the time the photograph was taken.
(LAC Photo # PA-102808)

DETAILS
Designation: **Model No:** MS.12   **Marks:**   **Role:** Reconnaissance Fighter
Service: RFC

SPECIFICATIONS

Manufacturer:	Morane-Saulnier Aircraft	
Crew/Passengers:	one pilot	
Powerplant:	one 80 hp Gnome rotary engine	
Performance:	Max Speed: 71.5 mph (15 km/h)	Cruising Speed:
	Service Ceiling: 13,123 ft (4,000 m)	Endurance: 2½ hours
Weights:	Empty: 849 lb (385 kg)	Gross: 1,441 lb (655 kg)
Dimensions:	Span: 36 ft 9 in (11.20 m)	Length: 22 ft 6¾ in (6.88 m)
	Height: 12 ft 10½ in (3.93 m)	Wing Area:
Armament:	one fixed forward Hotchkiss machine gun	
Cost:	Unknown	

Nieuport
SCOUT

The Nieuport 17 Scout was one of the most famous fighters of the First World War. Though of French design, this highly successful type was used by all Allied Air Forces. Nieuport Scouts first entered service in 1915 with the RNAS. The aircraft is often associated with the brilliant exploits of Allied aces such as Ball and Bishop of the RFC and Navarre and Nungesser of the Le Service Aeronautique (French

Air Force). Canadian Captain Billy Bishop began his operational career with the RFC flying a Nieuport Scout. He quickly achieved 47 victories flying this aircraft type and went on to become one of the leading aces of the First World War. He was awarded the Victoria Cross for flying a Nieuport in a daring solo pre-dawn raid on an enemy airfield.

The Nieuport 17 saw widespread use as a fighter by the British and French air forces during the First World War. B1566 is an airworthy replica of the Nieuport 17 Scout as flown by (later) Air Vice Marshal William "Billy" Bishop VC. It is maintained on display by the Canada Aviation Museum in Ottawa. (CF Photo)

DETAILS

Designation: **Model No:** 17   **Marks:**   **Role:** Fighter
Service: RNAS, RFC

SPECIFICATIONS

Manufacturer:	Nieuport	
Crew/Passengers:	one pilot	
Powerplant:	one 110 hp (82 kW) Le Rhone or 130 hp (96 kW) Clerget radial piston engine	
Performance:	Max Speed: 107 mph (172 km/h)	Cruising Speed:
	Service Ceiling: 17,500 ft (5,334 m)	Endurance:
Weights:	Empty: 825 lb (374 kg)	Gross: 1,233 lb (559 kg)
Dimensions:	Span: 26 ft 10 in (8.18 m)	Length: 18 ft 11 in (5.77 m)
	Height: 8 ft 0 in (2.44 m)	Wing Area:
Armament:	provisions for one fixed Lewis gun over the top wing or one Lewis and one synchronized forward-firing Vickers machine gun	
Cost:	Unknown	

North American
SABRE

The North American F-86 Sabre was first flown on 1 October 1947 and the aircraft quickly proved to be a highly successful design. It was the USAF's first swept-wing jet fighter. In 1949, with the formation of NATO, the Canadian government made the decision to re-equip the RCAF's front-line fighter squadrons with modern aircraft, and the F-86 Sabre was the type selected. An agreement was then reached between North American and Canadair Limited of Montreal to manufacture 100 F-86As in Canada. After the first prototype, designated CL-13 Sabre Mk I, Canadair immediately began production in earnest with an improved Mk II model. The Mark II was essentially an F-86E with an "all flying" tailplane to provide better flying characteristics as well as a flat windscreen. As a day fighter, the F-86 Sabre saw active combat service in Korea with three successively improved models (the F-86A, E & F models). The Sabres were primarily pitted against a contemporary jet adversary, the Russian-built MIG-15. By the end of hostilities, 792 MIGs had been shot down with a loss of only 76 Sabres, a victory ratio of 10 to 1. Although Canada did not send any fighter squadrons to Korea, pilots were sent there on exchange with the US Air Force. These pilots accounted for a total of 9 MIG-15s confirmed, 2 probables and 10 damaged. RCAF pilots flew a total of 1,036 sorties in Korea and were awarded seven U.S. Distinguished Flying Crosses, one Commonwealth Distinguished Flying Cross, and four US Air Medals. Of these pilots, only one was shot down and became a POW (Squadron Leader Andy MacKenzie was accidentally shot down by a USAF pilot). In addition, because the US could not produce the numbers of Sabres needed to sustain the war effort, Canada also supplied the USAF with 60 F-86 Sabre Mk 2s (USAF F-86E-6).

A Korean War-era USAF F-86 Sabre similar to those flown by RCAF exchange officers. (USAF Photo)

DETAILS

Manufacturer: North American and Canadair   **Designation:** F-86   **Model No:** A, E, F
Marks: Mk 1, 2, 4   **Role:** Fighter   **Service:** USAF

SPECIFICATIONS F-86E

Crew/Passengers: one pilot in ejection seat
Powerplant: General Electric J-47-GE-13 turbojet at 5,200 lbs (2,360 kg) thrust
Performance: Max Speed: 590 mph (949 km/h)   Cruising Speed:
Service Ceiling: 47,200 ft (14,386 m)   Range:
Weights: Empty: 10,434 lbs (4,737 kg)   Gross: 14,577 lbs (6,618 kg)
Dimensions: Span: 37 ft 11½ in (11.57 m)   Length: 37 ft 6 in (11.43 m)
Height: 14 ft 9 in (4.50 m)   Wing Area: 287.9 sq ft (26.74 sq m)
Armament: Six .50 calibre machine guns plus provisions for tanks, bombs, and rockets (unguided)
Original Cost: Unknown

NRC
PTERODACTYL FLYING WING

In 1946, the RCAF conducted an extensive test program on a tailless "flying wing" glider known as the Pterodactyl, developed by the National Research Council (NRC). The glider was constructed of wood and had a U shape, with twin side-by-side cockpits each with its own windscreen/canopy. It featured a retractable undercarriage fitted with hydraulically operated brakes. The glider was outfitted with extensive test instrumentation and was finished in a high-visibility, yellow paint scheme. The glider was typically towed on the end of a 350 ft nylon rope to altitude (6,000 – 10,000 ft) using a Dakota tow plane. The original test program was conducted in Namao, Edmonton, and then the glider was successfully towed across the country for further test flights in Arnprior, Ontario. The glider was struck off charge sometime after 1948.

The two men in this view give scale to the unique Pterodactyl VIII "flying wing" research glider tested by the RCAF in 1946. (LAC Photo # PA-175710)

DETAILS

Designation: **Model No:** **Marks:** Mk VIII **Role:** Glider
Service: NRC/RCAF

SPECIFICATIONS

Manufacturer: National Research Council
Crew/Passengers: crew of two; pilot and observer side by side under separate canopies
Powerplant: none
Performance: Max Speed: 140 mph   Landing Speed: 60 mph
Service Ceiling: 10,000 ft   Range:
Weights: Empty: Gross: 4,150 lb
Dimensions: Span: 46 ft 8 in   Length: 18 ft 0 in
Height: Wing Area:
Armament: None
Cost: Unknown

Percival
PROCTOR

The Percival Proctor was developed from a pre-war design from the same company, the Percival Vega Gull. The RAF had previously acquired 15 Vega Gulls for communications duties and for use by overseas Air Attachés. With the outbreak of the Second World War, both the RAF and FAA sought additional communications aircraft and radio training aircraft. The Percival Proctor then saw increased production and more than 1,100 aircraft were eventually built for both services. The aircraft performed very effectively in the communications role, and many squadrons, including Canadian units, also had Proctors on strength as "hacks."

Two views of the Percival Proctor as used by various squadrons of the RCAF; these are aircraft belonging to No. 438 Squadron. (Carl Vincent collection)

DETAILS

Designation: **Model No:** P.28, 30, 31, 34   **Marks:** Mk I, II, III, IV

Role: Communications Aircraft and Radio Trainer   **Service:** RAF, FAA

SPECIFICATIONS

Manufacturer:	Percival Aircraft	
Crew/Passengers:	one pilot and up to three passengers	
Powerplant:	one 210 hp De Havilland Gipsy Queen II in-line piston engine	
Performance:	Max Speed: 160 mph (257 km/h)	Cruising Speed: 140 mph (225 km/h)
	Service Ceiling: 14,000 ft (4,267 m)	Range: 500 mi (805 km)
Weights:	Empty: 2,370 lb (1,075 kg)	Max T/O: 3,500 lb (1,588 kg)
Dimensions:	Span: 39 ft 6 in (12.04 m)	Length: 28 ft 2 in (8.59 m)
	Height: 7 ft 3 in (2.21 m)	Wing Area: 202 sq ft (18.77 sq m)
Armament:	none	
Cost:	Unknown	

Panstwowe Zaklady Lotnicze Warszawa-Okecie SA
WILGA 2000

The PZL-104M Wilga 2000 is used as a glider tow plane for the Royal Canadian Air Cadet program. With the Cessna L-19 tow planes approaching 60 years of service, the RCAC was looking for a suitable replacement aircraft type. The Wilga 2000 had its origins in the Wilga design first developed in Poland in 1962. The prototype Wilga gave way to an improved design (Wilga 35) in 1969. Nine-cylinder radial air-cooled engines powered all these initial variants. The Wilga 2000 is essentially an improved version of the Wilga 35, developed by the Polish State Aviation Works in Warsaw-Okecie to appeal to Western markets, primarily through the incorporation of a Western-built engine and avionics. The newer design incorporates increased fuel capacity, a strengthened wing with integral fuel tanks plus shorter main wheel landing gear that features wheel fairings. In addition, the Wilga 2000 can be fitted with floats or wheels. The 300 horsepower engine installation on these aircraft also makes them excellent glider tow plane aircraft.

The Wilga 2000 is the newest type of tow plane to join in the Royal Canadian Air Cadet gliding program. The aircraft is being used in Comox, BC. (Photo courtesy of EADS)

DETAILS

Designation:	**Model No:** PZL-104M 2000	**Role:** Glider Towing	
TOS: 2005	**SOS:** In-Service	**No:** 1	**Service:** Royal Canadian Air Cadets

SPECIFICATIONS

Manufacturer:	Panstwowe Zaklady Lotnicze (PZL) Warszawa-Okecie SA (State Aviation Works)
Crew/Passengers:	Pilot and up to three passengers
Powerplant:	one 300 hp Textron Lycoming O-540-K1B5 engine
Performance:	Max Speed: 129 mph (208 km/h) · Cruising Speed: 118 mph (190 km/h)
	Service Ceiling: 13,510 ft (4,118 m)
Weights:	Empty: 1,984 lb (900 kg) · Maximum Take-off: 3,086 lb (1,400 kg)
Dimensions:	Span: 36 ft 5½ in (11.12 m) · Length: 26 ft 16½ in (8.10 m)
	Height: 9 ft 8½ in (2.96 m) · Wing Area: 161.5 sq ft (15.00 m²)
Armament:	None
Original Cost:	Approximately $100,000 US

Royal Aircraft Factory
F.E.2B

Initially used for reconnaissance, the Farman Experimental 2 two-seater biplane ended the "Fokker Scourge" over the Somme. Like the single-seat DH2, it was a "pusher" (i.e. the engine & propeller pushing from behind) and items floating about in the nacelle inevitably ended up being swept back into the propeller, sometimes with disastrous results. Armed with two or three Lewis guns and a camera, the observer sat far forward in the nacelle, directly in front of the pilot. Vulnerable to attacks from the rear, the F.E.2 was frequently shot down. During the summer of 1916, the Germans captured one of the first F.E.2ds when a British pilot inadvertently landed his new aircraft at an enemy aerodrome. The introduction of more advanced aircraft made the F.E.2 an ineffective fighter and by 1917 it was primarily used for bombing missions. Canadian crews saw service in the F.E.2B while attached to RFC units.

The F.E.2B was a pusher configuration fighter that later became a bomber. The pilot and gunner positions, one behind the other, can be seen here. (RAF & RCAF photos)

DETAILS

Designation:	**Model No:** F.E.2B	**Marks:**	**Role:** two seat fighter/bomber aircraft
Service: RFC			

SPECIFICATIONS

Manufacturer:	Royal Aircraft Factory	
Crew/Passengers:	crew of two: pilot and observer/gunner	
Powerplant:	one 160 hp Beadmore radial piston engine	
Performance:	Max Speed: 91½ mph (150 km/h)	Cruising Speed:
	Service Ceiling: 11,000 ft (3,300 m)	Range:
Weights:	Empty: 2,061 lb (935 kg)	Gross: 3,037 lb (1,378 kg)
Dimensions:	Span: 49 ft 9 in (14.56 m)	Length: 32 ft 3 in (9.83 m)
	Height: 12 ft 7½ in (3.07 m)	Wing Area:
Armament:	one or two flexible Lewis machine guns and provisions for light bombs	
Cost:	Unknown	

Royal Aircraft Factory
R.E.8

The (Reconnaissance Experimental) R.E.8, nicknamed "Harry Tate" (after a popular English music-hall comedian of that era) by its crews, was one of the most widely used two-seat reconnaissance aircraft used by the RFC on the Western Front during the First World War. It was also widely used in other theatres including Palestine, Egypt, Italy, and Russia. Essentially a further improved development of the R.E. 5 & 7 series of aircraft, the design provided for a stable photographic platform but its weak-nesses still included poor maneuverability due to slow response to controls and poor landing characteristics. Consequently, the type suffered heavy losses at the hands of enemy fighters. Despite this relatively poor record, the R.E.8 remained in service through the remainder of the war. Canadian aircrew and groundcrews consequently saw action with this type of aircraft while attached to RFC squadrons.

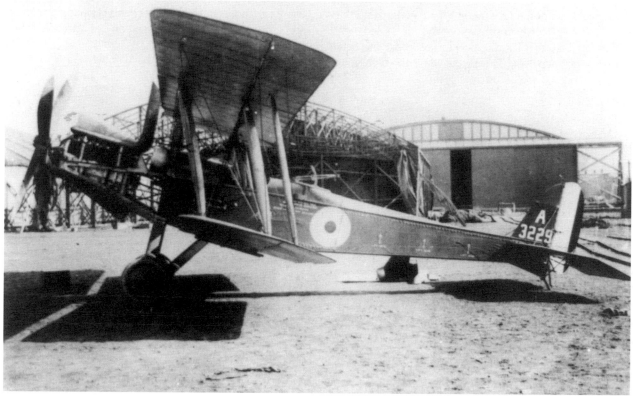

This view illustrates a R.E.8 aircraft undergoing maintenance, as evidenced by the missing engine cowlings. (LAC Photo # PA-123976)

DETAILS

Designation: **Model No:** R.E.8   **Marks:**   **Role:** two seat reconnaissance/light bomber aircraft
Service: RFC

SPECIFICATIONS

Manufacturer:	Royal Aircraft Factory	
Crew/Passengers:	crew of two: pilot and observer/gunner	
Powerplant:	one 150 hp RAF 4a twelve-cylinder engine	
Performance:	Max Speed: 103 mph (166 km/h)	Cruising Speed:
	Service Ceiling: 13,500 ft (4,115 m)	Endurance: 4 hr 15 min
Weights:	Empty: 1,803 lb (819 kg)	Gross: 2,678 lb (1,215 kg)
Dimensions:	Span: 42 ft 7 in (12.98 m)	Length: 27 ft 10½ in (8. 50 m)
	Height: 11 ft 4½ in (3.47 m)	Wing Area:
Armament:	one fixed forward Vickers machine gun and one flexible Lewis machine gun on a Scarff ring and up to 260 lb (113 kg) of bombs	
Cost:	Unknown	

Republic
THUNDERBOLT

Affectionately nicknamed "Jug," the P-47 Thunderbolt was one of the most famous American fighter aircraft of the Second World War. Perhaps ironically first conceived as a lightweight interceptor, the P-47 was actually developed as a heavyweight (7 ton) fighter/fighter–bomber and made its first flight on May 6, 1941. The first production model was delivered to the US Army Air Force in March 1942, and in April 1943 the Thunderbolt was flown on its first combat mission. Used as both a high-altitude escort fighter and a low-level fighter-bomber, the P-47 quickly gained a reputation for ruggedness and dependability. Its sturdy construction and air-cooled radial engine enabled the Thunderbolt to absorb severe battle damage and keep flying. During the war the P-47 served in almost every active war theater and in the forces of various Allied nations. Earlier production P-47B, -C, early -D and -G series aircraft were built with metal-framed "greenhouse" type cockpit canopies. Late -D series (dash 25 and later) aircraft and all -M and -N series production aircraft were given clear "bubble" canopies, which gave the pilot much improved rearward vision. By the end of the war, more than 15,600 Thunderbolts had been built. The RAF employed various marks of the Thunderbolt and the type was predominately employed in the Far East (India, Burma, etc) theatre. Canadian aircrew and ground crew were employed on Thunderbolts while attached to RAF squadrons.

The photograph illustrates the original Thunderbolt Mk I as used by the RAF in the Far East. The later Mk II Thunderbolt (P-47D-25) featured a revised bubble canopy and cut-down rear fuselage. (RAF Photo)

DETAILS
Designation: P-47   **Model No:** P-47C, P-47D-25/30   **Marks:** Mk I, II   **Role:** Fighter, Fighter Bomber
Service: RAF

SPECIFICATIONS Mk II
Manufacturer:	Republic Aircraft Ltd	
Crew/Passengers:	one pilot	
Powerplant:	one 2,300 hp Pratt & Whitney R-2800-59 Double Wasp radial piston engine	
Performance:	Max Speed: 427 mph (687 km/h)	Cruising Speed:
	Service Ceiling: 36,500 ft (11,125 m)	Range: 1,970 mi (3,170 km)
Weights:	Empty: 10,000 lb (4,536 kg)	Gross: 14,600 lb (6,622 kg)
Dimensions:	Span: 40 ft 9 in (12.42 m)	Length: 36 ft 2 in (11.02 m)
	Height: 12 ft 8 in (3.86 m)	Wing Area: 308 sq ft (28.61 m)
Armament:	Eight 0.5 in (12.7 mm) machine guns in the wings plus provisions for up to 2,000 lbs (907 kg) in bombs, rockets or fuel tanks	
Cost:	Unknown	

Saro
LERWICK

Developed to work alongside the very successful Shorts Sunderland flying boat, the smaller twin-engine Saro Lerwick also entered service with the RAF in 1938. Unfortunately the initial service trials revealed various deficiencies with the design; the Lerwick proved to have serious stability problems both in the air and on the water. However, wartime necessity saw the type introduced into service regardless of the deficiencies. Attempts to resolve the problems did not prove entirely successful. Consequently,

the type was quickly relegated to operational training duties and by 1941 was eventually withdrawn from service when suitable numbers of the more successful Sunderland aircraft were available. Although no Lerwick aircraft were officially on strength with the RCAF, in fact, two RCAF squadrons, Nos. 422 and 423, were initially equipped with Lerwick Mk I aircraft for operational training purposes before transitioning to the Sutherland aircraft type.

A view of the less-than-successful Saro Lerwick as used in training by No. 422 and 423 Squadron of the RCAF. (Comox AFM Photo)

DETAILS
Model No: S.36   **Marks:** Mk I   **Role:** Flying Boat/ASW Patrol   **Service:** RAF

SPECIFICATIONS

Manufacturer:	Saro Aircraft	
Crew/Passengers:	crew of six	
Powerplant:	two 1,375 hp Bristol Hercules II radial piston engines	
Performance:	Max Speed: 216 mph (348 km/h)	Cruising Speed: 166 mph (267 km/h)
	Service Ceiling: 14,000 ft (4,267 m)	Range:
Weights:	Empty:	Maximum Take-off: 33,200 lb (15,059 kg)
Dimensions:	Span: 80 ft 10 in (24.64 m)	Length: 63 ft 8 in (19.40 m)
	Height: 20 ft 0 in (6.10 m)	Wing Area: 845 sq ft (78.50 sq m)
Armament:	7 x .303 in (7.7 mm) machine guns in powered turrets plus provisions for up to 2,000 lb (907 kg) in bombs or depth charges	

Schweizer
GLIDER

The SCS 2-33 is a conventional tow-place tandem, inter-mediate-training sailplane, manufactured by Schweizer Aircraft Corporation of Elmira, New York. It is primarily of all metal construction with fabric covering on the fuselage and tail surfaces. It has a one-piece canopy for increased visibility. The wings are tapered in the outboard section and have dive-brakes incorporated. The 2-33 aircraft forms the mainstay of the Royal Canadian Air Cadets gliding program.

RCA Schweizer 2-33A Gliders. (CF Photos)

DETAILS

Designation: SCS **Model No:** 2-33A **Role:** Glider
TOS: 1975 **SOS:** In-service **Service:** RCA Ops Cadets

SPECIFICATIONS

Manufacturer: Schweizer Aircraft Corporation
Crew/Passengers: two pilots
Powerplant: none
Performance: Best 2-place gliding speed: (lift/drag) 23-1: 50 mph (80 km/h)
Best single-place gliding speed: (lift/drag) 23-1: 45 mph (72 km/h)
Minimum 2-place sinking speed: 42 mph (68 km/h) at 3.1 fps
Minimum single-place sinking speed: 38 mph (61 km/h) at 2.6 fps
Weights: Empty: 670 lbs (304 kg)   Gross: 1,040 lbs (472 kg)
Dimensions: Span: 51 ft 0 in (15.5 m)   Length: 25 ft 9 in (7.84 m)
Height: 9 ft 3½ in (2.83 m)   Aspect Ratio: 11.85-1
Original Cost: Unknown

Shorts
TYPE 184

The Shorts Type 184 was one of the most important seaplane designs to serve with the Royal Naval Air Service. Perhaps unusually the design never received a popular nickname. It was the first aircraft in the world to sink an enemy ship at sea by means of a torpedo attack. It was also the only aircraft to play an important part in the Battle of Jutland and it served at virtually every RNAS station. The design was conventional for the period and it was progressively improved throughout the war. This included the fitment of larger and more powerful engines. Canadian personnel were involved with Type 184 operations while attached to the RNAS.

The Shorts Type 184 seaplane of the RNAS was a very large single-engine floatplane. (CF Photo)

DETAILS

Designation:	**Model No:** 184	**Marks:**	**Role:** two seat seaplane
Service: RNAS			

SPECIFICATIONS

Manufacturer:	Shorts Aircraft	
Crew/Passengers:	crew of two: pilot and observer/gunner	
Powerplant:	one 240 hp Sunbeam piston engine	
Performance:	Max Speed: 88½ mph (142 km/h)	Cruising Speed:
	Service Ceiling: 9,000 ft (2,743 m)	Range:
Weights:	Empty: 3,703 lb (1,129 kg)	Gross: 5,363 lb (2,433 kg)
Dimensions:	Span: 63 ft 6 in (19.35 m)	Length: 40 ft 7½ in (12.38 m)
	Height: 13 ft 6 in (4.11 m)	Wing Area: 688 sq ft (63.92 sq m)
Armament:	one flexible Lewis machine gun on a Scarf ring in rear cockpit and up to 520 lb (236 kg) of bombs or one 15 inch torpedo	
Cost:	Unknown	

Shorts
STIRLING

Designed at the outset with four engines, the Shorts Stirling was the RAF's first four-engine heavy bomber to come into service. It was also the first to be used operationally and the first of its stable mates to be withdrawn from operational service. An unusual constraint to the Shorts design was the limitation of the wingspan to less than 100 feet in order to fit the standard RAF hangars of that era. Unfortunately, this limitation also proved to be the aircraft's chief drawback. While the Short Stirling was manoeuvrable and stable, the small wing area imposed relatively poor operational altitude capabilities when fully loaded. This fact, coupled with a limited bomb bay capacity, eventually led to Stirlings being switched to operational training, glider towing and transport roles. Canadian crews saw service in Stirlings while attached to RAF squadrons and conversion units.

This flight of Short Stirlings is from No. 1651 Heavy Conversion (Operational Training) Unit circa 1942. (RAF Photo)

DETAILS
Model No: S.29   **Marks:** Mk I, II, III, IV, V   **Role:** Bomber, Glider Tow Plane, Transport
Service: RAF

SPECIFICATIONS Mk III
Manufacturer:	Shorts Aircraft	
Crew/Passengers:	crew of seven or eight	
Powerplant:	four 1,650 hp Bristol Hercules XVI radial piston engines	
Performance:	Max Speed: 270 mph (435 km/h)	Cruising Speed:
	Service Ceiling: 17,000 ft (5,182 m)	Range: 2,010 mi (3,235 km)
Weights:	Empty: 43,200 lb (19,595 kg)	Maximum Take-off: 70,000 lb (31,751 kg)
Dimensions:	Span: 99 ft 1 in (30.20 m)	Length: 87 ft 3 in (26.59 m)
	Height: 22 ft 9 in (6.93 m)	Wing Area: 1,460 sq ft (135.63 sq m)
Armament:	8 x .303 in (7.7 mm) machine guns in powered turrets plus provisions for up to 14,000 lb (6,350 kg) in bombs	

Shorts
SUNDERLAND

Developed from the pre-war C-Class Empire flying boats developed for and used commercially by Imperial Airways, the Shorts Sunderland entered service with the RAF in 1938. The robust design was progressively improved and increasingly heavily armed. Readily able to attack and defend itself on long-range patrol missions, it earned the nickname the "Flying Porcupine" from its enemies because of these characteristics. Sunderlands used by Coastal Command participated in the destruction of 31 U-boats. Although no Sunderlands were officially on strength with the RCAF, in fact two RCAF squadrons, No. 422 and 423, were equipped with Sunderland Mk III aircraft. These Canadian-flown aircraft participated in the sinking of five U-boats and heavily damaged at least two

others. In addition, another submarine was sunk after a Sunderland of No. 423 Squadron homed two RCN destroyers onto the enemy vessel.

Two views of the Shorts Sunderland similar to those used by No. 422 and 423 Squadron of the RCAF. (CF & RAF Photos)

DETAILS

Model No: S.25   **Marks:** Mk III   **Role:** Flying Boat/ASW Patrol   **Service:** RAF

SPECIFICATIONS

Manufacturer:	Shorts Aircraft	
Crew/Passengers:	crew of thirteen	
Powerplant:	four 1,065 hp Bristol Pegasus XVIII radial piston engines	
Performance:	Max Speed: 212 mph (341 km/h)	Cruising Speed:
	Service Ceiling: 15,000 ft (4,570 m)	Range: 3,000 mi (4,828 km)
Weights:	Empty: 33,000 lb (14,969 kg)	Maximum Take-off: 58,000 lb (26,308 kg)
Dimensions:	Span: 112 ft 10 in (34.39 m)	Length: 85 ft 4 in (26.01 m) (Beaching Gear)
	Height: 32 ft 2 in (9.79 m)	Wing Area: 1,487 sq ft (138.14 sq m)
Armament:	12 x .303 in (7.7 mm) machine guns in powered turrets or fixed positions with twin 0.5 in (12.7 mm) machine guns in waist positions plus provisions for up to 4,960 lb (2,250 kg) in bombs or depth charges on a mobile bomb rack wound out under the wing from the fuselage	

Sopwith
CUCKOO

The Sopwith Cuckoo was a single-seat biplane torpedo bomber developed for the Royal Naval Air Service. It was the first landplane designed specifically to operate from ships as a torpedo bomber. The prototype first flew in 1917 and it featured conventional construction for the period. The wings folded for shipboard use. A sturdy wide-track divided undercarriage was fitted to facilitate the carriage of an externally mounted 18-inch torpedo. The Sopwith Cuckoo was a successful design and the type remained in post-war use. Canadian pilots saw service in the Cuckoo while attached to the RNAS.

The Sopwith Cuckoo was one of the world's first torpedo bombers. (LAC Photo # PA-06807)

DETAILS
Designation: **Model No:** T.1   **Marks:**   **Role:** single-seat torpedo bomber
Service: RNAS

SPECIFICATIONS
Manufacturer: Sopwith Aircraft and Blackburn Aeroplane & Motor Co
Crew/Passengers: one pilot
Powerplant: one 200 hp Sunbeam Arab piston engine
Performance: Max Speed: 103.5 mph (166 km/h)   Cruising Speed:
Service Ceiling: 12,100 ft (3,960 m)   Range: 420 mi (676 km)
Weights: Empty: 2,199 lb (993 kg)   Gross: 3,883 lb (1,761 kg)
Dimensions: Span: 45 ft 9 in (13.94 m)   Length: 28 ft 6 in (8.69 m)
Height: 10 ft 8 in (3.25 m)   Wing Area: 566 sq ft (52.58 sq m)
Armament: one 18 in Mk IX torpedo carried below the fuselage
Cost: Unknown

Sopwith
PUP

The Sopwith Pup quickly became a favorite with pilots of the Royal Naval Air Service. It was superior to the Fokker D.III and more than a match for any of the new Halberstadt and Albatros scouts. Armed with a single synchronous machine gun, it was lighter and less dangerous than its successor, the Sopwith Camel. Although underpowered, pilots liked the plane because it was maneuverable and fast. It could climb and hold its altitude better than any other fighter. In August 1917, the Sopwith Pup was the first aircraft to land aboard a moving ship, the Royal Navy's HMS *Furious*. Canadian crews saw service with Sopwith Pups while attached to the Royal Naval Air Service.

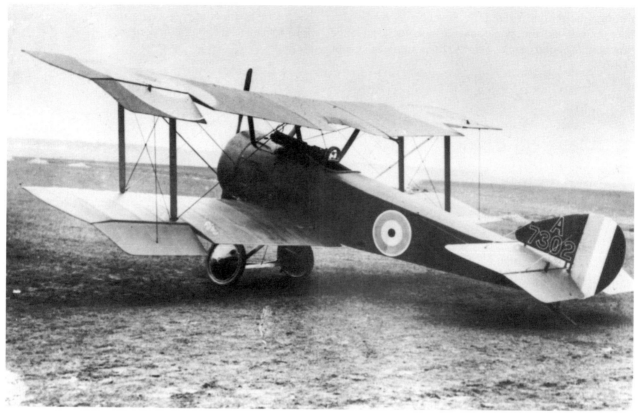

The Sopwith Pup was a well-liked small biplane fighter, which preceded the more famous Sopwith Camel. The Pup was regarded as one of the most pleasant of all the British aircraft to fly in the First World War. (LAC Photo # PA-06396)

DETAILS

Designation: **Model No:** 9901   **Marks:**   **Role:** single seat fighter
Service: RFC, RNAS

SPECIFICATIONS

Manufacturer:	Sopwith Aircraft	
Crew/Passengers:	one pilot	
Powerplant:	one 80 hp Le Rhone 9C or 100 hp Gnome Monosoupape radial engines	
Performance:	Max Speed: 106 mph (161 km/h)	Cruising Speed:
	Service Ceiling: 18,500 ft (5,639 m)	Endurance: 3 hours
Weights:	Empty: 1,225 lb (555 kg)	Gross:
Dimensions:	Span: 26 ft 6 in (8.08 m)	Length: 19 ft 3¾ in (5.86 m)
	Height: 9 ft 5 in (2.87 m)	Wing Area:
Armament:	one fixed forward .303 Vickers machine gun	
Cost:	Unknown	

Sopwith
1 & 1/2 STRUTTER

Known officially as the Sopwith Type 9700, the nickname by which the aircraft is best remembered ("Strutter") was due to the W-arrangement of struts supporting the centre section of the top wing. The outer ones were about half the length of the outer inter-plane struts, hence 1 & 1/2 struts. Originally a two-seater reconnaissance/fighter biplane, the first British aircraft to go into service had an interrupter gear, permitting a fixed machine gun to fire through the propeller disc. The Royal Naval Air Service later introduced the single-seat version for long-range bombing. On the single-seater, 224 pounds of bombs could be carried internally in a 12-cell compartment immediately aft of the cockpit, vice the 130-pound load of the two-seater. The RNAS was more tolerant of organizational diversity than the RFC, so it was more enterprising and experimental in its approach to matters of aircraft design and supply. Therefore, on 1 April 1918, when a fully loaded 1 & 1/2 Strutter was flown off the forward turret of the battlecruiser *Australia*, it rapidly replaced the Short Seaplane as shipborne reconnaissance airplane as well as providing a fleet fighter component.

The RNAS naval wings used the Sopwith 1 1/2 Strutter aircraft extensively, and Canadian crews used this aircraft while attached to the RNAS. (RCAF Photo)

DETAILS

Designation:	**Model No:** 9700	**Marks:**	**Role:** Fighter/Bomber
Service: RNAS			

SPECIFICATIONS

Manufacturer:	Sopwith Aviation Company		
Crew/Passengers:	one pilot or one pilot and one observer/gunner		
Powerplant:	one 130 hp Clerget radial piston engine		
Performance:	Max Speed: 115 mph (185 km/h)	Cruising Speed:	
	Service Ceiling:	Range:	
Weights:	Empty:	Gross:	
Dimensions:	Span: 33 ft 6 in (10.21 m)	Length: 25 ft 3 in (7.97 m)	
	Height:	Wing Area:	
Armament:	One or two 0.303 (7.7 mm) calibre Vickers machine guns; one fixed and one flexible mount plus provision for 130 lb (59 kg) for two-seat or 240 lb (109 kg) of bombs for single-seat aircraft		
Cost:	Unknown		

Sopwith
TRIPLANE

The Sopwith Triplane was an attempt by the Sopwith experimental department for a radically new fighter to succeed the nimble Sopwith Pup. The three narrow chord wings provided plenty of lift, ensured manoeuvrability and gave the pilot the widest possible field of view. The airframe was stressed to accept the 110 hp Clerget rotary engine. Later Triplanes were fitted with the more powerful 130 hp version of the engine, which considerably improved the performance. Very few bracing wires were used externally on the wings, which led to some structural weakness on some versions of the aircraft manufactured with lighter gauge bracing wires. The first aircraft began service trials with the RNAS in 1916 and were immediately successful. Used by various RNAS squadrons, in

Canadian history, the most famous of all the aircraft were the Triplanes of "B" Flight of No. 10 (Naval) Squadron. Flown by legendary Canadian aces such as Raymond Collishaw, the aircraft of "Black" Flight accounted for 87 enemy aircraft between May and July of 1917. Sub-Lieutenants Raymond Collishaw, E.V. Reid, J.E. Sharman, G.E. Nash, and W.M. (Mel) Alexander constituted the original Canadian members of the Black Flight. The Black Flight gained its name through the extremely dark khaki-brown colour of the aircraft, complete with black cowlings and wheel disks; a unique and non-standard colour scheme. The Tripes or Tripehounds, as they were affectionately known, were eventually to be replaced by the equally successful Sopwith Camel.

Canadians in the RNAS No. 10 Sqn "Black Flight" made the Sopwith Triplane, shown here, famous. Each of the aircraft in the Flight had black markings and a name commencing with "Black" (i.e. Black Maria, Black Death, Black Roger, Black Prince and Black Sheep). (LAC Photo # PA-006395)

DETAILS
Designation: **Model No:**   **Marks:**   **Role:** Fighter
Service: RNAS

SPECIFICATIONS
Manufacturer: Sopwith Aviation Co. Ltd.
Crew/Passengers: one pilot
Powerplant: one 110 hp (82 kW) or 130 hp (96 kW) Clerget radial piston engine
Performance: Max Speed: 117 mph 188 km/h)   Cruising Speed:
Service Ceiling: 20,500 ft (6,248 m)   Endurance: 2¾ hours
Weights: Empty: 1,101 lb (499 kg)   Gross: 1,541 lb (698 kg)
Dimensions: Span: 26 ft 6 in (8.07 m)   Length: 18 ft 10 in (5.73 m)
Height: 10 ft 6 in (3.20 m)   Wing Area: 231 sq ft (21.46 sq m)
Armament: provisions for one or two forward-firing Vickers machine guns
Cost: Unknown

Vickers
GUNBUS

The Vickers Fighting Biplane 5 was the first aircraft specifically designed as a fighter for the Royal Flying Corps. It featured unstaggered, equal-span wings with a tail boom of steel tubing with wooden struts. The fuselage nacelle had a blunt aluminum nose on top of which was fitted a Lewis machine gun on a pillar mount. With its engine mounted behind the cockpit, it was the first pusher to enter service during the First World War. Commonly referred to as the "Gunbus," it was armed with a moveable, forward firing machine gun. Vulnerable to attack from the rear, the Gunbus was soon replaced by more advanced single-seat fighter aircraft. Canadian crews saw service in F.E.2Bs while attached to RFC units.

This view of the Vickers F.B. 5 Gunbus clearly illustrates its pusher configuration and nose-mounted machine gun. (RAF Photo)

DETAILS
Designation: **Model No:** F.B.5   **Marks:**   **Role:** Fighter
Service: RFC

SPECIFICATIONS
Manufacturer:	Vickers Aircraft	
Crew/Passengers:	crew of two	
Powerplant:	one 100 hp Gnome Monosoupape radial piston engine	
Performance:	Max Speed: 182 mph (113 km/h)	Cruising Speed:
	Service Ceiling: 8,990 ft (2,740 m)	Range:
Weights:	Empty: 1,219 lb (553 kg)	Gross: 2,050 lb (930 kg)
Dimensions:	Span: 36 ft 5 in (11.1 m)	Length: 27 ft 3 in (8.30 m)
	Height: 11 ft 2 in (3.40 m)	Wing Area:
Armament:	1 or 2 Lewis machine guns	
Cost:	Unknown	

Vickers
VICTORIA

Designed from the outset as a troop-carrying transport, the Vickers Victoria was an adaptation of the company's previous bomber designs. Using the wing design from the Vickers Vimy bomber and mating a fuselage design from commercial equivalents, the resulting Victoria was successful as a troop transport. The Victoria was progressively updated and metal surfaces were replaced with wooden ones. Victorias saw most of their service in the Middle East. The Victoria and its sister type Valentia built the foundations of the RAF's Transport Command and helped develop civilian air routes in the Middle East. As war erupted, the lack of suitable transport ensured that the Victorias, although obsolete, remained in service. In 1940, Victorias were also pressed into offensive operations as light bombers flying night attacks. As late as 1943, some were still flying on communication duties. Canadian aircrew flew Victorias while attached to RAF squadrons.

Obsolete by the start of the Second World War, the Vickers Victoria was nevertheless pressed into service in the Middle East by the Royal Air Force. (RAF Photo)

DETAILS
Model No: **Marks:** Mk I, II, III, IV, V, VI   **Role:** Transport   **Service:** RAF

SPECIFICATIONS Mk VI

Manufacturer:	Vickers Aircraft	
Crew/Passengers:	crew of two and up to twenty-three fully equipped troops	
Powerplant:	two 660 hp Bristol Pegasus III.3 radial piston engines	
Performance:	Max Speed: 130 mph (209 km/h)	Cruising Speed:
	Service Ceiling: 18,300 ft (5,578 m)	Range: 800 mi (1,288 km)
Weights:	Empty: 9,806 lb (4,448 kg)	Gross: 17,600 lb (7,983 kg)
Dimensions:	Span: 87 ft 4 in (26.62 m)	Length: 59 ft 6 in (18.14 m)
	Height: 17 ft 9 in (5.41 m)	Wing Area: 2,178 sq ft (202.34 sq m)
Armament:	None originally but subsequently provision for self-defensive machine guns and light bombs on underwing racks	

Vickers
VILDEBEEST

The Vickers Vildebeest was an ungainly looking three-seat general purpose biplane that first flew in April 1928. It saw service as a torpedo bomber, as an army cooperation aircraft and as a light bomber. Later variants were intended to replace the Westland Wapiti and Fairey IIIF biplanes. Clearly obsolete by the outbreak of the Second World War, approximately 100 Vildebeests of various marks were still in service. Necessity meant the Vildebeest plus an improved variant, the Vickers Vincent, had to continue in operational service. The last front-line operations were flown by No. 36 and 100 (RAF) Squadron as late as 1942, shortly before the fall of Singapore. Canadian crews saw service in Vildebeest aircraft while attached to RAF squadrons.

Torpedo-armed Vickers Vildebeest biplanes were used against Japanese shipping in the Far East. (RAF Photo)

DETAILS
Model No: 132   **Marks:** Mk I, II, III, IV, V   **Role:** Utility   **Service:** RAF

SPECIFICATIONS Mk I

Manufacturer:	Vickers Aircraft	
Crew/Passengers:	crew of three	
Powerplant:	one 660 hp Bristol Pegasus IIM3 radial piston engine	
Performance:	Max Speed: 142 mph (229 km/h)	Cruising Speed:
	Service Ceiling: 17,000 ft (5,182 m)	Range: 1,250 mi (2,012 km)
Weights:	Empty: 4,229 lb (1,918 kg)	Max T/O: 8,100 lb (3,674 kg)
Dimensions:	Span: 49 ft 0 in (14.94 m)	Length: 36 ft 8 in (11.18 m)
	Height: 17 ft 9 in (5.41 m)	Wing Area: 728 sq ft (67.63 sq m)
Armament:	One forward-firing .303 in (7.7 mm) machine gun and one flexible Lewis gun in the aft cockpit plus provision for up to 1,000 lb (454 kg) in bombs or torpedoes	

Vickers
WARWICK

The Vickers Warwick was a larger stable mate to the better known Vickers Wellington bomber. Like the Wellington, the Warwick featured geodetic construction. The aircraft was initially designed with the less than successful Rolls Royce Vulture engines, but the significant problems with that engine necessitated a change to more reliable Pratt & Whitney Double Wasp or Bristol Centaurus radial engines. Delays in production also meant a role change and the initial Warwick variant was developed into an air-sea rescue vehicle capable of carrying an airborne lifeboat. Subsequent variants were used in both coastal command and transport roles. Canadian crews flew Warwick aircraft while attached to RAF Coastal Command squadrons.

Coastal Command flew the GR Mk V variant of the Vickers Warwick as shown here in standard colours but with D-Day invasion stripes added to the fuselage. (LAC Photo # PA-133287)

DETAILS

Model No: 284   **Marks:** Mk I, II, III, V   **Role:** Bomber, Air-Sea Rescue, Transport
Service: RAF

SPECIFICATIONS GR Mk II

Manufacturer:	Vickers Aircraft	
Crew/Passengers:	crew of seven	
Powerplant:	two 2,500 hp Bristol Centaurus VI radial piston engines	
Performance:	Max Speed: 262 mph (422 km/h)	Cruising Speed:
	Service Ceiling: 19,000 ft (5,791 m)	Range: 3,050 mi (4,908 km)
Weights:	Empty: 31,125 lb (14,118 kg)	Maximum Take-off: 51,250 lb (23,247 kg)
Dimensions:	Span: 96 ft 9 in (29.49 m)	Length: 68 ft 6 in (20.88 m)
	Height: 18 ft 6 in (5.64 m)	Wing Area: 1,006 sq ft (93.46 sq m)
Armament:	6 x .303 in (7.7 mm) machine guns; one each in nose and tail and four in powered dorsal turret plus provision for up to 12,250 lb (5,557 kg) in bombs or depth charges	

Vickers
WELLESLEY

The Vickers Wellesley was the first of the Vickers designs to employ the unique geodetic construction of the famed designer, Barnes Wallis. Originally submitted against a biplane requirement for a light bomber, the Wellesley was a two-seat, low wing monoplane design. Unusually, the payload was intended to be carried in underwing panniers to preserve the integrity of the fuselage construction. The Wellesley was a successful pre-war design and the RAF's Long Range Development Flight used the type in setting a 1938 world long distance record, flying from Egypt to Australia. By the outbreak of the Second World War, Wellesleys had been replaced in RAF's Bomber Command by twin-engined bombers such as Hampdens, Whitleys and Wellingtons. Largely obsolete by the start of hostilities, Wellesleys played a small but important part in the Middle East and North Africa campaigns along with various other pre-war designs. Canadian crews had some experience with the Vickers Wellesley while attached to RAF squadrons.

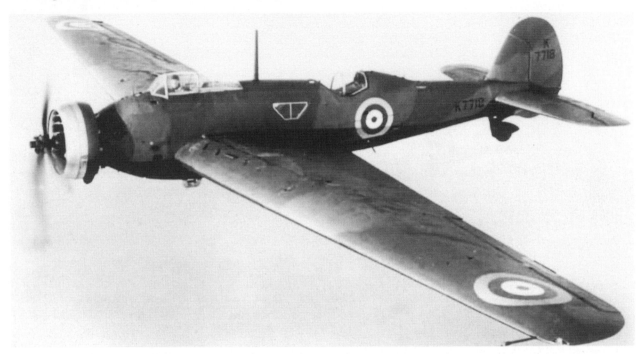

The unusual-looking Vickers Wellesley featured "geodetic" construction pioneered by famed engineer Sir Barnes Wallis. (Comox AFM Photo)

DETAILS
Model No: 246   **Marks:** Mk I, II   **Role:** Bomber
Service: RAF

SPECIFICATIONS Mk I
Manufacturer:	Vickers Aircraft
Crew/Passengers:	crew of two
Powerplant:	one 950 hp Bristol Pegasus XX radial piston engine

Performance:	Max Speed: 228 mph (367 km/h)	Cruising Speed: 188 mph (303 km/h)
	Service Ceiling: 33,000 ft (10,058 m)	Range: 1,110 mi (1,786 km)
Weights:	Empty: 6,369 lb (2,889 kg)	Maximum Take-off: 11,100 lb (5,035 kg)
Dimensions:	Span: 74 ft 7 in (22.73 m)	Length: 39 ft 3 in (11.96 m)
	Height: 12 ft 4 in (3.76 m)	Wing Area: 630 sq ft (58.53 sq m)
Armament:	one forward firing .303 in (7.7 mm) and one flexible Vickers machine guns in rear cockpit plus provision for up to 2,000 lb (907 kg) in bombs in underwing panniers	

Vickers
WELLINGTON

The Vickers Wellington, affectionately known as the "Wimpy," (after J. Wellington Wimpy, Popeye's friend) was armed with twin .303 in (7.7 mm) machine guns in the nose and tail turrets. It also had 2 manually operated .303 guns in the beam positions and could carry a 4,500 lb (2,041 kg) bomb load. Its slow speed, limited ceiling, and small bomb capacity soon made the Wellington obsolete, although one significant design advantage was Sir BarnesWallis's geodetic latticework fuselage construction. This made the Wimpy extremely tough, and it often survived battle damage which would have destroyed other aircraft. Its other nickname, "The Flying Cigar," alluded to the shape of the fuselage as seen in profile. After

it proved early on the inadequacy of the turret firepower in fending off attacking fighters during daylight attacks, the Wellington went on to build a great reputation for reliability and ruggedness in night bombing operations. In April 1941, the aircraft were the first to drop the deadly "block-buster" bomb, during a raid on Emden, and they helped to initiate the Pathfinder target-indicating tactics. No Wellingtons were "officially" on RCAF strength in the war but in fact eleven RCAF bomber squadrons flew them in the European theatre from 1941until 1944. A further two RCAF squadrons, No. 407 and 415, flew Wellingtons on Coastal Command missions. No. 407 Squadron sank four U-boats with Leigh-light equipped Wellingtons.

At right, a Canadian crew hamming it up for the camera in front of their Coastal Command Wellington. Inset, a dramatic night-time view of a Royal Air Force Wellington Mk. I. (CF & RAF Photos)

DETAILS
Model No: 415, 406, 417, 448, 455, 467   **Marks:** Mk IC, II, Ill, X, XII, XIII, XIV   **Role:** Bomber/ASW Patrol
Service: RAF

SPECIFICATIONS Mk III

Manufacturer:	Vickers Aircraft	
Crew/Passengers:	crew of eight	
Powerplant:	two 1,130 hp Rolls Royce Merlin X piston engines	
Performance:	Max Speed: 235 mph (378 km/h)	Cruising Speed:
	Service Ceiling: 19,000 ft (5,791 m)	Range: 1,540 mi (2,478 km)
Weights:	Empty: 18,650 lb (8,459 kg)	Maximum Take-off: 29,500 lb (13,381 kg)
Dimensions:	Span: 86 ft 2 in (26.26 m)	Length: 60 ft 10 in (18.54 m)
	Height: 17 ft 5 in (5.31 m)	Wing Area: 840 sq ft (78.04 sq m)
Armament:	eight .303 in (7.7 mm) machine guns in powered turrets or fixed positions plus provision for up to 4,500 lb (2,041 kg) in bombs or depth charges	

Vought
CORSAIR

The Vought Corsair was probably the best American naval fighter of the Second World War. First flown in 1939, the Corsair was characterized by its inverted gull, upward folding wings. This feature allowed for a large diameter propeller while reducing the length of the undercarriage. Equipped with a powerful radial engine, the type was progressively improved and served with many nations for the next 30 years. Although early operational experience proved the aircraft was not the easiest design to land on a carrier deck, the Royal Navy was anxious to introduce the aircraft into service under Lend-Lease arrangements. First used by the RN on the *Tirpitz* raids in 1943, the design also quickly gained favour with the British fleet in the Pacific. In the closing months of the war, July and August 1945, RN Corsair squadrons No. 1841 and 1842 from the aircraft carrier HMS *Formidable* carried the war to the Japanese mainland by conducting strikes against the Tokyo region. On 9 August 1945, in the course of a shipping strike in Onagawa Bay, Lt R. Hampton (Hammy) Gray of the Royal Canadian Volunteer Naval Reserve, flying a Corsair, won a posthumous Victoria Cross. Pressing home an attack on a Japanese destroyer in spite of intense anti-aircraft fire, his aircraft was struck repeatedly. He still scored a direct hit, sinking the destroyer, but then fatally crashed. He became the only Second World War member of the RCN to win the highest decoration of the British Commonwealth.

This is a view of the unusual looking Vought Corsair with its inverted gull wing arrangement, similar to the aircraft flown by Lt(N) Hampton Gray, VC. This aircraft is a restored example displayed in the colours of the French Navy. (Author's collection)

DETAILS
Designation: **Model No:** F4U-1D, FG-1D   **Marks:** Mk III, IV   **Role:** Fighter, Strike Fighter
Service: RN

SPECIFICATIONS Mk IV

Manufacturer:	Vought Aircraft Ltd
Crew/Passengers:	one pilot
Powerplant:	one 2,250 hp Pratt & Whitney R-2800-8 Double Wasp radial piston engine

Performance:	Max Speed: 415 mph (668 km/h)	Cruising Speed: 261 mph (420 km/h)
	Service Ceiling: 34,000 ft (10,363 m)	Range: 1,562 mi (2,514km)
Weights:	Empty: 9,100 lb (4,128 kg)	Maximum Take-off: 12,100 lb (5,488 kg)
Dimensions:	Span: 39 ft 8 in (12.09 m)	Length: 33 ft 4 in (10.16 m)
	Height: 15 ft 1 in (4.60 m)	Wing Area: 305 sq ft (28.33 m)
Armament:	Four 0.5 in (12.7 mm) machine guns in the wings plus provision for up to 2,000 lbs (907 kg) in bombs, rockets or fuel tanks	
Cost:	Unknown	

Vultee
VENGEANCE

Primarily in response to British interest, Vultee developed a two-seat dive bomber in 1940, which was to become known as the Vengeance. The British Purchasing Commission placed an initial order for 200 aircraft from Vultee along with a further 200 aircraft to be built under license by Northrop. Additional orders then followed. Few of these aircraft actually reached Britain, however, with almost the entire order being diverted to the Far East for use by RAF, RAAF or Indian Air Force squadrons.

A number of aircraft were also retained by the USAAF. In RAF service, the Vengeance was operationally employed to good effect in the Burma theatre. As the war progressed, the RAF transferred some Vengeance aircraft to the Fleet Air Arm for use as target tugs. Additionally, some aircraft were used by the RAF in smoke-laying operations. Canadian crews saw service with Vengeance aircraft while attached to RAF or FAA squadrons and units.

The Vultee Vengeance was a relatively little known but useful dive bomber design employed by both the RAF and RN. (Comox AFM Photo)

DETAILS

Model No: V-72   **Marks:** Mk I, II, III, IV   **Role:** Dive Bomber, Target Tug
Service: RAF

SPECIFICATIONS Mk I

Manufacturer:	Vultee & Northrop Aircraft	
Crew/Passengers:	crew of two	
Powerplant:	one 1,600 hp Wright R-2600-A5B Cyclone radial piston engine	
Performance:	Max Speed: 275 mph (443 km/h)	Cruising Speed: 235 mph (378 km/h)
	Service Ceiling: 22,500 ft (6,858 m)	Range: 1,400 mi (2,253 km)
Weights:	Empty: 9,725 lb (4,411kg)	Maximum Take-off: 14,300 lb (6,486 kg)
Dimensions:	Span: 48 ft 0 in (14.63 m)	Length: 39 ft 9 in (12.12 m)
	Height: 15 ft 4 in (4.67 m)	Wing Area: 332 sq ft (30.84 sq m)
Armament:	4 x .30 in (7.62 mm) forward firing machine guns plus twin 0.30 (7.62 mm) machine guns in rear cockpit plus provision for up to 2,000 lb (907 kg) in bombs	

Westland
LYNX

Developed within an Anglo-French helicopter agreement, the Westland Lynx first flew in 1972. The Westland Lynx was simultaneously developed in army and naval variants. It was an advanced lightweight military helicopter featuring an overall compact design with single four-blade semi-rigid main rotor blades mounted on a monobloc rotor head. The very successful helicopter could be armed with a wide variety of weapons and possessed a cabin large enough to carry useful loads in both army and navy configurations. Ordered into service for both the British Army and the Royal Navy, the Westland Lynx has been progressively upgraded through the years and has seen combat operations with both services. Canadian exchange officers flew British Westland Lynx helicopters during the first Gulf War.

The Westland Lynx was employed by both the British Army and the Royal Navy during the first Gulf War and flown by Canadian exchange pilots. This image depicts a variant of the Lynx belonging to the Dutch Navy deployed from the Dutch ship HNLMS *Van Galen* in the background. (RN Photo)

DETAILS
Designation: **Model No:**   **Marks:** Various

Role: Anti-Submarine, Anti-Surface and Battlefield Helicopter   **Service:** RN, British Army

SPECIFICATIONS Naval Variant

Manufacturer:	Westland Helicopters
Crew/Passengers:	crew of two and up to ten troops or six stretchers plus attendant
Powerplant:	two 1,120 hp Rolls Royce Gem 42 turboshaft engines

Performance:	Max Speed: 180 mph (289 km/h)	Cruising Speed: 131 mph (211 km/h)
	Hover Ceiling: 10,600 ft (3,230 m)	Range: 368 mi (593 km)
Weights:	Empty: 6,040 lb (2,740 kg)	Maximum Take-off: 10,750 lb (4,876 kg)
Dimensions:	Rotor Diameter: 42 ft 0 in (12.80 m)	Length: 49 ft 9 in (15.17 m)
	Height: 11 ft 5 in (3.48 m)	Rotor Disc Area: 1,385 sq ft (128.71 sq m)
Armament:	None	
Cost:	Unknown	

Westland
WHIRLWIND

The Westland Whirlwind was the first single-seat, twin-engine fighter to serve with the Royal Air Force. First flown in 1938 prior to the war, the design is not well known despite having seen successful combat. Production delays meant that the type did not begin service until 1940. Its four heavy 20 mm cannon armament and long range compared to contemporary fighters made it attractive for long range escort and interdiction missions. However, its unique Peregrine engines caused some maintenance reliability problems and its high landing speed also caused some accidents. Canadian pilots flew Whirlwind aircraft while attached to RAF squadrons. The Whirlwinds were withdrawn from operational service by the end of 1943.

Two views of the Westland Whirlwind illustrating its unusual lines. (DND Photos)

DETAILS

Designation:	**Model No:**	**Marks:** I	**Role:** Fighter
Service: RAF			

SPECIFICATIONS Mk I

Manufacturer:	Westland	
Crew/Passengers:	one pilot	
Powerplant:	two 885 hp Rolls-Royce Peregrine piston engines	
Performance:	Max Speed: 360 mph (579 km/h)	Cruising Speed:
	Service Ceiling: 30,300 ft (9,235 m)	Range: 800 mi (1,287 km)
Weights:	Empty: 8,310 lb (3,769 kg)	Gross: 11,388 lb (5,166 kg)
Dimensions:	Span: 45 ft 0 in (13.72 m)	Length: 32 ft 9 in (9.98 m)
	Height: 11 ft 7 in (4.32 m)	Wing Area: 250 sq ft (23.23 sq m)
Armament:	four 20 mm cannon and provision for 1,000 lb (454 kg) of bombs	
Cost:	Unknown	

Messrs Frederick Sage & Co.
AIRSHIPS

The SSZ and C classes of non-rigid airships were progressive improvements of non-rigid designs used by the RNAS and RFC for coastal patrol and defence in the First World War. The SSZ class was a non-rigid design with a boat-shaped control car featuring an aluminum-covered wood (ash) frame. Its Rolls-Royce engine was specifically designed for an airship application. The forward cockpit carried a wireless transmitter. It also featured three fins.

Part of a post-war Imperial gift to Canada of aeronautical equipment included some SSZ and C-class airships, kite balloons and other lighter than air equipment. While never put to use for the intended purpose, the equipment was carefully stored at Camp Borden. Some of the gasbag material became patching material for hangar roofs and one of the gondolas was converted as a crash rescue snowmobile.

A post-World War I Imperial gift to Canada included a number of SSZ-type airships as shown here. (LAC Photo # PA- 62280)

DETAILS

Designation:	**Model No:** SS "Z"	**Marks:**	**Role:** Coastal Patrol Airship
TOS: 1919	**SOS:** ?	**No:** ?	**Service:** CAF

SPECIFICATIONS

Manufacturer:	Messrs Frederick Sage & Co.	
Crew/Passengers:	crew of two	
Powerplant:	75 hp Rolls Royce Hawk water cooled piston engine	
Performance:	Max Speed: 53 mph (85 km/h)	Cruising Speed:
	Service Ceiling:	Range:
Weights:	Empty:	Gross:
Dimensions:	Diameter: 32 ft 0 in (9.75 m)	Width (including fins): 39 ft 6 in (12.04 m)
	Length: 143 ft 4 in (43.69 m)	Height: 47 ft 0 in (14.33 m)
	Volume: 70,000 cu ft (1,982 cu m)	
Armament:	One machine gun plus provision for two 110 lb (50 kg) bombs	
Cost:	Unknown	

RNAS Kingsnorth
AIRSHIPS

The SSZ and C classes of non-rigid airships were progressive improvements of non-rigid designs used by the RNAS and RFC for coastal patrol and defence in the First World War. The SS "C" or Coastal Star class was a non-rigid design with a distinctive tri-lobe section envelope fitted with six ballonets. The control car was plywood covered and featured glass portholes. Part of a post-World War I British Imperial gift to Canada of aeronautical equipment included some SSZ and C-class airships, kite balloons and other lighter than air equipment. While never put to use for the intended purpose, the equipment was carefully tucked away in the stores section at Camp Borden. Some of the gasbag material would become patching material for hangar roofs and one of the gondolas would end up as a crash rescue snowmobile. The Air Board and early RCAF did not throw things out; money was just too scarce.

The photo on the bottom is a poor but interesting view of an RNAS C-type airship. A post-World War I Imperial gift to Canada included a number of SS C-type airships; the airships never flew but their construction material was cannibalized for various uses at Camp Borden, including an early snowmobile as shown here. (LAC Photo # 62279 & RCAF Photo)

DETAILS

Designation:	**Model No:** SS "C"	**Marks:**	**Role:** Coastal Patrol Airship
TOS: 1919	**SOS:** ?	**No:** ?	**Service:** CAF

SPECIFICATIONS

Manufacturer: RNAS Kingsnorth
Crew/Passengers: crew of four
Powerplant: one 240 hp Fiat & one 110 hp Bleriot water cooled piston engine
Performance: Max Speed: 86 mph (138 km/h)   Cruising Speed:
Service Ceiling: Range:
Weights: Empty: Gross:
Dimensions: Width (including fins): 50 ft 0 in (15.24 m)   Length: 217 ft 0 in (66.14 m)
Height: 88 ft 9 in (27.05 m)   Volume: 210,000 cu ft (5,947 cu m)
Armament: Lewis machine guns plus provision for two 230 lb (104 kg) and two 110 lb (50 kg) bombs
Cost: Unknown

Missiles and Remotely Piloted Vehicles

Altair CU-163 (CF).

Boeing
BOMARC

The BOMARC missile was designed by Boeing and the Michigan Aeronautical Research Centre. The controversial Boeing CIM-10B BOMARC nuclear-armed surface-to-air interceptor missile equipped No. 446 and 447 Squadron in North Bay, Ontario and La Macaza, Quebec, respectively for North American air defence from 1961 to 1972. The missile was initially guided from the ground and then switched to an internal seeker for the terminal homing phase of the flight. Along with used CF-101 Voodoo interceptors, the missile was introduced to defend Canadian airspace after the cancellation of the sophisticated Avro CF-105 Arrow interceptor. As indicated in the 1971 White Paper on Defence; The BOMARC missiles sited in Canada were an important contribution in the days when a full anti-bomber defence existed to defend urban-industrial targets as well as to protect the deterrent, which consisted largely of the US bomber force. The deployment by the USSR of a missile force numbering in the thousands then considerably altered the strategic situation. The BOMARCs had become highly vulnerable to a missile attack since they could not be dispersed like aircraft. Moreover, the Canadian BOMARCs were sited to defend the eastern part of North America, whereas the preponderance of the US land-based strategic retaliatory forces was located in the US mid-west. Since no compre-

hensive defence of population against missile attack was available in the foreseeable future, the government then concluded there was no longer sufficient reason to continue to deploy BOMARCs in Canada, and this system was retired.

The BOMARC shown was one of the 26 missiles maintained ready for use by the 446 (SAM) Squadron at RCAF Station North Bay. (CF Photo)

DETAILS

Designation: IM-99B **Model No:** CIM-10B **Marks:** **Role:** Guided Missile
TOS: 1961 **SOS:** 1972 **No:** 56 **Service:** RCAF/CF

SPECIFICATIONS

Manufacturer:	Boeing Aircraft Corp
Crew/Passengers:	None
Powerplant:	1 x 50,000 lb Aerojet General LR59-AG-13 liquid propellant motor and 2 x 14,000 lb Marquardt RJ43-MA-3 ramjet engines

Performance:	Max Speed:	Cruising Speed:
	Service Ceiling: 70,000+ ft (21,336 m)	Range: 400 mi (644 km)
Weights:	Empty:	Gross: 15,500 lb (7,031 kg)
Dimensions:	Span: 18 ft 2 in (5.54 m)	Length: 47 ft 4 in (14.43 m)
	Height: 10 ft 3 in (3.12 m)	Wing Area:
	Fuselage Diameter: 34.6 in (0.88 m)	
Armament:	Nuclear warhead (US controlled)	
Cost:	Unknown	

Teledyne-Ryan
FIREBEE

The Teledyne-Ryan Firebee drone was acquired by the RCAF to provide training for interceptor crews, probably in anticipation of the procurement of the CF-105 Arrow interceptor. At the same time, two Lancaster Mk 10 aircraft were reactivated from storage to act as "mother" ships for the drones. The Lancaster modifications were carried out by Fairey Aviation and included fitting of Firebee launch racks under each wing along with the associated electrical wiring and control units. The Lancasters were then operated by the Central Experimental Proving Establishment and the drones were primarily planned for testing and evaluating of present and proposed weapons systems. After release from the launch aircraft, the Firebees under remote control could climb to 40,00 feet in approximately 10 minutes and could be made to perform any manouevre of which contemporary high performance aircraft were capable. An airborne duration of 1 hr 20 minutes was typical. The drones could also be fitted with wingtip mounted radar reflector pods to ensure optimum radar energy reflection. Assuming the drone was not shot down, recovery was achieved by means of a two-stage parachute, which had a built-in flotation system. Refurbishment and re-use for up to 15 operational flights was possible.

Two RCAF Lancaster Mk10s were modified as launch and control platforms for the the Teledyne-Ryan Firebee drones in Canadian service. A Firebee can be seen here mounted on the outboard wing pylon. Recovery of the drones was accomplished via parachute. (CF Photo)

DETAILS

Designation:	**Model No:** KDA-4 or Q2A	**Marks:**	**Role:** Target Drone
TOS: 1957	**SOS:** 19??	**No:** 30	**Service:** RCAF

SPECIFICATIONS

Manufacturer:	Teledyne-Ryan
Crew/Passengers:	None
Powerplant:	1,000 lb (454 kg st) thrust Fairchild K-20 jet engine

Performance:	Max Speed: 610 mph (976 km/h)	Cruising Speed: 575 mph (920 km/h)
	Service Ceiling: 42,500 ft (12,960 m)	Stalling Speed: 162 mph (259 km/h)
Weights:	Empty: 1,181 lbs (536 kg)	Gross: 1,849 lb (839 kg)
Dimensions:	Span: 11 ft 2 in (3.40 m)	Length: 17 ft 3 in (5.26 m)
	Height: 5 ft 10 in (1.79 m)	Wing Area:
Armament:	None	
Cost:	$45,000	

Advanced Ceramics Research
SILVER FOX

As part of its continuing exploration into the potential utility of uninhabited aerial vehicles (UAVs), the Canadian Forces purchased the Silver Fox mini UAV system produced by Advanced Ceramics Research of Tucson, Arizona. Thales Systems Canada was the prime contractor in the acquisition of this system, which was initially for a two-year period of combined concept development and experimentation. The Silver Fox mini UAV systems included the UAV platforms themselves plus associated payloads, ground control stations, remote video terminal, spares support for two years, ground support equipment, documentation, training and shipping containers. They were primarily based out of the DRDC facility at Suffield, Alberta, but were operated across Canada by various CF organizations on a shared basis. The Silver Fox mini UAV system was also employed during one of the phases of the Atlantic Littoral ISR Experiment, which took place on Baffin Island and across Atlantic Canada in August 2004.

The CU-167 Silver Fox. (Advanced Ceramics Research Photo)

DETAILS

Designation: CU-167	**Model No:**	**Marks:**	**Role:** Tactical Mini UAV
TOS: 2004	**SOS:**	**No:** 9	**Service:** CF

SPECIFICATIONS Silver Fox

Manufacturer:	Advanced Ceramics Research	
Powerplant:	one model aircraft engine	
Performance:	Max Speed:	Cruising Speed: 80 mph (129 km/h)
	Max Ceiling: 1,000 ft (305 m)	Endurance: 10 hours
Weights:	Empty: 134 lb (60.8 kg)	Max: 170 lb (77.1 kg)
Dimensions:	Span: 7 ft 0 in (2.13 m)	Length: 5 ft 0 in (1.52 m)
	Height:	Wing Area:
Armament:	none	
Cost:	$649,000 for the system, including training and service support	

General Atomics
ALTAIR

Between 22 and 31 August 2004, the CFEC (Canadian Forces Experimentation Centre) tested a single CU-163 Altair UAV from CFB Goose Bay. Despite its being given a CF designation and serial number (163301), the Altair was not purchased by DND. Instead this aircraft (as with the I-GNAT UAV before it) was on short-term lease from its US manufacturer, General Atomics, after the company announced that it had been awarded a DND contract in February of 2004. These CFEC tests were part of ALIX,

the Atlantic Littoral ISR (Intelligence Surveillance and Reconnaissance) Experiment. Three different scenarios were to be tested: a reconnaissance in support of EX *Narwhal* in Nunavut, a maritime surveillance and targeting mission in the Gulf of St. Lawrence (followed by an overflight of CFB Gagetown where the Altair operated alongside the Silver Fox mini UAV), then a final ISR mission over the Grand Banks.

The CU-163 Altair in CF colours. (CF Photo)

DETAILS

Designation: CU-163	**Model No:**	**Marks:**	**Role:** Surveillance UAV
TOS: 2004	**SOS:** 2004	**No:** 1	**Service:** Leased from General Atomics Aeronautical Systems Inc.

SPECIFICATIONS Altair

Manufacturer:	General Atomics Aeronautical Systems Inc.
Powerplant:	One 708 kW (950 shp) Honeywell TPE331-10T turboprop, flat rated at 522 kW (700 shp) for max continuous operation; McCauley three-blade, variable-pitch aluminum pusher propeller
Performance:	Max Speed: 259 mph (416 km/h) Cruising Speed: 81 mph (130 km/h)
	Max Ceiling: 60,000 ft (18,290 m) Range: 2,975 mi (4,787 km)
Weights:	Empty: Max: 7,000 lb (3,175 kg)
Dimensions:	Span: 84 ft 0 in (25.60 m) Length: 36 ft 2.4 in (11.03 m)
	Height: 11 ft 9½ in (3.59 m) Wing Area: 302 sq ft (28.06 sq m)
Armament:	none
Cost:	Leased from General Atomics Aeronautical Systems Inc.

Israeli Aircraft Industries
EAGLE

The Canadian Forces Experimentation Centre continued its ongoing UAV tests with Israeli Aircraft Industries' large Eagle-1 off the west coast of Vancouver Island on 11 July 2003. Israeli technicians ran the UAV through its paces in front of military observers from Canada, Britain,

France, and the US. The Eagle-1 follows the twin-boom pusher propeller arrangement of earlier Israeli UAVs. The Eagle-1 as tested was fitted with search radar in a large belly radome to suit it for maritime patrol of Canada's coastlines.

Two views of the Eagle UAV designated CU-160 Eagle as leased by the CF. (CF Photos)

DETAILS

Designation: CU-160   **Model No:**   **Marks:**   **Role:** Surveillance UAV
TOS: 2003   **SOS:** 2003   **No:** 1   **Service:** Leased from Israeli Aircraft Industries

SPECIFICATIONS Eagle

Manufacturer:	Israeli Aircraft Industries
Powerplant:	One 84.6 kW (113.4 hp) Rotax 914 F turbocharged engine, driving a two-blade pusher propeller
Performance:	Max Speed: 144 mph (231 km/h) — Cruising Speed:
	Operational Ceiling: 25,000 ft (7,620 m) — Range: 1,956 mi (3,148 km)
Weights:	Empty: 1,448 lb (657kg) — Max: 2,535 lb (1,150 kg)
Dimensions:	Span: 53 ft 5.7 in (16.30m) — Length: 29 ft 4 in (8.94 m)
	Height: 3m — Wing Area:
Armament:	none
Cost:	Leased from Israeli Aircraft Industries

SAGEM
SPERWER

In 2003, the Canadian Army hastily acquired an unmanned target acquisition and surveillance drone for deployment with Operation Athena in Afghanistan. The new system, known as the Sperwer UAV (unmanned air vehicle), was designed by SAGEM SA of France. Oerlikon Contraves of Saint-Jean-sur-Richelieu, Quebec, was the prime contractor in Canada. The system is launched by catapult and then recovered by parachute. For Op Athena, the Army purchased four drones, the associated ground data and launching equipment including vehicles, along with simulators for training. The all-weather drones have de-icing capability. A team of 28 CF personnel initially operated the system in Afghanistan. Most were from E Battery, 2nd Regiment, Royal Canadian Horse Artillery in Petawawa. For this initial mission, Air Force personnel oversaw areas such as airworthiness and maintenance. This successful initial deployment resulted in a number of losses of the air vehicles due to malfunctions. The Air Force subse-quently assumed program management for the Sperwer and additional platforms and system components were purchased in various batches. The Sperwer subsequently deployed on repeat occasions to Afghanistan.

Two views of the Sperwer UAV as deployed to Operation Athena in Afghanistan. (CF Photos)

DETAILS

Designation: CU-161 **Model No:** **Marks:** **Role:** Target Acquisition and Surveillance Drone
TOS: 2003 **SOS:** In-Service **No:** 13 **Service:** CF

SPECIFICATIONS

Manufacturer: SAGEM SA
Crew/Passengers: None
Powerplant: two-cylinder engine (made by Bombardier's Austrian subsidiary, ROTAX) generating 48 kW (65 hp) at 6500 rpm
Performance: Max Speed: 127 knots (235 km/h) Cruising Speed: 90 knots (167 km/h)
Service Ceiling: 16,400 ft (4,999 m) Range: 150 km
Weights: Empty: Gross:
Dimensions: Span: 14 ft 1 in (4.30 m) Length: 8 ft 10 in (2.70 m)
Height: ft 10 in Wing Area:
Armament: None
Cost: $33.8M for 4 UAVs with 2 Ground Control Stations, 1 launcher, 2 ground data terminals, 4 remote video terminals, and 3 simulators, plus 3 generator trailers, training, and support

Schreiner
VINDICATOR II

The Vindicator II was designed as a basic training target for the evaluation and testing of anti-aircraft 20 and 40 mm gunnery and low-speed missile systems, and for training personnel in the use of such weapon systems. It has been used as a target for Blowpipe, Javelin, ADATS, vertically launched Sea Sparrow surface-to-air missiles, and for Bofors 40 mm, Oto Melara 76 mm, Skyguard 35 mm and FAADS 20 mm gun systems. It can be used for shipboard and land-based operations, and precise flight profiles can be repeated or varied to meet the exact requirements of individual weapons, sensors and/or tracking systems. The system was acquired from Bristol Aerospace in July 1999. The target consists of a bullet-shaped fuselage; low-mounted, low aspect ratio tapered wings with endplate fins; and a ventral landing skid. It features all-composites (glass fibre and epoxy) construction. All major components can be easily removed from the fuselage. The modular construction combined with extensive use of quick-release fittings enables Vindicator to carry a wide range of payloads in its nose, mid and rear fuselage bays. Typical flight profiles include low-altitude attack and crossing patterns, low-altitude attack with a pop-up manoeuvre, continuously varying altitude, jinking, or any combination of these. The target is launched from a low-maintenance pneumatic mobile launcher (4.57 m; 15 ft launch stroke). A conventional skid landing or parachute recovery can be commanded either manually or automatically. The fail-safe system automatically shuts down the engine and deploys a parachute in the event of autopilot or sensor failure, and initiates automatic recovery if the command link is lost. After recovery, Vindicator can be readied for a new flight within 30 minutes.

The Vindicator II target drone has received the designation CU-162 while in CF-service. (CF Photos)

DETAILS

Designation: CU-162 **Model No:** **Marks:** **Role:** Target Drone
TOS: **SOS:** **No:** 20 **Service:** Leased from Schreiner Target Services Canada Ltd

SPECIFICATIONS Vindicator II

Manufacturer:	Schreiner Target Services Canada Ltd	
Powerplant:	One 26.1 kW (35 hp) UEL AR 731 rotary engine; two-blade pusher propeller	
Performance:	Max Speed: 200 mph (322 km/h)	Cruising Speed: 60 mph (97 km/h)
	Max Ceiling: 9,840 ft (3,000 m)	Range: 6.2 mi (10 km)
Weights:	Empty: 134 lb (60.8 kg)	Max: 170 lb (77.1 kg)
Dimensions:	Span: 8 ft 6 in (2.59 m)	Length: 8 ft 9 in (2.67 m)
	Height: 1 ft 8 in (0.51 m)	Wing Area: 18.6 sq ft (1.73 sq m)
Armament:	none	
Cost:	Leased from Schreiner Target Services Canada Ltd	

Glossary and Abbreviations

AESOP	Airborne Electronic Sensor Operator
ARMY COOP	Army Cooperation
ASW	Anti-Submarine Warfare
AWACS	Airborne Warning and Control System
BCATP	British Commonwealth Air Training Plan
CAF	Canadian Air Force (1919-1924)
CF	Canadian Forces (1968+)
CS	Combat Support
ECM	Electronic Counter Measures
eshp	engine shaft horsepower
EW	Electronic Warfare
FAA	Fleet Air Arm (Royal Navy)
JATO	Jet Assisted Take-off
kts	knots
LAC	Library and Archives Canada
NATO	North Atlantic Treaty Organization
nm	nautical miles
No.	Number; (Total) of aircraft type in service
OTU	Operational Training Unit
RAF	Royal Air Force
RAAF	Royal Australian Air Force
RCA	Royal Canadian Army
RCAF	Royal Canadian Air Force
RCN	Royal Canadian Navy
RFC	Royal Flying Corps
RN	Royal Navy
RNAS	Royal Naval Air Service
RNZAF	Royal New Zealand Air Force
SAR	Search and Rescue
SOS	Struck Off Strength
Sqn	Squadron
TOS	Taken On Strength
USAF	United States Air Force
USAAF	United States Army Air Force
USMC	United States Marine Corps
USN	United States Navy

Photograph Credits

The following images have been reproduced courtesy of the Department of National Defence, with the permission of the Minister of Public Works and Government Services. List is alphabetical.

Albacore (CF);
Albatross–(RCAF PL-132832);
Albemarle–(CF PL-40948);
Altair–(CF);
Anson–(CF); –PC-2492);
Arcturus–(CF IHD01-0137);
Argus–(RCAF);
Arrow–(CF PL-107092);
Aurora–(CF);
Avenger–(CF EKS-221);
Avro 504–(CF PCN 4621);
Avro Avian–(CF RE- 17383);
Avro Tutor–(CF CB69-1132);
B.E.2C–(CF RE-17403);
Back Cover–F-86
    Sabre–(CF PL-55764);
Baltimore–(RCAF);
Banshee–(CF);
Barkley Grow–(CAFM);
Beaufighter–(CF);
Beaufort–(CAFM);
Bermuda–(CAFM);
Bird Dog–(CF RE-69-1868);
BK117–(CF);
Blenheim–(RCAF);
Boeing 247D–(CAFM);
Boeing 707–(CF);
BOMARC–(CF);
Bombay–(CAFM);
Boston (Havoc); –(RCAF);
Brewster Buffalo–(CAFM);
Bristol Fighter–(CF);
Bristol Freighter–(CF PL-63126);
Buffalo–(CF);
Burgess-Dunne–(CF RE-17706);
C-5–(CF);
Camel–(CF PCN- 4592);
Canso–(RCAF);
Caribou–(CF PL-140543);
Catalina–(CAFM);
CF100–(CF PL-54505);
Challenger–(CF ISC 87-038 +
    NBC 87-120-10);

Chinook–(CF);
Chinook–(CF);
Chinook–(CF);
Chipmunk–(CF PCN–5597);
Comet–(CF PCN 252 and
    PCN-253);
Cormorant–(CF);
Cornell–(CF PCN–3878);
Cosmopolitan–(RCAF);
Courier–(CAFM);
Crane–(CF);
D.H. 4–(RCAF);
Dakota–(CF);
Dash 7–(CF ILC81-265);
Dash 8–(CF ISC87-394);
Defiant–(CAFM);
Delta–(CF);
Dolphin–(CF M-948);
Dragonfly–(RCAF);
Eagle–(CF);
Expeditor–(CF);
F.E.2B–(RCAF);
Fairchild 51–(CAFM);
Fairchild 71–(CF PMR-77-242);
Fairchild Argus– (RCAF);
Fairchild FC2L–(CAFM);
Fairey Battle–(CAFM);
Falcon–(CF);
Felixstowe F.3–(CF PL-114749);
Firebee–(CF);
Firefly–(CF);
Fleet Fawn–(CF PL-1954);
Fleet Finch–(CF RNC-1572-3);
Flying Fortress–(RCAF);
Fokker DVII–(RCAF);
Fox Moth–(CF RE68-17940);
Freedom Fighter–(CF);
Fulmar–(CAFM);
Gipsy Moth–(CF CF-377-39
    and CAFM Photo);
Goblin–(CF PL-5954);
Goose–(RCAF);
Griffon–(CF);

H-21–(CF);
Hadrian–(RCAF);
Halifax–(RCAF); PL-10457);
Hampden–(CF); PL-3052);
Harrow–(CAFM);
Harvard–(CF RNC-266);
Havard II–(CF);
Hawk–(CF CK2004-0065-18d);
Hellcat–(CAFM);
Hercules–(CF);
Hornet–(CF); –AEC83-1213
    and ?);
Hotspur–(RCAF);
Hudson–(CAFM & CF);
HUP-3–(CF);
Hurricane–(CF PCN-3986);
Iroquois–(CF);
Jenny–(CF RNC-1383-2);
Jet Ranger–(CF);
Jet Ranger–(CF);
Kaydet–(RCAF);
King Air–(CF);
Kiowa–(CF);
Kittyhawk–(CF PL 8346);
KR-34–(CF RE-17379);
L-182–(CF PCN 67-857);
Labrador–(CF);
Lancaster–(CF);
Lerwick–(CAFM);
Liberator–(RCAF);
Lincoln–(CF RE -19785-2);
Lockheed T-33–(RCAF)
Lynx–(CF SL2006-0181-04[1]);
Lysander–(CAFM);
M0-2B–(RCAF);
Mailwing–(CF);
Martinsyde F.6–(CF AH-296);
Maryland–(CAFM);
Master–(CAFM);
Mentor–(CF RE-68-1767);
Meteor–(CF RE68-1612);
Mitchell–(RCAF & CAFM);
Mosquito–(CAFM);

Musketeer/Sundowner–
    (CF PPC 87-174 + ?);
Mustang–(CF);
NA-44–(RCAF);
Neptune.–(CF);
Nieuport Scout–
    (CF PL-140914);
Nomad–(CF);
Nomad–(CF);
Non-Rigid SS "C" Type Airship
    (RCAF);
Norseman–(RCAF);
Northstar–(RCAF);
Otter–(CF PL-123361);
Oxford–(CAFM);
Prentice–(CAFM);
Puffer–(RCAF);
Roc–(CAFM);
S-51–(RCAF);
S-55–(RCAF);
S-58–(CF);
Sabre–(CF PC-2144 + PCN
    67-962);
Schweizer–(CF);
TN2002-0693-05c &
TN2002-0693-09c);
SE-5A–(CF RE-18453);
Sea Fury–(CF REC82-2067);
Sea King–(CF HSC 99 -1113 -3
    and ISC00-0736-14);
Seafire–(CF RE68-1777);
Sentry–(CF); –IS2002-2799);
Shark–(RCAF);
Shorthorn–(CF);
Shorts Type 184–(CF AH-574);
Silver Dart–(CF);
Silver Star–(CF);
Siskin–(CF RE -13717);
Skua–(CAFM);
Snipe–(CF PCN-4614);
Sopwith Strutter–(RCAF);
Sperwer–(CF IS2006-0279[1]);
Spitfire–(CF);

Starfighter–(CF AEC 74-23);
Starfighter–(RCAF);
Stranraer–(CAFM);
Sunderland–(CF);
Super Universal–(CF);
Swordfish–(CAFM);
Tiger Moth–(CF PCN 3880 &
RCAF);
Tomahawk–(CF PL-5578);
Tornado–(CF CK2005-0328-
21d.jpg);
Tracker–(CF);
Trimotor–(CAFM);
Tutor–(CF PCN-5322);
Twin Huey–(CF);
Twin Otter– (CF);
Typhoon– (CAFM & CF);
UAVs–(CF);
Vampire–(CF RNC-352);
Vancouver–(RCAF);
Vanessa–(CF PL-114868);
Varuna–(CF RE-19288);
Vedette–(CF RE-19960);
Velos–(CF RE -15800);
Vengeance– (CAFM);
Ventura–(CAFM);
Vickers Gunbus- (RCAF);
Vigil–(CF RE-17076);
Viking–(RCAF);
Vindicator II– (CF IM000749
& IM000752);
Viper–(CF DMR 72-443);
Vista–(CF RE-17369);
Voodoo–(CF);
Wapiti–(CF);
Wellesley– (CAFM);
Wellington–(CF PL-33320);
Whirlwind–(CF PL-8908 &
PL-8909);
Wildcat–(CAFM);
Wright–(CF RE-15819);
Yale–(CF PL-1427);
Yukon–(RCAF).

The following images have been reproduced courtesy of Library and Archives Canada:

Audax–(LAC PA-62981);
Avro 626–(LAC PA-133586);
B.E. 12.–(LAC PA- 006358);
Barracuda–(LAC PA-146652);
Cuckoo–(LAC PA-06807);
Curtiss H-16–
    (LAC PA-006393);
Curtiss HS-2L–
    (LAC PA-53337);
D.H.2– (LAC PA-006636);

D.H.6– (LAC PA-006368);
D.H.9–(LAC PA-006370);
Digby–(LAC PA-140642);
Fairey IIIC–(LAC PA-006752);
FK8–(LAC PA-000297);
Fleet Fort–(LAC PA-64009);
H.12– (LAC PA-006392);
Hawk Moth–(LAC PA-62799);
Horsa–(LAC PA-211504 and
    PA-133492);

HP 0/400–(LAC PA-006401);
Lockheed 212–(LAC #PA-64052);
Lockheed T-33–
    (LAC PA-67567);
Lodestar– (LAC PA-64763);
M0-2B–(LAC PA- 062407);
M1C–(LAC PA-006365);
Magister–(LAC C81438);
Non-Rigid SS "C" Type Airship
    (LAC PA- 62279);

Pacemaker–(LAC #PA-062723);
Parasol–(LAC PA-102808);
Privateer–(LAC PA-166980
    and PA-65976);
Pterodactyl–(LAC PA-175710);
Pup–(LAC PA-06396);
Puss Moth–(LAC PA-62938);
R.E.8–(LAC PA-123976);
Rambler–(LAC PA-62527);
Scout– (LAC PA-125919);

Sentinel–(LAC PA145833);
Super 71–(LAC PA-63184);
Taylorcraft–(LAC PA-162286);
Tomahawk–(LAC PA-136240);
Triplane–(LAC PA-006395);
Waco AQC-6–
    (LAC PA-RD001071);
Waco GG-15–(LAC PA-65385);
Walrus–(LAC PA-116626);
Warwick.–(LAC PA-133287)

Abbreviations: CAFM–Comox Air Force Museum; CF–Canadian Forces; LAC–Library and Archives Canada; RCAF–Royal Canadian Air Force

Bibliography and Suggested Reading

Arrowheads, The. *Avro Arrow: The Story of the Avro Arrow From Its Evolution To Its Extinction*. Erin, Ontario: Boston Mills Press, 1980.

Campbell, Christopher. *Aces and Aircraft of World War I*. Poole, Dorset: Blandford Press, 1981.

Canadian Aviation Historical Society (CAHS) Journal. Various editions, vols 4, 5, 7, 8 & 20.

Cheshire, Leonard. *Bomber Pilot*. Granada, Herts: Mayflower Publishing, 1975.

Childerhose, Chick. *Splash One Tiger*. Toronto: McClelland and Stewart Ltd., 1961.

Deere, David N. (ed.) *CNN War in the Gulf*. Atlanta: Turner Publishing, 1991.

Donald, David (ed.). *American Warplanes of World War II*. Connecticut: AIRtime Publishing, 1995.

Donald, David (ed.). *The Modern Civil Aircraft Guide*. Etobicoke, ON: Prospero Books, 1999.

Douglas, W.A.B. The Official History of the Royal Canadian Air Force,*The Creation of a National Air Force*. Vol 1 & 2. Toronto: University of Toronto Press, 1986.

Fletcher, David C. and Doug MacPhail. *Harvard! The North American Trainers in Canada*. San Josef, BC: DCF Flying Books, 1990.

Francillon, Rene J. *Lockheed Aircraft Since 1913*. London: Putnam Books, 1987.

From White-caps to Contrails: a History of a Modern Air Formation. Shearwater, N.S.: Canadian Forces Base Shearwater, 1981.

Gordon, John. *Of Men and Planes*. (Vol 1, 2 & 3), n.p., 1967.

Green, William. *The World's Fighting Planes*. New York: Doubleday Inc, 1968.

Griffin, J.A. *Canadian Military Aircraft (Serials & Photographs 1920-1968)*. Ottawa: Canadian War Museum, 1969.

Gunston, Bill. *Military Aviation Library United States World War II Aircraft*. London: Salamander Books, 1985.

Gunston, Bill. *The World's Military Aircraft*. London: Octopus Books,1983.

Harvey, J. Douglas. *Laughter Silvered Wings, Remembering the Air Force* II. Toronto: McClelland and Stewart Ltd., 1984.

Harvey, J. Douglas. *The Tumbling Mirth*. Toronto: McClelland and Stewart Ltd., 1983.

Jane's All The World's Aircraft 1985-1986. London: Janes Publishing, 1985.

Johnson, J.E. *Full Circle, The Story of Airfighting*. London: Chatto and Windus Ltd, 1964.

Kealey, J.D.F. and E.C. Russell. *A History of Canadian Naval Aviation 1918–1962*. Ottawa: Queen's Printer, 1965.

Kostenuk, S. and J. Griffin. *RCAF Squadrons and Aircraft*. Toronto: A.M. Hakkert Ltd., 1977.

Lewis, P.*The British Fighter Since 1912*. London: Putnam Books, 1979.

Lotz, Jim. *Canadians at War*. London: Bison Books, 1990.

March, Daniel J. (ed.). *British Warplanes of World War II*, Connecticut: AIRtime Publishing, 1998.

Milberry, Larry. *The Canadair Sabre*. Toronto: CANAV Books, 1986.

Milberry, Larry. *The CF-100*. Toronto: CANAV Books, 1981

Milberry, Larry. *The North Star*. Toronto: CANAV Books, 1982.

Milberry, Larry. *Sixty Years: The RCAF and CF Air Command 1924–1984*. Toronto: CANAV Books, 1984..

Mitchell, B.*The International Encyclopedia of Aircraft*. Toronto: Aerospace Publishing Ltd,. 1991.

Molson, K.M. and H.A. Taylor. *Canadian Aircraft Since 1901*. Stittsville, Ont: Canadian Wings Inc, 1982.

Mowthorpe, C.E.S. *Battlebags: British Airships of the First World War*. Stroud, UK: Alan Sutton Publishing Ltd, 1997.

Munson, Kenneth. *Aircraft of World War I*. Surrey: Ian Allan Ltd, 1967.

NBC Group. *A History of the Air Defence of Canada 1948–1997*. 71 Film Canada Inc, 1997.

Nolan, Brian. *Hero: the Buzz Beurling Story*. Toronto: Lester and Orpen Dennys Ltd, 1981.

Peden, Murray. *A Thousand Shall Fall*. Toronto: Stoddart, 1979.

Pickler, R. and L. Milberry. *Canadair—The First Fifty Years*. Toronto: CANAV Books, 1995.

RCAF Overseas, The. Vol 1, 2 & 3, Toronto: Oxford University Press, 1949.

Steward, Charles H. *A Record of Valour*, Toronto: 1987.

Swanborough, F.G. *United States Military Aircraft Since 1909*. London: Putnam Books, 1963.

Swanborough, F. G. *United States Navy Aircraft Since 1911*. London: Putnam Books, 1976.

Taylor, H.A. *Airspeed Aircraft Since 1931*. London: Putnam & Co, 1970.

Thetford, Owen. *Aircraft of the Royal Air Force*. London: Putnam & Co, 1977.

Thetford, Owen. *British Naval Aircraft Since 1912*. London: Putnam & Co, 1977.